The Great Texts
of the Bible

EDITED BY

JAMES HASTINGS

PSALMS XXIV · CXIX

VOLUME IV

Wm. B. Eerdmans Publishing Company
Grand Rapids, Michigan

Library of Congress Catalog Card Number: 58-13517

Published by special arrangement with Charles Scribner's Sons.

PRINTED IN THE UNITED STATES OF AMERICA

CONTENTS

—◆—

TOPICS.

TEXTS.

Psalms.

THE SECRET OF THE LORD.

LITERATURE.

Banks (L. A.), *The King's Stewards*, 142.

Brooks (P.), *New Starts in Life*, 271.

Clow (W. M.), *The Secret of the Lord*, 1.

Cowl (F. B.), *Digging Ditches*, 79.

Holland (C.), *Gleanings from a Ministry of Fifty Years*, 150.

Johnston (J. B.), *The Ministry of Reconciliation*, 323.

Jowett (J. H.), *Brooks by the Traveller's Way*, 172.

Keble (J.), *Sermons for the Christian Year* : Ascension Day to Trinity Sunday, 343.

Morrison (G. H.), *The Afterglow of God*, 366.

Potts (A. W.), *School Sermons*, 78.

Selby (T. G.), *The Divine Craftsman*, 142.

Simeon (C.), *Works*, v. 168.

Vaughan (C. J.), *Memorials of Harrow*, 270.

Literary Churchman, xxxviii. (1892) 45 (C. W. Whistler).

Sunday at Home, 1910, p. 629 (G. H. Morrison).

Treasury (New York), xvii. 404 (G. B. F. Hallock).

The Secret of the Lord.

The secret of the Lord is with them that fear him;
And he will shew them his covenant.—Ps. xxv. 14.

WHEN the Hebrew poet spoke of the secret of the Lord he meant the knowledge of the God of Israel, the unseen and eternal Jehovah. When he thought of them that fear Him, he remembered the stalwart saints who shall ever be the heroic leaders of the faith. He recalled Abraham coming out of Ur of the Chaldees with a wisdom and a knowledge that no Babylonian star-gazer ever divined. He thought of Jacob rising from his midnight dream at Bethel, saying in penitence and awe, " Surely the Lord is in this place; and I knew it not." He saw Moses at the burning bush, putting off the shoes from his feet, for the place whereon he stood was holy ground. He remembered Samuel coming out of the temple in the morning light, having heard the voice of God, with a message he dared not tell to Eli. Each of these had entered into a solemn experience. Each of them had come forth with a secret. A new and deeper understanding of God's ways, and thoughts, and purposes had been given them. He marks the law of their experience. It was the law of fear. They had that fear of God which is an awe and a reverence, a passion of desire to know, and a willingness to submit and to obey. Therefore God made known the secret to them.

¶ Thompson dwells on St. Paul's unspoken message, which, designated by the name of *wisdom*, he withheld from many of the Corinthians because they were not fit to hear it. He communicated it to the *spiritual* not to the *animal* man. Origen says that that which St. Paul would have called *wisdom* is found in the " Canticle of Canticles." Thompson dwells further on the hidden meanings of the Pentateuch, believing that there was " an inexhaustible treasure of divine wisdom concealed under the letter of Holy Writ." Thompson saw wise men whispering, and guessed that there were secrets; their presence discovered, they were open

3

secrets for such as he. "You have but to direct my sight, and the intentness of my gaze will discover the rest." [1]

¶ There were three courts in the Temple at Jerusalem. There was the outer court, where even the Gentiles who cared nothing for the God of Israel or the faith of the Hebrew people might freely come. There was the holy place with its sacred things, where only the Hebrew worshipper might walk. There was the most holy place, over which the veil of the Temple hung, and into whose unseen and unknown seclusion the high priest entered once every year, alone. There are these three courts in the life of a Christian man. There is the outer court, where a man who is living his life in the world must keep company with all who enter its circle. He must rub shoulders with the crowd, although he never forgets that they cannot enter into his secret. There is the holy place, where fellow-believers may pass, and speech and thought of the things of God have a gracious liberty. But there is the most holy place, and what passes there between God and the soul is to be kept with a guarded reticence until there is need for its being told. [2]

¶ When the ancient Jew approached his sanctuary, he found an outer court of the Temple full of activity with the coming and going of those who touched the whole natural life and the daily sacrifice on the altar. But behind lay the still silent room where the golden lamp burned and the bread of life was resting on the golden table. And behind again the silence of the Holy of Holies where man and God merge in union. Even so it is not the great activity, touching national issues—it is not even the sacrificial life of Dr. Paton that has most attracted me and, I believe, others. But here was a priest of the Most High God, in the sanctuary of whose heart the light burned and the bread of life was broken. And with reverent awe we knew that behind lay communion with the Inspirer and Hearer of Prayer. So that out of him from the Divine source flow "rivers of living water." Thus heaven touched earth through our intercourse, and the passion for service of his soul entered ours. [3]

The secret of the Lord, as the Psalmist conceives it, may be held to include (1) Knowledge; (2) Character; (3) Happiness. Knowledge is the secret of the Teacher, Character is the secret of the Friend, Happiness is the secret of the Lover.

[1] E. Meynell, *The Life of Francis Thompson* (1913), 223.
[2] W. M. Clow, *The Secret of the Lord*, 247.
[3] J. Marchant, *J. B. Paton*, 311.

I.

KNOWLEDGE.

1. Every teacher has his secret. He scans his scholars, eager to find a receptive mind to whom he can reveal it. When the responsive glance, the significant word, or the searching question reveals the student's promise, the teacher has an exquisite joy in revealing his secret.

¶ The great painters of the Middle Ages took pupils into their studios. To every aspirant they gave honest attention. When one came who was swift to understand his master's conceptions, eager to imitate his strength of line and purity of colour, humbly and patiently reverent in his zeal, the secret was disclosed. In our own day Edward Burne Jones became a disciple of Dante Gabriel Rossetti. He spent still and strenuous hours in copying his master's works, studying their distinction, and aspiring after their spirit. With a trembling heart young Burne Jones took his drawings to Rossetti to receive his judgment upon them. The honest painter looked at them in silence, and with a word of emotion he said, "You have nothing more to learn from me." He had entered into the master's secret. But mark the law. It is not to the carping critic, the scorning and cynical scholar, the contemptuous idler, that the secret is revealed. The secret is "with them that fear."[1]

> God keeps His holy mysteries
> Just on the outside of man's dream. . . .
> Yet, touching so, they draw above
> Our common thoughts to Heaven's unknown;
> Our daily joy and pain advance
> To a divine significance.[2]

2. There is a mystery in every Christian life. When the words are said in our hearing, "The secret of the Lord is with them that fear him," they seem to give a momentary glimpse of the truth. There is a secret in such lives, and that secret is God's. He has to do with them. There is a communication between their souls and Him. He has told them a secret, and they keep it.

---

[1] W. M. Clow, *The Secret of the Lord*, 4.
[2] E. B. Browning.

Others may see that they have a secret; but intermeddle with it they cannot. There is only one way to attain it—by going through the same process as these have gone through. We may not at present think it worth our while to do so, or we may have an undefined dread of the supposed difficulty and irksomeness of that process: but at least let us lay it up well in our hearts that there is such a process, and such an end; that the Christian's life is a reality, whether we ever attain that life or not; a mystery, whether we be ever initiated into that mystery or not; let us accept and reverence the inspired declaration that "the secret of the Lord is with them that fear him."

¶ The more of a man a man is, the more secret is the secret of his life, and the more plain and frank are its external workings. A small and shallow man tries to throw a mystery about the mere methods of his life, he tries to make his ways of living seem obscure. Where he goes, how he makes his fortune, whom he talks with, what his words mean, who his friends are—he is very mysterious about all these, and all because the secret of his life is really weak, because he is conscious that there is no really strong purpose of living which he himself understands. It is a shallow pool which muddies its surface to make itself look deep. But a greater man will be perfectly frank and unmysterious about these little things. Anybody may know what he does and where he goes. His acts will be transparent, his words will be intelligible. Yet all the while every one who looks at him will see that there is something behind all, which escapes the closest observation. The very clearness of the surface will show how deep the water is, how far away the bottom lies. There is hardly a better way to tell a great man from a little one.[1]

¶ *He always lived with his blinds up*, and you saw all the workings of his mind. Had he not been steeped in the spirit of love he could never have survived the self-exposure which was a habit with him. But his very caprices were always unselfish, and he could afford to let his friends look him through and through.[2]

> As in some cavern dark and deep,
>   My soul within me here lies low,
> Where, veiled, she dreams in wondrous sleep
>   Of things I may not know.

[1] Phillips Brooks, *New Starts in Life*, 272.
[2] *Love and Life: The Story of J. Denholm Brash* (1913), 163.

And if perchance she wake awhile,
  I probe her radiant eyes in vain :
She turns from me with misty smile
  And, sighing, sleeps again.[1]

3. God may be expected to keep some things hidden. In the most intimate and sacred of our friendships it is not for us to say what secrets shall be made known to us, and what secrets shall be guarded from our cognizance. A government reserves to itself the right of saying what information may be imparted to its friends, and what, for sufficient reasons, shall be kept back. A general on the battle-field, whilst putting safe and suitable selections of news at the service of authorized war correspondents, cannot allow them unlimited access to his plans. It is necessary to respect official reserve. And is not the temper which accepts such conditions binding on a true servant of God? Let God Himself choose the things He sees fit to make known to us. If we live in reverent and believing fellowship He will treat us as confidants, and our knowledge of His methods and purposes will surpass that of the world ; but at the same time we need to be told once and again that He cannot admit us to equality with Himself by making known the veiled things we petulantly demand. It ought to satisfy us if His heart trusts us, and He comes to us in forms of revelation withheld from the world. He who is thus initiated into His deep counsels and led to know His will makes few mistakes in his prayers, and the faith he cherishes does not suffer the bitterness of disappointment or betrayal.

¶ I have heard Sir Clifford Allbutt and Signor agree that the necessity or, perhaps better, the love of the mysterious, was an essential and valuable part of the human mind; far from being all disadvantageous or an impediment to progress, it had been in the main a stimulus towards something transcending man's best efforts. Signor said: " It is in fact the poetic element; and what in the superstitious mind is mere dread, in Browning and Tennyson is aspiration. You cannot take away the mysterious from man, he cannot do without it." [2]

¶ One of the most beautiful of the Bishop's sonnets

---

[1] Laurence Alma Tadema.
[2] M. S. Watts, *George Frederic Watts*, ii. 177.

was composed at Trondhjem on August 12, 1888. It runs
thus :—

> And was it there—the splendour I behold?
> This great fjord with its silver grace outspread
> And thousand-creeked and thousand-islanded?
> Those far-off hills, grape-purple, fold on fold?
> For yesterday, when all day long there rolled
> The blinding drift, methinks, had some one said
> "The scene is fair," I scarce had credited;
> Yet fairer 'tis than any tongue hath told.
> And *it was there!* Ah, yes! And on my way
> More bravely I will go, though storm-clouds lour
> And all my sky be only cold and grey;
> For I have learnt the teaching of this hour:
> And when God's breath blows all these mists afar,
> I know that I shall see the things that are.[1]

4. Knowledge comes by obedience. It would be hopeless to
try to tell the secret, even for the sake of inducing others to
treasure it for themselves. The fact is that the secret might be
told, and told in the best of words, without its ceasing to be a
secret to those who heard. Words are necessary in religious as
in other matters; but there is no fear of their telling anything
which ought not to be told: first, because the secret is designed
for all, and revealed to all who will listen to it; and next, because
it lies deeper far than the understanding, and never becomes the
possession of any man till he takes it into his heart. For the
obedience by which comes knowledge is the obedience of the
heart. Obedience to law, and acts of worship arising out of fear
of penalty, are merely hiding from God among the trees of the
garden. Even obedience from duty can never be a satisfactory or
final state; it is merely educational, to make manifest defect of
life. "I was alive without the law once; but when the commandment came, sin revived and I died." When the glory of the Lord
has filled all the courts of His temple, man's outward nature
becomes reconstituted, not after the law of a carnal commandment, but after the power of an endless or indissoluble life. The
tree of knowledge becomes one with the tree of life which is in
the midst of the city, and on both sides of the river of life,
proceeding from the throne of God and of the Lamb.

[1] F. D. How, *Bishop Walsham How*, 399.

¶ I have known more than one Highland saint who never had any intellectual training. They had had little schooling, they never were at college, and their libraries were of the scantiest kind. Yet in every true sense of the word they were men of culture; their language was choice and their thoughts large and just; and they had singular power in complicated questions of seizing on the things that really mattered. What was the secret of that mental clarity?—" If any man willeth to do his will." To God they had prayed—in Christ's name they had wrestled—they had clung to the right and beaten down the wrong; until at last that life of deep obedience—that faithfulness to God in what was least—all unexpectedly had reached their intellect, and made it a sphere of mastery and joy.[1]

> Just to ask Him what to do
>   All the day,
> And to make you quick and true
>   To obey.
> Just to know the needed grace
>   He bestoweth,
> Every bar of time and place
>   Overfloweth.
> Just to take thy orders straight
>   From the Master's own command.
> Blessed day! when thus we wait
>   Always at our Sovereign's hand.[2]

5. Obedience is rendered easy by sympathy and an open mind. The man who is full of himself, bent on his own will, seeking his own ends, is not in a frame of mind to have the secret of the Lord revealed to him: probably he does not want it, or wish to have it revealed to him. It is a check upon him. He does not want the key to the Kingdom of Heaven, because he has no wish whatever to enter into it. To enter into the Kingdom of God is to do the will of God, and to try to love it, and the will of God is human duty—what is due from us to God as poor, weak, ignorant creatures at the best; coming we know not whence, going we know not whither; seeing but a little way into things; living by faith, by trust in the power over us, trust in the good about us, trust in the good in other people; and what is due from us to

[1] G. H. Morrison, *The Wings of the Morning*, 19.
[2] F. R. Havergal.

others, for we are related to each other as brethren, because we are all related to God as the Father over all.

¶ "See how that noble fellow Collingwood leads the fleet into action!" exclaimed Nelson at the battle of Trafalgar, as he looked on the ship of his second bearing down upon the French line under a press of sail. "Ah! what would Nelson give to be here!" exclaimed Admiral Collingwood at the same moment. It seemed as if the two heroic men were animated by one spirit; as if by completeness of sympathy they knew each other's thoughts. And have we not all seen something like this in our own experience? Have we not known persons so congenial in thought and feeling that scenes in nature lighted up their faces with the same delight, or cast over them the shadows of thoughtfulness and awe; sights of distress and tales of sorrow drew forth from them kindred tears of compassion; a noble poem or an eloquent oration awakened in their bosoms the same pure and generous emotions? And such, too, is the power of sympathy between man and God. Just as a man tells his secret only to his friends, knowing that it would often be unsafe, and at other times impossible, to tell it to others; and just as they, knowing his great aim and motive, can make more of a nod or look or word than others can of a lengthened statement; so God reveals, as He did to Abraham His friend in the matter of Sodom's destruction, the depth of His mind and will to them who fear Him, and who by fearing Him have been made like Him; and they, loving in general as God loves, and hating in general as God hates, enter as others cannot into the meaning and spirit of God's declarations.[1]

II.

CHARACTER.

1. God unveils His character by entering into friendly relations with man. It is always a sign of deepening friendship when people begin to open their inner rooms to us. To be made the depository of a rare secret is to be sealed as a friend. When any one tells us a secret joy, it is a mark of intimacy; when any one unveils to us a secret grief, it is a proof of the closest fellowship. When we are taken from the suburbs of a man's being to the centre, it is a proof of an enriching communion. "No longer do I call you servants; but I have called you friends; for all things

[1] J. B. Johnston, *The Ministry of Reconciliation*, 335.

that I heard from my Father I have made known unto you."
Is there not something tenderly suggestive in the word which
tells us that "when they were alone, he expounded unto them"?
When He had His familiar friends to Himself, He told them His
secrets and showed them His covenant.

> Are these the tracks of some unearthly Friend,
>   His foot-prints, and his vesture-skirts of light,
>   Who, as I talk with men, conforms aright
> Their sympathetic words, or deeds that blend
> With my hid thought;—or stoops him to attend
>   My doubtful-pleading grief;—or blunts the might
>   Of ill I see not;—or in dreams of night
> Figures the scope, in which what is will end?
> Were I Christ's own, then fitly might I call
> That vision real; for to the thoughtful mind
> That walks with Him, He half unveils His face;
> But when on earth-stain'd souls such tokens fall,
> These dare not claim as theirs what there they find,
> Yet, not all hopeless, eye His boundless grace.[1]

2. Fellowship with God is the secret of the highest character
in man. If a man admires, reveres and attaches himself to any
one, he is naturally led to imitate him; and the tendency of all
worship is to make a man like his God. The deities of heathen-
dom are the product of the vain imaginations, unholy passions
and guilty fears of their votaries, and the contemplation of them
continues to quicken the foul source whence they have issued.
The sins as well as the sorrows of those who follow after other gods
are multiplied. And the worshippers of the true God are, in
accordance with this principle of our nature, brought to godliness,
induced and taught to love and hate, to approve and condemn,
according to the perfect model. In every one that fears God,
there is a real and growing assimilation.

¶ Some words of Kingsley's written in 1872, in which he
defines a "noble fear" as one of the elements of that lofty and
spiritual love which ruled his own daily life, may explain why he
speaks of entering the married state with "solemn awe and self-
humiliation," and why he looked upon such married Love as the
noblest education a man's character can have: "Can there be
true love without wholesome fear? And does not the old Eliza-

[1] J. H. Newman.

bethan 'My dear dread' express the noblest voluntary relation in which two human souls can stand to each other? Perfect love casteth out fear. Yes; but where is love perfect among imperfect beings, save a mother's for her child? For all the rest, it is through fear that love is made perfect; fear which bridles and guides the lover with awe—even though misplaced—of the beloved one's perfections; with dread—never misplaced—of the beloved one's contempt. And therefore it is that souls who have the germ of nobleness within, are drawn to souls more noble than themselves, just because, needing guidance, they cling to one before whom they dare not say, or do, or even think an ignoble thing. And if these higher souls are—as they usually are—not merely formidable, but tender likewise, and true, then the influence which they may gain is unbounded—both to themselves, and to those that worship them." [1]

3. To enjoy this fellowship we must "fear" the Lord. In order to read any one's secret we must respect him. You cannot show the real secret of your life, the spring and power of your living, to any man who does not respect you. Not merely you will not, but you cannot. Is it not so? A man comes with impertinent curiosity and looks in at your door, and you shut it in his face indignantly. A friend comes strolling by and gazes in with easy carelessness, not making much of what you may be doing, not thinking it of much importance, and before him you cover up instinctively the work which was serious to you, and make believe that you were only playing games. So it is when men try to get hold of the secret of your life. No friendship, no kindliness, can make you show it to them unless they evidently really feel as you feel, that it is a serious and sacred thing. There must be something like reverence or awe about the way that they approach you. It is the way in which children shut themselves up before their elders because they know their elders have no such sense as they have of the importance of their childish thoughts and feelings.

¶ You must believe that there is something deep in nature or you will find nothing there. You must have an awe of the mystery and sacredness in your fellow-man, or his mystery and sacredness will escape you. And this sense of mystery and sacredness is what we gather into that word "fear." It is the

[1] *Charles Kingsley*, i. 154.

feeling with which you step across the threshold of a great deserted temple or into some vast dark mysterious cavern. It is not terror. That would make one turn and run away. Terror is a blinding and deafening emotion. Terror shuts up the apprehension. You do not get at the secret of anything which frightens you, but fear, as we use the word now, is quite a different emotion. It is a large, deep sense of the majesty and importance of anything, a reverence and respect for it. Without that no man can understand another. And so "the secret of a man is with them that fear him."[1]

¶ We have listened to some sweet melody, and we cannot escape from its gracious thraldom. It pervades the entire day. It interweaves itself with all our changing affairs. We hear it in our work and in our leisure; when we retire to rest and when we awake. It haunts us. The analogy may help us to some apprehension of what is meant by the fear of God. The man who fears God is haunted by God's presence. God is an abiding consciousness. God is "continually before him." Everything is seen in relationship to God. The Divine presence pervades the mind and shapes and colours the judgment. Here are two descriptions from the Word of God, in the contrast of which the meaning will be made quite clear. "God is not in all his thoughts." The Eternal does not haunt his mind. Everything is secularized, and nothing is referred to the arbitrament of the Divine Will. He is not God-possessed. "Pray without ceasing." Here is the contrasted mind, from which the sense of God is never absent. Like an air of penetrating music the Divine presence pervades the exercise of all his powers. He is God-haunted, and in the consciousness of that presence he lives and moves and has his being. He fears God.[2]

III.

HAPPINESS.

1. The secret of happiness is love. The people of God love Him, and He loves them; their habitual feeling is that their affection and gratitude bear no proportion to the greatness of His claims. Like the penitent disciple who had had much forgiven, they can solemnly appeal to His omniscience and say, "Lord, thou knowest all things; thou knowest that I love thee." And He loves them with a love which has a height and depth, and

---

[1] Phillips Brooks, *New Starts in Life*, 275.
[2] J. H. Jowett, *Brooks by the Traveller's Way*, 173.

length and breadth passing knowledge—a love which has thrown open to them the book of Nature that their eyes might be filled with its beauty and their souls with its truth—a love which sings sweet songs in the carol of the bird, in the murmur of the brook, in the whispering of the breeze, and in the joyous music of the domestic hearth—a love which covers the earth with golden grain, and casts abundance into the lap of life—a love which has toiled, and bled, and died that the soul of man might be taken from the spoiler who has held it under his cruel and polluting sway, and be brought under the dominion of its rightful Lord and made fully happy, and that for ever, in His fellowship.

¶ He looked out on the world through the eyes of Love, and that is why it was to him ever beautiful in its infinite variety, and in its amazing friendliness. He lived to be seventy-one as the world counts years, but even then he was Youth and Joy—in the best sense of the word he refused to grow up.[1]

¶ Though Mr. Paynter was a deeply spiritual man, there was nothing in his life or speech to suggest gloom; certainly there was not in his looks. Many a laugh have we had together, over some amusing incident or story, in the lighter interludes of life; and though he himself rarely told a story, yet sometimes he would make a "dry" remark, which showed that the sense of humour was not absent. He was a happy man—happy in all the domesticities of his home and family life—happy among his flowers—happy in his work—happy always in doing good to others, and all because he was happy in God, and had learned what St. Paul meant when he said, "All things are yours."[2]

> Just to recollect His love,
>   Always true;
> Always shining from above,
>   Always new.
> Just to recognize its light
>   All-enfolding;
> Just to claim its present might,
>   All-upholding.
> Just to know it as thine own,
>   That no power can take away.
> Is not this enough alone
>   For the gladness of the day?[3]

[1] *Love and Life: The Story of J. Denholm Brash* (1913), 8.
[2] S. M. Nugent, *Life Radiant: Memorials of the Rev. F. Paynter*, 228.
[3] F. R. Havergal.

2. We learn the secret of happiness as we try to express our love in noble character and unselfish conduct. Men are so constituted that obedience is its own reward. There is no delight so deep and true as the delight of doing the will of Him whom we love. There is no blessedness like that of the increasing communion with God and of the clearer perception of His will and mind which follow obedience as surely as the shadow follows the sunshine. There is no blessedness like the glow of approving conscience, the reflection of the smile on Christ's face.

To have the heart in close communion with the very Fountain of all good, and the will in harmony with the will of the best Beloved; to hear the Voice that is dearest of all ever saying, "This is the way, walk ye in it"; to feel "a spirit in my feet" impelling me upon that road; to know that all my petty deeds are made great, and my stained offerings hallowed by the altar on which they are honoured to lie; and to be conscious of fellowship with the Friend of my soul increased by obedience—this is to taste the keenest joy and good of life, and he who is thus "blessed in his deed" need never fear that that blessedness will be taken away, or sorrow though other joys be few and griefs be many.

¶ To Florence Nightingale, communion with the Unseen meant something deeper, richer, fuller, more positive than the fear of God. The fear of God is the beginning, but not the end, of wisdom, for perfect love casteth out fear. It was for the love of God as an active principle in her mind, constraining all her deeds, that she strove.[1]

¶ The income from his books and other sources, which might have been spent in a life of luxury and selfishness, he distributed lavishly where he saw it was needed, and in order to do this he always lived in the most simple way. To make others happy was the Golden Rule of his life. On August 31 he wrote, in a letter to a friend, Miss Mary Brown: "And now what am I to tell you about myself? To say I am quite well 'goes without saying' with me. In fact, my life is so strangely free from all trial and trouble that I cannot doubt my own happiness is one of the talents entrusted to me to 'occupy' with, till the Master shall return, by doing something to make other lives happy."[2]

---

[1] Sir Edward Cook, *The Life of Florence Nightingale*, i. 50.
[2] S. D. Collingwood, *The Life and Letters of Lewis Carroll*, 325.

3. And thus we are brought round again to knowledge. For the final verdict upon the realities of religion rests not with the highest intellect, but with the purest heart. Humboldt tells that the Arab guide employed in one of his desert journeys had such a keen and highly trained power of vision that he could see the moons of Jupiter without a telescope, and that he gave the date when one of those moons was eclipsed, a date afterwards verified by the traveller on his return to Europe. The watch-maker, the line-engraver, the microscopist, who for years have been poring over minute objects a few inches from the face, could not emulate the feat of the Arab whose eye had been trained for a lifetime by use in the desert, and might possibly doubt the fact. In that respect the man of science himself, with his wide know-ledge, exact observation, many accomplishments, was inferior to his unlettered guide. A devout soul seeks wistfully after God, accustoms its faculties to discern and interpret His signs, and acquires a vision penetrative beyond that of his neighbour.

¶ In one of his saddest poems—in the series entitled "Men and Women"—Browning tells the story of Andrea del Sarto, who was called the faultless painter of Florence. In his youth he had loved and married a woman of rare and radiant beauty. He rendered to her an almost worshipping homage. He longed to lift her to the high plane of thought and desire and holy ambition on which he moved. But she was a shallow, thin-natured, mean-souled woman. She was the woman who smeared with a careless fling of her skirt the picture he had painted in hours of spiritual ecstasy. She was the woman who craved him for his hard-earned money that she might spend it at the gaming-table with her dissolute companions. Browning sets down the tragedy of their years with his usual unerring insight. It was not that she dis-appointed him, robbed his hand of its power, dulled his mind, shadowed his heart, and, as he foresaw, would sully his fame. It was this more piteous thing, that he could not disclose himself to her. She was not able to see and to understand him at his highest and noblest. She never discerned the moral majesty of his mind or the spiritual hunger of his heart. The poet sets the sorrow of it all in a sigh, which is the climax of his story.

> But had you—oh, with the same perfect brow,
> And perfect eyes, and more than perfect mouth,
> And the low voice my soul hears, as a bird
> The fowler's pipe, and follows to the snare—
> Had you, with these the same, but brought a mind!

Lover he was, with the lover's secret, but she brought no mind, and the lover's secret she never knew. For the lover's secret is only with them that fear.[1]

4. The nearer we live to Christ, the further shall we see into the Unseen and discern the secret of God. The vision of the godly man, like that of the prophet at Bethel, pierces into the unseen, and he is sensible of things to which others are blind. If he cannot envisage horses and chariots of fire, the vindicating ministries of the covenant, he can read the terms of the covenant in letters clear as the stars, and these revelations are enough, and assure as perfectly as glimpses of the hosts God leads. Doubts and misgivings are dispelled by spiritual insight. In the things which, to a worldly mind, suggest the anger of Heaven, he is made to see occasions which discipline the character into higher fitness for receiving the awaiting blessings of an immutable covenant.

¶ For many years a lady made her livelihood by taking Greenwich time round to the jewellers' shops in the small towns to the west of London. She was the daughter of a watchmaker, and possessed an excellent chronometer which had been bequeathed by her father. When necessary, the authorities of the Observatory kindly regulated it. Every Friday she went to Greenwich, got the standard time, and carried it to her clients, who paid a small fee for the service rendered. She belonged to the old dispensation, and may stand for one of its types. Many provincial towns, and even private firms of watchmakers, are now in direct electric connexion with Greenwich, and get the standard time every day. . . . In the United States of America, every post office is linked with the Observatory at Washington. Under the earlier Covenant, men who wished to learn of the things of God had to avail themselves of the ministries of the prophets, or sit at the feet of scholars, whose office it was to interpret the books of the law. But under the New Covenant the regenerate soul is brought into direct contact with God, and acquires Divine wisdom, not by listening to a neighbour, but by heeding swift inward impressions wrought by the wonderful Spirit of God.[2]

Love touch'd my eyes—these eyes which once were blind,
　　And, lo! a glorious world reveal'd to view,
A world I ne'er had dream'd so fair to find.
　　I sang for gladness—all things were made new.

---

[1] W. M. Clow, *The Secret of the Lord*, 10.
[2] T. G. Selby, *The Divine Craftsman*, 175.

'Twas Love unstopp'd my ears, and every sound
　　Borne through the silence seem'd a psalm of praise:
Bird-song, child-laughter—yet o'er all I found
　　Thy voice the music of my happy days.

Love chang'd life's draught and made the water wine,
　　And through my languid senses seem'd to flow
Some pow'r enkindled by the fire divine,
　　Some inspiration I can ne'er forego.

Love rais'd the dead to life—and never more
　　Can many waters quench th' eternal flame.
Love open'd wide the everlasting door,
　　And bade us enter, callèd by His name.[1]

[1] Una, *In Life's Garden*, 6.

WAITING COURAGEOUSLY.

LITERATURE.

Bright (W.), *Morality in Doctrine*, 115.
Craig (R.), *Rock Plants with Gospel Roots*, 27.
Dyke (H. van), *Manhood, Faith and Courage*, 53.
Jowett (J. H.), *From Strength to Strength*, 65.
Maclaren (A.), *Creed and Conduct*, 15.
Newman (J. H.), *Sermons on Subjects of the Day*, 47.
Spurgeon (C. H.), *Morning by Morning*, 243.
    „   „   *Metropolitan Tabernacle Pulpit*, xxiii. (1877), No. 1371.
Steel (T. H.), *Sermons in Harrow Chapel*, 315.
Vaughan (J.), *Sermons in Christ Church, Brighton*, 2nd Ser., 51.
Wynne (G. R.), *In Quietness and Confidence*, 50.
Christian World Pulpit, xliv. 321 (C. S. Horne) ; liii. 136 (H. Black) ; lvii.
    27 (J. G. Rogers) ; lviii. 401 (J. H. Jowett).
Church of England Magazine, xxxiv. 168 (R. W. Dale).
Church of England Pulpit, lx. 286 (C. Wordsworth).
Churchman's Pulpit : Sermons to the Young, xvi. 406 (R. G. Soans).
Twentieth Century Pastor, xxx. 20 (A. B. Macaulay).

WAITING COURAGEOUSLY.

Wait on the Lord:
Be strong, and let thine heart take courage;
Yea, wait thou on the Lord.—Ps. xxvii. 14.

THIS is the concluding verse of a psalm which glows with lofty faith, and yet is clouded by a sense of depression. The magnificent opening, with its fulness of glad, exuberant energy, its high-hearted disclaimer of all fear in view of a host of enemies, and its fervid avowal of one supreme desire—to dwell in the Lord's house and to gaze upon His beauty—is followed up by entreaties which represent a change of mood. It is one of those transitions so common in the Psalter, which make it so truly human a book. Acting on the invitation, "Seek ye my face," the Psalmist begs his Lord not to cast him away, not to forsake him; he describes himself as an orphan whom God will adopt, and he glances tremblingly at a contingency which would surely have overwhelmed him—

What if no faith were mine, to see
Thy love in realms where life shall be?

But the psalm goes back to the major key at last, and in the closing verse prayer passes into self-encouragement. The heart that spoke to God now speaks to itself. Faith exhorts sense and soul to "wait on Jehovah." The self-communing of the Psalmist, beginning with exultant confidence and merging into prayer thrilled with consciousness of need and of weakness, closes with bracing him up to courage, which is not presumption, because it is the fruit of waiting on the Lord. He who thus keeps his heart in touch with God will be able to obey the ancient command, which had rung so long before in the ears of Joshua and is never out of date, "Be strong and of a good courage"; and none but those who wait on the Lord will be at once conscious of weakness and filled with strength, aware of the foes and bold to meet them.

I.

WAITING.

The word "walk" describes almost the whole of Christian life, and so does this word "wait"; for, rightly understood, waiting is active as well as passive, energetic as well as patient, and to wait upon the Lord necessitates as much courage as warring and fighting with enemies. It may seem an easy thing to wait, but it is one of the postures which a Christian soldier learns only with years of teaching. Marching and quick-marching are much easier to God's warriors than standing still. There are hours of perplexity when the most willing spirit, anxiously desirous to serve the Lord, knows not what part to take. Then what shall it do? Vex itself by despair? Fly back in cowardice, turn to the right hand in fear, or rush forward in presumption? No, but simply wait.

¶ The English Prayer-Book version of the Psalms gives a quaint but beautiful rendering of the phrase "Wait on the Lord." It runs, "O tarry thou the Lord's leisure." This rendering brings out the exact meaning of the word "wait," which we have interlarded and lost sight of by making it mean such things—and legitimately enough—as prayer. It just means "wait." Wait for Him as you would wait at the trysting-place for a friend who does not come. Wait for Him, and wait, and wait until He does come.[1]

> When He appoints to meet thee, go thou forth.
>   It matters not
> If south or north,
>   Bleak waste or sunny plot.
> Nor think, if haply He thou seek'st be late,
>   He does thee wrong;
> To stile or gate
>   Lean thou thy head, and long!
> It may be that to spy thee He is mounting
>   Upon a tower,
> Or in thy counting
>   Thou hast mista'en the hour.

[1] Hugh Black.

But, if He come not, neither do thou go
    Till Vesper chime;
Belike thou then shalt know
    He hath been with thee all the time.[1]

1. Let us wait with *faith*. It is faith that secures the Divine blessing—persistent, expectant faith. He cannot be said to wait upon God who disbelieves that God will come to his aid, or who doubts whether He will. Loitering about to see if anything will turn up is not the same thing, by any means, as waiting for a particular person to appear, or a particular event to happen. Faith and expectation characterize the latter condition as distinct from the former. And these qualities belong to the very nature of the exercise of "waiting on God." The more unwavering a man's faith is, in fact, and the higher he stretches on tiptoe of expectation, the more accurately may he be described as a man waiting on God. "My soul," cries the Psalmist, "waiteth for the Lord more than they that watch for the morning." How eager he represents himself to be by that figure of the anxious watchers scanning the eastern skies for signs of daybreak! And how confident, too! For more surely than the sun shall climb up over the horizon and dispel the shadows of night, his God, he believes, shall cause His face to shine upon him. His God and our God— it is not to immensity or infinity, or some dimly comprehended and overwhelming attribute, precariously personified, that we look up for help and a response to our supplications. It is to the living, self-revealing God, who hath "of old time spoken unto the fathers in the prophets," and who "hath at the end of these days spoken unto us in his Son."

¶ There is a school of philosophy, much current in our day, which tells us that religious truth is relative to the individual; the way to test a religion is to live it. If the philosophy of the pragmatists be right, then few forms of religious creed can claim better witness to their truth than that wherein Florence Nightingale lived and moved and had her being. She had "remodelled her whole religious belief from beginning to end," and had "learnt to know God" in the years immediately preceding her active work in the world. Her belief helped to sustain her natural courage amidst the horrors of Scutari, and the fever and the cold of Balaclava. It inspired the life of arduous labour to which she

[1] T. E. Brown, *Old John and Other Poems*, 244.

devoted herself on returning from the East. It informed her unceasing efforts for the health of the Army and the people, for the reformation of hospitals, for the creation of an art of nursing. Does some one doubt whether any vital force can have proceeded from a belief in Law as the Thought of God, and suggest that to herself as to others she was offering a stone instead of bread? It was not so. To her the religion which she found was as the body and blood of the Most High.[1]

¶ In the early spring of 1881 Captain Catherine Booth and her intrepid lieutenants, Florence Soper, Adelaide Cox, and Ruth Patrick, began life in Paris. With her own hand Catherine raised the flag at Rue d'Angoulême 66, in Belleville. Here was a hall for six hundred, situated in a court approached by a narrow street. The bulk of the audience that gathered there night after night were of the artisan class. Some were young men of a lower type, and from these came what disturbance there was. The French sense of humour is keen, and there were many lively sallies at the expense of the speakers and singers on the platform. Meetings were held night after night, and for six months the Capitaine was never absent except on Saturdays. Those were days of fight, and she fought, to use her own phrase, like a tiger. She had to fight first her own heart. She knew her capacity, and God had done great things through her in England. The change from an audience of five thousand spell-bound hearers in the circus of Leeds to a handful of gibing *ouvriers* in the Belleville quarter of Paris was indeed a clashing antithesis. A fortnight passed without a single penitent, and Catherine was all the time so ill that it was doubtful if she would be able to remain in the field. That fortnight was probably the supreme trial of her faith. The work appeared so hopeless! There was nothing to see. But for the Capitaine faith meant *going on*. It meant saying to her heart, "You may suffer, you may bleed, you may break, but you shall go on." She went on, believing, praying, fighting, and at last the tide of battle turned.[2]

2. Let us wait with *patience*. Patience is just the other side and the practical side of faith. Faith is the breath of life to the religious man. Without faith he cannot live. But there may be, and there often is, a faith which is extremely lacking in patience, a faith which is even impatient, a faith which, in the name of God, almost rebukes God for His leisure with the world, and with the

---

[1] Sir Edward Cook, *The Life of Florence Nightingale*, i. 488.
[2] J. Strahan, *The Maréchale* (1913), 51.

Church, and with ourselves. We know it to be a Christian duty
to be patient with our fellow-men; have we ever thought of the
necessity and the duty of being patient with God? Let us have
patience with God. And this patience, about which the Bible is
full, is not the sickly, complaining counterfeit of it which we often
hear of under the name of patience; it is the power to suffer, the
power to sacrifice, the power to endure, the power to die, and, if
need be, sometimes harder as it is, to continue to live for His sake.
Let us wait God's time. If there were no other reason why we
must wait God's time, this is one, and one all-powerful—because He
knows the whole, and because we know only a part. The Psalmist
cries out, under protracted and aggravated trials, "Lord, *how* long?"
but he never complains or murmurs, "Lord, this is *too* long!"

¶ It is worthy of remark that Bishop King's first Charge
elicited warm commendation from the prelate who, of all the
Bishops at that time on the Bench, possessed the acutest and
most vigorous intellect. Bishop Magee, of Peterborough, wrote
on November 28, 1886:—

"What I write specially to thank you for is simply one
sentence in your Charge—a very pregnant one, and to me, I
confess, a new one—it is, 'The Soul is impatient of the Mediatorial
Kingdom.' This is a thought which runs out very far and very
deep under all our Christian life. The '*im*patient,' instead of the
'patient, waiting for Christ,' is seen, when we come to think of it,
to be the source of no small part of our ecclesiastical and even our
personal errors and troubles." [1]

> Say, did impatience first impel
>   The heaven-sent bond to break?
> Or, couldst thou bear its hindrance well,
>   Loitering for Jesu's sake?
>
> Oh, might we know! for sore we feel
>   The languor of delay,
> When sickness lets our fainter zeal,
>   Or foes block up our way.
>
> Lord! who Thy thousand years dost wait
>   To work the thousandth part
> Of Thy vast plan, for us create
>   With zeal a patient heart. [2]

[1] G. W. E. Russell, *Edward King, Bishop of Lincoln,* 122.
[2] J. H. Newman, *Verses on Various Occasions.*

3. Let us wait with *assurance*. According to our English
Versions, the 62nd Psalm begins with the words, " Truly my soul
waiteth," or " My soul waiteth only upon God." The adverbs do
not matter at present, but the verb does. What the Psalmist
actually wrote, as we can see from the word which he used, was,
" My soul is silent unto God." The same expression occurs elsewhere in the Old Testament. It is a very striking one. The
condition of silence before God, inward silence, with every fret
and murmur and disturbing thought hushed, was recognized as
the condition suitable for hearing the still small voice of the
Eternal One. Those that achieved it were rewarded. And have
we no experiences of our own to corroborate the testimony of
these Old Testament writers ? Matthew Arnold tells us that—

> From the soul's subterranean depth upborne
> As from an infinitely distant land,
> Come airs and floating echoes and convey
> A melancholy into all our day.

But other airs and other echoes as well are upborne from the
depths of the soul. There is conveyed into the day of the soul
that waits upon God and is silent unto Him a peace and a quiet
sense of assurance that passes all understanding. Language
cannot describe the source and nature of these inward ministries
of strength and consolation, but the soul knows that God has
responded to its waiting.

¶ " Does it hurt you severely ? " one asked of a friend who lay
with a broken arm. " Not when I keep still," was the answer.
This is the secret of much of the victoriousness we see in rejoicing
Christians. They conquer the pain and the bitterness by keeping
still. They do not ask questions, or demand to know why they
have trials. They believe in God, and are so sure of His love and
wisdom that they are pained by no doubt, no fear, no uncertainty.
Peace is their pillow, because they have learned just to be still.
Their quietness robs trial of its sharpness, sorrow of its bitterness,
death of its sting, and the grave of its victory.[1]

4. Let us wait with *prayer*. Let us call upon God and spread
our case before Him; tell Him our difficulty, and plead His
promise of aid. In dilemmas between one duty and another, it is
sweet to be humble as a child, and to wait with simplicity of soul

[1] J. R. Miller.

upon the Lord. It is sure to be well with us when we feel and know our own folly, and are heartily willing to be guided by the will of God. Let us remember that God has always loved intervals. Intervals there are generally, if not always, in His best dealings with His children—intervals before He bestows His greatest blessings, intervals before He answers prayer. And a great part of man's education lies in these intervals. The intellect is humbled, the heart is curbed, faith is trained, hopes are pointed, promises are sweetened, God is magnified. And are they not the growing times of mercies—the darkness brought in for no other end than that the light may be seen in it?

¶ By prayer we link ourselves on to the inexhaustible riches of God. How it comes that, when I pull a switch down in my study, the room is flooded with light no man can say, save that by doing so I have linked my need on to the great centre of light energy in the town. So, all that we can say about those who keep their hearts open towards God and in the love of Christ is that by this means they link their weakness on to the grace and strength of the Eternal. But, mark you, the electric current does not break into my room of itself when my need arises. I have to make a way for it, and more, *I have to keep that way open*.[1]

¶ Prayer was the white flame at the very centre of his life. To the throne of Grace, with unfailing mindfulness and with childlike simplicity, he would bring, day by day, his friends, his people, those in special sorrow, sickness, or sin; so filling his petitions with engrossed and concentrated intercession for them in their needs that he became wholly forgetful of his own. Once, when I had been ill, he said to me, "I have prayed for you night and morning for five months." And I knew that it was true. In his long life it was true of thousands of others. And he believed, with such intensity and simplicity of conviction as no man can ever have surpassed, that every word of intercession that he uttered went straight to a heavenly Father's ear, and found an answering chord in a heavenly Father's heart.[2]

> Unanswered yet, the prayer your lips have pleaded,
>   In agony of heart these many years?
> Does faith begin to fail? Is hope departing,
>   And think you all in vain those falling tears?
> Say not the Father hath not heard your prayer;
> You shall have your desire sometime, somewhere.

[1] Archibald Alexander.
[2] Frances Balfour, *Dr. MacGregor of St. Cuthberts*, 532.

Unanswered yet, though when you first presented
   This one petition at the Father's Throne,
It seemed you could not wait the time of asking,
   So urgent was your heart to have it known?
Though years have passed since then, do not despair;
The Lord will answer you sometime, somewhere.

Unanswered yet? Nay, do not say ungranted;
   Perhaps your part is not yet wholly done;
The work began when first your prayer was uttered,
   And God will finish what He has begun.
If you will keep the incense burning there,
His glory you will see sometime, somewhere.

Unanswered yet? Faith cannot be unanswered,
   Her feet are firmly planted on the rock;
Amid the wildest storms she stands undaunted,
   Nor quails before the loudest thunder shock.
She knows Omnipotence has heard her prayer,
And cries, It shall be done—sometime, somewhere.

5. Let us wait with *regularity*. The most prominent feature of our waiting is too often its spasmodic character. Now and then we draw near to God, but by fits and starts, with long intervals of indifference and prayerlessness between. And that is just about as hopeless as it would be to expect to keep ourselves clean by bathing once a week. Daily our strength drains away, both physical and spiritual, and as the one must constantly be replenished, so must the other. Even earnest bursts of effort at intervals do not count for anything like so much as the quiet, constant keeping in the love of God. Volcanic eruptions have done something to transform the earth's surface, but not nearly so much, geologists tell us, as the quiet, constant forces, the sun, the rain, frost, heat, and wind. And it is by the regular daily waiting, far more than by the infrequent upheaval of desire, that the power of God and the likeness of Christ pass slowly but visibly into the lives of His people. It is the daily meeting with God in spirit, the daily thought of one's humble task as God's call to us to serve Him, the daily sense that we are His children, destined and called in Christ to fellowship with Him, the sense that we are not alone in our little corner, but that He is all about us, so that we live and move and have our being in Him, like islands in

some great sea—it is that, repeated and continued till it becomes the habit of the spirit, that transfigures life and lifts it to blessedness and power.

¶ It is related of Schwabe the German astronomer that, wishing to determine the relation between sun-spots and earth-magnetism, he gave himself to the recording of the varying appearances of the sun's surface. For forty-two years the sun never rose a single morning free of clouds above the flat horizon of the plain at Dessau where Schwabe lived but his patient telescope was there to confront it! The man of science believes in Nature. He waits for it, in the faith that it is, and that it is the rewarder of those that diligently seek it. If only Christian people would realize that it is infinitely more worth their while to wait thus patiently upon God, what wonders of Spirit-filled lives we should see ![1]

¶ The other day I stumbled across a little book in which he wrote the names of those for whom he prayed, and the day of the week on which he interceded for them. It was a revelation—for one would have thought that many of those names had been forgotten by him years before. There is a great unity in the list; they all sorely needed the Divine help. He also prayed daily by name for the members of his family, and each worker of our Church on the Foreign Field was remembered by him. With the map before him he interceded for the many nations of the world.[2]

II.

COURAGE.

As many as are the conflicts and perils and hardships of life, so many are the uses and the forms of courage. Courage is necessary, indeed, as the protector and defender of all the other virtues. Courage is the standing army of the soul, which keeps it from conquest, pillage, and slavery. Unless we are brave we can hardly be truthful, or generous, or just, or pure, or kind, or loyal. "Few persons," says a wise observer, "have the courage to appear as good as they really are." You must be brave in order to fulfil your own possibilities of virtue. Courage is essential to

---

[1] Archibald Alexander.
[2] *Love and Life: The Story of J. Denholm Brash*, 65.

guard the best qualities of the soul, and to clear the way for their action, and make them move with freedom and vigour.

Courage, an independent spark from Heaven's throne,
By which the soul stands raised, triumphant, high, alone;
The spring of all true acts is seated here,
As falsehoods draw their sordid birth from fear.

If we desire to be good, we must first of all desire to be brave, that against all opposition, scorn, and danger we may move straight onward to do the right.

¶ The Rev. Henry Parnaby, M.A., writes: "Only six days ago I had a long talk with the surgeon who attended Principal Simon in Liverpool — Dr. Armour — and he told me something very characteristic of the old Principal. When his trouble had reached a certain stage, Dr. Armour suggested to Dr. Simon that by a very delicate and difficult operation he could be cured. The operation, however, was attended with very great risk, and possibly Dr. Simon would not survive. The decision was left to him, and he took a week to think over it. He went off and consulted his family, and returned a week later to announce that he had decided not to undergo the operation. His reason was this. He was in such dreadful and continuous pain that he felt he would go into the operation with eagerness, because it promised an end of his trouble either by cure or death. He felt that he would welcome this as an end of his pain, and that therefore he would be displaying an unwillingness to endure the purifying pain which he accepted as a means of spiritual discipline from God. Dr. Armour assures me that never in all his wide experience has he found another patient who could give so courageous and honourable a reason for declining to undergo an operation.[1]

¶ One winter night the Maréchale and two young comrades, Blanche Young and Kate Patrick, went out with shawls on their heads, and made their way to one of the boulevard cafés. The leader passed the door, and passed it again. She turned to her lieutenants and said, "You have never known your Maréchale till now; you see what a coward she is!"
"No, no, no!" they both protested.
At last she put her hand on the door, pushed it open, and went in. A man in a white apron was selling drink. Going up to him, she said, "May I sing something?"
He stared open-mouthed.

[1] F. J. Powicke, *David Worthington Simon*, 297.

Trembling from head to foot, she repeated, "I should like to sing something,"

"Very well!"

She began:

> Le ciel est ma belle patrie,
> Les anges y font leur séjour;
> Le soldat qui lutte et qui prie
> Y sera bientôt à son tour.

While she sang, Blanche chimed in with her guitar and her second voice. As they proceeded, the smoking, drinking, and card-playing ceased, and every face was turned towards them. They sang on:

> En marche, en marche,
> Soldats, vers la patrie!
> En marche, en marche,
> Soldats, vers la patrie!

When they had finished the hymn, the Maréchale thanked her audience, adding that they could hear her again at Rue Auber Hall; and that she knew a Friend, of whom she wished to tell them. As she and her comrades turned to walk out, the man in the white apron bowed, as if they had done him a service.

"May I come another time?" said the Maréchale.

"Certainly, Mademoiselle!" [1]

1. What is the source of courage? It is waiting on the Lord. That is the truest and deepest source of courage. To believe that He is, and that He has made us for Himself; to love Him, and give ourselves up to Him, because He is holy and true and wise and good and brave beyond all human thought; to lean upon Him and trust Him and rest in Him, with confidence that He will never leave us nor forsake us: to work for Him, and suffer for His sake, and be faithful to His service—that is the way to learn courage. Without God what can we do? We are frail, weak, tempted, mortal. The burdens of life will crush us, the evils of sin will destroy us, the tempests of trouble will overwhelm us, the darkness of death will engulf us. But if we are joined to God, we can resist and endure and fight and conquer in His strength. This is what the Psalmist means in the text, "Wait on the Lord; be of good courage, and he shall strengthen thine heart."

[1] J. Strahan, *The Maréchale* (1913), 114.

Had we the strength !—Have we perhaps the strength,
Who have all else beside ? Are we not men ?
Is not the Universe our dwelling-place ?
And therefore perfectly in truth for us
Is not the utmost wholly possible ? . . .
O, with the baffled and the resolute
Vanguard of liberal humanity,—
O to so purge our lives of the mild hours,
Our hearts of humble longings and meek hopes,
Our minds of customs and credulities,
That we may find the days wholly fulfilled
And lightened of the Spirit—all the days
And all things and ourselves, rich and revealed
In the majestic meanings and the might
And passion and pure purpose of the soul ![1]

¶ Torstensohn was one of the generals formed in the school of
Gustavus Adolphus. To him that great commander transmitted
the prosecution of the Thirty Years' War. Physically, he was
so shattered and dislocated by disease and deformity that he
could neither walk nor ride on horseback. He had to be carried
at the head of his forces in a litter. Yet no commander of his
age was so resistless and terrible in his onset and so invariably
victorious. Let us be loath to accept infirmity as an excuse for
uselessness. A naturalist asks : "How is it that the golden-
crested wren, apparently so weak and helpless, can fly right
across the North Sea from Norway ?" Because God knows how to
fix strange energy within delicate organisms. Our very infirmities
through resolution and grace may give us special efficacy.[2]

2. How does waiting on God sustain our courage ?

(1) Our heart is strengthened by waiting upon God, because
we receive a mysterious strength through the incoming of the
Eternal Spirit into our souls. No man can explain this, but
many of us know what it is. How wonderfully do the secret
springs of omnipotence break into the feeble soul and fill it with
might in the inner man. Through the sacred anointing of the
Holy Ghost we have been made to shout for joy. He that made
us has put His hand a second time to the work, and restored to us
the joy of His salvation, filled our emptiness, removed our weakness, and triumphed in us gloriously.

[1] G. C. Lodge, *Poems and Dramas*, ii. 137.
[2] W. L. Watkinson.

¶ That these days at the Keswick Convention in 1889 were a turning-point in Mr. Macgregor's life, there is not the smallest doubt. That they made his later ministry what it was, is equally certain. To say that he sometimes appeared to claim for this experience and its effects more than the facts altogether warranted, is only to say that, though remarkably enlightened and strengthened by God's Spirit, he remained a fallible human being. But no one who knew George Macgregor, either as a man or a minister, before that crisis and after it, could question that he found then a new secret of strength both for his own life and for his work.[1]

(2) Waiting upon God makes men grow small, and dwarfs the world and all its affairs, till we see their real littleness. Set your great troubles before the infinite God, and they will dwarf into such little things that you will never notice them again. " He taketh up the isles as a very little thing," and " the nations are as a drop of a bucket"; and this great God teaches us to look at earthly things in the same light as He does, till, though the whole world should be against us, we can smile at its rage. Our worst ills are utterly despised when we learn to measure them by the line of the Eternal.

¶ Sometimes in the country on a night in early summer you may shut the cottage door to step out into an immense darkness which palls heaven and earth. Going forward into the embrace of the great gloom, you are as a babe swaddled by the hands of night into helpless acquiescence. Your feet tread an unseen path, your hands grasp at a void, or shrink from the contact they cannot realize ; your eyes are holden ; your voice would die in your throat did you seek to rend the veil of that impenetrable silence.

Shut in by the intangible dark, we are brought up against those worlds within worlds blotted out by our concrete daily life. The working of the great microcosm at which we peer dimly through the little window of science; the wonderful, breathing earth; the pulsing, throbbing sap; the growing fragrance shut in the calyx of to-morrow's flower; the heart-beat of a sleeping world that we dream that we know; and around, above, and interpenetrating all, the world of dreams, of angels and of spirits.

It was this world which Jacob saw on the first night of his exile, and again when he wrestled in Peniel until the break of day. It was this world which Elisha saw with open eyes ; which Job knew when darkness fell on him ; which Ezekiel gazed into

[1] Duncan C. Macgregor, *George H. C. Macgregor*, 111.

from his place among the captives; which Daniel beheld as he
stood alone by the great river, the river Hiddekel.

For the moment we have left behind the realm of question
and explanation, of power over matter and the exercise of bodily
faculties; and passed into darkness alight with visions we cannot
see, into silence alive with voices we cannot hear. Like helpless
men we set our all on the one thing left us, and lift up our
hearts, knowing that we are but a mere speck among a myriad
worlds, yet greater than the sum of them; having our roots in
the dark places of the earth, but our branches in the sweet airs
of heaven.[1]

(3) Nothing can give us greater courage than a sincere
affection for our Lord and His work. Courage is sure to
abound where love is fervent. Look among the mild and gentle
creatures of the brute creation and see how bold they are when
once they become mothers and have to defend their offspring.
A hen will fight for her chicks, though at another time she is
one of the most timid of birds. Gilbert White, in his *Natural
History of Selborne*, tells of a raven that was hatching her
young in a tree. The woodman began to fell it, but there she
sat; the blows of the axe shook the tree, but she never moved,
and when it fell she was still upon her nest. Love will make
the most timid creature strong; and if you love Christ you will
defy all fear, and count all hazards undergone for Him to be your
joy. In this sense, too, perfect love casteth out fear; it "hopeth
all things, endureth all things," and continues still to wait upon
the Lord.

¶ In February 1894 she had two of the finest campaigns of
her life—at Havre and Rouen. The turbulent beginning at
Havre was graphically described by her friend the Princess
Malsoff, who accompanied the Maréchale in order to have a
taste of the *vie apostolique*. "There was a great tumult in the
'Lyre Havraise.' The Maréchale had come to publish the word
of love and salvation. An immense crowd forced itself into the
hall, and who would have dared believe that they had all come
simply to present the world with the most scandalous, the most
vulgar and odious spectacle that one can imagine? When the
Maréchale rose with great dignity and calm . . . she could not
make herself heard. Every word was interrupted; one could
see that it was a prepared stroke. One might imagine oneself to

[1] Michael Fairless, *The Roadmender*, 86.

be in an asylum. But she did not let herself be discouraged ; she persevered; she walked straight into the midst of the infuriated crowd. She did not tame these wild beasts, but she came out victorious all the same. Tall, beautiful, calm, sustained by her divine conviction and with the strength of a great heart, she came back again and again—our admirable Maréchale ! . . . In the midst of this infernal and ridiculous tumult a few *élite* souls felt a noble enthusiasm for this young woman who battled alone against a hostile and wicked crowd. They came to grasp her hand, to express their admiration for her and their shame for those who had broken the simplest laws of hospitality, politeness, and civilization. Blessed be our Maréchale; in her the whole *Armée du Salut* was personified that night in its strength, its faith, its persevering love." [1]

> The Master knows ; He can but see
> How willingly, how joyfully
> I would within His vineyard stay
> To bear the burden of the day,
> And yet He bids me stand apart
> With folded hands and longing heart.
> I see at morn the happy throng
> Pass by my door with jest and song.
> They seem so glad, they seem so gay,
> So ready for the busy day.
>
> And when at eve they homeward go
> Sometimes with weary steps and slow,
> But laden with the sweet new wine,
> And purple clusters of the vine,
> And precious sheaves of golden grain
> To recompense their toil and pain ;
> But that the Lord doth choose for me,
> I fain within their ranks would be.
>
> Yet though I can but hope and wait,
> I am not sad or desolate.
> For every day with bounty free
> The Master bringeth gifts to me.
> From out His life there seems to shine
> A wondrous glory into mine.
> My life ! how dark and how unclean,
> How poor and fruitless has it been.

[1] J. Strahan, *The Maréchale* (1913), 62.

But sure the seed He planted there
That should have grown so tall and fair
Must now, at last, begin to spring
Beneath such heavenly nourishing.

And if, perchance, I fail to see
The thought of God concerning me,
I leave in peace my fallow field
Till love divine shall make it yield.
And when at last the corn and wine
Of all His harvests shall be mine,
Then shall I know, or soon, or late,
They also serve who stand and wait.

THE TRANSIENCE OF SORROW.

LITERATURE.

Crosthwait, E. G. S., *Heavenward Steps*, 78.

Davies (D.), *Talks with Men, Women and Children*, i. 17.

Hutton (R. E.), *The Crown of Christ*, i. 547.

Ingram (A. F. W.), *The Secrets of Strength*, 199.

Maclaren (A.), *The Wearied Christ*, 241.

Raleigh (A.), *The Way to the City*, 79.

Rawnsley (R. D. B.), *Sermons Preached in Country Churches*, i. 118; iii. 120.

Spurgeon (C. H.), *Morning by Morning*, 134.

Wilkinson (J. B.), *Mission Sermons*, ii. 255.

Winterbotham (R.), *Sermons*, 214.

Christian World Pulpit, xxxiii. 233 (H. P. Liddon); xxxv. 314 (R. B. Brindley).

Homiletic Review, xlix. 222 (F. Smith).

Treasury (New York), xxi. 951 (G. B. F. Hallock).

THE TRANSIENCE OF SORROW.

His anger is but for a moment;
In his favour is life:
Weeping may tarry for the night,
But joy cometh in the morning.—Ps. xxx. 5.

THERE is an obvious antithesis in the first part of the text, between "his anger" and "his favour." Probably there is a similar antithesis between "a moment" and "life." For although the word rendered "life" does not usually mean a *lifetime*, it *may* have that signification, and the evident intention of contrast seems to require it here. So, then, the meaning of the first part of the text is, "the anger lasts for a moment; the favour lasts for a lifetime." The perpetuity of the one and the brevity of the other are the Psalmist's thought. Then, if we pass to the second part of the text, we observe that there is a double antithesis there also. "Weeping" is set over against "joy"; the "night" against the "morning." And the first of these two contrasts is the more striking if we observe that the word "joy" means, literally, "a joyful shout," so that the voice which was lifted in weeping is conceived of as now being heard in exultant praise. Then, still further, the expression "may endure" literally means "come to lodge." So that Weeping and Joy are personified. Two guests come— one, dark-robed and approaching at the fitting season for such— "the night"; the other bright, coming with all things fresh and sunny, in the dewy morn. The guest of the night is Weeping; the guest that takes its place in the morning is Gladness.

Thus the two clauses of the text suggest substantially the same thought, and that is the persistence of joy and the transitoriness of sorrow. The one speaks of the succession of emotions in the man; the other, of the successive aspects of the Divine dealings which occasion these. The whole is a leaf out of the Psalmist's own experience. The psalm commemorates his deliverance from some affliction, probably a sickness. That is long gone past; and the tears that it caused have long since dried up. But this shout of joy of his has lasted all these centuries, and is like to be immortal.

¶ It was Paget himself who had taught us, years before, through his best-known volume, *The Spirit of Discipline*, to consider carefully the meanings and contrasts of *accidie*, and of *tristitia*, and of "the sorrow of the world." I asked him once—it was on a walk ove. the Col de Chécouri at Courmayeur—to expand for me afresh his understanding of the phrase he used to quote from Spinoza: *Tristitia est hominis transitio a majore ad minorem perfectionem.* He answered gravely and almost in a whisper, "I can never understand Spinoza, but I am quite certain he was right there."[1]

I.

Seasons of Sorrow.

1. Sorrow comes in the night. It comes in the night of *worldly reverses*. These may not be the worst misfortunes in life, but only those who experience them know their poignancy. It is no small thing to have the savings of a lifetime swept away. Perhaps the storm came, the flood fell, the fire burned, a friend proved false, the crash of plans arrived, a blunder in judgment happened—and the accumulation of years has gone. It represented our toil and tears and thought and love. But it perished in an hour. It promised us happiness and independence in old age. But the promise failed. Tears do not turn dust to diamonds. Riches on wings fly faster from us than to us. To cry over fortune lost is no wiser than for the miller to weep over water that has flowed past.

2. Sorrow becomes our guest in the night of *broken health*. The powers once were vigorous. We ran to our task. Caution was scorned. Life seemed made to combat. We had the strength of Hercules. But something broke. We came against a stone wall. We reached a limit. Our wings were clipped. Suddenly we discovered that the race must be won by swifter feet than ours. Possibly we complain as a recent prisoner of pain who

---

[1] Archbishop Davidson, in *Francis Paget, Bishop of Oxford*, xviii.

said, " I cannot see why people should be born into a world like
this to suffer. Could I have seen my life from the beginning, and
had I been consulted as to whether I should live to suffer, I
certainly would have chosen never to have been." Possibly we
have money; but pain hurts the rich and poor alike. Possibly we
are religious; but pain hurts both the infidel and the Christian.
Possibly we deny pain or endure it as heroically as Epictetus, the
Phrygian philosopher-slave, in the Roman court, who said, when
his master with some instrument of torture cruelly twisted his
servant's leg, " If you go on you will break it "; and who also said
calmly, without expressing any of the anguish he felt when his
brutal master did go on, " I told you that you would break it."
Possibly you despise the old suffering house in which you live as
did this same ancient thinker, and define yourself as " an ethereal
existence staggering under the burden of a corpse." But whatever attitude we sustain towards pain, it wrings the stifled cry
from our heart, and our face often feels the burning touch of
a tear.

¶ Heine, suffering great physical agony, living in his mattress
grave, has given us verse upon verse of sweet sadness—sometimes
bitter in harsh complaining against God and man; while James
Thomson, in his great poem on London, "The City of Dreadful
Night," even says that, could he not have made a less miserable
world, he would not be God for all His glory—a horrible utterance,
but yet the answer of a man who has been made heartsick by the
poverty and misery of East London, the sight of innumerable
children who never know childhood, so soon does life curse them.[1]

3. Sorrow comes to tarry with us in the night of *bereavement*.
It may be only for an infant whose beauty was never caught by
a camera, and whose innocent feet were too fair to walk other
than streets of the city of God. It may be for a friend or a lover
who, in the sweet old days, went out of our life and left us for an
imperishable treasure only the sacred memories of hours that can
never return. After these many years, were a cross-section made
of our soul, we feel that the image of that blessed being would be
found mirrored thereon. It may be for a mother, whose voice
will never again this side the stars call her child; or for a father,
whose big, brave life will no more bid us follow the path of virtue.

[1] F. Lynch.

We know that to-day in the little city of the dead, hard by the city of the living, sleeps the dust of our sacred dead, or under other skies they who are dead to us walk forgetful of old ties and obligations. So onward we all go, each bearing his burden of sorrow.

¶ In some instances the Indian mothers literally cry their eyes out; and if you ask a blind woman how she lost her vision, she may answer that it was by weeping too hard for her lost relatives, and dimness of sight is attributed to the same cause. The wailings of an Indian over his lost relative, and especially of a mother over her lost children, are piercing and heart-rending; but it is pleasant to see the contrast in this respect between those who are still ignorant of the Gospel and such as have received it. The Christian converts have now learned to accept their bereavements as from God's hand in silence and submission, and their mute grief is more impressive than the loud lamentation of the heathen.[1]

¶ Scarlet fever in its most virulent form appeared in Carlisle (where Dr. Tait was then Dean), and, of the six little daughters whose presence had brought radiance to the Deanery, the heart-broken parents were called, within the space of a few weeks, to part with all except the infant who had just been born. One by one, between the 10th of March and the 10th of April, they were laid in the single grave in Stanwix Churchyard. The last entry which has been quoted from the diary was dated March 2. The entry which immediately succeeds it is as follows:—

" *Thursday, 8th May* 1856.—I have not had the heart to make any entry in my journal now for above nine weeks. When last I wrote I had six daughters on earth; now I have one, an infant. O God, Thou hast dealt very mysteriously with us. We have been passing through deep waters : our feet are well-nigh gone. But though Thou slay us, yet will we trust in Thee. . . . They are gone from us, all but my beloved Craufurd and the babe. Thou hast re-claimed the lent jewels. Yet, O Lord, shall I not thank Thee now ? I will thank Thee not only for the children Thou hast left to us, but for those Thou hast re-claimed. I thank Thee for the blessing of the last ten years, and for all the sweet memories of their little lives—memories how fragrant with every blissful, happy thought. I thank Thee for the full assurance that each has gone to the arms of the Good Shepherd, whom each loved according to the capacity of her years. I thank Thee for the bright hopes of a happy re-union, when we shall meet to part

---

[1] Bishop W. C. Bompas, *Northern Lights on the Bible*, 55.

no more. O Lord, for Jesus Christ's sake, comfort our desolate
hearts.   May we be a united family still in heart through the
communion of saints—through Jesus Christ our Lord." [1]

4. Sorrow comes in the night of the *consciousness of sin*.   In
the dim glimmer of the fire on the hearth the angel of penitence
brings to our notice stains on our garment which, she assures us,
would look a thousand times worse if we saw them in the proper
light—saw them as others see them, and, above all, as God sees
them.   She tells us that such marks can never be removed; that
there are also upon our countenance ugly scars which will always
disfigure it; that it is a hopeless thing when a man has lost his
good name; that when that is lost there is nothing worth keeping.   She tells us, too, that even those stains which others may
not detect God sees; that sin is sin, whether it be secret or open;
and that, the wide world over and in every age, " the wages of sin
is death."

> Yearly I till the vale and sow the seed,
>   But in the furrow rots the golden grain;
>   My labour is accursed, and all in vain,—
> The very earth revolteth at my deed.
> God saith no man shall slay me, though I plead
>   Daily for death. He placed this scarlet stain
>   Here on my brow, and agonizing pain
> Gnaws me beneath it—yet He gives no heed.
> Enoch reproacheth me—the guileless lad—
>   With eyes too like that other's, long since dead;
>   Remorse engulfs me in her sanguine flood;
> I build this City, else I should go mad;
>   But, as I work, the frowning walls turn red
> And all the towers drip crimson with *his* blood. [2]

II.

THE SOJOURN OF SORROW.

1. Sorrow always comes with a mission.   It has a message
from God to human life.   You may get two diametrically opposite
motions out of the same machine.   The same power will send one

---

[1] *Life of Archbishop Tait,* i. 189.
[2] Lloyd Mifflin.

wheel revolving from right to left, and another from left to right, but they are co-operant to grind out at the far end the one product. It is the same revolution of the earth that brings blessed lengthening days and growing summer, and that cuts short the sun's course and brings declining days and increasing cold. It is the same motion that hurls a comet close to the burning sun and sends it wandering away out into the fields of astronomical space, beyond the ken of telescope, and almost beyond the reach of thought. And so one uniform Divine purpose fills the life, and there are no interruptions, however brief, to the steady, continuous flow of God's outpoured blessings. All is love and favour. Anger is masked love, and sorrow has the same source and mission as joy. It takes all sorts of weather to make a year, and all tend to the same issue of ripened harvests and full barns.

¶ I grudged not our noble, lovely child, but rather do delight that such a seed should blossom and bear in the kindly and kindred paradise of my God. And why should not I speak of thee, my Edward! seeing it was in the season of thy sickness and death the Lord did reveal in me the knowledge and hope and desire of His Son from heaven? Glorious exchange! He took my son to His own more fatherly bosom, and revealed in my bosom the sure expectation and faith of His own eternal Son! Dear season of my life, ever to be remembered, when I knew the sweetness and fruitfulness of such joy and sorrow![1]

¶ "We will not complain of Dante's miseries," said Carlyle; " had all gone well with him as he wished it, Florence would have had another prosperous Lord Mayor, but the world would have lost the *Divina Commedia.*"

¶ There came to Glasgow, not so long ago, a pianist of an excellent reputation. I read the *Herald's* criticism on him, and there was one thing in it that I noted specially. The *Herald* said that he had always been brilliant—always been wonderful as an executant—but now there was a depth of feeling in him that had never been present in his work before. A day or two afterwards, preaching in a suburb, I met a relative of the pianist. And we fell to talk of him, and of the *Herald*, and of the *Herald's* criticism on him. And he said to me, " Did you notice that? And do you know what was the secret of the change? *It was the death of his mother eighteen months ago.*" He was an only son, unmarried, and he had been simply devoted to his mother. And

---

[1] Edward Irving, in *Life* by Mrs. Oliphant, i. 247.

then she died, and he was left alone, and all the deeps were broken up in him. And now he played as only he can play who knows what life and death are, and what sorrow is.[1]

> The dark brown mould's upturned
>   By the sharp-pointed plow,
> And I've a lesson learned.
>
> My life is but a field
>   Stretched out beneath God's sky,
> Some harvest rich to yield.
>
> Where grows the golden grain,
>   Where faith,—where sympathy?
> In a furrow cut by pain.[2]

2. Sorrow tarries only for the night. It takes its departure whenever its mission is fulfilled. A thunder-storm is very short when measured against the long summer day in which it crashes; and very few days have thunder-storms. It must be a bad climate where half the days are rainy. If we were to take a chart and prick out upon it the line of our voyage, we should find that the spaces in which the weather was tempestuous were brief and few indeed as compared with those in which it was sunny and calm.

¶ Referring to the discipline which God's love makes Him use, David says, "For his anger is but for a moment: his favour is for a lifetime. Weeping may come in to lodge at even, but joy cometh in the morning." There may be weeping. There shall be joy. Weeping won't stay long. There is a morning coming, always a morning coming, with the sunshine and the chorus of the birds. Love's discipling touch that seems at the moment like anger is only for a moment. (The printer wanted to change that word "discipling" to "disciplining"; but God's tenderness comes to us anew when we realize that disciplining with its sharp edge means the same as discipling, with its softer, warmer touch.) The loving favour is for always, a lifetime of eternal life.[3]

¶ A tourist writes of stopping at Giesbach to look at the wonders of its waterfalls. The party had to pass over one of the falls on a slender bridge through the drenching water, with the wild torrents dashing beneath. It was a trying experience. But

---

[1] G. H. Morrison, *The Afterglow of God*, 92.
[2] M. D. Babcock, *Thoughts for Every-Day Living*, 167.
[3] S. D. Gordon, *Quiet Talks on Service*, 210.

once through, a glorious picture burst upon them. There were rainbows above, beneath, and circling on all sides. So the spray of sorrow falls now, and we may have to walk through floods and pitiless torrents, and all may seem a strange, inexplicable mystery. But there will come a time when we shall have passed through these showers of grief, and when we shall stand amid the splendour of rainbows on the shores of glory. Then we shall understand, and see love in every pang and tear.[1]

> From the sunshine of Thy dwelling
>   Thou hast sent me this new day,
> Laden with Thy love excelling,
> Tidings of Thy glory telling
>   To refresh my way.

> Good and perfect gifts are lying
>   Wrapt within its folds of light,
> Pledges of a faith undying,
> That earth's sorrow and its sighing
>   Will but last a night.[2]

3. There is a balance of good in the world, using the word "good" in the lowest sense, that is, looking merely on man's animal life, and regarding him only as a denizen, for a little, of this material world. Men are busy, men are happy; far more happy, at least, than miserable. Some few are miserable utterly; all are more or less unhappy at times, and for a little. Yes! that is just it, just what the text says—"for a little"; the dark time is "for a moment." The brighter times stretch on, and flow into each other, and go far to fill up the life.

¶ The proportion of solid matter needed to colour the Irwell is very little in comparison with the whole of the stream. But the current carries it, and a trace of dye-stuff will stain miles of the turbid stream. Memory and anticipation beat the metal thin, and make it cover an enormous space. And the misery is that, somehow, we have better memories for sad hours than for joyful ones, and it is easier to get accustomed to "blessings," as we call them, and to lose the poignancy of their sweetness because they become familiar, than it is to apply the same process to our sorrows, and thus to take the edge off them. The rose's prickles are felt in the flesh longer than its fragrance lives in the nostrils,

---

[1] J. R. Miller, *Week-Day Religion*, 81.
[2] G. Matheson, *Sacred Songs*, 57.

or its hue in the eye. Men have long memories for their pains as compared with their remembrance of their sorrows.[1]

¶ To her friend Miss Nicholson, whose sympathy brought her much strength and peace, Florence Nightingale wrote in 1846: "My imagination is so filled with the misery of this world that the only thing in which to labour brings any return, seems to me helping and sympathizing *there*; and all that poets sing of the glories of this world appears to me untrue: all the people I see are eaten up with care or poverty or disease. I know that it was God who created the good, and man the evil, which was not the will of God, but the necessary consequence of His leaving free-will to man. I know that misery is the alphabet of fire, in which history, with its warning hand, writes in flaming letters the consequences of Evil (the Kingdom of *Man*), and that, without its glaring light, we should never see the path into the Kingdom of God, or heed the directing guide-posts."[2]

III.

THE SUPPLANTER OF SORROW.

1. "Joy cometh in the morning." There are two figures presented before us, the dark-robed and the bright-garmented. The one is the guest of the night, the other is the guest of the morning. The verb which occurs in the first clause of the second half of the text is not repeated in the second, and so the words may be taken in two ways. They may either express how Joy, the morning guest, comes, and turns out the evening visitant, or they may suggest how we took Sorrow in when the night fell, to sit by the fireside, but when morning dawned—who is this sitting in her place, smiling as we look at her? It is Sorrow transfigured, and her name is changed into Joy. Either the substitution or the transformation may be supposed to be in the Psalmist's mind. Both are true.

¶ Does not the whole teaching of the Cross say that sorrow and pain alone wake us up to reality, and that trial is a truer refiner of character than pleasure? Of course, this is not our first impression; it needs a revelation to tell it, or at all events to interpret our own experience. You have a proof of that in a

---

[1] A. Maclaren, *The Wearied Christ*, 243.
[2] Sir Edward Cook, *The Life of Florence Nightingale*, i. 58.

child's wonder at the expression, "Blessed are they that mourn";
for how should a happy, careless child divine such a mystery?
Life alone can apply the meaning of these words of Christ, or
explain how true they are; for, indeed, they are only subjectively
true, deriving their truth not from sorrow and pain in themselves,
but from the tempers on which they fall; so that they are not
true always—to some never true. Yet how deep they are, and
how such convictions alone can make this life intelligible or
tolerable! That is a blessed faith which feels that there cannot
be clouds and gloom for ever—which, ever resting in conviction of
what God is, hopes and knows that "joy cometh in the morning."[1]

> Say not that darkness is the doom of light,
>   That every sun must sink in night's abyss,
>   While every golden day declines to this,
> To die and pass at evening out of sight.
> Say rather that the morning ends the night,
>   That death must die beneath the dayspring's kiss—
>   Whilst dawn the powers of darkness shall dismiss,
> And put their dusky armaments to flight.
> Man measures life in this wise; first the morn,
>   And secondly the noontide's perfect prime,
>   And lastly night, when all things fade away:
> But God, ere yet the sons of men were born,
>   Showed forth a better way of marking time—
>   "The evening and the morning were the day."[2]

2. We can anticipate the morning even in our night of sorrow.
Even in the midst of the snow and cold and darkness of Arctic
regions, the explorers build houses for themselves of the very
blocks of ice, and within are warmth and light and comfort and
vitality, while around is a dreary waste. There may be two
currents in the great ocean; a cold one may set from the Pole
and threaten to chill and freeze all life out, but from the Equator
there will be a warm one which will more than counterbalance
the inrush of the cold. And so it is possible for us, even when
things about us are dark and gloomy, and flesh and natural
sensibilities all proclaim to us the necessity of sadness—it is
possible for us to be aware of a central blessedness, not boisterous,
but so grave and calm that the world cannot discriminate between
it and sadness, which yet its possessors know to be blessedness

---

[1] *Life and Letters of the Rev. F. W. Robertson*, 281.
[2] Ellen Thorneycroft Fowler, *Verses, Wise or Otherwise*, 200.

unmingled. Left alone, we may have a companion; in our
ignorance we may be enlightened; and in the murkiest night of
our sorrow we may have, burning cheerily within our hearts, a
light unquenchable.

¶ A traveller entered Milan Cathedral at the dawn of day.
The sunbeams fell on the eastern windows. Every pane of
glass revealed its beauty. The images of apostle, prophet, angel,
and Christ were seen in all their glory. The sun swept on to
his zenith and then drove his chariot behind the western Alps.
As he did so he flung his beams upon the western windows of the
great shrine. Then the glories they contained appeared. Not a
figure remained without its light. All the richness of colour and
symbolism appeared. So the passing of time and the shining of
the consolations of faith into a life transform sorrow into joy and
gloom into glory.[1]

> Oh, deem not they are blest alone
>   Whose lives a peaceful tenor keep;
> The Power who pities man, hath shown
>   A blessing for the eyes that weep.
>
> The light of smiles shall fill again
>   The lids that overflow with tears;
> And weary hours of woe and pain
>   Are promises of happier years.
>
> There is a day of sunny rest
>   For every dark and troubled night:
> And grief may hide an evening guest,
>   But joy shall come with early light.[2]

[1] F. Smith, in *Homiletic Review*, xlix. 224.
[2] W. C. Bryant, *Poems*, 39.

ROOM TO LIVE.

Literature.

Adams (J.), *Sermons in Syntax*, 51.
Ainsworth (P. C.), *The Pilgrim Church*, 201.
Clow (W. M.), *The Secret of the Lord*, 333.
Ellis (J.), *Through Christ to Life*, 52.
Miller (J. R.), *Week-Day Religion*, 1.
Morrison (G. H.), *The Afterglow of God*, 143.
Christian World Pulpit, lxxix. 253 (B. J. Gibbon); lxxx. 158 (C. F. Perry).
Treasury (New York), xii. 175 (T. W. Anderson).

ROOM TO LIVE.

Thou hast set my feet in a large place.—Ps. xxxi. 8.

THE idea is common in the Psalms of distress as restraint, irksome confinement. The man in trouble is shut up: he is in a strait place. Consequently the idea of deliverance takes the form of enlargement. The distressed man is led out of a narrow gorge into a wide plain. He dwells now in a broad place. He enjoys the sense of ample space. "Thou hast set my feet in a large place." We have the same figure, although our use of it is perhaps not so common, in our own language. We talk of "straitened circumstances," and again of "room to breathe" and "elbow room."

I.

STRAITENED CIRCUMSTANCES.

There are agencies and influences always operating, whose nature it is to reduce life to a narrow area. The most potent are sin, trouble, and grinding toil.

1. The narrowing effect of *sin*, more than of anything else, seems to be suggested by these words. There is the inherited weakness and the encircling contagion—within us, the evil tendency; without us, the unhallowed opportunity. Sometimes a man accepts the pressing solicitation of evil, or yields to the hot-handed grip of the world's desire; and then with a demeaned dignity and lowered self-respect, he measures life and finds he has but a few square feet in which to stand and call himself a fool. He measures his shame and his weakness—his poor failure—and he says, Life is a narrow place.

¶ When William Blake the poet was an old man, there came a lady one day to see him. She was beautiful and rich, and she

had the world at her feet, as we express it. Blake looked at her,
as with a look of pity he put his hand upon her head and said,
" My child, may God make the world as beautiful to you as it has
been to me." Let a young man have a pure imagination and his
world will be a world of glory. He may be poor, and his days
may be monotonous, but life will be clad for him in royal
splendour. And that is where the curse of sin comes in, defiling
and polluting everything. Let it once creep into the imagination,
and everything bright and beautiful is gone.[1]

> So dear to Heav'n is saintly chastity
> That when a soul is found sincerely so,
> A thousand liveried angels lackey her,
> Driving far off each thing of sin and guilt,
> And in clear dream, and solemn vision,
> Tell her of things that no gross ear can hear,
> Till oft converse with heav'nly habitants
> Begin to cast a beam on th' outward shape,
> The unpolluted temple of the mind,
> And turns it by degrees to the soul's essence,
> Till all be made immortal: but when lust
> By unchaste looks, loose gestures, and foul talk,
> But most by lewd and lavish act of sin,
> Lets in defilement to the inward parts,
> The soul grows clotted by contagion,
> Imbodies, and imbrutes, till she quite lose
> The divine property of her first being.
> Such are those thick and gloomy shadows damp
> Oft seen in charnel-vaults and sepulchres,
> Lingering, and sitting by a new-made grave,
> As loth to leave the body that it lov'd,
> And link't itself by carnal sensuality
> To a degenerate and degraded state.[2]

2. *Trouble and adversity* make life a small room. It is true
that at times a stone pillow brings a man, like dreaming Jacob,
near heaven, but generally the heart is full of unsatisfied longings,
of unutterable thoughts. We are shut in by sordid circumstances,
like the lark by its cheap cage, or we drag behind us a chain of
anxiety and regret; we are clogged by ill-health or mean cares;
parts of our being lie waste, or yield crops that cause pain and
shame. At times the sky is grey, the heart full of bitterness.

[1] G. H. Morrison, *The Afterglow of God*, 143.
[2] Milton, *Comus*.

All is so flat and depressing, and no outlook promises better weather to come.

¶ In every life are there not strange events, unlooked-for catastrophes, heartbreaking bereavements, mysterious contradictions, unfathomed problems shed all along our path, in which it seems as though by some sudden combination the very heavens are blotted out? Do we not sometimes feel like the pelican in the wilderness or the stranger left by the caravan to die alone in a dry and thirsty land where no water is? Life's heaviest blows often come most unexpectedly. Death appears, and our astonishment is even greater than our grief. Losses arise, and we are petrified with surprise as our treasure disappears in the most unlikely directions. Friends and comrades fail us, and amazement almost chokes us. Have we not times in which prayer fails and hope dies down to a poor flicker, and we can do nothing and think nothing, and when we feel as dead men that cumber the ground? Do we not know what it is to walk about with that sickening of heart which makes our food like bitter herbs, and in the morning makes us wish for evening and at night makes us long for morning? [1]

¶ From physical weakness, mental distress, or it may be from the faults of others, some lives remain weak and feel it, and, with lessening resources, find increasing pain. To such the following incident will appeal: "I was strongly touched one day," says Dr. Gregory, "by the bedside of an energetic and elastic man of business, sanguine and successful and with a splendid flow of spirits, who was suddenly struck down by illness. With trembling finger and with moistened eyes he pointed to an illuminated text hung in front of him at the foot of his bed, 'Have mercy upon me, O Lord; for I am weak'—a new and strange experience for one in the flower of manhood, who had hitherto known only high-toned health. He said, 'Do you see that?' I answered, 'Yes, and God sees it and hears it too.' 'Ah,' said he, 'I got them to put it there that I might look at it and then from it to God.'" [2]

3. The *monotony of our tasks* has a narrowing effect on life. The young just entering life find it full of novelty and aglow with romance. All things are possible to them. The world is open before them. They are conscious of latent powers. They see great opportunities. They will go far. They will climb

[1] W. Bramwell Booth.   [2] J. Ellis.

high. "Thou hast set my feet in a large room," they are well able to say. But as they grow older, and find their place in the world, and settle down to their work, the glamour vanishes. They find that their sphere is small, their abilities limited, and their opportunities few. The wide horizon of youth contracts. Work loses its novelty. It becomes wearisome and monotonous, and they are ready to cry, "Thou hast set my feet in a small room!"

¶ The girl who goes to the marriage altar, her head full of romance, wakes up from love's young dream to discover that her life is a ceaseless round of cooking, sweeping, dusting, and tidying. Her husband perhaps works in a factory, where he feeds a machine, the same machine, or stokes a fire, the same fire, all day long, and six days a week. I have seen a girl in a factory lining a box with paper, and then lining another box with paper, and continuing to line boxes with paper the livelong day. Oh, for an outdoor life![1]

> The close and subtle clasping of a chain,
> Formed not of gold, but of corroded brass,
> Whose links are furnished from the common mine
> Of everyday's event, and want, and wish;
> From work-times, diet-times, and sleeping-times:
> And thence constructed, mean and heavy links
> Within the pandemonic walls of sense
> Enchain our deathless part, constrain our strength,
> And waste the goodly stature of our soul.
>
> Howbeit, we love this bondage; we do cleave
> Unto the sordid and unholy thing,
> Fearing the sudden wrench required to break
> Those claspèd links. Behold! all sights and sounds
> In air, and sea, and earth, and under earth,
> All flesh, all life, all ends, are mysteries;
> And all that is mysterious dreadful seems,
> And all we cannot understand we fear.
> Ourselves do scare ourselves; we hide our sight
> In artificial nature from the true,
> And throw sensation's veil associative
> On God's creation, man's intelligence;
> Bowing our high imaginings to eat
> Dust, like the serpent, once erect as they;

[1] B. J. Gibbon.

Binding conspicuous on our reason's brow
Phylacteries of shame; learning to feel
By rote, and act by rule (man's rule, not God's!),
Until our words grow echoes, and our thoughts
A mechanism of spirit.[1]

II.

Large Room.

There are two ways in which the smallest room can be enlarged indefinitely—one by lifting the roof, the other by pushing back the walls. And in those two ways, by taking off the roof of life until we see God, and knocking away the walls of time until we see eternity, each of us may occupy—and should occupy, as many do—the largest room on earth.

i. Add God to Life.

1. Let us add the thought of God to life. God alone can deal effectively with our sin. He alone can give deliverance. And what happens to the man who resolutely takes his place in the battle against sin—his own sin, the world's sin? Day by day the soul within him, which has its birthplace and its goal beyond the stars, asserts itself, as it discovers larger rights and possibilities, and an ever surer hope of victory gives vision not bounded by life's most pressing and persistent circumstance. Day by day it becomes more apparent that the life of the soul is circled by a horizon that its most daring dreams have never scanned, and that for the pure-hearted the dusty, choking, hand-to-hand encounter with sin holds promise wider than the world. Let us remember that, if in this day of much striving we are growing sick and weary, we are not fighting for the little patch of trampled earth beneath our feet, where the grass and the flowers have been beaten into common dust. We are fighting for the right and fitness to enter the land that is very far off, where, by the river of nameless peace, men have life because they see God. Surely the life that finds room for a fight like that is a wide life!

¶ If our faith is to be true, we need the simple, direct sense

---

[1] E. B. Browning, *A Sea-side Meditation.*

of God the Father that we had as children—we need that expanded into a sense of the great, living God. What was dear to us in our childhood's religion is purified and preserved and strengthened by the wider range which the expansion of our life has opened up. In one of Shakespeare's sonnets he writes:

> When to the sessions of sweet silent thought
> I summon up remembrance of things past,
> I sigh the lack of many a thing I sought,
> And moan the expense of many a vanish'd sight:
>> But if the while I think on thee, dear friend,
>> All losses are restor'd, and sorrows end.

Now what Shakespeare wrote about this friendship, we may apply to the time in which we are living. It is the thought of God which lifts us up above the melancholy of the past, and delivers us from the weakness that morbid regret instilled into our hearts. We believe in a God of our life who is able to develop our growth. We learn from Jesus to recognize in God's handling of us that any outward change, however unwelcome, must be accompanied by an inward access of moral strength. Whatever God takes from us in that way comes back to us in another form, enriched, enlarged.[1]

2. The thought of God will reveal a purpose in trouble. We shall realize that "in every sorrow of the heart, Eternal Mercy bears a part." God's good purpose runs through our saddened hours. It is then that pride dies and sympathy is born. But if we forget God we reverse this order of things. We grow narrower and colder and harder. We drift into cynicism and pessimism. We are the worse instead of the better for our tears. There is an old saying attributed to Christ that has a double significance. It runs: "He that is near Me is near the fire." To be near the fire is to be tested, perhaps scorched and made hard. But it is also to be warmed and cheered, and the double action is felt by each disciple. Attempts at serious, earnest living will always involve pain, but it will be pain that is compensated by stronger and sweeter strength. Life is neither all sunshine nor all gloom. A restless devil and a changing world will account for discomforts, and there are moments of intense dreariness, gloom, bitterness, and woe. Then I am with you, says the Lord, as a Comforter able to help, to bring Lazarus from the dead; and this

[1] J. Moffatt.

is more than we dare ask for or can realize. As the chaplain said to the dying Highlander—"Geordie, 'tis just Jesus"; and where the cloud appears Jesus is not far away.

¶ Mr. A. C. Benson has described in *The House of Quiet* the life of a man who had attained, after a youth of unstable health, to an apparently sound constitution, and was now living out a full and happy and useful life in London. Suddenly his old delicacy of health reappeared. He consulted an eminent physician. He came out of the consulting-room with a virtual sentence of death. "To say farewell to the bustle and activity of life; to be laid aside on a shelf like a cracked vase, turning as far as possible my ornamental front to the world; to live the shadowed life, a creature of rules and hours—a degrading and humiliating rôle." But he accepted the will of God. He took up his cross. He passed into "The House of Quiet," expecting only the peace of a difficult resignation. But in "The House of Quiet" a new life began. An unexpected feeling of the possibilities of life dawned. His perceptions became more delicate. The gush of morning air, the liquid song of birds, the sprouting of the green buds, the babble of the stream gave a new delight. His intellectual life grew strong, eager, discerning. A quickened taste for pure and noble reading, and a fresh joy in beauty, filled him with rapture. Then there swelled within him a more deliberate intention of enjoying simple things and of expecting beauty in homely life. At last he awoke to his true service. He had hitherto looked on at life around him with a dimmed eye and dulled ear. Now all the cries of the sick and the pained, and all the eager and appealing voices of the young and wistful, and all the soft, low sobbing of the bereaved fell upon his ears. All the needs, daily and clamant, of his neighbours rose up in appeal. This broken man, walking on the edge of death's abyss, gave up his life and used his feeble strength to help and to comfort others. He found that he had entered a new world. He no longer lived in the isolation of the strong, the successful, the selfish. New felicities swelled within his heart. New and unhoped-for strength was given. His life became a life of faith and love; and that rest which is our deepest satisfaction is always their first-born child.[1]

The cry of man's anguish went up unto God:
    "Lord, take away pain—
The shadow that darkens the world Thou hast made,
    The close-coiling chain

[1] W. M. Clow, *The Secret of the Lord*, 333.

That strangles the heart, the burden that weighs
  On the wings that would soar;
Lord, take away pain from the world Thou hast made,
  That it love Thee the more!"

Then answered the Lord to the cry of His world:
  "Shall I take away pain
And with it the power of the soul to endure,
  Made strong by the strain?
Shall I take away pity that knits heart to heart,
  And sacrifice high?
Will ye lose all your heroes that lift from the fire
  White brows to the sky?
Shall I take away love that redeems with a price,
  And smiles at its loss?
Can ye spare from your lives that would climb into Mine
  The Christ on His cross?"

3. The thought of God will change grinding toil into a sweet
ministry.

(1) We shall realize that our sphere is God-appointed. The
place in which we find ourselves is the place in which the Master
desires us to live our life.

Thou cam'st not to thy place by accident;
It is the very place God meant for thee.

There is no haphazard in this world. God leads every one of His
children by the right way. He knows where and under what
influences each particular life will ripen best. One tree grows
best in the sheltered valley, another by the water's edge, another
on the bleak mountain-top swept by storms. There is always
adaptation in nature. Every tree or plant is found in the locality
where the conditions of its growth exist, and does God give more
thought to trees and plants than to His own children? He places
us amid the circumstances and experiences in which our life will
grow and ripen the best. The peculiar discipline to which we are
each subjected is the discipline we severally need to bring out in
us the beauties and graces of true spiritual character. We are
in the right school. We may think that we would ripen more
quickly in a more easy and luxurious life, but God knows what is
best; He makes no mistakes.

¶ Too often the Christian thinks that he could "walk and please God" if he might first readjust the pathway to his own liking. But surely it is not so. Our work, our home, our appointed circle of intercourse, our temperament, our past, He has made them. It is ours not to re-arrange His plan, but to follow Him along it. There is an instructive passage in the life of Madame de la Mothe Guyon. At an early stage of her blessed walk with God, peculiar trials beset her home life. She had learnt to taste the deep sweetness of solitary communion with the Lord in order to renew her strength for duty. But day by day this was made impossible in ways exquisitely trying. For a time her spiritual prosperity was greatly disturbed. But soon she saw that even in this there lay hidden the will of God, and that *while the difficulty lasted* she was accordingly to welcome it as from Him. By His grace she did so, and with the surrender, with the trust, there came to her a larger and fuller experience of peace than she had ever known when time seemed at her own disposal.[1]

¶ There is a work for all of us, and there is a work for each, work which I cannot do in a crowd, or as one of a mass, but as one man, acting singly, according to my own gifts, and under a sense of my personal responsibility. There is no doubt associated work for me to do. I must do my work as part of the world's great whole, or as a member of some great body. But I have a special work to do, as one individual, who by God's plan and appointment has a separate position, separate responsibilities, and a separate work; if I do not do it, it must be left undone. No one of my special fellows can do that special work for me which I have come into the world to do; he may do a higher work, a greater work, but he cannot do my work. I cannot hand over my work to him, any more than I can hand over my responsibilities or my gifts.[2]

(2) We shall regard all the tasks of life as golden opportunities to further a great purpose. After having seen the sordidness and meanness and littleness of things, David still held that life is a grand, free, glorious gift, that it is liberty and opportunity and hope. What was the secret of his wide and worthy view of life? How had he escaped these narrower and meaner thoughts that crowd into men's minds and belittle their lives? He had laid hold upon God. He looked at life through the Divine purpose. He found the high and noble meaning of the dusty parable that

---

[1] H. C. G. Moule, *All in Christ*, 207.
[2] Ruskin.

men call the day's work. When he talks of life as a large room,
it is really his way of saying, "Thy service is perfect freedom."
If life is lived to God, then it is wider than any man can measure.

¶ The Booth children were left in no mist of doubt as to their
future.   There was an end, a point, a purpose, in their life.   They
grew up in an atmosphere of decision.   Many children are made
timid, diffident, ineffective by their training.   They are constantly
told how naughty they are, till they begin to believe that they
are good for nothing.   The Booth parents acted on a different
principle.   They had faith in their children and for their children.
When Katie was still a little girl in socks, her mother would say
to her, "Now, Katie, you are not here in this world for yourself.
You have been sent for others.   *The world is waiting for you.*" [1]

¶ It was the strange fancy of a little child, writes George
MacDonald, as he stood on a summer's evening looking intently
and thoughtfully at the great banks of clouds piled like mountains
of glory about the setting sun: "Mother, I wish I could be a
painter."   "Why, my child?"   "For then I would help God to
paint the clouds and the sunsets."   It was a strange and beautiful aspiration.   But our commonest work in this world may be
made far nobler than that.   We may live to touch hues of loveliness in immortal spirits which shall endure for ever.   Clouds dis-
solve and float away.   The most gorgeous sunset splendours
vanish in a few moments.   The artist's canvas crumbles and his
wondrous creations fade.   But work done for Christ endures for
ever.   A life of simple consecration leaves a trace of imperishable
beauty on everything it touches.   Not great deeds alone, but the
smallest, the obscurest, the most prosaic, write their record in
fadeless lines.[2]

¶ It is possible to bring near that far-distant world and to
hold it in our hearts.   When the soul's revealing-glass is brought
to bear upon it—when eternity swims like a new world into our
ken—how differently does life look in the light of that revelation !
The light of eternity playing about the things of time, how it
changes everything !   How differently now shall our life be led,
once that vision has begun to be ours !   In this light we see our
life and work at a new angle, and we change our minds as to the
things that are big with importance and the things that are of
little value.   We see that things are large or small, not so much
from the comparison they make with one another, but according
as they have in them the elements of eternal meaning and

        [1] J. Strahan, *The Maréchale* (1913), 10.
        [2] J. R. Miller, *Week-Day Religion*, 90.

purpose. As to our life's work, it is not so much what we are
doing or where we are doing it, as it is how we are doing it and
with what purpose in view. The case is well put by Professor
Drummond in his own clear-cut way. " An office is not a place
for making money, it is a place for making character. A workshop is not a place for making machinery, it is a place for making
men. . . . A school of learning is not so much a place for making
scholars, as a place for making souls. And he who would ripen
and perfect the eternal element in his being will do this by
attending to the religious uses of his daily task, recognizing the
unseen in the seen, and so turning three-fourths of each day's life
into an ever-acting means of grace." In his picturesque study of
Lazarus brought back to earth again from heaven, Browning
seeks to show the effect that the heavenly vision will have on a
man who must still walk the earth. It will mean for him a
reversal of the world's judgments as to the meaning of things
and the proportion of values. And it will mean for those who
watch him a feeling of his unfitness for playing his part as a
successful man of the world in the affairs of this life.

> The man is witless of the size, the sum,
> The value in proportion of all things,
> Or whether it be little or be much.[1]

¶ The type may be as crude and clumsy as were the first
wooden pieces of Faust and Gutenberg, but if the thought be deep
and great the imperfection of the medium through which it finds
its way to the mind is of small account; the conditions in which
we pass this mortal life may be hard and uncongenial, but if they
convey spiritual truths to us, and make us aware of spiritual
realities, it were cowardly to complain and ignorant to rebel.
The wise traveller, to whom the great scenery or the great art of
the world is accessible, does not waste his time on the discomforts
of travel or allow his thoughts to dwell on the shortcomings of
his inn. The measure of a man's soul is his ability to disregard
the hindrances and concentrate his energy on the achievement;
to put aside the accidents of a relation, a work, an opportunity,
and grasp the reality. If there is, as a wise poet has told us, a
soul of goodness in things evil, there is much more certainly a
soul of beauty within the form of all relations and duties and
works; and he who is able to carry all his relationships, duties,
and work to the mount where the patterns are, to the light of the
spiritual order where these mortal things instantly put on immortality, has read the open secret and pierced the mystery of life.[2]

[1] J. B. Maclean, *The Secret of the Stream*, 145.
[2] H. W. Mabie, *The Life of the Spirit*, 282.

God and Man are free.
Where Freedom is, no other cause is sure.

Is Purpose then Foreknowledge?—Human will
May yield and fail to win the victory:
And God Himself, it may be, turns and bends
His purposes to further human ends,
Stooping to serve His servant; so that still
We find no Purpose that is Prophecy.
But where both wills, the human and Divine
Are yoked together, where God ratifies
The struggling purposes of man,—there lies
The law unchangeable, the fixed decree
That nought in earth or heaven shall undermine.[1]

ii. Add Eternity to Life.

By bringing eternity into life we make it a large place. Everything we do has an effect, an effect upon ourselves, that is eternal. That is the recognition of eternity, and to bring this conception into life is to make it a very wide room. We find life small and tedious because the work we do seems so petty and ineffective. What we do to-day we have to do again to-morrow, still again the third day, and so continually. The baker bakes his bread, but to-morrow it is all eaten and he has to bake another batch, and day after day to go on baking. It seems hopeless to try to feed his customers. "My work is never done," we constantly hear. It is generally the housewife who says it. What is the use of cooking, sweeping, dusting and tidying, when to-morrow she has to cook, sweep, dust and tidy again, and all the to-morrows of her life to repeat the programme? Our work seems so futile that the life spent in doing it appears petty, small, unworthy. Yes; but it is so in appearance only. It is not really so. By our daily work we are manufacturing for eternity. We are making, or we are marring, characters that will last for ever. We are developing, or we are destroying, souls that will go on with this handiwork upon them into eternity. We are fitting, or we are unfitting, ourselves to dwell for ever in the holy light of God.

¶ If this life is all, then the horizon is near, and the whole scope and outlook of man's highest life cramped and fettered. To

[1] Roger Heath, *Beginnings*, 56.

many a soul it would be a bondage almost as grim as the bondage
of Egypt. "Mas'r," pleads Tom, the slave of *Uncle Tom's Cabin*,
as he is threatened with death, "after ye've killed the body there
ain't no more ye can do. You may whip me, starve me, burn me,
it'll only send me sooner where I want to go." From the fire and
water, the cruel terror of his fellow, this pure and beautiful soul
was to pass to its vindication and eternal rest. We are always
reaching our limits; there are things we cannot do, ideals we
cannot attain, powers we cannot conquer, service we cannot render,
but with the breaking of the morning when the spirit enters the
Homeland, then surely we must believe we shall see those limits
crossed. We shall be in a wealthy place, there will be a fuller,
richer life.[1]

> 'Tis a long road home;
>   But sleep for aching eyes,
>   Rest for weary feet,
>   For striving hearts a prize,
>   Silence still and sweet,
> Wait at the end of the long road home.

> 'Tis a hard road home;
>   Many faint and lag
>   Beneath the heavy pack,
>   With feet and hearts that drag,
>   But none looks back—
> We know there's an end to the hard road home.

> 'Tis a dark road home,
>   With shadows long and deep,
>   Where timid travellers fall,
>   And scarce their path may keep;
>   But the Light that shines for all
> Gleams at the end of the dark road home.

[1] C. F. Perry.

THE BEATITUDE OF FORGIVENESS.

Literature.

Adams (J.), *Sermons in Syntax*, 45.

Dunbar (J. W.), *The Beatitudes of the Old Testament*, 129.

Keble (J.), *Sermons for the Christian Year* : Lent to Passiontide, 260.

Mackay (J. J.), *Recent Letters of Christ*, 124.

Meyer (F. B.), *The Directory of the Devout Life*, 15.

Price (A. C.), *Fifty Sermons*, i. 345.

Ritchie (A.), *Sermons from St. Ignatius' Pulpit*, 42.

Smellie (A.), *In the Hour of Silence*, 303.

Wilmot-Buxton (H. J.), *In Many Keys*, 102.

Children's Pulpit : Second Sunday after Christmas, ii. 204.

Church of England Pulpit, xxviii. 301.

Church Year Book, 1912, p. 49.

THE BEATITUDE OF FORGIVENESS.

Blessed is he whose transgression is forgiven, whose sin is covered.
Blessed is the man unto whom the Lord imputeth not iniquity,
And in whose spirit there is no guile.—Ps. xxxii. 1, 2.

THESE words form the preface to a psalm generally understood
to have been written in connexion with the great sin of David's
life. It sings of that happy time when he had repented of his
iniquity, when he had sought mercy and had found it, and then
poured out the joy of his heart. It is no marvel that his pent-up
feelings burst forth in such words as these, for the experience
through which he had passed had been peculiarly dark and bitter.
He tells here of the misery which he had undergone. He had
kept silence, he says, with the result that his very bones had
waxed old, and his moisture had been turned into the drought of
summer. He would not confess, he would not repent. To a man
with the open nature of David that would mean unspeakable
wretchedness, but he persevered in it month after month till the
mission of Nathan the prophet broke through his sulky reserve,
and let loose the springs of his being. And then how measureless
his peace and joy ! Probably no man has ever felt more deeply
than he the blessing of forgiveness. He entered into a new world,
and being a poet he could not refrain from giving expression to
his bliss in this beautiful poem, which begins with the outburst,
" Blessed is he whose transgression is forgiven, whose sin is
covered."

¶ This psalm has been selected by the Church for one of the
" seven penitential psalms." It forms a part of the service of the
synagogue on the great Day of Atonement. Yet it is almost as
much jubilant as penitent. The writer, while very sensible of his
sin, is still more sensible of the fact that his sin is pardoned.
While his first words breathe content and gratitude, his last are a
shout of rejoicing (ver. 10).[1]

[1] G. Rawlinson.

69

¶ Ewald says: "The song is manifestly ancient, original throughout, evidencing a strong spirit. Hardly could the inner misery of a lacerated heart, together with the higher happiness of one again reconciled and healed, be described with more inwardness, impressiveness, and power than here. The harder the struggle in his heart, so much more glorious is the victory, so much more limpid and joyous is the stream of the earnest word. The colour also of the language is Davidic, and there is no reason to doubt that it was sung after the transaction recorded in 2 Sam. xii."

I.

THE REALITY OF FORGIVENESS.

Forgiveness is a reality on God's part, because sin is a reality on our part. Forgiveness, or justification, is sometimes spoken of as "treating the sinner as though he had not sinned." This, however, is but loose, figurative language. Forgiveness implies sin, disobedience to God's law. Therefore God is bound, as the Righteous One, to take account of sin. He must condemn or pardon it. And our Lord Himself speaks of forgiveness as a definite act. "Son, be of good cheer; thy sins be forgiven thee."

1. The Psalmist views sin under three aspects.

(1) First, he calls it *transgression*. In its literal sense this means separation, or rending apart, or departure, and so comes to express the notion of apostasy and rebellion. All sin is a departure from God. It is treacherous rebellion. That is to say, it has relation not only to a law, but to a Lawgiver. It is not merely a departure from what is right, it is treason against God. It not only breaks some impersonal ideal of duty, but it is an act of rebellion against a loving Will which is in definite relations to me. And so it assumes a far graver and more solemn aspect than when we think of it as being merely a breach of law, a traversing of duty, a crime against conscience, or society, or public opinion, or expediency, or some abstract idea of morality. It is all these, but it is something much worse than these. The inmost recesses of the ugliness and wickedness of the wicked and ugly thing is this, that it throws into disorder our relations to a living person, that it is rebellion against the Living God.

¶ There is in man an instinct of revolt, an enemy of all law, a rebel which will stoop to no yoke, not even that of reason, duty, and wisdom. This element in us is the root of all sin—*das radicale Böse* of Kant. The independence which is the condition of individuality is at the same time the eternal temptation of the individual. That which makes us beings makes us also sinners. Sin is, then, in our very marrow, it circulates in us like the blood in our veins, it is mingled with all our substance. Or rather I am wrong: temptation is our natural state, but sin is not necessary. Sin consists in the voluntary confusion of the independence which is good with the independence which is bad; it is caused by the half-indulgence granted to a first sophism. We shut our eyes to the beginnings of evil because they are small, and in this weakness is contained the germ of our defeat. *Principiis obsta*—this maxim dutifully followed would preserve us from almost all our catastrophes. We will have no other master but our caprice—that is to say, our evil self will have no God, and the foundation of our nature is seditious, impious, insolent, refractory, opposed to and contemptuous of all that tries to rule it, and therefore contrary to order, ungovernable and negative. It is this foundation which Christianity calls the natural man. But the savage which is within us, and constitutes the primitive stuff of us, must be disciplined and civilized in order to produce a man. And the man must be patiently cultivated to produce a wise man, and the wise man must be tested and tried if he is to become righteous. And the righteous man must have substituted the will of God for his individual will, if he is to become a saint.[1]

(2) Then another aspect of sin rises before the Psalmist's mind. This evil which he has done, which probably was the sin in the matter of Bathsheba, was not only rebellion against God, but it was, according to this text, in the second clause, " a sin," by which is meant literally *missing an aim*. So this word, in its pregnant meaning, corresponds with the signification of the ordinary New Testament word for sin, which also implies error, or missing that which ought to be the goal of our lives. That is to say, whilst the former word regarded the evil deed mainly in its relation to God, this word regards it mainly in its relation to ourselves, and that which before Him is rebellion—the assertion of our own individuality and our own will, and therefore in separation from His will—is, considered in reference to ourselves, fatally missing the mark to which our whole energy and effort ought to be

[1] *Amiel's Journal* (trans. by Mrs. Humphry Ward), 164.

directed. All sin, big or little, is a blunder. It is a blunder even if it hits what it aims at, for it aims at the wrong thing. So doubly, all transgression is folly, and the true name for the doer is " Thou fool ! " For every evil misses the mark which, regard being had to the man's obvious destiny, he ought to aim at. " Man's chief end is to glorify God and to enjoy Him for ever " ; and whosoever in all his successes fails to realize that end is a failure through and through, in whatever smaller matters he may seem to himself and to others to succeed.

¶ Full of far deeper love for what I remember of Turner himself, as I become better capable of understanding it, I find myself more and more helpless to explain his errors and his sins. His errors, I might say, simply. Perhaps, some day, people will again begin to remember the force of the old Greek word for sin ; and to learn that all sin is in essence—" Missing the mark " ; losing sight or consciousness of heaven ; and that this loss may be various in its guilt ; it cannot be judged by us.[1]

(3) But the Psalmist sees in his own past behaviour not only rebellion and failure, but *iniquity*—that is, something twisted or distorted. His conduct is thus brought into contrast with the right line of the plain, straight path in which we ought to walk. We have the same metaphor in our own language. We talk about things being right and wrong, by which we mean, in the one case, parallel with the rigid law of duty, and in the other case, " wrung," or wavering, crooked and divergent from it. There is a standard as well as a Judge, and we have to think of evil not only as being rebellion against God and separation from Him, and as, for ourselves, issuing in fatal missing of the mark, but also as being divergent from the one manifest law to which we ought to be conformed. The path to God is a right line ; the shortest road from earth to Heaven is absolutely straight.

¶ Every person of a mature age, and in his right mind, remembers turns or crises in his life, where he met the question of wrong face to face, and by a hard inward struggle broke through the sacred convictions of duty that rose up to fence him back. It was some new sin to which he had not become familiar, so much worse perhaps in degree as to be the entrance to him consciously of a new stage of guilt. He remembers how it shook his soul and even his body ; how he shrunk in guilty anticipation from the

---

[1] Ruskin, *Modern Painters*, v. pt. ix. chap. xii. (*Works*, vii. 441).

new step of wrong; the sublime misgiving that seized him, the awkward and but half-possessed manner in which it was taken, and then afterward, perhaps even after years have passed away, how, in some quiet hour of the day or the wakeful hour of night, as the recollection of that deed—not a public crime, but a wrong, or an act of vice—returned upon him, the blood rushed back for the moment on his fluttering heart, the pores of his skin opened, and a kind of agony of shame and self-condemnation, in one word of remorse, seized his whole person. This is the consciousness, the guilty pang, of sin; every man knows what it is.[1]

2. Corresponding to the three terms for sin, there are three expressions to signify its removal. The first word means taken away or lifted off, as a burden from aching shoulders. It implies more than holding back penal consequences; it is the removal of sin itself, and that not merely in the multitudinousness of its manifestations in act, but in the depth of its inward source. This is the metaphor which Bunyan has made so familiar by his picture of the pilgrim losing his load at the cross. The second ("covered") paints pardon as God's shrouding the foul thing from His pure eyes, so that His action is no longer determined by its existence. The third describes forgiveness as God's not reckoning a man's sin to him, in which expression hovers some allusion to cancelling a debt.

(1) Sin is here pictured as a burden, lying on the soul. Every sin we commit is making that burden larger and heavier. We do not say it is *felt* to be heavier; that would be the *sense of sin*. The burden is there, whether it be felt or not, and it always grows. If the burden of his sin remains on any sinner it will sink him into ruin. Surely, then, he is a happy man whose burden of sin is lifted off. "Oh, the blessedness of the man whose burden of sin is lifted off!" Why is he a blessed man? Because when the burden of sin goes, other things must go with it. When this burden is lifted off, the sentence of death against the sinner is cancelled for ever, the gates of hell are closed against him and will never open to admit him, and heaven's gates are open in a new sense, in that they never can be closed till he is inside.

¶ The most persistent symbol of Conscience in this first stage is the " burden "—a simple but picturesque emblem of a sense of

[1] T. T. Munger, *Horace Bushnell*, 218.

guilt. It is on him, though behind him; it is oppressive, though it leaves his limbs all free for action or advance; it is rather felt than seen. Somewhat characteristic it is of Bunyan's Christian that this burden of his is "great." [1]

¶ In 1881, when he was nearing his end, Dante Gabriel Rossetti, though an agnostic, became very anxious for confession and absolution. It was suggested to him that absolution was contrary to his pronounced views. But he said, "I don't care about that. I can make nothing of Christianity, but I only want a confessor to give me absolution of my sins," adding, "I believe in a future life—what I want now is absolution for my sins, that's all." [2]

(2) Again, sin is pictured as inward pollution and filthiness, which must be covered before there can be true blessedness. But not every kind of "covering" will suffice. Many ways of covering sins bring no blessing, but a curse. Some people spend much time and trouble, and exercise great ingenuity, in covering up their sins. They dig deep graves in which they seek to bury them, but every sin they bury is going to have a resurrection. Such coverings never bring any blessedness. "He that covereth his sins shall not prosper." The Psalmist tried for a year to bury his sin. Did he succeed? Was it a happy year? Note what he says about that time: "When I kept silence, my bones waxed old through my roaring all the day long. For day and night thy hand was heavy upon me: my moisture is turned into the drought of summer." When he is brought to a right frame of mind he no longer tries to cover up his sin, but says, "My sin is ever before me." "I acknowledge my sin unto thee, and mine iniquity have I not hid."

¶ Bees in their hives, when there is anything corrupt and too large for them to remove, fling a covering of wax over it, and hermetically seal it, and no foul odour comes from it. And so a man's sin is covered over and ceases to be *in evidence*, as it were, before the Divine Eye that sees all things. He Himself casts a merciful veil over it and hides it from Himself. [3]

(3) The third picture of sin is perhaps the most striking of all. It means: "I am a debtor, over head and ears in debt, but

[1] J. A. Kerr Bain, *The People of the Pilgrimage*, i. 51.
[2] A. C. Benson, *Life of D. G. Rossetti*, 71.
[3] A. Maclaren.

the debt is not charged or reckoned against me at all." Still
more, it means: "I am guilty, yet the righteous Judge justly
pronounces me *not guilty.*" How can that be possible? Let
the Apostle Paul explain. He says that "David describes the
blessedness of the man to whom the Lord imputeth righteousness
without works," and he quotes the text to prove this. David
did not say one word about "righteousness without works." What
does St. Paul mean by saying he did? The simple fact is that
St. Paul supplements David; he gives the positive side, in addition to David's negative side of the double transaction. St. Paul
has his eye on Christ. If sin is not reckoned or charged against,
or put to the account of, the believing sinner, it is because it has
been imputed, reckoned, charged against, or put to the account
of Christ. And if "righteousness without works" is imputed,
reckoned to, or put to the account of, the believing sinner, it is
because of what Christ had done. "Him who knew no sin he
made to be sin on our behalf; that we [who knew no righteous-
ness] might become the righteousness of God in him."

¶ A very common idea of the object of the gospel is, that it
is to show how *men may obtain pardon*; whereas, in truth, its
object is to show how *pardon for men has been obtained,* or rather
to show how God has taken occasion, by the entrance of sin into
the world, to manifest the unsearchable riches of holy compassion.
I have observed that even the phrase *free offer of pardon* is so
interpreted that the very existence of the pardon is made to
depend on the acceptance of the offer. The benefit of the pardon
does most assuredly depend on its being accepted, but the
pardon itself is laid up in Christ Jesus, and depends on nothing
but the unchangeable character of God.[1]

3. *The condition of forgiveness.*—The last clause of the text,
"In whose spirit there is no guile," seems to refer to the frank
sincerity of a confession. He is not like the self-righteous sinner
who tries to tell lies to God, and, attempting to deceive Him,
really deceives only himself. Whoever opens his heart to God,
makes a clean breast of it, and without equivocation or self-
deception or the palliations which self-love teaches, says, "I
have played the fool and erred exceedingly"—to that man, the
Psalmist thinks, pardon is sure to come.

[1] *Letters of Thomas Erskine of Linlathen,* i. 379.

The great question before the mind of the Psalmist is how the burden of sin may be removed not from the Divine side, but from the human, and so he states one necessary condition to that removal—confession: "I said, I will confess my transgressions unto the Lord; and thou forgavest the iniquity of my sin" (ver. 5). Sin must be confessed before it is removed. Till a man confesses his sins he hugs them to himself, and refuses to part with them. When he truly confesses them he puts them away by an act of will. Not till then are they removed. God *cannot* forgive the man who is impenitent, for that man will presently sin again. He cannot forgive, much as He longs so to do, because there is an obstacle in the way. Repentance removes that obstacle; it opens the door to the exercise of God's forgiving grace. The moment we repent we are pardoned.

¶ Excellent as repentance may be in itself, and quite independent of all results, yet the one ultimate test of it is amendment —amendment, and nothing else. We have done wrong and are sorry for it. What is the test of the value of our sorrow? Our doing the same thing no more. We desire to be forgiven. We pray to God for that forgiveness. What is to us the certain seal that He has heard our prayer, and by the power of His Son's Cross has finally forgiven us? The seal is that we have been enabled to sin so no more. Put it how you will, you must always come back to that. I do not say that no repentance is worth anything which is followed by further falls. God forbid. I do not say that God never forgives until He also makes the sin impossible. God forbid. But I do say that to *us*—to *us* there is no other proof either of the genuineness of our repentance, or of the certainty of God's forgiveness.[1]

II.

THE BLESSEDNESS OF FORGIVENESS.

In all the benedictions of the Bible the thing brought prominently into notice is not the outward circumstances but the inner state or life of the man who is blessed. Blessedness does not depend on outward possessions, such as worldly goods, or lands, or high birth, or erudite culture. Indeed, there are words of Christ which suggest that they who stand possessed of these

[1] Archbishop Temple.

things will find it harder to enter that Paradise which has not yet
faded from our world, and to pass through the gates of that city
which are before our eyes, if only they were opened to discern
them. When He repeated the Sermon of the Mountain-Heights
and of the Dawn to the multitudes that stood breathless beneath
its spell, He said, " Woe unto you that are rich. Woe unto you
that are full. Woe unto you, ye that laugh." He did not mean
that such would be necessarily excluded, but that entrance into
blessedness would be hard for them.

1. The forgiven soul enjoys the blessedness of deliverance. The
very essence of the benediction is the exquisite sense of transgression forgiven, sin covered. This royal sinner knew the felicity
in its full range. Through all those weary months of sullen
silence which followed David's murder and adultery, he was a
most miserable man. He knew that his Divine Judge had not
pardoned him. He was conscious all the time of lying under the
withering condemnation of God. He felt that his iniquity lay
naked and open to the eye of Him with whom he had to do. He
might to some extent conceal his fault from his fellows, but in all
its hideous enormity it was exposed to the gaze of the Searcher of
hearts. Could the king have any peace or comfort under that
continual sense of the silent sentence of Heaven on his conduct ?
O what a joyful man he was when the grace of God enabled him
to confess, " I have sinned," and the sweet response came, " The
Lord also hath put away thy sin " ! When he contrasted the
sordid wretchedness of the preceding months with his condition,
now that the springs of his better nature had found vent, would
he not feel that he was in the seventh heaven ? It was not
enough for him to say that his transgression was forgiven: he
had to supplement that with this other word, that his sin was
covered, in order to utter fully his felicity. His Judge had
pardoned him, how much was that ! But was it not even more
that his Heavenly Father had blotted out his foul guilt, so that
it should be never seen or remembered more ?

¶ Whatever I have studied of the Epistles of St. Paul, and
this has been for many years, and with as much yearning eagerness and breathless awe as I have felt in nothing except the
words of the Lord Jesus, has tended to the confirmation of the

old evangelic interpretation of them, in which perhaps I should
not have seen my way so clearly but for their accordance with
my own "experience." All that unutterable sense of sin, that
terrible deadly fight with evil, those strivings of the Spirit I went
through, and more; all that deliverance, that liberty of the
Gospel, that being justified by faith in Christ, that peace with
God, that shedding abroad by the Holy Ghost of the love of God
in the heart, that coming in of the "new creation"; all the shades
and lights of experience since then. Twenty-three years of such
experience, which inwardly is as great and as simple a fact as the
facts of seeing and hearing, make me unable to receive, even to
perceive, any other interpretation. And I have met with such
scores and hundreds who strike hands with me in life and death
on these great matters that it is settled "without controversy"
to me.[1]

¶ When Saul Kane, the ill-living prodigal whose "rake's
progress" John Masefield has so vividly set forth in his poem
The Everlasting Mercy, suffered his instant conversion, an immediate and wonderful glory filled his soul.

> I did not think, I did not strive,
> The deep peace burnt my me alive;
> The bolted door had broken in,
> I knew that I had done with sin.
> I knew that Christ had given me birth
> To brother all the souls on earth,
> And every bird and every beast
> Should share the crumbs broke at the feast.
>
> O glory of the lighted mind,
> How dead I'd been, how dumb, how blind.
> The station-brook to my new eyes,
> Was babbling out of Paradise,
> The waters rushing from the rain
> Were singing, "Christ has risen again."
> I thought all earthly creatures knelt
> From rapture of the joy I felt.
> The narrow station-wall's brick ledge,
> The wild hop withering in the hedge,
> The lights in huntsman's upper storey
> Were parts of an eternal glory,
> Were God's eternal garden flowers.
> I stood in bliss at this for hours.

[1] *Letters of James Smetham*, 234.

O clover tops, half-white, half-red,
O beauty from beyond the dead,
O blossom, key to earth and heaven,
O souls that Christ has new forgiven.

2. The forgiven soul is blessed, because the whole character
and life are lifted to a higher plane. No man can pass from
darkness to light, from alienation to reconciliation, without being
marvellously transformed by the experience. His whole nature
is changed. That is what we mean when we contrast the effect
on the human soul of the gospel of grace with that produced by
the preaching of mere morality and legality. Sinai thunders at
us in vain, and the most eloquent exposition of the beauty of
virtue is apt to leave a soul very much where it found it; but let
a sinner come to believe that Christ died for him, that God so
loved Him that He spared not His own Son, but delivered Him
up for the transgressor, and that in the fountain thus opened for
sin and for uncleanness his sins have been washed away for ever,
then that forgiven soul will become a living mass of gratitude, of
love, of devotion to Him whose grace has saved him. Through
all his subsequent life he will be a changed man. He will hate
iniquity and love holiness. We cannot say that he will never sin
again, but never again can he feel toward sin as he did in the days
before he had drunk this wine of heaven. His character will be
radically altered, and the life will answer, more or less truly, to
the character.

¶ You stand in some valley, and however brightly the sun
may shine, there are shadows; you climb to the summit of some
lofty hill, and it is all sunshine, and no shadows there. Even so,
if you rest satisfied with forgiveness of sins merely, brightly as
that exhibits God's love, and wonderful as is the grace of it, your
peace, and joy, and rest will be all imperfect. Come up into the
heavenly places in Christ Jesus; get upon the high tableland of
a really *Christ-life*; go on to the realization of all the " happinesses "
which are linked on to forgiveness; be a little child, and take
God at His word about them, without cavil or question; and then
your whole life will be sunlit indeed. Difficulties and sorrows
and temptations you may have, and they may multiply as you go
on; but you will *look down* upon them, instead of being *over-
shadowed* by them: and you will see, what in the valley of a low

life you cannot see, how God's love lights them all up, and how in very truth they all work together for your good.[1]

3. Happy is he whose sin is forgiven, because new relations are established between God and the soul. To have passed through this experience not only changes a man's character, it puts him permanently on a new footing with God. The pardon comes to him as but one part of what we call the Divine scheme of salvation. Henceforth he does not think of the Almighty as his Judge, but rather as his Heavenly Father. He has been adopted into the family of the Most High, and he knows that all the privileges of adoption, in time and eternity, are secured to him. Christ has become to him as an elder Brother, who is preparing a place for him in that region of the blessed which is to be hereafter their common home.

This is a side of Christian truth which has not always received the attention it deserves—a neglect the more to be regretted that the doctrine furnishes the reply to the objection sometimes made, that "justification" presents our relations with God in salvation in too exclusively "legal" a light. It would do so if it stood alone; but it does not stand alone. Adoption, by certain writers, has been treated as part of justification—as the positive side of it, in *acceptance*. But this is not warranted. If it is wrong to merge, as many do, God's character as Judge in that of Father, it is as wrong to merge His character as Father in that of Judge, and to overlook the fact that God's relation to us is personal as well as judicial. God does not merely pardon the sinner by way of legal acquittal. There is the outflow of paternal tenderness, paternal forgiveness, paternal grace (cf. the Prodigal, Luke xv. 20–24); and the soul that comes to Him is received by Him into a relation of sonship—not merely that forfeited sonship which was its destination by creation, but a relation of honour, nearness, and privilege, analogous to Christ's own. "If children, then heirs; heirs of God, and joint-heirs with Christ" (Rom. viii. 17).

> Here are we dark and weak, yet are we not
> Excluded from Thy glorious family;
> Pain to Thy children is a transient lot;
> We suffer, that from sin we may be free.

[1] A. C. Price.

Angels and men, the prophet and the child,
　These all are what they are by gift of Thine;
No break or gulf is there; the undefiled
　Are tenderly made one by birth divine.

If but a letter of the all-perfect name,
　If but a mark of the celestial pen,
Distinguish us, we will, despising shame,
　Abjuring self, live boldly among men.

Named after God! a little like to Him,
　In whom the entireness of the name divine
Brightly involved was once by woes made dim,
　But now unfolded shines, yet more to shine.[1]

[1] T. T. Lynch, *The Rivulet*, 202.

The Guiding Eye.

LITERATURE.

Bourdillon (F.), *Handfuls*, 24.
Brown (J. Baldwin), *The Sunday Afternoon*, 278.
Hackett (W. S.), *The Land of Your Sojournings*, 37.
Knight (G. H.), *Abiding Help for Changing Days*, 27.
Matheson (G.), *Words by the Wayside*, 16.
Meyer (F. B.), *Christian Living*, 78.
Stone (C. E.), *Children's Sunday Afternoons*, 186.
Vaughan (J.), *Sermons* (Brighton Pulpit), New Ser., xiii. (1876), No. 989.
Voysey (C.), *Sermons*, ii. (1879), No. 1.
Clergyman's Magazine, 3rd Ser., xii. 96 (H. G. Youard).
Literary Churchman, xx. (1874) 95.
Sunday Magazine, 1880, p. 140 (R. H. Smith).

THE GUIDING EYE.

**I will instruct thee and teach thee in the way which thou shalt go:
I will counsel thee with mine eye upon thee.—Ps. xxxii. 8.**

IT was at the end of a long and bitter trial that this promise was
given to the Psalmist. It was by passing through doubt, perplexity, and despair that he was taught at last to find his way
by the light of God. He had tried long and desperately to be his
own guide, to trace out a path for himself through life, and it was
after many wanderings, and many shameful falls, and much
misery, that he was forced to confess that it is not in man that
walketh to direct his steps, and that his only way of safety is to
give himself up to One who will guide him better than he can
guide himself. Feeling his ignorance, and perplexed at times by
uncertainty as to his duty, he besought the Lord to teach and to
guide him; and the Lord heard him and answered him, bringing
strength to his weakness, light into his darkness, and showing him
the way in which he should walk.

¶ The beautiful suggestiveness of the Authorized Version, "I
will guide thee with mine eye," need not be wholly lost, though
the Revised Version shows that the Hebrew does not mean that
"a look is enough." It means that with a Divine word of counsel
in the ear, and the eye of Providence watching from above, the
traveller in the pathway of life will be safe.[1]

I.

OUR NEED OF GUIDANCE.

1. We need guidance because we may deliberately reject God.
There are those who may be called the unbridled: the men who
care for no restraint; whose whole life is a challenge, "Who is
the Lord, that we should serve him?" The Psalms are full of

[1] W. T. Davison.

the description of them. They escape the eye and the hand of God to all appearance. But do they indeed escape? The mere men of the world are the worst of slaves; and of all men they are the most limited, checked, compelled, by the hand of God. A hard bar meets them at every turn, a check at every breath. God rules them though it be with a rod of iron. Blind to the glance of His eye, they must writhe under the pressure of His hand.

¶ The pupil spoke: "You said once that the tramcar comes to a standstill if it loses connexion with the aerial wire. I know that very well. Would that my friends who are atheists and pagans knew what a relief it is to find the connexion again. It is like diving in crystal-clear sea-water after perspiring in the heat of the dog-days on a dusty high-road. The heart grows light; the systematic ill-luck ceases; one has some success, one's undertakings prosper, one can sleep at night, and neurasthenia ceases. I remember how, after a night of debauchery, the most beautiful landscape at sunrise looked ghastly; while after a night of quiet sleep the same scene looked paradisal. When we gain the certainty, and the belief founded on certainty, that life is continued on the other side, then we find it easier on this one, and do not hunt after trifles till we are weary. Then we discover the divine lightheartedness of which Goethe speaks, which finds expression in a certain contempt of honours and distinction, promotion and money. We become more insensible to blows and abuse. Everything goes more softly and smoothly. However dark the surroundings may be, we become self-luminous, so to speak, and carry the little pocket-lamp hope with us."[1]

2. There are those whose hearts are divided between God and the world, and who need constraint to keep them in the right way. Some things are already settled in their minds on the subject of the duties and the issues of life. They know already that there is no blessing that is really worth anything but God's. They would weep bitterly, and feel that life was utterly impoverished, if God's presence were gone from it, and they were just left to make the best of a world that they love too well. But they will not risk too much in seeking the Kingdom of God and His righteousness. One eye is always on the world, if the other is on God. They have their comforts, their luxuries, their

[1] A. Strindberg, *Zones of the Spirit*, 111.

pleasures, their possessions, which fill as large a space as the higher things in the horizon round which they sweep their sight. They are not ungodly, they are not indifferent to the benediction of Heaven. But there is a great dead weight to be lifted, a great back-longing to be overcome. They have to be driven in the way which they say they love, and to the end which they profess to desire more than worlds. How many Christians have to be driven in the way of life, at a cost of pain to them, and patience to Him, which God alone knows!

¶ It looks to me now like a kind of humble russet-coated epic, that seven years' settlement at Craigenputtock; very poor in this world's goods, but not without an intrinsic dignity greater and more important than then appeared. It is certain that for living in and thinking in, I have never since found in the world a place so favourable. And we were driven and pushed into it, as if by Necessity, and its beneficent though ugly little shocks and pushes, shock after shock gradually compelling us thither! "For a Divinity doth shape our ends, rough-hew them how *we* will": often in my life have I been brought to think of this, as probably every considering person is; and, looking before and after, have felt, though reluctant enough to believe in the importance or significance of so infinitesimally small an atom as oneself, that the Doctrine of a Special Providence is in some sort natural to man. All piety points that way, all logic points the other;—one has, in one's darkness and limitation, a trembling faith, and can at least say with the Voices, "*Wir heissen euch hoffen*,"—if it *be* the will of the Highest.[1]

¶ Do you at all recollect that interesting passage of Carlyle in which he compares, in this country and at this day, the understood and commercial value of man and horse; and in which he wonders that the horse, with its inferior brains and its awkward hoofiness, instead of handiness, should be always worth so many tens or scores of pounds in the market, while the man, so far from always commanding his price in the market, would often be thought to confer a service on the community by simply killing himself out of their way? Well, Carlyle does not answer his own question, because he supposes we shall at once see the answer. The value of the horse consists simply in the fact of your being able to put a bridle on him. The value of the man consists precisely in the same thing. If you can bridle him, or, which is better, if he can bridle himself, he will be a valuable creature

---

[1] Carlyle, *Reminiscences*, ii. 244.

directly. Otherwise, in a commercial point of view, his value is either nothing, or accidental only. Only, of course, the proper bridle of man is not a leathern one; what kind of texture it is rightly made of, we find from that command, " Be ye not as the horse or as the mule which have no understanding, whose mouths must be held in with bit and bridle." You are not to be without the reins, indeed; but they are to be of another kind: " I will guide thee with mine eye." So the bridle of man is to be the Eye of God; and if he rejects that guidance, then the next best for him is the horse's and the mule's, which have no understanding; and if he rejects that, and takes the bit fairly in his teeth, then there is nothing left for him than the blood that comes out of the city, up to the horse-bridles.[1]

3. There are those who desire and who willingly accept God's guidance. To such God says, " I will instruct thee and teach thee in the way which thou shalt go: I will counsel thee with mine eye upon thee." He will take a personal interest in them. For the guide of men is no Epicurean God, loftily serene and impassive, but one whose interest in the world, whose care for the world, brought Him to live in it that He might share its burden and pain. The gospel is the revelation of how much He cares; of how much the happiness of His creation, the order of His government, and the satisfaction of His heart depend on the way man takes. He has created a being of wonderful and complex powers, capable, if guided aright, of doing godlike work in the universe, or capable of making it an Aceldama, a Gehenna of wailing and death. And the great work of Heaven is to guide him; to make him know, trust, and love his guide. Truly " thou shalt guide me with thy counsel, and afterward receive me to glory." When Christ has won this trust from a human spirit, His redemptive work is done.

¶ To obey the will of the Lord is the secret first of all, of safety—security. " All things work together for good to them that love God." From the moment a planet wheels into its path round the sun, there is nothing that can harm that planet, but just as soon as a star wanders from its orbit, and goes plunging headlong into the depths of space, it is liable to come into clash and crash with the universe of God. I have seen a great piece of machinery that would fill an immense building. Now, suppose

[1] Ruskin, *A Joy for Ever*, §18 (*Works*, xvi. 28).

that in that great piece of machinery, one little wheel, as small, it may be, as a shilling, should drop out of its place and fall into the midst of the machinery, that colossal mechanism moving round and round and round would grind this little wheel among its larger wheels into fragments, if not into powder. The Universe is one great Machine, and God is the Motive Power of it, and when a soul drops out of its place in this great machinery, and falls among the great wheels of God's purpose, it is ground into powder, unless the grace of God puts that wheel back into its place in the vast system. The moment that you find out what the will of God is, and drop into your place, all the universe moves with you, and all the universe moves for you, the whole Godhead is back of you, the wisdom of God, and the power of God, and the love of God, and the grace of God; and you are as absolutely sure and safe as God is. And so Peter says: "Who is he that shall harm you if you be followers of that which is good?"[1]

II.

GOD'S METHOD OF GUIDING US.

1. God guides His people by imparting to them understanding. There is a threefold assurance in the text: I will make thee wise; I will point out to thee the way; I will fix Mine eye upon thee. God will do something *in* the man. He shall yet be instructed more deeply than ever, and shall find himself never too old to learn. God will do something *round about* the man. He shall have the guidance of circumstances, of closed and opened doors, which only the wise can understand. Finally, this man being a backslider of proven weakness, God will watch him with fixed attention to correct the least slip. Providential care is shown to be a very complex thing, operating along many lines which converge to the great result. But more particularly for our purpose, it is largely an *inward* thing, dealing first and foremost with the mind rather than with the circumstances, according to this initial promise, "I will make thee wise." Probably circumstances are much more nearly right than people admit, and where failure arises the man himself is generally at fault. Also, men can never be saved from the outside or by the most favourable circumstances. Deliverance must be wrought supremely by

[1] A. T. Pierson.

an inward grace illuminating the mind and making men circum-
spect and self-adaptive to win the mastery over life's conditions.
It is written that God did not stay the flood, but Noah, being
warned by Him, prepared an ark for the saving of his house. The
grand resource and secret of the Most High in the protecting of
His children is this gift of wisdom.

The name "Wisdom" pervades the Old Testament, bringing
the glimmer of jewels and visions of a good woman's face as
tokens of its power to adorn and enrich life. In the text a
smaller word is used, indicating circumspection or intelligence;
yet that is but wisdom applied practically. The assertion is that
we may be made wise to think God's thoughts after Him, intelligent to recognize the meaning of His way with us, and when
understanding fails—as fail sometimes it will—patient to endure
with a great trust. Mere acquiescence cannot be the end of our
faith. He has called us friends—not puppets. Trials and griefs
have no inevitable efficacy. In every different destiny of joy
and sorrow, health and sickness, help and injury, there lie hidden
both a use and a misuse, both a blessing and a curse, and only
active wisdom can choose the better part.

¶ Many still think of God in the way Omar Khayyám thought
of Him—as an infinite Chess-player, with the world for His
board. There stand bishops and knights and pawns, each on its
own square and perhaps untouched for long intervals. But every
piece is moved from time to time by the inexorable Hand, and
sooner or later every piece is sacrificed for ends that it cannot
know. Our duty is simply to trust that God is winning the
game in His own way. Thus do the uninstructed ones most pitifully
talk, taking the name of the Lord their God *in vain*—finding faith
a poor futility. They cast their burden upon the Lord in quite
the wrong sense, for they lay only the blame of it on Him. They
think themselves not so much led through the world as dragged
through it, like a child's toy across the parlour floor, meeting with
a bump here and a bump there; and having caught a gleam of
religious truth from the nursery or the pulpit, they feel it right
to say without conviction, "I suppose the bumps are all for my
good." They are puppets in the hand of the Inscrutable One:
they are not made wise.[1]

¶ A lady put the universal difficulty to me in a simple but
complete statement. "My troubles," she said, "come from the

[1] W. S. Hackett, *The Land of Your Sojournings*, 79.

unkindness of other people, and they are very hard to bear
because I know they are not God's will. Unkindness cannot be
His will." Her complaint well-nigh covers all the dreary catalogue of human suffering. Nearly always it is " somebody's fault."
The cotton corner which spreads want over an English county, the
opened lamp in the coal-mine which darkens a hundred homes,
the careless workmanship at the drain which slays the darling of
the household, the heartbreak of a fruitless search for employ-
ment—these surely are not the will of your Heavenly Father.
Now it is quite true that Atlantic storms may be beyond control.
But nothing hinders men from building ships strong enough to
weather them. There may be limits which we know not to the
miraculous betterment of circumstances outside, but there is no
limit to God's power to build up His saints inwardly in strength.
He may be barred out of a thousand hearts, but He need not be
barred out of mine. And this gospel is ennobling because it is
educative. It may be doubted if "God tempers the wind to the
shorn lamb," but it is not at all doubtful that He expects men to
invent warmer clothing. The blessings of Providence are not for
idlers, but for those who are willing to learn wisdom.[1]

2. God guides His own not by force, but by love. The eye is
the indicator of the desire ; the lips command ; the hand compels.
The lips can plead, but there is an inner plea which the eye alone
urges. Those who know the language of the eye have mastered
the language of the soul. It implies that a sympathy is already
established. When the glance is understood and obeyed, there is
perfect concert of mind and heart. A heart tuned to sympathy
with the Divine purposes and hopes, leaps forth in glad obedience.
It sees no meanings anywhere so joyfully as those which it reads
in the eye of God.

¶ What is it that makes thy life an intenser note than the
music of the stars ? Is it not just the fact that thou art free,
just the circumstance that there is no iron belt around thee?
What is this marvellous thing thou callest thy will ? Wherein
does its glory differ from the glory which the heavens declare ?
Is it not just in this, that thou art not *compelled* to come in ?
There is a guidance for thee, but it is not a star's guidance; it is
a guidance of the eye. It is the only guiding which a will can
get without dying. Wouldst thou be driven like a star ? then
must thou cease to be free. The heavens declare God's glory;

[1] W. S. Hackett.

but it is the glory of His hands. Who shall declare the glory of His Spirit? Not a star however bright, not a pulseless thing however fair; only something that can throb and strive and choose. He will not guide thee by aught but His eye. He will not *compel* thee to bear His cross. He will not sacrifice the joy of being loved to the pride of being obeyed. He will draw thee, but He will never drive thee; He shall guide thee only with His eye.[1]

¶ Is God your leader?—or does He only rein you in? Are you personally conscious of the vast difference between these two experiences? It is well to be held back from sin, no doubt, but the joy of the God-directed, sanctified man is certainly beyond that of the horse and mule which have no understanding, and whose mouth must be held in with bit and bridle. There is no holiness of a radical sort without Divine, positive, everyday guidance. This differs not only in degree but in kind from negative restraint. The latter may be no more than the rebuke or cry of our own alarmed conscience. Conscience is born with us, born with every man. We possess it without choice of our own. It is liable to error like other human faculties, even though of inestimable value. But God intends us to know Him of our own free choice, and much more intimately than by laws written involuntarily upon our heart. Those latter we have in common with the heathen. They operate upon our fears. Guidance appeals to our faith. "I will guide thee with mine eye," is a promise to God's people which goes far ahead of conscience, and so universally is it intended to be enjoyed that it was given even long before the coming of our Lord. But there is no guidance of this highest kind without the eager and abiding desire for it—a desire strong enough in its faith and intensity to survive during the severest trial and suffering.[2]

3. God guides us, not by showing us at the outset the whole road that lies before us, and instructing us beforehand which turn to take, and what to do in each difficult place; but, step by step, as we go along, He reveals the path to us, and shows us how to walk. We should be appalled were we to see at a glance all that He sees. He does not guide us so. He Himself sees all; but He shows it to us, bit by bit, as we can bear the sight, and as it is needful for us to know. When we accept God's guidance, we

---

[1] G. Matheson, *Words by the Wayside*, 17.
[2] J. Rendel Harris, *Life of F. W. Crossley*, 165.

experience more and more the warm, cherishing, quickening sunlight, the light of God's countenance, shining on, gladdening, and glorifying the life. We escape, too, all that is bitter in the school of discipline, all harm, all loss, all death. Nothing malign, nothing sorrowful, can lurk for a spirit in the path in which it is guided by the eye of God; while the life-path brightens as it travels, opening into a sphere of boundless activity, of glorious beauty, of perfect blessedness, as it nears the bounds of the eternal world.

¶ My parents founded every action, every attitude, upon their interpretation of the Scriptures, and upon the guidance of the Divine Will as revealed to them by direct answer to prayer. Their ejaculation in the face of any dilemma was, " Let us cast it before the Lord ! " So confident were they of the reality of their intercourse with God, that they asked for no other guide. They recognized no spiritual authority among men, they subjected themselves to no priest or minister, they troubled their consciences about no current manifestation of " religious opinion." They lived in an intellectual cell, bounded at its sides by the walls of their own house, but open above to the very heart of the uttermost heavens.[1]

4. God's guidance meets all possible circumstances and conditions. The eye has infinite capability of expression, and speaks all languages. It thus meets and fits any character, in all its feelings, and in all its circumstances, every moment. And yet it is actually personal. Other "guidings," such as laws, or books, or commands, are general, and the same to everybody. The look of " the eye " is essentially individual; it brings the Guider and the guided into the closest association: " I will guide *thee* with mine eye."

¶ Of all bodily organs the most expressive is the eye. I can read in the eye of a friend far more than he utters with the tongue. It is the most accurate of all the heart's dial-plates. It can express joy or grief, entreaty or reproof, approval or dislike. Parents and children, or brothers and sisters, living in the same home, can hold conversations with each other, even in the presence of strangers, by the language of the eye. Small signs pass between them thus which a stranger neither sees nor understands. And just so, those who live in close intercourse with God learn to

---

[1] Edmund Gosse, *Father and Son*, 14.

read what may be called the glances of His eye, small indications
of His will which strangers to heart-fellowship with Him cannot
read at all.[1]

5. God's guidance is unerring; it never fails. We read in the
Old Testament that God guided His people in various ways—by
angels, by dreams, by visions, by prophets, by priests, by Urim
and Thummim, by signs and wonders. Although God no longer
guides man by these special or extraordinary agencies, yet we may
be as certain of God's guidance now as though we saw Him in the
heavens with His eye upon us and His finger pointing to the
course He desires us to take. By an instinct, by an impression,
by a sense of duty, by an exercise of judgment, by the advice of
others, by a book, by a sermon, by a passage of Scripture, by
helping us in one direction, by hindering us in another—these are
the ordinary methods or agencies by which God is ever guiding
those who obey His guidance. We are as a vessel being steered
to port. There is One with us whose eye is always on the
compass, and whose hand, so to speak, is always on the wheel of
life. By His eye and by His hand every movement of a man's
life is guided. That hand and that eye are hidden, are unnoticed;
but night and day they are in action, ever performing their
guiding work till we reach the haven of God's everlasting rest.
We may make false moves at times, at times appear to get out of
our providential track; but somehow, so long as the Divine eye
is upon us and the Divine hand directs us, we go not far astray,
and in the end reach our God-appointed port.

¶ Keble recalled to men the teaching of Bishop Butler on the
moral nature of the evidence by which spiritual convictions were
reached. To the mere reason, this evidence could not get beyond
suggestive probabilities; but these probabilities were used, by the
living spirit of man, as an indication of the personal Will of God,
which could be read by the soul that was in tune with that Will.
So probabilities became certitudes. "I will guide thee with mine
Eye," was Keble's favourite example of the mode in which Divine
truth touched the soul. By deep glimpses, by rare flashes, by a
momentary glance, the Eye of God could make us aware of Truths
far beyond the understanding of reason. Such Truths possessed
authority, which we could not dissect or critically examine.

[1] G. H. Knight, *Abiding Help for Changing Days*, 30.

They were revelations of the mind of Him with whom we had to deal.[1]

¶ There is a tender awe in knowing that there is some One at your side guiding at every step, restraining here, leading on there. He knows the way better than the oldest Swiss guide knows the mountain trail. He has love's concern that all shall go well with you. There is a great peace for us in that, and with it a tender awe to think who He is, and that He is close up by your side. When you come to the splitting of the road into two, with a third path forking off from the others, there is peace in just holding steady and very quiet while you put out your hand and say, "Jesus, Master, guide here." And then to hear a Voice so soft that only in great quiet is it heard, softer than faintest breath on your cheek, or slightest touch on your arm, telling the way in fewest words or syllables—that makes the peace unspeakable.[2]

> Not like the angel with drawn sword,
>   Neither with rod threat'ningly;
> Leadst Thou, Lord, but fulfill'st Thy word,
>   "I will guide thee with Mine eye."
>
> We see Thee not, but Thou seest us,
>   Be where we may, Thou art nigh;
> Whisp'ring, timid or valorous,
>   "I will guide thee with Mine eye."
>
> Dark days come and our path is dark,
>   We know not to go or fly;
> From the sky falls, like trill of lark,
>   "I will guide thee with Mine eye."
>
> Ah, Lord, we're wayward and we're weak,
>   Our gladness changing to sad sigh:
> O keep Thou us as Thou dost speak,
>   And guide us ever with Thine eye.[3]

[1] H. S. Holland, *Personal Studies*, 78.
[2] S. D. Gordon, *Quiet Talks on Personal Problems*, 154.
[3] A. B. Grosart, *Songs of the Day and Night*, 33.

THE GOODNESS OF GOD.

Literature.

Arnold (T.), *Sermons*, v. 163.
Ballard (F.), *Does it Matter what a Man Believes?* 234.
Bosanquet (C.), *The Man after God's own Heart*, 82.
Holland (H. S.), *Vital Values*, 36.
Simeon (C.), *Works*, v. 240.
Smith (Mrs. Pearsall), *The God of all Comfort*, 90.
Symonds (A. R.), *Fifty Sermons*, 280.
Vaughan (J.), *Sermons to Children*, i. 57.
Voysey (C.), *Sermons*, xv. (1892), No. 31.
Christian World Pulpit, lxii. 145 (R. F. Horton).
Expositor, 2nd Ser., iv. 410 (S. Cox).

THE GOODNESS OF GOD.

O taste and see that the Lord is good :
Blessed is the man that trusteth in him.—Ps. xxxiv. 8.

1. No man who looks thoughtfully around him and within can
fail to feel at times, as Plato felt, that he needs some wiser and
more certain guidance than his own if he is ever to learn what
God really is; that God Himself must speak to him and show
Himself to him if he is to be sure that God is good, friendly,
accessible. Even if we believe that God has spoken to us and
shown Himself to us, that we have seen Him in Christ Jesus and
found Him altogether good, yet at times, when the burden of
all this unintelligible and self-contradictory world lies heavily
upon us, or when our own life is darkened by some misery to
which there seems neither relief nor end, we lose our assurance; we falter where we firmly trod: God seems to shroud
Himself in some inaccessible heaven, to retire behind thick clouds
we cannot penetrate, to become doubtful to us once more, so that
we can no longer see or say that He is good.

It is an unspeakable relief and comfort to hear any voice which
assures us, in clear and cordial tones, that God *is* good, despite our
doubts and fears, that the sun of His love is shining down on the
world, though it be hidden from us by the dark clouds that hang
about our hearts. And if the voice be that of a man such as
we are, yet better and wiser than we are, and wiser and better
mainly because he has passed through many such experiences as
those by which we are troubled and has found out what they
mean—then surely he can give us not comfort only, but the
very succour that we most need.

2. Now the author of this psalm stands in the front rank of
those poets who have devoted themselves to the study of the
ethical aspects and problems of human life, and he is able to

interpret the inner world of character and motive and passion with a precision and a delicacy, a truth and a power never surpassed. Confessedly also, despite the grievous transgression he so bitterly rued, he was a man after God's own heart; a man whose goodness was not of the narrow, ascetic, forbidding type which repels men, but of that large, cordial, and manly type which is most winning and attractive. Nor can we well doubt that his experience was wider and more varied than ours, embraced more radical vicissitudes, swept a larger circle, covered more distant extremes. And not only did he run through the whole gamut of human experience, but at the very time he sung this psalm he was involved in those clouds of undeserved loss, pain, reproach, under which we too often lose our faith in the goodness of God. It would have been pardonable if, under stress of so hard and unmerited a fate, he had brooded over it till the goodness of God had become as doubtful to him as it often becomes to us under the lesser strain of trials not to be compared with his. But it is from the thick darkness of his adversity that he comes forth, with manly and cheerful courage, to assure us that the Lord is good, and to dwell enjoyingly on the blessedness of the man who trusts in Him. Such a testimony, given by such a man at such a moment, may well touch and reassure our hearts. What are our powers of insight as compared with his? or what our troubles as compared with his? That, with his powers, he saw no reason to doubt the goodness of the Lord; that, under his burden, he held fast his confidence in God—this should at least bring some little hope to our hearts when they are heavy and doubtful and sad. And if we believe that he was not only a poet, but an inspired poet, we have in his words a Divine revelation as well as the result of his own illuminated reason and far-reaching experience. It is God who speaks to us and assures us that He is good, and will do us good, however we doubt or distrust Him.

¶ The following letter was written by Canon Liddon to Dr. King, Bishop of Lincoln, one of his oldest friends, in the second week of his illness, which was destined to proved fatal: "God has laid His hand very heavily upon me; and I have been through the fire—I greatly needed it. Nothing [is] more wonderful in Him than His goodness to such as I am. Pray for me, that I may learn how to be humble and patient, and that this visitation (in the Day of Account) may not be seen to have been as nothing—or worse than nothing—instead of a great means of grace."[1]

> Lifelong our stumbles, lifelong our regret,
>   Lifelong our efforts failing and renewed,
>   While lifelong is our witness, "God is good,"
> Who bore with us till now, bears with us yet,
> Who still remembers and will not forget,
>   Who gives us light and warmth and daily food;
>   And gracious promises half understood,
> And glories half unveiled, whereon to set
> Our heart of hearts and eyes of our desire;
>   Uplifting us to longing and to love,
> Luring us upward from this world of mire,
>   Urging us to press on and mount above
>   Ourselves and all we have had experience of,
> Mounting to Him in love's perpetual fire.[2]

I.

THE APPROACH TO GOD.

1. The Psalmist invites us to put God to the most practical of tests. "O taste and see." Of our five senses taste is the most homely; of our five senses taste is the most personal; for what we see, and hear, and smell, and touch, we share with others, but in a peculiarly personal sense the taste is our own. As the proverb says: "There is no disputing about taste." Moreover, the sense of taste is a peculiarly gracious gift of the Creator to us, for, so far as we can tell, we might easily be nourished with food which we did not taste, and all those processes of digestion might go on unconsciously, like the feeding of an engine. But He has given us this faculty of taste, by which we discriminate the different flavours of the food we eat, and get a relish from variety. Now, it is this one of the senses—the most homely, the most personal, and the most gratuitous—that is taken as the image to be used for urging upon us the experience of God. "Taste" is the command. It is as if God came to us with this generous proposal, "I would not have you choose Me until you have tasted Me, nor would I force Myself upon you unless your

---

[1] *Life and Letters of H. P. Liddon*, 384.   [2] Christina G. Rossetti.

taste decide." In a marvellous way He puts Himself at our disposal for us to try. "Taste and see that the Lord is good."

¶ There is an Indian story of a queen who "proved the truth by tasting the food." The story tells how her husband, who dearly loved her, and whom she dearly loved, lost his kingdom, wandered away with his queen into the forest, left her there as she slept, hoping she would fare better without him, and followed her long afterwards to her father's court, deformed, disguised, a servant among servants, a cook. Then her maidens came to her, told her of the wonderful cooking, magical in manner, marvellous in flavour and fragrance. They are sure it is the long-lost king come back to her, and they bid her believe and rejoice. But the queen fears it may not be true. She must prove it; she must taste the food. They bring her some. She tastes and knows. And the story ends in joy. "O taste and see that the Lord is good."[1]

2. The secret of goodness can be found only by personal experience. Men know what sin is, by experience. They do not know what holiness is, and they cannot obtain the knowledge of its secret pleasure, till they join themselves truly and heartily to Christ, and devote themselves to His service—till they "taste," and thereby try. One may ask, Of what value, of what distinct force and bearing, as an evidence of truth, is this appeal to experimental proof? To this we may answer, first, that while the mere fact of any religious or ethical system making such an appeal would by no means prove its truth, for a false system might profess to do the same, still no system could be true which shrank from it. It would argue a consciousness of being untrue to the realities of things, otherwise it would not fear the ordeal of experience. So far, therefore, it is a fair presumption in favour of the Bible that throughout its language, expressed or implied, is "Taste and see." And this presumption, it is next to be observed, rises into positive inductive proof, in proportion to the duration, extent, and diversity of the trial. As in experimental philosophy we arrive at a general law by an induction of particular instances, and the result is satisfactory in proportion to the multiplication of concurring instances and the absence of antagonistic ones, so is it with the argument for the Bible as derived from experimental proof. In this case the induction is overwhelming.

[1] Amy Wilson Carmichael, *Things as they are in India*, 253.

From the beginning it has been undergoing this ordeal.   Millions
have tried it, and have set to their seal that God's Word is true.
From age to age the testimony has rolled on, swelling in its progress into one mighty and majestic volume.   And thus, borne on
the echoes of successive generations, the voice of that testimony
has reached our ears, and the burden of its cry is still the same,
" O taste and see that the Lord is good: blessed is the man that
trusteth in him."

¶ It is in his inner experience of the glorified Christ that we
are to look for the secret and source of Raymund Lull's doctrine
and life—what he thought, what he was, what he suffered.   And
this must be true of all true missionaries.   They do not go out
to Asia and to Africa to say, " This is the doctrine of the Christian
Church "; or, " Your science is bad.   Look through this microscope
and see for yourselves and abandon such error "; or, " Compare
your condition with that of America and see how much more
socially beneficial Christianity is than Hinduism or Confucianism
or Islam."   Doubtless all this has its place—the argument from
the historic evidences of Christianity, the argument from the
coherence of Christianity with the facts of the universe, the
argument from fruits.   But it is also all secondary.   The primary
thing is personal testimony: " This I have felt.   This He has
done for me.   I preach whom I know." [1]

> Experience bows a sweet contented face,
>   Still setting to her seal that God is true:
>   Beneath the sun, she knows, is nothing new
> All things that go return with measured pace,
> Winds, rivers, man's still recommencing race:—
>   While Hope beyond earth's circle strains her view,
>   Past sun and moon, and rain and rainbow too,
> Enamoured of unseen eternal grace.
> Experience saith, " My God doth all things well ":
>   And for the morrow taketh little care,
>   Such peace and patience garrison her soul:—
>   While Hope, who never yet hath eyed the goal,
> With arms flung forth, and backward floating hair,
> Touches, embraces, hugs the invisible. [2]

3. This is a mode of proof available to every man, without
distinction or exception.   It requires neither learning nor logic to

---

[1] R. E. Speer, *Some Great Leaders in the World Movement*, 46.
[2] Christina G. Rossetti, *Verses*, 105.

conduct it. The appeal is simply this, "Taste and see; trust in the Lord and thou shalt be blessed." Whatever doubts there might have been before the time of our Lord Jesus Christ, there can be little doubt now that this experience of the great souls is meant to be the experience of every soul. For ever since our Lord and Master came to us in that homely speech of His, and proposed that we should taste Him, eat His flesh, and drink His blood, and ever since He reminded us that it is in that kind of intimate personal communion that life comes, and not otherwise, He has made it clear that there is with Him no selection. He does not choose the people at His banquet; He does not say, "Let the rich or let the worthy come." The whole point of it is, "Go out into the highways and hedges, and compel them to come in"; "whosoever will, let him drink"; "come, buy wine and milk without money and without price."

¶ Madame Guyon possessed the feminine rather than the masculine relation between the soul and God; but that is the beauty of this relation—that it does not depend upon sex or age; it is equally significant to the woman as to the man. There is something essentially delicate and sweet in this woman-soul opening to God. Follow the process. She comes in stillness and quietness and solitude to wait upon Him. She utters His name, and pauses; she says a word to Him, and waits to listen; she will not speak much, lest she should not hear. Presently she hears; it is the response, He is coming. "Oh, my soul, be still; hush thy words; He is here!" He speaks, and now she speaks again, and presently from speech to silence she comes into the sanctuary of His presence, and there it is all still—activity which does not move. Oh, the joy, the rapture of what seems passionless passion! He is speaking, she is hearing; the soul is throbbing on the heart of God. What a marvellous experience it is, this tasting God![1]

¶ Has the love of Christ worked any real change in our feelings towards God? Has there broken out yet in our hearts the beautiful bright spring of thankfulness, or the deep fount of holy sorrow? Have we ever felt the promptings of remorse, the pangs of penitence, as we thought of the goodness of God in giving us Jesus Christ? . . . Has the goodness of the Lord ever got a hold of our hand and turned us right round, and begun to lead us gently along the road that ends in a new mind about God, a mind

[1] R. F. Horton.

at peace with Him? That is what God's goodness leads to. If you have not seen the sunshine streaming down that lane, the sun has never shone for you. If you have never heard that in the patter of the rain, it has yet to fall a new way for you. If the sweetest voice you ever heard on earth never sounds in that strain, there is a music in it yet for you. If your father's wisdom, your teacher's help, your friend's love have not pointed out this track, there is a meaning in them hitherto missed by you. Oh, never say you have known the goodness of God as it can be known, as He would have it known, if it does not sometimes make you bow your head in your prayer and stop speechless, and nearly break your heart. Speak not of God's goodness if it has not cast you at the feet of Christ; if it has not made you feel after and find the hem of His garment, and hold on for dear life.[1]

4. The test must be applied under certain conditions, if the result is to prove satisfactory. Look at verses 13 and 14 of this psalm. Does a man want that taste of God? Then "Keep thy tongue from evil, and thy lips from speaking guile. Depart from evil, and do good; seek peace, and pursue it." The tongue that is to taste God must be true, the lips into which that food is to pass must be pure, and the life must be a life that is compatible with so high a companionship and so intimate a communion. "Oh, then," you say, "it is impossible to me; for my lips are unclean, and my tongue is untrue; what you say is possible for the good is not possible for me, the bad." But read on to verse 18—"The Lord is nigh unto them that are of a broken heart, and saveth such as be of a contrite spirit." So it appears that there are two conditions for this tasting of God. The one is that you shall be perfectly pure in heart and speech, and then you can taste Him; but if you are not pure, if you are defiled with sin, then you shall be contrite and broken-hearted, and your God will come that you may taste Him. It is not His intention that any should go unfed at the banquet which He has laid for the children of men.

¶ A very popular picture of Watts which usually holds the spectator spellbound is taken from the Arthurian Epic. Riding through the forest, with its tangled vegetation graphically painted, Sir Galahad has suddenly caught a glimpse of the mystic Sangreal, which was concealed from all ordinary vision.

[1] R. W. Barbour, *Thoughts*, 30.

> The times
> Grew to such evil that the holy cup
> Was caught away to Heaven, and disappear'd.

The knights of King Arthur had gone in search of this hidden
treasure. At the same time and in the same place, one could see
it and another could not. The knights had the vision of the Grail
in proportion to their purity. To some of them who saw it, it
appeared veiled with a luminous cloud. But Sir Galahad, the
knight of pure heart and unselfish living, who lost himself to save
himself, beheld the glorious thing itself, clear and distinct. It is
at this supreme moment when the heavenly vision appears to him
that he is painted by the artist. He dismounts from his white
horse, and stands bareheaded with fascinated eyes gazing upon the
glorious vision revealed to him in the luminous sky through a
break in the trees, and lighting up his face and armour. . . . The
inner meaning of the subject will come to us as the view of the
Grail came to Sir Galahad, when our eye is single and our heart
is pure, suddenly and unexpectedly; and we shall find that the
idea which underlies the whole picture, and makes it lovely with
a loveliness far surpassing that of hue and form so vividly de-
lineated, is an intensely modern one, and as applicable to our
day as to the far-off times of King Arthur.[1]

II.

THE DISCOVERY OF THE GOODNESS OF GOD.

1. The soul that tastes makes a great discovery; it finds that
God is good. It is a stupendous act of courage by which the soul
of man pushes through the tangled jungle of natural powers
that stop his progress and embarrass him; and thrusts himself
through; and emerges into the open spaces under a clear sky;
and finds himself face to face with God. Those powers have had
him as their own. He has been their creature, their captive
prey. He has been carried to and fro by feeling, instincts,
desires, appetites, interests, ambitions. So he has grown. So
it has always been. Passions, fears, hates, joys, loves—these
welled up from unknown sources; these made him their puppet.
Whither they impelled he went. They were strong in their grip.
They were terribly, horribly real.

[1] Hugh Macmillan, *The Life-Work of G. F. Watts*, 175.

Yet through all this wild riot the spirit thrust its way, like a tender blade through the grass and stony soil. Up it came. It showed itself a new and strange force amid the mob of tyrannous impulses that tugged and strained to beat it down. Still it persevered; still it insisted; still it drew itself upward, beyond all that clung and encumbered, seeking still the intangible, the unseen. It threw all competing experiences aside, it pressed on towards a secret goal of its own; it strove, it wrestled, it sought in all strange places, and on lonely mountain-peaks, and in hidden silences. It sought something that haunted and fled, and escaped and returned; and was very near, yet very far; something that for ever evoked and yet for ever evaded. It sought it through blundering incantations and bloody rites, and down by foul ways and by weird devices. It sought and failed, and cried aloud in its failure and cut its flesh with knives; it tore itself, it foamed, it went mad. It lost itself in obscure magic. Yet still it sought that which its heart desired.

At last out of a wilderness of effort, strewn with the wreckage of a thousand false hopes, it arrived; it found; it felt; it touched; it knew. Lo! this, this is God. This is what explains all. This is it. This is the experience that it craved; this is the consummation; this is religion. "O taste and see" (so man cried) "how gracious the Lord is!" Spirit and spirit meet. Soul and God are one. How deep the ·peace! How keen the joy! Blessed! blessed is the man that putteth his trust in Him.[1]

¶ In the Divinity Hall at Aberdeen John Duncan was impressed with Dr. Mearns's prayers to the "Great King," and his cogent reasonings convinced him intellectually of the existence of the living God. The gain was to him invaluable. "It was Dr. Mearns," he frequently said to me, "who satisfied me of the existence of God"; and through life he remembered the debt with lively gratitude. But the conviction had been reached by a logical process, without any more direct mental perception; rather his reason accepting, than his mind seeing it. The next stage of light seems almost to belong to the operation of the Spirit of God, and to involve on his part a special resistance in not following it up to spiritual fruit. It was the breaking in of a light which he looked back upon to the last as an era in his life,

[1] H. Scott Holland, *Vital Values*, 40.

and spoke of as a season of indescribable joy. His own words to me were nearly if not exactly these : "I first saw clearly the existence of God in walking along the bridge at Aberdeen; it was a great discovery to me; I stopped and stood in an ecstasy of joy at seeing the existence of God." I think he also added, "I stood and thanked God for His existence." To another friend he said, "When I was convinced that there was a God, I danced on the Brig o' Dee with delight."[1]

> Expecting Him my door was open wide:
>   Then I looked round
>   If any lack of service might be found,
> And saw Him at my side :—
>   How entered, by what secret stair,
>   I know not, knowing only He was there.[2]

¶ I shall never forget the hour when I first discovered that God was really good. I had of course always known that the Bible said He was good; but I had thought it only meant He was religiously good; and it had never dawned on me that it meant He was actually and practically good, with the same kind of goodness as He has commanded us to have. The expression, "the goodness of God," had seemed to me nothing more than a sort of heavenly statement, which I could not be expected to understand. And then one day I came, in my reading of the Bible, across the words, "O taste and see that the Lord is good," and suddenly they meant something. "The Lord is good," I repeated to myself. What does it mean to be good? What but this, the living up to the best and highest that one knows. To be good is exactly the opposite of being bad. To be bad is to know the right and not to do it, but to be good is to do the best we know. And I saw that, since God is omniscient, He must know what is the best and highest good of all, and that therefore His goodness must necessarily be beyond question. I can never express what this meant to me. I had such a view of the real actual goodness of God that I saw nothing could possibly go wrong under His care, and it seemed to me that no one could ever be anxious again. And over and over since, when appearances have been against Him, and when I have been tempted to question whether He had not been unkind, or neglectful, or indifferent, I have been brought up short by the words, "The Lord is good"; and I have seen that it was simply unthinkable that

---

[1] A. Moody Stuart, *Recollections of John Duncan*, 17.
[2] T. E. Brown, *Old John and Other Poems*, 181.

a God who was good could have done the bad things I had imagined.[1]

¶ The Lord's goodness surrounds us at every moment. I walk through it almost with difficulty, as through thick grass and flowers.[2]

¶ He took his pain and all the trials of his days, and said, "They say there is a better land, but it is hard to believe." Thus he was a true pilgrim, for it is only stupid people who think that the vision of the loveliest city in the loveliest land dims the pilgrim's eyes to the fair beauties of this world. He did not make the most of two worlds; but as he lived to be worthy of that city with foundations, God counted him worthy to find along the dusty road of traffic and toil and pain the well of deep joys which only the true pilgrim can discover. These wells were at many stages of the day's road: he found one deep spring of pure, sparkling water in the morning reading of the Bible and hymn-book; another when his hands were clasped in prayer.[3]

2. The true standard of goodness we find in Jesus Christ. Ordinary human nature measures its purity and nobility by itself, by the customs of society, by the decrees of law courts, by the maxims of current philosophy. The blessed life takes its estimate from the doctrine and spirit of Jesus. This means a higher-toned goodness which we call holiness, and applies only to those who, besides being virtuous in their actions, are possessed with an unaffected enthusiasm of goodness, and besides abstaining from vice, regard even a vicious thought with horror. Here is an ideal which ordinary ethics not only do not reach, but do not even attempt. When Jesus says, "If ye know these things, blessed are ye if ye do them," the test is as spiritual as it is practical. "These things" include what He referred to as a pure heart; an inner life, that is, which is utterly true to both the great commands, as He interpreted and emphasized them. How much more this means than the honesty which keeps men out of prison, and the kindness which makes daily life tolerable, no words are needed to show. The blessed life receives Christ Jesus as Lord; that is the open secret of its ethical and spiritual superiority to every other life.

(1) The hope of the world lies in its vision of goodness, in its

---

[1] Mrs. Pearsall Smith.   [2] R. W. Barbour, *Thoughts*, 107.
[3] *Love and Life: The Story of J. Denholm Brash*, 198.

realization of character. The only radical and final remedy for human misery is in the remoulding of human character. It is a potent truth, alike for good and ill, that character is influenced by environment. But it is even more true and potent that environment is influenced by character. The elevation of individual character is an old highway to social happiness, but it is confessedly difficult, and many eager philanthropists have sought for shorter cuts. Sooner or later, however, the return has to be made to the only road. What it all comes to is that the blessed life is ultimately the only hope of humanity. Christendom may sadly fail to teach or to exemplify this hope. But that is not the failure of Christianity. For the needs of the whole world, Christianity has never yet been tried. The modern Christian, like the ancient Israelite, is continually forsaking the true God to worship idols. Hence the Church's impotence to bless the world. But if only the profession of Christianity did mean on all hands the embodiment of the blessed life, full churches would be but a small fraction of the result. Much more may be affirmed with no less truth—even this, that the curses of civilization (which may well alarm unbelief) would come to an end as surely as noxious bacteria in sunlight; society would be leavened with even more certainty than yeast leavens dough; human sorrows would be brought to their natural and tolerable minimum; and the nations would be in such assurance of permanent peace that the millions expended on murderous battleships could be utilized for the abolition of poverty and the enrichment of humanity.

¶ There is one signal service which the appeal of the Christian character is peculiarly apt to render in the cause of faith. It is often the only power which can confront the steady, surreptitious, miserable pressure with which the sins of Christians fight against the work of Christ. It may be that the contest between these two forces covers by far the greater part of the whole battlefield; and that, while critics and apologists, with their latest weapons (or with the latest improvement of their old ones), are charging and clashing amid clouds of dust—with the world still thinking that here at last is the real crisis—the practical question between belief and disbelief is actually being settled for the vast majority of men by the silent and protracted conflict between the consistent and the inconsistent lives of those who alike profess themselves Christians; the conflict between the contrasted experience of Christ's Presence manifest in goodness, and Christ's Name dishonoured in hypocrisy, or blindness, or indifference.[1]

(2) Goodness is attainable through faith in Christ. For men and for nations alike, life is largely if not wholly made up of habits. The blessed life, whether on the large or the small scale, is certainly a question of blessed habit. But this is not the whole case. Destiny, we know, turns on character, just as character is decided by habits. But habits are neither more nor less than the repetition of acts. Let the first act be worthy, then let repetition confirm it, and habit becomes not only easy but the sure prophecy of destiny. The true beginning of the blessed life is plain, viz., to receive Christ Jesus as Lord. The repetition of that supreme act of the soul, as each day dawns and throughout all the duties it brings, is the pledge of the habit which makes character. That character not only ensures destiny but contributes in the interim to other characters and destinies on every hand. Social reform yields no hope of any golden age without purified and ennobled individual character. For that, there is no such ideal or guarantee on earth as the blessed life which is "rooted and built up" in Jesus Christ.

¶ In June, G. F. Watts wrote asking Shields to lunch any day at Little Holland House. He knew nothing of the work Shields was commencing, but said: "I should like to have an occasional chat about serious art. I wish you would kindly send me a line and tell me the correct colours for the draperies of Faith. I know you are an authority." To which Shields replied: "For answer to your question and compliment, I am no 'authority.' I know none on the subject but the Authority of the Word revealed. Paul declared Faith is God's gift. She is heaven-born. She is the assurance of heavenly things to mortals shut in by sensuous things, therefore the skies' hue is hers, her mantle and her wings: and for her robe, white—unspotted. And this because they who seek righteousness by works fail of that which only Faith gives. The 'fine linen of the Saints' symbolizes their righteousness in the Apocalypse, and it is said that their robes were made 'white in the blood of the Lamb.' If I seek where alone I look to find, this is what is given me, and it is the best I can offer in response to your question. I bow to tradition only where it agrees with the written Word."[2]

---

[1] Francis Paget, Bishop of Oxford, 178.
[2] E. Mills, Life and Letters of Frederic Shields, 309.

3. Having once tasted, we must continue tasting. Those who have once tasted of God, have contracted a passion that grows in being fed. Because they have tasted they must come again and again to stay an appetite which, though always being met, is always on the increase. The tasting of this meat is not to be the tasting of an occasional delicacy, it is to be the eating of daily bread.

¶ There was a man who once lived in a place where, close to his house, he had a spring of water. At a little distance from him, there was another spring. We shall call the spring close to his house, " the nether spring," and the other, a little way off, "the upper spring." So he had the nether and the upper spring. The nether spring looked very pleasant when the sun was shining; the water sparkled in its rays; yet, when looked at more closely, the water was black and dark, and very often grew muddy, and the flowers on the side of it never lasted long; and people who drank a great deal of the water from the nether spring seemed to grow sick. The other spring, a little way off, came out of the rock; it required a great deal of patience to get it; but if the cup was held long enough, it would always get filled, and you were never sick from it.

Now this man who lived in the cottage near the nether spring always went to it; he did not like the trouble of going to the upper spring. He had not sufficient patience. So it went on for many years. At last he came to the nether spring and it was dry, not a drop of water in it. So he was obliged to go to the upper spring; he had to wait some time, but at last he had a cup of nice, pure water. It was so sweet, and he enjoyed it much. He had never before tasted such water. The nether spring flowed on again, but ever after he went to the upper; and when asked why he went so far, he said, " I cannot leave the upper spring; having once tasted it, I cannot go back to the nether spring."[1]

III.

SATISFACTION IN THE GOODNESS OF GOD.

1. Those who discover the goodness of God are content to trust Him. To be religious is to trust God, and to do that is to be free from the fear of evil. He who trusts shall not be afraid

[1] James Vaughan.

of evil tidings, his heart is fixed, trusting in the Lord. To be religious is to keep God's commandments, and the path of rectitude cannot but be the path of happiness. Of course we must not disguise the fact that to be truly religious is to deny one's self and to take up the cross. But even that carries with it its own blessedness. Suffering and sacrifice for the good of another bring to one's soul a peculiar sweetness and satisfaction. How much more must this be the case when it is done for God! "Take my yoke upon you," said Christ, not concealing that His religion is a yoke, " and ye shall find rest unto your souls."

¶ Miss Trotter was penurious in small things, but her generosity could rise to circumstances. Her dower was an annuity from the estate of Mortonhall. She had a contempt for securities, and would trust no bank with her money, but kept all her bills and banknotes in a green silk bag that hung on her toilet-glass. On each side of the table stood a large white bowl, one of which contained her silver, the other her copper money. One day, in the course of conversation, she said to her niece, " Do ye ken, Margaret, that Mrs. Thomas R—— is dead ? I was gaun by the door this morning, and thought I would just look in and speer for her. She was very near her end, but quite sensible, and expressed her gratitude to God for what He had done for her and her fatherless bairns. She said she was leaving a large, young family with very small means, but she had that trust in Him that they would not be forsaken, and that He would provide for them. Now, Margaret, ye'll tell Peggy to bring down the green silk bag that hangs on the corner of my looking-glass, and ye'll tak' twa thousand pounds out o' it, and gi'e it to Walter Ferrier for behoof of thae orphan bairns; it will fit out the laddies, and be something to the lassies. I want to make good the words, that 'God wad provide for them,' for what else was I sent that way this morning, but as a humble instrument in His hands ? "[1]

2. He who has tasted the goodness of God and has learned the secret of happiness will seek to share his experience with others. Fire will cease to have either heat or light as it burns, before the blessed life will be hidden away in heart-secrecies, buried like the one talent in useless seclusion. Every man or woman who rises above carnality and custom and selfishness into the pure brightness and calm strength of communion with Christ

[1] J. A. Doyle, *Susan Ferrier*, 18.

must go on to exemplify His word, "Ye are the salt of the earth; ye are the light of the world." Egoism is as intolerable without altruism as altruism is impossible without egoism. In the blessed life there is no conflict between these two. Rather do they supplement and stimulate each other. The human self, by very reason of its enrichment beyond utterance through receiving Christ Jesus as Lord, will never cease to feel, and act upon the feeling—

> O that the world might taste and see
> The riches of His grace!
> The arms of love that compass me
> Would all mankind embrace.

¶ When persons only wish for the happiness of another, and when they never pass a day without doing a kindness, how can they be otherwise than happy? And when difficulties are very great they have only to ascend to the level of doing the will of God; they will be happy still. If they are determined to act rightly, to live as the best men and women have lived, there is no more difficulty of unbelief. They see, not having seen, they go out trusting in God, but not knowing whither they go. There is no delight in life equal to that of setting the world right, of reconciling things and persons to one another, by understanding them, not by embittering them. True sympathy with every one is the path of perfect peace.[1]

¶ A poor man came home one day and brought five peaches: nice beautiful peaches. He had four sons; he gave one to each and one to his wife. He did not say anything, but just gave them. At night he came home again, and then he said, "How were the peaches—all nice?" I will tell you what each of the four boys said.

The eldest boy said, "Oh yes, father, delicious. I ate my peach, and then I took the stone very carefully, and went and planted it in the garden, that we may have another peach-tree some day." "Well," said the father, "very prudent; look out for the future."

Then the little boy said, "Oh, father, 'twas exceedingly nice. I ate all mine, and mother gave me half hers, and I threw away the stone." "Well," said the father, "I am glad you liked it, but perhaps if you had been a little older, you would have acted differently."

The second boy said, "Yes, father, I will tell you what I did with mine; I picked up the stone my little brother threw away,

[1] B. Jowett, in *Life and Letters*, ii. 402.

broke it, and ate the kernel; I enjoyed that exceedingly; but I did not eat my peach, I sold it. I could buy a dozen peaches with what I got for it." The father said, "That may be right, but I think it was a little covetous."

Then he said to the third boy, "Well, Edward, what did you do with your peach?" Edward came forward reluctantly; but in answer to his father, he replied, "I took it to poor little George, who is sick down the lane. He would not take it, so I left the peach on his bed and ran away."

Which of the four peaches was sweetest? "Taste and see" the way to enjoy anything.[1]

[1] James Vaughan, *Sermons to Children*, i. 67.

GOD OF NATURE AND GOD OF GRACE.

LITERATURE.

Davies (J. A.), *Seven Words of Love*, 165.
Dearden (H. W.), *Parochial Sermons*, 68.
Gray (W. A.), *The Shadow of the Hand*, 198.
Hanks (W. P.), *The Eternal Witness*, 142.
Maclaren (A.), *A Year's Ministry*, ii. 211.
Christian World Pulpit, xxxiv. 188 (W. G. Horder) ; xl. 169 (L. Abbott) ;
    lxxv. 60 (E. E. Newell).
Church Times, July 28, 1911 (J. W. Horsley).
Preacher's Magazine, vii. 439 (R. Brewin).
Twentieth Century Pastor, xxviii. (1911) 201 (J. E. Flower).

GOD OF NATURE AND GOD OF GRACE.

Thy lovingkindness, O Lord, is in the heavens;
Thy faithfulness reacheth unto the skies.
Thy righteousness is like the mountains of God;
Thy judgements are a great deep.—Ps. xxxvi. 5, 6.

THE landscape from which the Psalmist has borrowed his lessons
in all probability lay beside him while he mused. We imagine
him at the time a fugitive from Saul. He is hid in some desert-
retreat, with the everlasting hills round about him, and the gleams
and the shadows of a summer noon overhead. He had been cast
out from the comforts of an earthly home, but God was his
dwelling-place and his refuge. Hunt him as men might, they
could not drive him where Jehovah's righteousness did not environ
him, and the wings of His lovingkindness stretch to shadow and
protect. Out there, amidst the silence and restfulness of nature,
God's breath was about him to cool and to strengthen, and His
voice spoke comfort and peace. So the Psalmist speaks little of
himself. He mentions his trials and perils only for the sake of
dismissing them. From the wickedness and the craft of men he
is fain to turn to the goodness and the faithfulness of God, of
which all things around were eloquent.

¶ I was struck with the fact that Scripture is adapted to every
land, on Sunday week, as I sat in the little English Church at
Zermatt, right under the shadow of the gigantic Matterhorn, and
read such passages as these on its walls: "Ye frost and cold,
bless ye the Lord, praise Him and magnify Him for ever." "Ye
mountains and hills, bless ye the Lord, praise Him and magnify
Him for ever." And as day after day I moved about in a land
where in every direction the eye rested on gigantic peaks,
whose crests were often lost in the clouds, these words were ever
rising in my mind: "Thy righteousness is like the mountains of
God."[1]

[1] W. Garrett Horder.

I.

THE LOVINGKINDNESS OF GOD.

"Thy lovingkindness, O Lord, is in the heavens."

The "mercy" or "lovingkindness" of which the Psalmist speaks is very nearly equivalent to the New Testament "grace." Both mean substantially this—active love communicating itself to creatures who are inferior, and who might have expected something else to befall them. Mercy is a modification of love, inasmuch as it is love to an inferior. The hand is laid gently upon the man, because if it were laid with all its weight it would crush him. It is the stooping goodness of a king to a beggar. And mercy is likewise love in its exercise to persons that might expect something else, being guilty. As a general coming to a body of mutineers with pardon and favour upon his lips, instead of with condemnation and death, so God comes to us forgiving and blessing. All His goodness is forbearance, and His love is mercy, because of the weakness, the lowliness, and the ill desert of us on whom the love falls.

1. As the heavens are high above the earth, so God's lovingkindness evermore transcends man. Far above the towers that men's hands have reared, the waves that the tempests uplift, the peaks that the earth has heaved, the heaven stretches its distant curtain, embracing but surmounting them all. And so with the mercy of our God. It is the one all-enfolding, all-transcending fact in God's moral universe, lifting itself far above the region of human experience and analogy. It is high; we cannot attain to it. It is far above man's mercies, for our "goodness extendeth not to God's," and while "greater love hath no man than this, that a man lay down his life for his friends," God "commendeth his love toward us, in that, while we were yet sinners, Christ died for us." It is far above man's deserts, for we are "not worthy of the least of all the mercies, and of all the truth" which He showeth to His servants. It is far above man's sins, for high as he has heaved the mountains of his provocations, God's mercy can transcend the loftiest. It is far above man's prayers and conceptions, for

as the heavens are higher than the earth, so are His ways higher
than our ways, and His thoughts than our thoughts, and He " is
able to do exceeding abundantly above all we ask or think."

> Great God ! I stood beneath the skies one night,
> When all Thy stars were out, serene and clear,
> And tried to think of Thee, and feel Thee near,
> When, suddenly, a sense of all Thy might,
> Thy times to come, Thy wonders out of sight,
> Struck chill on me—my spirit reeled for fear ;
> Scarce certain of the ground I stand on here,
> I shrank abased beneath Thy awful height ;
> When soft as dew, a word of Holy Writ
> Fell on my troubled mind ; "Thy mercy, Lord,
> Is greater than the heavens"—then all above,
> Around, beneath, took comfort from the word ;
> For 'twas as if the heavens were newly lit
> With their best, brightest star—the Star of Love.

2. Like the face of the summer sky, the lovingkindness of
God is unalterable. The earth which the sky overshadows has
seen many mutations. " Surely the mountain falling cometh to
nought, and the rock is removed out of its place. The waters
wear the stones; thou washest away the things that grow out of
the dust of the earth." Rivers have altered their courses. The
sea has shifted its ancient bounds. Forests have sunk in swamps.
Empires have risen and fallen. The grass rustles and the lizards
bask by the broken columns of cities that pulsed with the
interests and sounded with the traffic of busy men. Generation
after generation has come and gone, and the place that knew
them once knows them no more for ever. Beneath there is
nothing but flux, restlessness, change. But the sky has looked
down on it all, serene and unvarying, amidst all the overturning
and mutations of the countless years. Time writes no wrinkles
on its steadfast blue. Orion hangs his glittering sword, and the
Pleiades weave their mystic braids, just as they did for Isaac
when he went forth to the field to meditate at the eventide; for
Abraham when God took him out from his tent, and bade him
look up to heaven with the promise of a seed that should be as
the stars of heaven for multitude ; for Adam when the first day
faded over him, and the glories of the night revealed themselves

amidst the balm and the silences of an unstained Eden. So with the mercy of God. All down the ages His covenant has stood, ordered in all things and sure amidst all changes, free from variableness or any shadow of turning. As the heavens that were formed of old "continue unto this day according to God's ordinance," so does the word that is settled there.

¶ Miss R. having told Dr. Duncan that a young man had said at a meeting that "there was not mercy in God from everlasting —there could not be mercy till there was misery," he said, "God is unchangeable; mercy is an attribute of God. The man is confounding mercy with the exercise of mercy. There could not be the exercise of mercy till there was misery; but God was always a merciful God. You might as well say that there could not be justice in God till there were creatures towards whom to exercise punitive justice."[1]

3. Like the canopy of heaven, the lovingkindness of God is all-embracing. "The noblest scenes of earth," it has been said, "can be seen and known but by few; it is not intended that man should live always in the midst of them; he injures them by his presence, he ceases to feel them if he be always with them. But the sky is for all. Bright as it is, it is not 'too bright or good for human nature's daily food.' It is fitted in all its functions for the perpetual comfort and exaltation of the heart." No rough hand can sully the clear blue vault above, as it unfolds its splendour and dispenses its blessings for a worldful at once, and that without money or price. Be your dwelling-place on the bleakest and dreariest swamp, without a tree or a hill to diversify its surface, you have still overhead a picture of loveliness and of mystery as often as you choose to look up. Thread the narrowest thoroughfare of a crowded town, and far above the filth and squalor, between the eaves of the tall and tottering tenements that enclose you, there are strips of clear blue sky, reminding you that, whatever be the restlessness, the sorrow, and the vice below, there is nothing above but beauty, purity, and peace. So again with the mercy of our God; it is exceeding broad. It is the attribute of all attributes that is ever engirdling and over- shadowing us, making its existence known through a thousand channels, in a thousand ways. Mercy is the very sphere in which

[1] David Brown, *Memoir of John Duncan*, 422.

we live and move; it is swift as the light of heaven, near to us as its circling breaths. And it is just as free. Rich and poor, high and low, all have alike a share in it. And as it is the gift of God to all, so is it the gift of God to all in all circumstances, throughout every change of their changing lives.

¶ The Doctor must keep his temper: this is often worse to manage than even his time, there is so much unreason, and ingratitude, and peevishness, and impertinence, and impatience, that it is very hard to keep one's tongue and eye from being angry; and sometimes the Doctor does not only well, but the best when he is downrightly angry, and astonishes some fool, or some insolent, or some untruth doing or saying patient; but the Doctor should be patient with his patients, he should bear with them, knowing how much they are at the moment suffering. Let us remember Him who is full of compassion, whose compassion never fails; whose tender mercies are new to us every morning, as His faithfulness is every night; who healed all manner of diseases, and was kind to the unthankful and the evil; what would become of us, if He were as impatient with us as we often are with each other? If you want to be impressed with the Almighty's infinite loving-kindness and tender mercy, His forbearance, His long-suffering patience, His slowness to anger, His Divine ingeniousness in trying to find it possible to spare and save, think of the Israelites in the desert, and read the chapter where Abraham intercedes with God for Sodom, and these wonderful "peradventures." [1]

¶ My fear is not of expanding, but of contradicting, the Gospel which we are sent to preach; not of seeing too strong a testimony in the Bible to the will of Him in whom is light and no darkness at all, but of limiting its testimonies to meet my narrow conceptions; not of exaggerating the duty of the Church to be a witness against all hard and cruel conceptions of our Father in Heaven, which lead to a confusion between Him and the Spirit of Evil, but of not perceiving how manifold are the ways in which that duty should be fulfilled. I am sure that if the Gospel is not regarded as a message to all mankind of the redemption which God has effected in His Son; if the Bible is thought to be speaking only of a world to come, and not of a Kingdom of Righteousness and Peace and Truth with which we may be in conformity or in enmity now; if the Church is not felt to be the hallower of all professions and occupations, the bond of all classes, the instrument of reforming abuses, the admonisher of the rich,

[1] Dr. John Brown, *Horæ Subsecivæ*, ii. 35 (appendix).

the friend of the poor, the asserter of the glory of that humanity which Christ bears—we are to blame, and God will call us to account as unfaithful stewards of His treasures.[1]

II.

THE FAITHFULNESS OF GOD.

" Thy faithfulness reacheth unto the skies."

God's faithfulness is in its narrowest sense His adherence to His promises. It implies, in that sense, a verbal revelation, and definite words from Him, pledging Him to a certain line of action. He hath said, and shall He not do it? He will not alter the thing that is gone out of His lips. It is only a God who has actually spoken to men that can be a "faithful God." He will not palter with a double sense, keeping His word of promise to the ear, and breaking it to the hope. And not only His articulate promises, but also His own past actions, bind Him. He is always true to these; and not only continues to do as He has done, but discharges every obligation which His past imposes on Him. The ostrich was said to leave its eggs to be hatched in the sand. Men bring men into positions of dependence, and then lightly shake responsibility from careless shoulders. But God accepts the cares laid upon Him by His own acts, and discharges them to the last jot. He is a "faithful Creator." Creation brings obligations with it—obligations on the creature, obligations on the Creator. If God makes a being, God is bound to take care of the being that He has made. If He makes a being in a given fashion, He is bound to provide for the necessities that He has created. According to the old proverb, if He makes mouths it is His business to feed them. And He recognizes the obligation. His past binds Him to certain conduct in His future. We can lay hold on the former manifestation, and we can plead it with Him. "Thou hast been, and therefore Thou must be." "Thou hast taught me to trust in Thee; vindicate and warrant my trust by Thy unchangeableness." So His word, His acts, and His own nature, bind God to bless and help. His faithfulness is the

[1] *Life of Frederick Denison Maurice*, ii. 227.

expression of His unchangeableness. "Because he could swear by no greater, he sware by himself."

¶ I believe that love and righteousness and justice in God mean exactly the same thing, namely, a desire to bring His whole moral creation into a participation of His own character and His own blessedness. He has made us capable of this, and He will not cease from using the best means for accomplishing it in us all. When I think of God making a creature of such capacities, it seems to me almost blasphemous to suppose that He will throw it from Him into everlasting darkness, because it has resisted His gracious purposes towards it for the natural period of human life. No, He who waited so long for the formation of a piece of old red sandstone will surely wait with much long-suffering for the perfecting of a human spirit.[1]

1. The faithfulness of God reaches to *the clouds of sin and remorse.*—Think of David after his terrible fall. The clouds gathered round him then as they never gathered before. As he had sowed, so he was reaping; and no sufferings are so terrible or so testing as the sufferings that are the obvious outcome and natural retribution of a man's own follies and crimes. What of the darkness that envelops him then—when the sword that he had lifted against Uriah was turned against himself, and he experienced in the sins of his family the reproduction of his own, to the overshadowing and embitterment of his later years? Youth gone from him, his spirit crushed—does the man lose his hope and let go his hold on the promise of a truth-keeping God? Behind clouds such as these, does he fail to grasp and to cling to the faithfulness he spoke of in the years long gone by? Listen: "Although my house be not so with God; yet he hath made with me an everlasting covenant, ordered in all things, and sure: for this is all my salvation, and all my desire, though he make it not to grow." Yes, whom God loves He loves throughout, and He loves to the end.

¶ A friend once showed an artist a costly handkerchief on which a blot of ink had been made. "Nothing can be done with it now, it is absolutely worthless." The artist made no reply, but carried it away with him. After a time he sent it back, to the great surprise of his friend, who could scarcely recognize it. In a most skilful and artistic way he had made a fine design in India ink, using the

---

[1] *Letters of Thomas Erskine of Linlathen,* ii. 242.

blot as a basis, making the handkerchief more valuable than ever. A blotted life is not necessarily a useless life. Jesus can make a life beautiful though it has been marred by sin.[1]

2. The faithfulness of God reaches to *the clouds of trouble.*— God has hid His Church ere this in the mountain mists and in the deep places of the earth, till they were dead or vanished that sought its life.

¶ You remember the story of the godly family whose home lay across the track a returning army was expected to follow, when flushed with victory and athirst for rapine and blood. "Be a wall of fire unto us, O God," was the prayer which the father put up as he knelt at the household altar ere retiring for the night, and having thus committed himself and his circle to the hands of a preserving God, he and they together laid them down in peace, and took their quiet rest, knowing who it was that made them dwell in safety. The night-watches hastened on, morning came, and the family awoke. All was unwontedly dark and still when they rose. There was no light from chink or from window, nor sound of stirring life around. Noiselessly, and all unseen, the hand whose protection they craved stole forth from the wintry heavens, not, indeed, in the shape of a wall of fire, but in something as sufficient and safe—in wreath upon wreath of driven snow. Meanwhile the foe had passed by, and had gone on his way, and those whom he threatened breathed freely, for they knew that their tabernacle was at peace.[2]

III.

The Righteousness of God.

"Thy righteousness is like the mountains of God."

1. The idea in the mind of the Psalmist was that the righteousness of Jehovah is fixed and unchangeable. Men's ideas of righteousness may change. Those of one age may differ from those of another; one land may have a different standard from that of another. But in spite of this there is an everlasting, an unchanging righteousness in God. Nothing in this world so impresses the mind with the idea of unchangeableness as the great mountains.

---

[1] *Twentieth Century Pastor*, xxviii. (1911) 252.
[2] W. A. Gray, *The Shadow of the Hand*, 15.

The dwellings of men in the valleys are ever undergoing change; at every visit something new strikes one—the fields which men cultivate produce their different crops, the forests on the mountain sides grow denser and taller, the rivers alter their course, even the sea is restless, now receding from and now encroaching on the land; but the great mountains seem to be lifted to a realm beyond change. The snow upon them, it is true, is ever melting; the glaciers between them are ever moving, but the granite rock beneath seems ever the same. The generations of men who dwell beneath them live their little life and pass away; year after year new and wondering eyes look up to these mountains, but there they stand, the most impressive symbol of permanence in a world of change.

(1) *The mountains are stable and permanent.*—The mountains were thought to be the most ancient parts of the earth, the framework on which the Great Architect of the Universe had builded; next the earth generally; and then the world, or, in the Hebrew sense, the fruitful, habitable part of the earth. So in the Athanasian Creed, "The Father eternal, the Son eternal, and the Holy Ghost eternal." Eternal and changelessly the same throughout eternity, and therefore we do not read, "Thou wast God from everlasting," or, "Thou wilt be God world without end"; but, "Thou art God, the same past, present, and to come." As we look up to-day, so have the successive generations of men lifted up their eyes to the mountains that speak to each of an unimaginable and almost limitless past.

¶ Stand at the mountain's foot and look up at its high head, and remember how it has braved many a storm which hissed itself out of breath over it, and it still remains to-day scarred like a veteran, it is true, but yet proud and firm on the victorious field.

> His proud head the airy mountain hides
> Among the clouds; his shoulders and his sides
> A shady mantle clothes; his curling brows
> Frown on the gentle stream, which calmly flows;
> While winds and storms his lofty forehead beat,—
> The common fate of all that's high and great.

It was not yesterday that it was reared; it will not fall to-morrow; but it has seen generation after generation come and go, with all their faith and fear, their love and lust, their weal and woe; and to-day it looks down upon another race which trusts and trembles, sins and sorrows, loves and laughs, as though they were the first that mountain ever looked upon. Oh! if it could only speak, it would tell us how the actors constantly change on the stage of Time; that the play, now tragic, now comic, oftenest common-place, is always the same, and that it has seen it acted over and over again; and yet it looks on with no tired look. Whenever you see the mountain, you see that which is very old, and that which is very young. The signs of its age are also the symbols of its youth. It transmutes the furrows of its old age into the dimples of childhood's laughter. Perpetual youth is the preroga-tive of the old mountain. *It* lasts, lives on—

Eternal pyramids, built not with hands,
  From linked foundations that deep-hidden lie,
Ye rise apart, and each a wonder stands!
  Your marble peaks, which pierce the clouds so high,
Seem holding up the curtain of the sky;
  And there, sublime and solemn, have ye stood,
While crumbling Time, o'er-awed, passed reverent by,
  Since Nature's resurrection from the flood,
Since earth, new born, again received God's plaudit, "Good!"

How many races have ye seen descend
  Into Time's grave, the lowly with the great;
How many kingdoms seen asunder rend,
  How many empires fall, how many centuries end?[1]

(2) *The righteousness of God is more permanent than the mountains.*—Though the mountains *seem* as if they did not change, yet they *do* change. The atmospheric influences which play upon them *do* alter them, though the alteration may be imperceptible to men who can observe them only for a few brief years. But absolutely without change is the righteousness of God. How is God's righteousness shown? Most of all in His kindness. And so Isaiah says, "For the mountains shall depart, and the hills be removed; but my righteousness shall not depart from thee, neither shall the covenant of my peace be removed, saith the Lord that hath mercy on thee." There *is* one thing in this universe of change which is absolutely without change, and that is the eternal righteousness: "I the Lord change not; therefore ye, O sons of Jacob, are not consumed." Here is a resting-place

---

[1] J. A. Davies, *Seven Words of Love*, 168.

for our souls. In this world nothing abides in one stage. We move from childhood to youth, from youth to manhood, from manhood to old age, from old age to the unseen world, but God changes not. We pass into new relationships, from being children to being parents, from having to serve to having to govern, from the active government of manhood to the quiescent stage of old age; friends drop from our side, old bonds are broken, new bonds are formed; but in the midst of this sea of change, where the waters are ever in movement, now receding, now advancing, there *is* a rock which abides—the righteousness of God. There is one point on which the eye can rest. There is one spot on which the foot can be planted. There is one place of anchorage for the soul—the rightousness of God.

¶ Geologists tell us that these giants of Bernese mountains are but a third now of their original height, and we know how, to quote Ruskin, "The hills, which, as compared with human beings, seem everlasting, are in truth as perishing as they, their veins of flowing fountain weary the mountain heart, as the common pulse does ours; the natural force of the iron crag is abated in its appointed time, like the strength of the sinews in a human old age; and it is but the lapse of the larger years of decay which, in the sight of the Creator, distinguishes the mountain range from the moth and the worm." Yet God and His attributes, and even His relations to man, remain unchanged, and from this treasury Isaiah picks out the two jewels of kindness and peace for our thankful contemplation.[1]

¶ Arthur Clough, whose early death prevented him from becoming the foremost poet of the age, and who passed through many spiritual vicissitudes, felt and expressed this in his noble lines:

> It fortifies my soul to know
> That, though I perish, Truth is so:
> That, howsoe'er I stray and range,
> Whate'er I do, Thou dost not change.
> I steadier step when I recall
> That, if I slip, Thou dost not fall.[2]

2. The righteousness of God is like the great mountains in its power to inspire awe, wonder, and reverence. The great

[1] J. W. Horsley, in *The Church Times*, July 28, 1911.
[2] W. Garrett Horder.

height of mountains, the vastness of their bulk, and their far-reaching extent overawe the spectator, and dwarf him into insignificance in their presence. Their dark and frowning crags, their awful chasms, and their mysterious yet gigantic forms shut his lips in silent awe, and chasten his thoughtless spirit into seriousness and reflection. If they should fall upon him he is crushed like an insect by the foot. A thunder-storm among the mountains is an awful thing. Once experienced, it will never be forgotten. The Law of Moses was fitly given amid thunderings and lightnings and a great earthquake among the mountains of Sinai. Like the great mountains the righteousness of God is an awful thing. When we are first convinced of sin and stand in the presence of God we tremble and cry out for fear.

¶ "So Christian turned out of his way to go to Mr. Legality's House for help: but behold, when he was got now hard by the Hill, it seemed so high, and also that side of it that was next the wayside, did hang so much over, that Christian was afraid to venture further, lest the Hill should fall on his Head; wherefore there he stood still; and wotted not what to do. Also his burden now seemed heavier to him than while he was in his way. There came also flashes of fire out of the Hill that made Christian afraid that he should be burned: here therefore he sweat, and did quake for fear." [1]

(1) The real greatness of the mountains appears only as we approach them. We look up at them from the valleys and fancy that an hour's climb will bring us to their summit. It seems as if we could shoot an arrow to the top; but we begin to climb, and as we climb they seem to lift their heads higher and higher. And so it is with the righteousness of God. Until we begin to strive after it, it seems within easy reach; it is only when we begin the long ascent that its height is really felt, and the higher we go the loftier does it appear. The man who has climbed highest in the way of righteousness knows best how great is the distance he has yet to climb. Indeed, to the man who has not begun to strive after righteousness, it seems most easy of attainment. It seems to him far easier to be righteous than to be learned, or muscular, or inventive. He stands more amazed at some great work of art, or literature, or mechanical contrivance than at the sight of righteousness in man. And

[1] Bunyan, *Pilgrim's Progress* (Cambridge edition), 152.

why ? The one can be apprehended by the eye and the other can be apprehended only by the heart, and his heart has not been trained by the pursuit of righteousness to appreciate its glory. Righteousness is only spiritually discerned. It cannot be seen by the eye, or heard by the ear, or felt by the hand. It needs a deeper faculty. The delicate, subtle fancy of poetry, or the grace of art, or the exquisite suggestiveness of the noblest music is not discerned by the uncultured. Preparation is needed before any of these can be discerned. And the beauty of holiness, which is only another name for righteousness, is not revealed save to those who, by striving after it, have realized the difficulty and glory of its attainment. Only those who have begun to walk in the way of righteousness know how lofty, how far off, how difficult to reach, is the position to which the great Master, Christ, calls us when He says, " Be ye therefore perfect, even as your Father which is in heaven is perfect."

¶ About ten days ago we started from the valley of Zermatt, which is itself some thousands of feet above the level of the sea, and for nearly five hours were climbing up to the well-known Gorner Gratz, and when we reached it, the Matterhorn, instead of seeming nearer, positively seemed farther off, the distance to the summit appeared greater. When we were in the valley the lower mountains around its base seemed to lessen the distance, and only when these were scaled could we realize its awful height.[1]

(2) The summits of the mountains are clearly revealed only as the sun lifts the clouds. And so it is with the righteousness of God. Clouds and darkness are round about Him, until Christ, the Sun of Righteousness, arises, and brings Him into view. Before, all was mystery and gloom to men. Their eyes could not pierce the cloud. They feared as they entered therein. But on the mystery Christ threw His revealing light, so that the clouds were lifted and all stood out in startling clearness. And then men began to realize that the righteousness which seemed so repellent was but the vesture of love ; nay, that there could not be any real righteousness unless, at its very heart, there was the fire of love ; just as there could not be any verdure or beauty on the earth but for the central core of fire within.

[1] W. Garrett Horder.

I stand upon the mount of God,
  With sunlight in my soul;
I hear the storms in vales beneath,
  I hear the thunders roll.

But I am calm with Thee, my God,
  Beneath these glorious skies;
And to the height on which I stand
  Nor storms nor clouds can rise.

Oh, this is life! Oh, this is joy!
  My God, to find Thee so!
Thy face to see, Thy voice to hear,
  And all Thy love to know.

3. Mountain chains have been a refuge for the oppressed in
all ages. Liberty, bruised and broken on the level plain, has fled
into the mountain ranges and there has found a refuge. Out of
the level plains of Egypt Israel escapes and finds its life in the
rocky ranges of Mount Horeb. In the mountains of Palestine the
Israelites escape from Moabitish hosts on the east of them and the
Philistine hosts on the south of them. In the mountain caves of
En-gedi David hides from the persecuting hosts of Saul. In the
mountains Greece finds its escape from the overwhelming Persian
hosts. In the mountains of Switzerland liberty is cradled, while
all over Europe despotism is triumphant. In the mountains of
Northern Italy the Waldenses keep alive the Protestant religion
before Protestantism has been born.

We are not accustomed to think that God is a refuge because
of His righteousness. We rather, perhaps, think His righteousness closes His heart to us in our sinfulness. Perhaps we will say
that a good man, a benevolent man, a merciful man, will serve as
a refuge to us in our hour of need, but not a man strong in his
righteousness. And yet, if we will consider a little, it is not the
righteousness, it is the unrighteousness, of men that makes them
unmerciful and therefore repellent. One man repels another, not
because the first man is too righteous to have mercy, but because
he is not righteous enough. The men that are fighting scepti-
cism are half sceptics. The man who only half believes is at
enmity with the man who does not believe at all, because he is in

perpetual fear lest his half-belief shall be taken away from him; but he who is anchored, by a chain that cannot be broken, to the eternal verities has no fear, and therefore has a heart open to all argument and all reasons, and considers them with patience and gentleness. So it is a dormant sense of unrighteousness in us that makes us afraid of the unrighteous.

¶ In that marvellous story, Hawthorne's *Marble Faun*, when Miriam has fallen into a great sin and comes to Hilda, and Hilda will not receive her because of that sin, bidding her not come nearer, and Miriam cries, "Because I have sinned I need your friendship the more," Hilda replies, "If I were one of God's angels, incapable of stain, I would keep ever at your side and try to lead you upward. But I am a poor, lonely girl, and God has given me my purity, and told me to take it back to Him unstained, and I dare not associate with the criminal lest I carry back to Him a stained and spotted garment." It is the consciousness of a dormant impurity in the pure Hilda that makes her dread to receive to her heart the impure as her companion. It is not Hilda's perfection of righteousness, it is her imperfection, that makes her fail as a refuge to poor, sinful, despairing Miriam. Now, God's righteousness is of the kind that never can be harmed.[1]

IV.

THE JUDGMENTS OF GOD.

"Thy judgements are a great deep."

By "judgments" are not meant merely the acts of God's punitive righteousness, the retributions that destroy evil-doers, but all God's decisions and acts in regard to man. Or, to put it into other and briefer words, God's judgments are the whole of the "ways," the methods of the Divine government. So St. Paul, alluding to this very passage, when he says, "How unsearchable are his judgments," adds, as a parallel clause, meaning the same thing, "and thy ways past finding out." That includes all that men call, in a narrower sense, judgments; but it includes, too, all acts of kindness and loving gifts. God's judgments are the expressions of His thoughts, and these thoughts are thoughts of good and not of evil.

[1] Lyman Abbott.

Perhaps it was the great and wide sea that the Psalmist thought of while he spoke—the secret of whose depths only Omniscience could see, the noise of whose billows only Omnipotence could still. Or perhaps it was some land-locked lake, on whose shining surface he looked down, as it crisped with the breezes or slept in the calms of a long summer day. But in either case, the picture yields a ready lesson: "Thy judgments," he says, "are a great deep." It is the one touch that is needed to enhance the description; for what were mercy, faithfulness, and righteousness, without infinite wisdom to plan and direct the whole? But this wisdom is evermore a great deep, unsearchable and unfathomable, whether it lies in the heart of God as His purpose, or in the word of God as His statutes, or in the ways of God as His Providence. "Canst thou by searching find out God? Canst thou find out the Almighty unto perfection? It is high as heaven; what canst thou do? deeper than hell; what canst thou know? The measure thereof is longer than the earth, and broader than the sea." "O the depth of the riches both of the wisdom and knowledge of God! How unsearchable are his judgments, and his ways past finding out!"

1. The deep means mystery. We cannot escape the mystery in life, it is true, just as we cannot explore all ocean's secrets. But it is not wisdom to think we have touched bottom because the plummet ceases to descend. The plumb line slackens in our hands. But that may mean only that life is too deep for our pessimists' soundings, which have never gone deeper than the shifting surface tides. What is the obscurity of the sea? Not that which comes from mud, or anything added, but that which comes from depth. As far as a man can see down into its blue-green depths they are clear and translucent; but when the light fails and the eye fails, there comes what we call obscurity. The sea is clear, but our sight is limited.

¶ Here towers Vesuvius; there at its feet lie the waters of the bay. So the Righteousness springs up like some great cliff, rising sheer from the water's edge, while its feet are laved by the sea of the Divine judgments, unfathomable and shoreless. The mountains and the sea are the two grandest things in nature, and in their combination sublime; the one the home of calm and silence, the other perpetual motion. But the mountain's roots are deeper than the depths of the sea, and though the judgments are a mighty deep, the righteousness is deeper, and is the bed of the ocean.[1]

2. The righteousness of God is seen in His judgments. In God's nature the mountain height answers back to the sea deep; the great deep of judgment reflects the mountain summits of righteousness in its clear calm. We need to remember this great truth of the unity of God's purpose in the world; for the age which disputes most passionately the justice of God's judgments is the age which most completely ignores or opposes His commands. A man on the cliff can look much deeper into the ocean than a man on the level beach. The farther we climb the farther we shall see down into the " sea of glass mingled with fire " that lies placid before God's throne. Let us remember that it is a hazardous thing to judge of a picture before it is finished, of a building before the scaffolding is pulled down; and it is a hazardous thing for us to say about any deed or any revealed truth that it is inconsistent with the Divine character. Let us wait a bit! " Thy judgments are a great deep." The deep will be drained off one day, and we shall see the bottom of it. Let us judge nothing before the time.

¶ If we believe in the Father and His good purpose towards us, what we require of affliction and of suffering, what we have a right to require, is this, that it should be felt to be helping us and purifying us. God gives us a natural sense of justice, implanting it deep in our hearts; and it is through this sense of justice that all the best victories of humanity have been won. . . . The Father cannot have it in His heart that we should merely be crushed and silenced by our punishment; that we should submit, simply because there is no way out, as a little bird submits to be torn by a hawk. If our submission is like that, it is worth nothing; it only plunges our spirit in deeper darkness.[2]

¶ One night when I was recently crossing the Atlantic, an officer of our boat told me that we had just passed over the spot where the *Titanic* went down. And I thought of all that life and wreckage beyond the power of man to recover and redeem. And I thought of the great bed of the deep sea, with all its held

---

[1] A. Maclaren.
[2] A. C. Benson, *Thy Rod and Thy Staff*, 106.

treasure, too far down for man to reach and restore. "Too far down!" And then I thought of all the human wreckage engulfed and sunk in oceanic depths of nameless sin. Too far gone! For what? Too far down! For what? Not too far down for the love of God! Listen to this: "He descended into hell," and He will descend again if you are there. "If I make my bed in hell, thou art there." "Where sin abounded, grace did much more abound." "He *bore* our sin"; then He got beneath it; down to it and beneath it; and there is no human wreckage lying in the ooze of the deepest sea of iniquity that His deep love cannot reach and redeem. What a Gospel! However far down, God's love can get beneath it![1]

[1] J. H. Jowett, *Things That Matter Most* (1913), 17.

LIFE AND LIGHT.

LITERATURE.

Benson (E. W.), *Boy-Life*, 32.

Brooks (P.), *Sermons Preached in English Churches*, 89.

Cooke (G. A.), *The Progress of Revelation*, 3.

Creighton (M.), *The Heritage of the Spirit*, 185.

Matheson (G.), *Leaves for Quiet Hours*, 192.

Morrison (G. H.), *The Unlighted Lustre*, 30.

Stone (D.), *The Discipline of Faith*, 31.

Thackeray (F. St. John), *Sermons Preached in Eton College Chapel*, 105.

Vaughan (J.), *Sermons* (Brighton Pulpit), viii. (1871), No. 742; xxii. (1883), No. 1232; xxiii. (1883), No. 1259.

Cambridge Review, ix. Supplement No. 232 (R. Machray).

Christian Commonwealth, xxxii. (1912) 437 (R. J. Campbell).

Christian World Pulpit, xvi. 106 (J. B. Heard); xx. 392 (J. B. Tinling).

Church of England Pulpit, lxiii. 76 (M. P. Maturin).

Churchman's Pulpit: The Epiphany, iii. 286 (G. F. Terry).

Preacher's Magazine, v. (1894) 97 (C. New).

Sunday Magazine, 1881, p. 702 (J. Robertson).

LIFE AND LIGHT.

For with thee is the fountain of life:
In thy light shall we see light.—Ps. xxxvi. 9.

ST. AUGUSTINE asks, "What is the fountain of life, unless Christ?" and he adds, "He who is the Fountain is the Light." Our Lord said, "Whensoever I am in the world, I am the light of the world"; and again, "I am the light of the world; he that followeth me shall have the light of life." This is further explained by St. John, with reference to our Lord as the Word: "That which hath been made in him is life, and the life was the light of men." Thus we have continually associated together as in the text the two ideas of life and light, both finding their fullest meaning in our Lord Jesus Christ. As gifts or possessions from Him and through Him, we cannot separate them. The presence of the one bespeaks the presence of the other, and each the recreating presence of the Spirit of God. Light necessarily comes to us if there is life, and life necessarily issues when light enters.

¶ On some of the Alpine passes there are rude shelters for distressed travellers, but they are only shelters; they hold no food, no water, no light, no warmth; the man they have saved may perish within their walls. The Redeemer is sometimes thought of as a mere refuge to flee to from condemnation. How imperfect that is; for though we are saved from condemnation we have as many wants as heart-beats; but when the eyes of the refugee are opened he sees a home there, and everything he needs for all time, for all events, for all perfection. We flee to Him for safety, but He puts this song into our mouth:

> Thou, O Christ, art all I want,
> More than all in Thee I find.[1]

> [1] Charles New.

I.

The Source of Life.

"With thee is the fountain of life."

1. God is the fountain of life in the merely physical sense. He has life in Himself, and He communicates His life in multitudinous forms. He does not derive His life: it rises eternally in Himself. The life we need is ever flowing from God. All the life in the universe, visible and invisible, is from Him. Vegetable life with its myriad forms, in hedgerow, garden, forest, and field; animal life from the tiniest animalculæ to the mammoths of Eastern lands; human lives—which die, we are told, at the rate of nearly 4000 every hour, their places being taken by as many more; lives in the unseen world, the innumerable inhabitants of the unseen state. Space throbs and palpitates with life. What a conception it gives of the almightiness of our Heavenly Father! Of all this life He is the source.

2. But life is more than physical existence; it is fellowship with the Unseen. When God passed from the formation of His other creatures to the creation of man, He added something over and above what they had, something direct from Himself to make life; He "breathed into his nostrils the breath of life; and man became a living soul." Sin changed the base of life; it made another base necessary. God put all life into His Son. And that life which is in Christ is the real spring and essence of all that constitutes true human life. There must be generation from Him; there must be contact with Him; there must be union with Him to make life—life properly so called—the life which is the being of a man—the life that fulfils the end of life—the life that is for ever and for ever. The beginning of life, then, man's real life, is oneness with the Lord Jesus.

¶ Life in the Old Testament is primarily the physical, earthly life, the sum of energies which make up man's actual existence. The soul separated from the body does not cease to be, but it forfeits its portion in the true life. Two factors, however, were latent in the Old Testament conception from the beginning, and became more and more prominent in the course of the later development. In the first place, the radical element in life is activity. Mere physical existence is distinguished from that essential life which consists in the unrestricted play of all the energies, especially of the higher and more characteristic. In the loftier passages of the Psalms, more particularly, the idea of "life" has nearly always a pregnant sense. It is associated with joy, prosperity, peace, wisdom, righteousness; man "lives" according as he has free scope for the activities which are most distinctive of his spiritual nature. God Himself is emphatically the "living one." He is the creative, ever-active God—sufficient to Himself, the source of all reality and power. Life is His supreme attribute, distinguishing Him from men with their thousand weaknesses and limitations. The other factor in the Old Testament conception is even more important in its bearing on later thought. Since God alone possesses life in the highest sense, fellowship with Him is the one condition on which men can obtain it. "With thee is the fountain of life." In the higher regions of Old Testament thought, life and communion with God are interchangeable ideas. The belief in immortality is never expressly stated, but, as Jesus Himself indicates, it was implicit in this knowledge of a God "who was not the God of the dead, but of the living."[1]

3. And this life is conveyed to man through Christ. He secures it for us by the surrender of His own life, His sacrifice on Calvary, thus making it possible for the Father to bestow it righteously on us who are unworthy of it. And He, Christ crucified and alive again, is the medium of its communication. Again and again He claims, and it is claimed for Him, that He is the Author of life. "I am come," He says, "that they might have life, and that they might have it more abundantly"; "He that hath the Son hath life; and he that hath not the Son of God hath not life"; "The gift of God is eternal life through Jesus Christ our Lord"; "God hath given to us eternal life, and this life is in his Son." The Father is the fountain, but, said Christ, "If any man thirst, let him come unto me and drink."

¶ Like the great aqueducts that stretch from the hills across the Roman Campagna, His Incarnation brings the waters of the fountain from the mountains of God into the lower levels of our nature, and the fetid alleys of our sins. The cool, sparkling treasure is carried near to every lip. If we drink, we live. If

[1] E. F. Scott, *The Fourth Gospel*, 235.

we will not, we die in our sins, and are dead whilst we live. Stop the fountain, and what becomes of the stream? It fades between its banks, and is no more. You cannot live the life of the animal except that life be joined to Him. If it could be broken away from God it would disappear as the clouds melt in the sky, and there would be nobody, and you would be nowhere. You cannot break yourself away from God physically so completely as to annihilate yourself. You can do so spiritually; some do it, and the consequence is that they are dead! You can be made alive from the dead, if you will lay hold on Jesus Christ, and get His life-giving spirit into your heart.[1]

(1) The fountain is *mysterious* in its origin. This is perhaps the thought that first occurs to any one who stands by the rushing fountain pouring forth its stream of life; and the mystery has led the uninstructed nations to curious conjectures as to the origin of these fountains.

¶ Some years ago the engineers engaged in constructing the water-works of the city of Beyrout set themselves to the task of exploring the caverns from which issues the permanent supply of the Dog River. After great labour and repeated expeditions they succeeded in penetrating to a distance of three-quarters of a mile into the heart of the mountain; but as they passed onward from lake to torrent, now under lofty dome, and again through narrow and tortuous channels, the water was undiminished in its volume, and finally a roaring cataract barred their progress and forbade them to search farther into the secret of the living stream.

So is it that life, after all our inquiries into its nature and origin, remains hidden from us. We are conscious of its existence, we can see its effects, but in itself it is a mystery, even as the great Giver of it, the Fountain of Life, dwells in thick darkness. We can only say, " In his hand is the breath of all living." In Him we " live, and move, and have our being."[2]

(2) The fountain is *free and full* in its flow. The people of the East call water the "gift of God"; and so throughout Scripture the invitation is repeated in various forms: "Ho, every one that thirsteth, come ye to the waters." "If any man thirst, let him come unto me and drink." For "the gift of God is eternal life through Jesus Christ our Lord." This stream of spiritual life, though in its origin far above the level of human

[1] A. Maclaren.
[2] J. Robertson, in *Sunday Magazine*, 1881, p. 703.

nature, bursts forth in our nature, and at a level within reach of the poorest and the vilest. At the lowest point of the humiliation of the Son of God it was manifested. Though springing from the bosom of the eternal hills it runs in the valleys, and he that would have life must first know the power of death. The Rock of Ages cleft for us is the point at which we receive the gift of God, and we receive it without money and without price.

¶ The water of the fountain will flow of its own necessity. It is in its very nature that it must flow if only we do not wilfully hinder it. It is always flowing into an open heart.[1]

(3) The fountain of life *brings life* wherever it flows.

¶ One of the most striking of all the fountains of Syria is the fountain of Fijeh, in Anti-Lebanon, which furnishes at one spring from the solid rock three-fourths of the waters of the river Barada, the ancient Abana of Damascus. The traveller pitches his tent under the walnut-trees that overhang the fountain; lulled to sleep by it at night, he hears it at every waking hour; and when the rising sun pierces through the thick foliage its rays fall upon the sparkling river, rushing on with undiminished strength. By night and by day, when swollen by the rains of winter, and after all the snow on the highest heights has disappeared, for six long months of drought, the fountain pours forth its stream of life. And the nodding oleanders dip their flowered heads in its stream, and the poplars and walnut-trees draw their deep life from its waters, and orchards and gardens flourish along its banks, and it scatters life and beauty wherever it goes. But let us leave for a little the narrow valley in which it holds its course, and as we bend off to the left and its sound fades away on the ear, let us observe how vegetation gets scantier and poorer, till, within sight and almost within hearing of the river, we stand in a dry, parched wilderness. Proceeding still across the arid waste we reach the summit of a hill that is burnt up by the summer sun, and we have before us a view that is unparalleled in the East, perhaps unequalled in the world. A plain of vast extent is bounded on all sides by barren deserts, but in its centre, embedded in a belt of living green, is a city of a hundred and fifty thousand souls, for the river is there, and whithersoever the river comes there is life.[2]

(4) The water of the fountain is always *seeking to rise* to the level from which it came. This makes the very life and beauty of the fountain. So will it be with "the fountain of life." It will

---

[1] James Vaughan.

[2] J. Robertson, in *Sunday Magazine*, 1881, p. 704.

always be mounting to the height, the heavenly height from which it sprang, bearing us up and up to that world from which it came; and though it never reaches it, it will aspire to it; it will always be nearing it, continually approaching the heaven of its birth, the God of its creation.

¶ It is difficult to be always true to ourselves, to be always what we wish to be, what we feel we ought to be. As long as we feel that, as long as we do not surrender the ideal of our life, all is right. Our aspirations represent the true nature of our soul much more than our everyday life.[1]

> Alas! long-suffering and most patient God,
> Thou needst be surelier God to bear with us
> Than even to have made us! Thou aspire, aspire
> From henceforth for me! Thou who hast Thyself
> Endured this fleshhood, knowing how as a soaked
> And sucking vesture it can drag us down
> And choke us in the melancholy Deep,
> Sustain me, that with Thee I walk these waves,
> Resisting!—breathe me upward, Thou in me
> Aspiring, who art the way, the truth, the life,—
> That no truth henceforth seem indifferent,
> No way to truth laborious, and no life,
> Not even this life I live, intolerable![2]

II.

THE SOURCE OF LIGHT.

"In thy light shall we see light."

God is "the Father of lights." The sun and all the stars are only lights kindled by Him. It is the very crown of revelation that "God is light, and in him is no darkness at all." Light seems to the unscientific eye, which knows nothing about undulations of a luminiferous ether, to be the least material of material things. All joyous things come with it. It brings warmth and fruit, joyfulness and life. Purity, and gladness, and knowledge have been symbolized by it in all tongues. The Scripture uses light, and the sun, which is its source, as an emblem for God in His holiness and blessedness and omniscience.

[1] Max Müller.   [2] E. B. Browning.

The Psalmist saw the world all full of seekers after light; he was a seeker after light himself. What he had discovered, and what he wanted to tell men, was that the first step in a hopeful search after light must be for a man to put himself into the element of light, which is God. The first thing for any man to do who wanted knowledge was to put himself under God, to make himself God's man; because both he who wanted to know and that which he wanted to know had God for their true element and were their best and did their best only as they lived in Him.

¶ When I try to describe to myself this thought of David about man's seeing all light in the light of God, no picture like the picture of a true and docile childhood seems to me to express it. A child in his father's house learns everything within the intelligence and character of his father, who has provided all things there, and is perpetually throwing light upon their proper use. Everything has its own qualities, but those qualities are made distinct and vivid to the child by their relation to the master of the house. Not purely in themselves, but in his father's use of them and in their relationship to him does the child come to know the tools of the workshop, the furniture of the parlour, and all the apparatus of domestic life. So, I believe, it is with the child's knowledge of the larger house, the world-house, of which God is the Father.[1]

1. Nothing is seen in its own light—not even a visible thing. A landscape is not seen in its own light; it is perceived very much in the light of yesterday. How little of what you see is mere perception! Every sight of nature is tinged with the light of memory. The poet looks from the bridge at midnight upon the rushing waters; but what he sees is not the flowing tide; it is a tide of memory that fills his eyes with tears. You listen to the babbling of the brook; but what you hear is not the babbling, it is the utterance of a dear name. You visit Rome, you visit Jerusalem, you visit Greece; do you see any of these by its own light? No; they are all beheld by the light of yesterday; there is their glory, there lies their gold! "Even so," cries the Psalmist, "it is with this world; if you want to see it, you must look at it by the light of another world—God's coming world." He does not mean that when we quit the scenes of earth we shall have bright light in heaven. It is more than that. It is for the scenes

---

[1] P. Brooks, *Sermons Preached in English Churches*, 104.

of earth he wants the heavenly light. He says you cannot interpret your own skies without it. We often say that in the light of eternity earthly objects will fade from our sight. But the Psalmist says that, until we get the light of eternity, earthly objects will never be in our sight. It is by the light of the Celestial City—the City which has no need of the sun—that alone we can tell what here is large and what here is small.

¶ Jesus knew the streets of Jerusalem and the lanes of Galilee and the history of His mysterious Hebrew people, and the hearts of the lilies and the souls of men; but He knew them all differently from the way in which the Hebrew scribes and scholars knew them. To Him they were all full of light. There is no other description of His knowledge that can tell its special and peculiar character like that. It was all full of light. And the other peculiarity of it was just as clear. It was full also of God. He knew everything as God's child in God's house. The history of the prophets and the heart of the lily both meant something about His Father. These two peculiarities belonged together. The world was full of light to Him because it was full of God. It was God's light in which He saw the deeper light in everything.[1]

2. If we need God's light to appreciate natural beauty and to grasp intellectual truth, much more do we need it to apprehend spiritual realities. It is in communion with Him who is the Light as well as the Life of men that we see a whole universe of glories, realities, and brightnesses. Where other eyes see only darkness, we behold "the King in his beauty, and the land that is very far off." Where other men see only cloudland and mists, our vision will pierce into the unseen, and there behold "the things which are," the only real things, of which all that the eye of sense sees are the fleeting shadows, seen as in a dream, while these are the true, and the sight of them is sight indeed. They who see by the light of God, and see light therein, have a vision which is more than imagination, more than opinion, more than belief. It is certitude. Communication with God does not bring with it superior intellectual perspicuity, but it does bring a perception and an experience of spiritual realities and relations, which, in respect of clearness and certainty, may be called sight. Many of us walk in darkness, who, if we were but in communion with

[1] P. Brooks, *Sermons Preached in English Churches*, 105.

God, would see the lone hillside blazing with chariots and horses of fire. Many of us grope in perplexity, who, if we were but hiding under the shadow of God's wings, would see the truth and walk at liberty in the light which is knowledge and purity and joy.

(1) *It needs a God to make God known.*—Light has this property, that it is at once the vehicle and that which is borne by the vehicle; it is the revelation and its channel, and this twofold property of light remains the same whether we regard it as the old school of physicists did—as an actual emanation of particles; or as the new school do—as only an undulation or vibration of some invisible ether itself at rest. The oft-quoted line of the poet, that we may rise from nature up to nature's God, then, is either a truism or a sophism; a truism if we mean only that nature reveals something of God's character while it conceals the rest; a sophism, if we mean that man, by the unassisted light of his natural faculties, is able to discover the invisible things of God. We can know God only by Himself. The light must be Divine by which we see that there is anything whatever Divine to see and behold.

¶ When Dante has reached the Ninth of the Heavenly Spheres he catches his first glimpse of the Godhead, the Central Point on which "Heaven and all Nature hangs," surrounded by nine circles of fire, which he is told are the nine choirs of angelic beings. But though he can see them in their operation, his vision is too imperfect to see them as they are. He must drink of the River of Light. Then he beholds the Rose of the Blessed, with its myriads of saints. But still he is unable to see God. The Virgin Mary procures this grace for him, and gazing on the Central Point he sees three circles, like rainbows, and, being illuminated by a flash of Divine Light, he comprehends the mystery of the Holy Trinity and of the Incarnation.

(2) *Only in God's light can we truly see ourselves.*—We wish really to know ourselves, our own real being and position. What are we? Where do we stand in the scale of God's creation, as God sees us? We are so many things wrapped up in one; we are, alas! a mass of contradictions—so very different at different times. What am I? What am I, as an angel sees me? As truth sees me? As God sees me? What am I? I grow so perplexed when I go down into the dark depths of my own soul.

No natural light can clear up this. There must be a light from outside, a light from above. "In thy light," the soul will have to say at last out of all its searchings—"in thy light shall I see light." Down in those hidden crevices of my own innermost, blackest being, Lord, give me light to see clearly what I am.

¶ "John Leech," says Dean Hole, "had an original and effective method of reprimanding his children. If their faces were distorted by anger, by a rebellious temper, or a sullen mood, he took out his sketch book, transferred their lineaments with a slight exaggeration to paper, and showed them, to their shameful confusion, how ugly naughtiness was." [1]

3. The full effulgence of the Divine Light was manifested in Christ, who is both God and the Revealer of God. He is the light which alone is uncreated light, "bright effluence of bright essence increate"—language which Milton strangely enough has applied to material light, but which is inappropriate unless applied to Him who is the true Sun of Righteousness. As for material light, however subtle and ethereal, it is not Divine; the creature is not to be confounded with the Creator in this way. The language of the Psalmist is more careful and guarded: Thou "coverest thyself with light as with a garment." Light, in fact, is like a garment, or veil, or fleecy cloud, across the moon's disc, which part reveals and part conceals. So it is of all the material works of God, and hence the allegory of the ancients was not inexact which represented nature by the symbol of the veiled Isis. There is something seen through the veil, but more remains behind which we cannot see through. The same symbol was seen in the sanctuary, where a thick curtain hung between the Holy Place and the Most Holy of All; that curtain, woven within and without with cherubim, signifying this, that what was seen was the multiform appearance of creation, of which the cherubim were the symbol, while behind was that which no man hath seen or can see—God in Himself.

(1) *Christ lights up the unlighted lustre in our nature.*—Conversion is the lighting up of our nature with the spark of God's Holy Spirit out of heaven. When a man is converted he does not get new brains; he does not get new senses or capacities; he is still surrounded by the old relationships, and he still moves in

[1] R. E. Welsh, *God's Gentlemen*, 41.

the selfsame world. But men have been heard to tell the story of their conversion, and they have said, " The stars seemed new to me, and even the sun shone differently." And we have known men who had made every one round them miserable develop into true gentlemen when God met with them. Nor can any one move among our peasantry, and see the wisdom and weight and power of certain characters, without perceiving how much it has meant for them that they have known the living and true God. What has happened to them? Have they received new faculties? No, it is not that—the lustre was always there. But the light of all light has entered their circuit now, and the spark that is God's has kindled the spiritual candle: it is not a difference of added lustre; it is just that the lustre has been lighted up.

¶ The doctrine of conversion played so large a part in Bishop Wilkinson's life that it demands a few words, because it is so often misunderstood. Conversion, in its perverted sense, is often used to describe a sort of mental crisis in which, under the influence of hysterical excitement and rhetorical intoxication, the spirit is hypnotized into an experience so abnormal that it often has a permanent effect on character, and has in retrospect the appearance of a Divine interposition. That was not what Wilkinson meant by conversion. He believed, indeed, that it often came suddenly upon the soul, but that it was only a natural step in a chain of circumstance, like the parting of the avalanche from the snowfield. What he meant by it was a realization of truth, of the personal relation with God, so vivid and indubitable that the soul could never be in any doubt as to its redemption and its ultimate destiny. But he believed that this might be a tranquil and reasoned process, though in the case of sin-stained lives he was inclined to feel that the break with the past must often be of the nature of an instantaneous revulsion, a sudden perception of the hideousness of sin, and a dawning of the light of God.[1]

(2) *Christ sheds light for us on the manifold paths of duty.*—It is wonderful how, when a man lives near God, he comes to know what he ought to do. That great Light, which is Christ, is like the star that hung over the Magi, blazing in the heavens, and yet stooping to the lowly task of guiding three wayfaring men along a muddy road upon earth. So the highest Light of God comes down to be a Lantern for our paths and a Light for our feet.

[1] A. C. Benson, *The Leaves of the Tree*, 116.

Now the light comes just as we are ready to obey the will of the Most High. Abraham had to leave his home and go out, not knowing whither he went. Moses had to return from the home he had in Midian to the country where they had sought his life. The people of Israel had to journey into the great and terrible wilderness. The prophets had to pass through stern ordeals. The apostles must leave all and follow Christ. St. Paul must bow his neck under the yoke of Him whom a moment before he was persecuting, and say, "Lord, what wilt thou have me to do?" And do we not know that the light of God is most fully in our souls when by Divine grace we are uprooting self-indulgence and self-will?

¶ To St. Francis of Assisi, as he set out to join the champion of the Church, Walter de Brienne, intoxicated with the idea that he himself was destined to become a great leader, came a vision at Spoleto. "Francis," called the voice of God, "who can make thee the better knight, the Master or the servant, the rich man or the poor?" "The Master," said Francis, "not the servant, the rich man, not the poor." Then said the voice: "But thou leavest the Master for the servant and the rich man for the poor." And Francis said: "What dost Thou will that I should do, O my Lord?" And the Lord said: "Turn thee back to thy own land, for the vision that thou didst see meant heavenly and not earthly equipment, and it shall be given thee by God and not by man." Obedient to the vision, Francis gave up all thought of rejoining the band of Assisan soldiers, and rode slowly home that day, revolving in his mind this grace vouchsafed of direction in the path of the Spirit. It must have been from this time that he felt it was to no mundane glory he was being guided, but rather to the glory which vanquishes the world. One wonders how the struggle shaped itself, how keen were the pangs which moved him, as one fair temporal hope after another took on the likeness of a phantasm and trembled into nothingness at the potent presence of these unwonted and unseen realities. One wonders how his spirit stirred and shook as their amazing intervention became indubitable; how the unequal contest agonized and astounded him; how, step by step, the spiritual gained upon the temporal, whilst his shrinking flesh cried aloud in the suffering of death. Only this we know: he obeyed, and, in obedience to the Will, he found the Way, the way of the Cross, Christ Jesus, from which he never swerved.[1]

[1] A. M. Stoddart, *Francis of Assisi*, 71.

Then fiercely we dig the fountain:
  Oh! whence do the waters rise?
Then panting we climb the mountain:
  Oh! are there indeed blue skies?
We dig till the soul is weary,
  Nor find the water-nest out;
We climb to the stone-crest dreary,
  And still the sky is a doubt!

Let alone the roots of the fountain;
  Drink of the water bright;
Leave the sky at rest on the mountain,
  Walk in its torrent of light;
Although thou seest no beauty,
  Though widowed thy heart yet cries,
With thy hands go and do thy duty,
  And thy work will clear thine eyes.[1]

[1] George MacDonald, *A Book of Dreams* (*Poetical Works*, i. 394).

Delighting in the Lord.

LITERATURE.

Conn (J.), *The Fulness of Time*, 117.

Cox (S.), *The Bird's Nest*, 238.

Houchin (J. W.), *The Vision of God*, 31.

Mackey (H. O.), *Miniature Sermons*, 1.

Maclaren (A.), *Sermons Preached in Manchester*, ii. 245.

Reynolds (H. R.), *Notes of the Christian Life*, 111.

Voysey (C.), *Sermons*, viii. (1885), No. 32.

Christian World Pulpit, xxvii. 93 (H. W. Beecher).

Church of England Magazine, xxxi. 139 (J. Ayre).

DELIGHTING IN THE LORD.

Delight thyself also in the Lord;
And he shall give thee the desires of thine heart.—Ps. xxxvii. 4.

1. THE anthem, " O rest in the Lord," taken from Mendelssohn's oratorio "Elijah," is composed of words which many persons imagine to be a text accurately quoted from the Bible. This is, however, nowhere to be found as Mendelssohn quotes it, but is a compilation of two separate verses. Scarcely any music could be sweeter to an anxious and weary heart than this pathetic song, " O rest in the Lord, wait patiently for Him, and He will give thee thy heart's desire." It seems cruel to say a word to detract from the gracious comfort and hope conveyed by the words. Yet we shall be gainers and not losers by greater accuracy and truth, and shall find the promise "He will give thee thy heart's desire" none the less fulfilled. Mendelssohn's made-up text is amply true, was true for him in fact as it has been true to so many of us in our varied lives and in the fulfilment of our heart's desires. Yet there is a higher truth still, and to that the Psalmist gives expression here. "Delight thyself also in the Lord; and he shall give thee the desires of thine heart."

2. The text might be correctly paraphrased, "Delight in the Lord, and then thou mayest trust thy desires; they will be the forerunners of blessings, the beginning of their own realization." "Blessed are they that hunger and thirst after righteousness, for they shall be filled." Delight thyself in the Lord, and thou wilt desire strongly only what is in harmony with His will, and best for thyself. All thy wishes will be brought into subjection to His will, and thou wilt crave only those things which He is ready and anxious to bestow upon thee.

¶ There are many beautiful psalms in the Psalter, but I am disposed to think that this psalm is the most beautiful of them all. There is a strain of old experience in it, of ripe and mellow wisdom, of thoughtful and tranquil affection, which at once stirs and calms our hearts. I can never read it but it calls up before me the figure of a venerable and kindly old man, who has seen much and endured much, but has at last won for himself a sacred tranquillity and peace which no change and no alarm can disturb; who, now that he is old, does not forget either that he has been young or what his hot, eager youth was like; and who, in the calm evening of his days, draws upon the accumulated stores of his knowledge and experience for the benefit of those in whom the fires of youth still burn hotly, and tries to save them from many a conflict, and many a defeat, by teaching them the secret of peace.[1]

¶ There is a passage in Wordsworth's *Prelude* which expresses both the craving and its satisfaction, with all the poet's high seriousness and moving simplicity. He had risen, in his unrest of mind, before the dawn. In the grey light of the morning, he brooded over his life and its meaning. As the sun rose and flooded meadow and stream and the far-off shining sea with light, and as the birds awoke to song and the labourer came forth with quiet and honest content to his work in the field, all the stillness and charm of the scene fell upon him with refreshing and renewing power.

> Ah! need I say, dear Friend! that to the brim
> My heart was full; I made no vows, but vows-
> Were then made for me; bond unknown to me
> Was given, that I should be, else sinning greatly.
> A dedicated Spirit. On I walked
> In thankful blessedness, which yet survives.[2]

I.

Practising the Presence of God.

1. Delighting in God means, to begin with, realizing the presence of God. If men will not sometimes think of God, He will become merely a name to them. If they glance toward Him only now and again, and with an unobservant and undesiring eye, He will become strange and shadowy, and will remain unknown. We do not become sure of God by mustering up the arguments for His being and His purpose in the world. No

---

[1] S. Cox, *The Bird's Nest*, 238.
[2] W. M. Clow, *The Secret of the Lord*, 219.

heart ever stood up in a passionate conviction of God's presence because it had been told that His footprints were marked upon the rocks. No mind was ever driven by the logic of history to assent with a deep persuasion to the personal providence of the Almighty. These things have their place and their power. They are byways of evidence in which a believing heart will sometimes walk. But the only certainty which can satisfy the mind and stir the heart is an ethical and a religious, a moral and a spiritual consciousness of God. Faith is an opening of the eyes that we may see. It is in prayer that we rise most swiftly and most convincingly into this faith which sees. It is in prayer that we have the sure consciousness of God. Even although a man may kneel with a haze over his mind and a chill upon his spirit, he will not kneel in vain.

¶ In the beginning of Brother Lawrence's noviciate, he spent the hours appointed for private prayer in thinking of God, so as to convince his mind of, and to impress deeply upon his heart, the Divine existence, rather by devout sentiments than by studied reasonings and elaborate meditations. By this short and sure method, he exercised himself in the knowledge and love of God, resolving to use his utmost endeavour to live in a continual sense of His Presence, and, if possible, never to forget Him more. When he had thus in prayer filled his mind full with great sentiments of that Infinite Being, he went to his work appointed in the kitchen (for he was cook to the Society). When he began his business, he said to God, with a filial trust in Him: " O my God, since Thou art with me, and I must now, in obedience to Thy commands, apply my mind to these outward things, I beseech Thee to grant me grace to continue in Thy presence; and to this end, do Thou prosper me with Thy assistance, receive all my works, and possess all my affections." . . . When he had finished, he examined himself how he had discharged his duty : if he found well, he returned thanks to God; if otherwise, he asked pardon; and, without being discouraged, he set his mind right again and continued his exercise of the *Presence* of God, as if he had never deviated from it. " Thus," said he, " by rising after my falls, and by frequently renewed acts of faith, and love, I am come to a state, wherein it would be as difficult for me not to think of God as it was at first to accustom myself to it."

As Brother Lawrence had found such comfort and blessing in walking in the Presence of God, it was natural for him to recommend it earnestly to others; but his example was a stronger inducement than any arguments he could propose. His very countenance was edifying; such a sweet and calm devotion appearing in it as could not but affect all beholders. And it was observed that in the greatest hurry of business in the kitchen, he still preserved his recollection and his heavenly-mindedness. He was never hasty nor loitering, but did each thing in its season, with an even, uninterrupted composure and tranquillity of spirit. " The time of business," said he, " does not with me differ from the time of prayer, and in the noise and clatter of my kitchen, while several persons are at the same time calling for different things, I possess God in as great tranquillity as if I were upon my knees at the Blessed Sacrament." [1]

2. Delighting in the Lord implies sympathy with His mind and character. It means that His pure and holy character is the absorbing object of thought, that in the contemplation of it the mind is free from all suspicions, all hard thoughts and rebellious feelings; that, while it dwells on this high theme with reverence and with awe, it also finds in it a source of deepest joy.

¶ Five years before he left us, one who has since his death been much in men's minds had an illness which was of a very critical character. For some days he said nothing, and he was supposed to be quite unconscious. After his recovery he referred, one day, to this, the presumably unconscious, part of his illness. " People thought," he said, " that I was unconscious, but the fact was that although I could not speak I heard all that went on in the room, and I was well occupied." To the question, " What were you doing ? " he answered, " By God's mercy, I could re- member the Epistle for the fourth Sunday in Advent, out of the Philippians, which begins, 'Rejoice in the Lord alway.' This I made a framework for prayer; saying the Lord's Prayer two or three times between each clause, and so dwelling on the several relations of each clause to each petition in the Lord's Prayer." How he did this he explained at some length, and then added, " It lasted me, I should think, four or five hours." To the question, " What did you do after that ? " he answered, " I began it over again. I was very happy: and, had it been God's will, did not wish to get better." [2]

3. Delighting in God means holding close communion with Him. Communion is that quiet, intimate, tender intercourse with

---

[1] Brother Lawrence, *The Practice of the Presence of God.*
[2] H. P. Liddon, *Passiontide Sermons*, 271.

God in which we may ask nothing, confess nothing, and cease
even from thanksgiving. We simply speak face to face with God
as a man speaks to his friend. Communion may pass beyond
speech into a calm and absorbing and yet strangely wakeful
silence. God is not content always with silence only. He loves,
we may truly believe, to hear the human voice rising and falling
in the accents of prayer. Samuel's childish treble when he cried,
"Speak, Lord; for thy servant heareth," was sweeter to Him
than the perfect music of a boy's clear young voice in a choir to
its leader. God misses "His little human praise," with its doubt
and fear trembling in every tone, when we pray only with the
inner whisper of our thought and meditation. But there are
times when the spirit of prayer may be too swift and too tender
for words. Every man is a possible mystic in the best sense of
that word, for every man may enter into that intercourse with
God in which the hours pass by in the silence of a perfect confidence.

¶ Wesley, in his *Journal* tells us again and again that when
worn and ill he cast himself without words on the bosom of God.
Chalmers declares that, when greatly wearied and distressed in
mind, he gave himself up to quietism, and was much refreshed.
These were both men of strong practical wisdom, and not moody
and dreamy recluses. We must not think that when Christ continued "all night in prayer to God" He stretched out the arms of
His petitions and thanksgiving in words which fell upon His own
ear. We can be sure that His time was passed in still meditation.
He rose into a rapture in which there was no speech, a silence
that was felt and loved of God. To Him the Father was

A presence felt the livelong day,
A welcome fear at night.[1]

¶ I see that every good and wise man who is held up to my
admiration and imitation in the Bible desired nothing less, and
could be satisfied by nothing less, than communion with God.
Every word in the Book of Psalms, in the Gospels, in the Epistles,
and in the Prophecies tells me this. They wished to know God,
not in a vague, loose sense, but actually to know Him as a
friend. Starting with no preparatory notions of God, but ready
to receive everything He told them, they welcomed each new
dispensation only because it told them something more of God;

[1] W. M. Clow, *The Secret of the Lord*, 181.

because it enabled them more intelligently, more practically, more literally to converse with Him. I observe that all their sorrow arose from the loss of God's presence, all their joy from the possession of it, all their pleasure in expecting heaven from anticipation of it. I observe that they shrunk from the contemplation of no side or phase of God's character, that His holiness and His mercy were equally dear to them, and that, so far from viewing them as separate, they could not admire one without the other. They could not delight in His love unless they believed that He would admit no sin into His presence, for sin and love are essentially hostile; they could not adore His holiness unless they believed that He had some way of removing their sinfulness and imparting His own character to them. The plain, obvious study of the Bible tells me this.[1]

4. Lastly, delighting in God means entire surrender to God's will. The highest attitude in prayer is not desire, or aspiration, or praise. It is surrender. In surrender we open our whole being to God as a flower opens itself to the sun, and we are filled, up to our measure, with His Divine energy. It is because man can be filled with the fulness of God that he has been chosen of God as His instrument in the world. In one true sense God set bounds to His power when He created man. He placed a further limit on Himself when He committed dominion to him. God now works through man, and if man will not work the works of God, the works of God remain undone.

¶ *Esther.*—But that must be the best life, father. That must be the best life.

Rufus.—What life, my dear child?

Esther.—Why, that where one bears and does everything because of some great and strong feeling—so that this and that in one's circumstances don't signify.

Rufus.—Yea, verily: but the feeling that should be thus supreme is devotedness to the Divine Will.[2]

¶ It is best to limit oneself to what is strictly necessary, to live austerely and by rule, to content oneself with a little, and to attach no value to anything but peace of conscience and a sense of duty done. It is true that this itself is no small ambition, and that it only lands us in another impossibility. No,—the simplest course is to submit oneself wholly and altogether to God. Every-

---

[1] *Life of Frederick Denison Maurice*, i. 132.
[2] George Eliot, *Felix Holt.*

thing else, as saith the Preacher, is but vanity and vexation of spirit. It is a long while now since this has been plain to me, and since this religious renunciation has been sweet and familiar to me. It is the outward distractions of life, the examples of the world, and the irresistible influence exerted upon us by the current of things which make us forget the wisdom we have acquired and the principles we have adopted. That is why life is such weariness! This eternal beginning over again is tedious, even to repulsion. It would be so good to go to sleep when we have gathered the fruit of experience, when we are no longer in opposition to the supreme will, when we have broken loose from self, when we are at peace with all men.[1]

> Blindfolded and alone I stand,
> With unknown thresholds on each hand;
> The darkness deepens as I grope,
> Afraid to fear, afraid to hope,
> Yet this one thing I learn to know
> Each day more surely as I go,
> That doors are opened, ways are made,
> Burdens are lifted or are laid,
> By some great law unseen and still,
> Unfathomed purpose to fulfil,
>   "Not as I will."
>
> Blindfolded and alone I wait;
> Loss seems too bitter, gain too late;
> Too heavy burdens in the load
> And too few helpers on the road;
> And joy is weak and grief is strong,
> And years and days so long, so long:
> Yet this one thing I learn to know
> Each day more surely as I go,
> That I am glad the good and ill
> By changeless law are ordered still,
>   "Not as I will."
>
> "Not as I will": the sound grows sweet
> Each time my lips the words repeat.
> "Not as I will": the darkness feels
> More safe than light when this thought steals
> Like whispered voice to calm and bless
> All unrest and all loneliness.

[1] *Amiel's Journal* (trans. by Mrs. Humphry Ward), 115.

"Not as I will," because the One
Who loved us first and best has gone
Before us on the road, and still
For us must all His love fulfil,
    "Not as we will." [1]

II.

THE SATISFACTION OF DESIRE.

1. Nothing more disastrous could happen than that God should gratify the desires of all men. If God were to permit for one short hour that all human desires should be satisfied, it is impossible to calculate the dire confusion and pitiless despair that would prevail. Ignorance would unsettle every natural law; selfishness would break down every barrier; oppression, lust, and rapine would leap forth with fury. It is true that prisons, hospitals, and workhouses might disgorge their occupants, poverty might leap into affluence, and diseases and devils be cast out of suffering humanity. The slave might snap his fetters, and many an oppressed sufferer might rush forth to freedom and to life; but amid the widespread despair excited by the greatest curse that had ever fallen on humanity, the prayer would ascend, " O God, take back our liberty; bind us once more by Thy laws; Thou, and Thou alone, knowest what is best for us. Fence us round with Thine ordinances; restore to us Thy government; let us know once more that Thou alone canst speak, and it shall be done; Thou alone command so that it shall stand fast ! "

¶ The fables, the philosophy, and the experience of all nations, are crowded with lessons that men are blind, and ignorant, and selfish, and know not what is best for them; that they cannot enumerate their mercies; that the overruling of an infinite Mind and Will is the only refuge for their ignorance, the only hope of the race. He must be a bold man, or a fool, who would dare to take his lot into his own government, and be the master of his own destiny. The same principle will apply equally well, if we suppose our merely human desires to be made the measure of God's benedictions to us—of the spiritual blessings which are of the greatest necessity for us. Some are longing for more power to work, when probably God sees that they want more patience to endure, more

[1] Helen H. Jackson, *Verses.*

power to feel. Some are ever yearning after new truth, when God sees that their need is to understand more fully the truth already within their reach.[1]

2. When we delight in God, we are freed from the distraction of various desires by the one master attraction. Such a soul is still as the great river above the falls, when all the side currents and dimpling eddies and backwaters are effaced by the attraction that draws every drop in the one direction; or like the same stream as it nears its end, and, forgetting how it brawled among rocks and flowers in the mountain glens, flows "with a calm and equable motion" to its rest in the central sea. When we possess God, all other desires are put in their right place. The presence of the king awes the crowd into silence. When the full moon is in the nightly sky, it makes the heavens bare of flying cloud-rack, and all the twinkling stars are lost in the peaceful, solitary splendour. So let delight in God rise in our souls, and lesser lights pale before it—do not cease to be, but add their feebleness, unnoticed, to its radiance. The more we have our affections set on God, the more shall we enjoy, because we subordinate, His gifts. The less, too, shall we dread their loss, the less be at the mercy of their fluctuations. The capitalist does not think so much of the year's gains as the needy adventurer, to whom they make the difference between bankruptcy and competence. If we have God for our "enduring substance," we can face all varieties of condition, and be calm, saying:

> Give what Thou wilt, without Thee I am poor,
> And with Thee rich, take what Thou wilt away.

¶ Some men make themselves God, without knowing what they are doing. The deity they appeal to is really their deeper, higher self. When they feel God's approval, it is really their own self-praise. When God reproaches them, it is their own self-rebuke. When they go apart from the world to hold communion with Him, it really is an entrance into their own self-consciousness. To other men some good fellow-man, more or less consciously and completely enlarged into an ideal of humanity, answers the same purpose, and is in reality their God. To still others, a vague presence of a high purpose and tendency felt in everything—Tennyson's "one increasing purpose," and Arnold's

[1] H. R. Reynolds, *Notes of the Christian Life*, 115.

"something not ourselves which makes for righteousness." This fulfils the end and makes the substitute for God. But none of these supply the place of a true Personality outside ourselves, yet infinitely near to us.[1]

3. To delight in God is to have a desire for spiritual good; and the desire for spiritual good never goes unsatisfied. No man ever prayed but in the moment he was a better and a wiser man. To go into the sanctuary of God is to understand. To let our requests be made known unto God is to gain the peace that passeth all understanding. As we pray, our sins are set in the light of God's countenance. We see the beauty of holiness. We behold the beauty of the Lord. We open the sluice-gates of the soul, and the swelling tides of God's love and grace flood within. New penitence, new resolves, new endeavours are born in the depth of the will. That truth is written large in the history of every saint. Prayer is a mode of power within to learn the mind of Christ. His words and deeds become memorable and significant to us. We sometimes receive a more vivid insight into what He was, and did, as we serve Him in the toilsome duties of life. But when we pray, then those spiritual changes which are vital, determining, eternal, take place within. F. W. H. Myers, in his poem on St. Paul, so full of the seer's insight into the history of the soul, has set this truth in impassioned verse. He is speaking of Paul's shame at his failure, and he conceives him in the pain of his penitence, seeking the presence and the peace of Christ.

> Straight to Thy presence get me and reveal it,
>   Nothing ashamed of tears upon Thy feet,
> Show the sore wound and beg Thine hand to heal it,
>   Pour Thee the bitter, pray Thee for the sweet.
>
> Then with a ripple and a radiance thro' me,
>   Rise and be manifest, O Morning Star!
> Flow on my soul, Thou Spirit, and renew me,
>   Fill with Thyself, and let the rest be far.

4. When we delight in the Lord, our desire is not so much to have as to be and do. We cease to crave exclusively for temporal good, for personal and physical gratification, for the

[1] *Phillips Brooks: Memories of his Life*, 457.

supply of what we call our wants, and we crave, instead, to be
what our Creator and Father wishes us to be, and to do what
He wishes us to do. Delighting in the Lord does not mean
ceasing to be human, ceasing to have wants and natural lawful
desires for success and happiness; it means that all these
native and lawful wishes become subordinate to a higher desire
still, so that, for its sake, we are willing to forgo all the rest.
We may be hungry and thirsty, yet our meat and drink will be
to do the will of Him who sent us here and to finish His work.
We may be poor and needy, but we shall esteem the words of
God and obedience to His law "better than thousands of gold and
silver," or, in other words of the Psalmist, "more than our
necessary food." We may be hungering for a love which is out of
our reach, or sorrowing for the loss of a love that can never return,
and yet find in God a love passing the love of woman. We may
be toiling all day, and our very sleep may be broken by festering
care, by even a holy anxiety to bring our work to completion, and
yet we shall find something better and higher than success in the
knowledge that we are working for God and doing our best and
so earning His approval. If the greatest and supreme of all our
delights is in being and in doing what God wills, nothing can
frustrate His purpose to give us our heart's desire.

¶ Christianity seeks not to cramp man's nature, saying to him
constantly, "Thou shalt not"; but it leads on, up to freer air and
wider space, wherein the soul may disport itself. It is God we
follow. Obeying God is freedom. Our souls are like closed
rooms, and God is the sunlight. Every new way we find in which
to obey Him we throw open a shutter. Our souls are as enclosed
bays, and God is the ocean. The only barrier that can hinder
free communication is disobedience. Each duty performed is the
breaking down of a reef of hindrance between our souls and God,
permitting the fulness of His being to flow in upon our souls.
It is when we remember the greatness of the nature which God
has given us that we come into a full understanding of our
relations to God. At some time every man comes to realize the
meaning of the life he is living; the secret sins hidden in his
heart rise against him. Then we would hide ourselves from God
if we could. But the only way to run from God is to run to
Him. The Infinite Knowledge is also the Infinite Pity.[1]

[1] *Phillips Brooks: Memories of his Life*, 630.

THE CROWNING OF THE YEAR.

LITERATURE.

Little (H. W.), *Arrows for the King's Archers*, 50.
Mursell (W. A.), *Sermons on Special Occasions*, 95.
Rylance (J. H.), in *The Complete Preacher*, ii. 180.
Spurgeon (C. H.), *Metropolitan Tabernacle Pulpit*, xxv. (1879), No. 1475.
Wilmot-Buxton (H. J.), *In Many Keys*, 265.
Wilson (J. M.), *Sermons Preached in Clifton College Chapel*, ii. 35.
Churchman's Pulpit : Harvest Thanksgiving, Pt. 97, p. 68 (T. B. Johnstone) ; Pt. 98, p. 81 (J. S. James).
Treasury (New York), xiv. 585 (J. D. M'Caughtry).

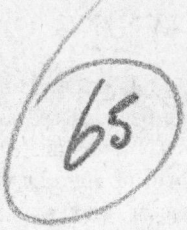

THE CROWNING OF THE YEAR.

Thou crownest the year with thy goodness;
And thy paths drop fatness.—Ps. lxv. 11.

In the midst of great political convulsions, of a shaking of nations and kingdoms, Jehovah had manifested His goodness to His people by sending down a blessing upon their flocks and their fields. The folds were full of sheep, the valleys stood so thick with corn that they laughed and sang; the garners were filled with all manner of store. Peace had been given to Zion as well as plenty. A year of blessing, temporal and spiritual, had been " crowned " by a secure provision against the drought and famine which had at one time threatened the chosen people.

I.

" Thou hast set a crown upon the year of thy goodness." Such is the literal rendering of the text. God is represented as setting the crown of completeness and perfection upon a long process. In the previous verses we have a graphic picture of how the grain is prepared. We see the plough at work, scooping out furrows and turning up ridges by one and the same process: and the Divine Co-operator dealing with both according to need and capacity. The furrows are naturally receptive of the streams which flow in abundance from those upper and invisible channels of God which are full of water; and what they thus receive, they hold and convey to the roots of the young plants. The turned-up ridges need to be settled down and closed well in upon the precious seed which they have received. The same rain that does the one does the other: fills the furrows and settles the ridges. Divine agriculture is economic of means, various in adaptations. But soon the surface becomes encrusted, and might imprison the tender blade, did not the gentler after-showers with their myriad drops come to soften the soil and make it easily permeable. And so, as eyes of wonder look on, and discreet judgment calculates how many dangers have been passed as the green crop carpets the earth, devotion exclaims, "The sprouting thereof thou dost bless."

God crowns the world of men as well as the world of nature. Human life and character and experience have their supreme culminating moments. Love comes to crown the solitary life. Success comes to crown legitimate ambition—not forgetting that there may be a true success in honourable failure. Influence comes to crown character. Friendship comes to crown the longings of the heart. Trust and confidence and admiration come to crown the life lived in honest toil, and with a single eye to the common welfare. But the culmination is a process : the crown is sometimes long deferred. It is deferred in nature, yet experience has taught us to expect it. It looks as if nothing were being done during the dreary, sterile months of winter. The earth seems to be dead, and God appears to have withdrawn. Yet if our hearing were acute enough, we might lay our ear to the ground in December and hear the pulse still beating in that mighty bosom, and by and by we shall behold again the riotous life of spring. We must not despond when there is a winter season in our mental growth, in our spiritual experience, in our church life. In these higher regions, the crown is often long withheld. But if a man is all the time reading, observing, studying, thinking, though there be no immediate visible result, there will come a moment of rapturous emancipation when he realizes that cold fetters, as it were, have fallen from his brain, and left him free to enter upon a richer and riper life of understanding. God has crowned the intellectual year.

¶ Tennyson was in his 81st year when he wrote " Crossing the Bar." He showed the poem to his son, who exclaimed, "That is the crown of your life's work." " It came in a moment," was the aged poet's reply. Yes, but however instantaneous was the inspiration, the hymn had behind it a lifetime of careful, painstaking, even fastidious work.

¶ Marcus Dods was a probationer for six years before being called to Renfield Church, Glasgow. During these years of waiting he was sometimes so discouraged as to think of giving up the ministry altogether. In a letter to his sister he wrote : "Do these two years and more waiting not show that I am seeking my work in the wrong direction, or why do they not show this, or how long would show this? Possibly you may say, 'Wait till some evident call to some other work arises'; but then, of course, evident calls enough would soon arise were I to put myself in the way of them, *e.g.*, were I to go along to Clark the publisher and ask him for some work, or go out to Harvey of Merchiston and ask him for some; whereas, so long as I keep myself back from such openings they are not a tenth part so likely to arise. But apart from growlery, let me give you a problem. I will give it you in the concrete, as being easier stated and easier apprehended. Is it right of me to wait and see whether I get a call or no, and let this decide whether I ought or ought not to take a charge? To me it seems not (though it's just what I'm doing), and on this ground, because in fact we find that God has often suffered men to enter the Church who were not worthy—because, that is, the call of the people does not always represent the call of God." He was afterwards Professor of Exegesis and Principal of the New College, Edinburgh.[1]

II.

The harvest crown comes as the reward of human labour. Man is called to be a co-worker with God. The sun and the rain may do their best, and the earth yield all its quickening powers, but the harvest would be but a heap of wild and tangled weeds without the constant work and toil of man. The earth will show its wondrous fecundity. Every seed that drops into its bosom must grow or die, and it is man's part to curb the wild extravagance of nature, to destroy that which is mere weed or worthless, in order that there may be room for the good to grow and ripen. God gives little even in nature without our toil; He never gives a rich and bounteous harvest unless we give our work, and care, and watchful supervision over its growth.

The world is but a great harvest-field, in which, each in his own place, we are called forth to take our part, and to do our share of labour. Neither by the structure of our nature, nor by the constitution of society, is there any room for the idler, or any possibility of true enjoyment and happiness without work. If we want to be truly happy, to attain in any measure to the real use and enjoyment of life, work of some kind we must have. There ought to be no play without work. No man is entitled to enjoyment who does not purchase it by labour. The sweetest holiday is that

---

[1] *Early Letters of Marcus Dods*, 198.

which we have earned by strenuous application. God has so made us that we must find our pleasure either *in* working, or as the *reward* of working.

¶ There are certain countries of such tropical luxuriance and fertility that you have only to tickle the earth with a hoe, and she laughs with a harvest. But you do not find the highest type of men where Nature is so kind. There is an enervating kindness. In these Northern lands men have a tussle with the earth to make her yield up her fruits, and they become the stronger for their battle with the elements. But they invariably find that God answers the prayer of their labour. There is a flourishing kitchen garden behind the hotel at Gairloch, reclaimed from the barest and barrenest bit of moorland I ever saw. All that countryside is just wild mountain, bare rock, shaggy heath, and desolate moor; to get a kitchen garden out of such a spot is a triumph. It must have needed some considerable faith to make the attempt, and it was justified. God is always ready to supply if man only has conscience enough to demand. "He is faithful that promised." [1]

¶ "My Father worketh hitherto, and I work." And I work! Say that too. If you destroy the sequence, life loses heart, and joy, and meaning, and value. Swing into line with the eternal energy, be a force among forces, a toiler, a producer, a factor, and life never loses its tone and flavour, its bead or glamour. There is no real taste to bread nor bliss in sleep for the idler. He is the doubter, the sceptic, the unhappy man. His idleness proclaims him diseased and decaying.[2]

Get leave to work
In this world—'tis the best you get at all;
For God, in cursing, gives us better gifts
Than men in benediction. God says, "Sweat
For foreheads," men say "crowns," and so we are crowned,
Aye, gashed by some tormenting circle of steel
Which snaps with a secret spring. Get work, get work;
Be sure 'tis better than what you work to get.[3]

III.

And yet the harvest is the gift of God, and should link man to God. Man can only do a little; he ploughs and sows, and

[1] W. A. Mursell.
[2] M. D. Babcock, *Thoughts for Every-Day Living*, 15.
[3] E. B. Browning.

makes what preparation he can, and then he has to sit down and wait. He can hasten nothing. If he goes out and waves his hands magically over the brown furrows, nothing happens; if he stamps and rages, he does but reveal his impatience, and emphasize his own impotence. He must work, and then he must wait; and there is something profoundly religious and infinitely suggestive in that waiting. What is he waiting for? God. For aught we know, God could do the work instantly; the harvest might follow immediately upon the seed-sowing, like the genii in the fairy tale. God could bring the gift at once on man's asking. But our world is not the world of the Arabian Nights. God chooses to wait on man's co-operation. He allows him to do so much that man is tempted to suppose that he is himself the author of the whole process of production. But man has not cleared up the mystery of growth by calling it Evolution. Whatever scientific explanation the human mind can offer of a harvest-field, the element of mystery remains precisely where it was before, and it is that element of mystery that makes us fall down and worship; it is that element of mystery that fills us with a wonder akin to prayer; it is that element of mystery that turns every flower into an altar, and makes a sanctuary of every cornfield. God thus keeps His hold of us by the persistence of the mysterious element in things. If we could explain the harvest, we could explain God, and our fairest vision would fade into the light of common day.

¶ In harvest time the Greek saw the good goddess Ceres bearing her golden sheaves; the modern farmer too frequently sees only the result of his own knowledge, or of the latest patent manure. We pity the poor heathen Greek; ought we not rather to pity ourselves?[1]

The seed was spread in the furrowed earth,
And nurtured long in the gloom it lay,
Till the beckoning hours led on its birth
And drew it up to the laughing day.
The young spring soothed and cherished the blade,
And summer 'stablished the stately stem,
And the Lord was glad of the thing He'd made,
The fair green ears and the fruit of them.

[1] H. J. Wilmot-Buxton.

Summer had worked her will, and past
With her world of green, and autumn arose
And over the prospering tillage cast
A glory of change; the marshalled rows
Of bearded barley and four-square wheat
And pale oats, bearing a hundredfold,
Ripened under her shapely feet,
And out of the green ear grew the gold.

God, how wonderful this the thing,
The new-old miracle Thou hast done,
This proud triumphant fashioning,
Through rains and wind and shine of the sun,
Of ripe and rich abundance, borne
To-day to the sheltering homes of men;
For us Thy Spirit among the corn
Has moved, and one has grown as ten.[1]

IV.

The crown of harvest is woven in the loom of winter. Out of December comes June. Out of the Cross is fashioned the Crown. Perpetual summer would be loss unutterable. Perpetual summer would be perpetual mockery. There is no greenness of the grass in June unless there be the chillness of November. God needs the one if He would make the other; fashions the glory out of the decay; lays the field under the grip of ice that it may be golden with the waving grain.

¶ If any one should ask me where I have seen, in the course of my journeyings, the freshest verdure and the greenest grass, I think I might surprise you with my answer. I have seen the tenderest foliage where the fire has recently swept through the forest. Whether it was because of the contrast provided by the blackened timbers or not, I cannot say, but the truth is I never saw such tender green as springs amongst the blackened embers of the forest fire. Certain it is I have never seen such graces as those that spring when the tribulation has passed by. Oh! what a scorching flame it was; but the grass grows green there, and the flowers spring tender there by reason of the fire. There was a soil prepared which has suited the tender growth. Thank God for the tribulation that makes us greener and tenderer in consequence.[2]

[1] J. Drinkwater, *Poems of Men and Hours*, 24.   [2] Thomas Spurgeon.

¶ I suppose there are many of us who are lovers of the Tweed. It is so beautiful, that river Tweed, and is so haunted by a hundred memories. And yet that river, in whose gentle murmuring we catch the echo of unforgotten voices, rises where everything is bleak and bare. There is no beauty that we should desire it there. There is only the desolate and lonely moor. There is no song, no shadowing of tree, no gathering of the great dead beside its waters. Out of that winter God has made its summer, and to that summer come a thousand pilgrims, who know not, for they have never seen, the bleak and barren region of its rise.[1]

¶ Christ was content to have His crown of glory fashioned in agony. He took to Himself a crown of thorns. He came to wear it, and He would have no other. After the miracle of the loaves the people would have crowned Him with an earthly crown, and He fled from them. He was afraid of them. He hid Himself in a quiet place. They wanted to give Him an honour He could not accept. They wanted to put around His brow the golden circlet of a brief popularity and a civic leadership. But He would not have it. There was a crown of thorns waiting for Him, and He would not be defrauded of it. There was a coronation day coming, and it must not be anticipated. He was going by a path that few would be willing to follow—unto an honour that few would be wishful to win. Oh, who is strong enough and brave enough to go on as Christ went treading underfoot the golden crown of gain and reaching out after the thorny crown of sacrifice? He chose between the crown that glitters and the crown that wounds. He refused the one that He might wear the other.[2]

It was a thorn,
And it stood forlorn
In the burning sunrise land:
A blighted thorn
And at eve and morn
Thus it sighed to the desert sand:

Every flower,
By its beauty's power,
With a crown of glory is crowned;
No crown have I;
For a crown I sigh,
For a crown that I have not found.

[1] G. H. Morrison, *The Afterglow of God*, 94.
[2] P. C. Ainsworth, *A Thornless World*, 194.

Sad thorn, why grieve?
Thou a crown shalt weave,
But not for a maiden to wear;
That crown shall shine
When all crowns save thine
With the glory they gave are gone.

For thorn, my thorn,
Thy crown shall be worn
By the King of Sorrows alone.[1]

V.

The crown of harvest is not for ornament and beauty only, but for utility and beneficence. The ripe grain becomes the seed of future harvests. The husbandman takes of his best corn, safe in his granary, and casts it into the earth. He sacrifices what is precious to him for the sake of the harvest in the future. So it is with those who work for worldly success. They sacrifice time, rest, ease, comfort; they deny themselves pleasure now that they may reap a rich harvest in the end. So must it be with those who sow for eternity. They must deny themselves, they must sow in tears, they must go forth weeping and bearing this good seed. Jesus, our Master, sowed in tears, sowed in the agony and bloody sweat. He sacrificed Himself that He might gather the glorious harvest of a world redeemed, of a Church bought with His Precious Blood. He gave up His Sacred Body, like a seed to be bruised and crushed by cruel hands, and to be sown in the furrow of the grave. But the harvest came. That Body sown in the weakness of death was raised in the power of the resurrection, and so Jesus reaped the harvest for Himself and for us His people.

¶ The story of a night of seemingly fruitless toil, which resulted in great blessing, is retold in the *Illustrated Missionary News.* Miss Harris, of Medak, in India, utterly tired out, was one evening about to return home, when the son of the head-man of an important village, who had been poisoned, was hurriedly brought into the compound. She saw it was impossible to save him, and yet she kept the night vigil, rendering him the most menial service—service hardly fit for the village scavenger. The father

[1] Owen Meredith.

and brothers watched all the time, and although the missionary
returned home utterly spent next morning, feeling as if nothing
had been accomplished, the chief and his family, as they watched,
had judged between Hinduism and the Gospel of Christ, and
within six months the whole of the large family of the village
chief was baptized; soon a church and school were founded in the
village, and from the chief's family there are now (so runs the
encouraging report) no fewer than ten evangelists and Bible-
women.

> A Sower went forth to sow;
> His eyes were dark with woe;
> He crushed the flowers beneath his feet,
> Nor smelt their perfume, warm and sweet,
> That prayed for pity everywhere.
> He came to a field that was harried
> By iron, and to heaven laid bare;
> He shook the seed that he carried
> O'er that brown and bladeless place.
> He shook it, as God shakes the hail
> O'er a doomed land,
> When lightnings interlace
> The sky and the earth, and his wand
> Of love is a thunder-flail.
>   Thus did that Sower sow;
> His seed was human blood,
> And tears of women and men.
> And I, who near him stood,
> Said: "When the crop comes, then
> There will be sobbing and sighing,
> Weeping and wailing and crying,
> Flame, and ashes, and woe."

> It was an autumn day
> When next I went that way.
> And what, think you, did I see?
> What was it that I heard,
> What music was in the air?
> The song of a sweet-voiced bird?
> Nay—but the songs of many,
> Thrilled through with praise and prayer.
> Of all those voices not any
> Were sad of memory;

But a sea of sunlight flowed,
A golden harvest glowed,
And I said: "Thou only art wise,
God of the earth and skies!
And I praise Thee, again and again,
For the Sower whose name is Pain."[1]

[1] R. W. Gilder, *The Sower.*

THE BURDEN-BEARING GOD.

Literature.

Ainsworth (P. C.), *A Thornless World*, 154.
Barrett (G. S.), *Musings for Quiet Hours*, 27.
Clifford (J.), *The Secret of Jesus*, 57.
Cuyler (T. L.), *Stirring the Eagle's Nest*, 39.
Dix (M.), *Christ at the Door of the Heart*, 195.
Forbes (J. L.), *God's Measure*, 175.
Hamilton (J.), *Works*, vi. 430.
Jowett (J. H.), *Thirsting for the Springs*, 41.
Maclaren (A.), *Expositions* : Psalms li.–cxlv., 93.
Matheson (G.), *Messages of Hope*, 145.
Morrison (G. H.), *The Afterglow of God*, 320.
Neville (W. G.), *Sermons*, 312.
Raleigh (A.), *Quiet Resting-Places*, 331.
Spurgeon (C. H.), *Metropolitan Tabernacle Pulpit*, xlix. (1903), No. 2830.
Talmage (T. de W.), *Sermons*, vi. 145.
Vaughan (J.), *Sermons* (Brighton Pulpit), ix. (1872), No. 793.
Christian World Pulpit, lii. 74 (T. Jones).
Church of England Pulpit, xxxviii. 195.
Clergyman's Magazine, 3rd Ser., ii. (1891) 247 (H. G. Youard).
Literary Churchman, xxxii. (1886) (M. Fuller), 355.

The Burden-Bearing God.

Blessed be the Lord, who daily beareth our burden.—Ps. lxviii. 19.

The occasion of this psalm was the removal of the ark to Zion after it had been returned by the Philistines. Under the figures of a military invasion and occupation and settlement of the land, David represents Jehovah as Leader conquering His enemies, possessing Himself of their land, choosing a city for the seat of His Empire, and advancing in triumphal procession to enter upon His chosen residence. In the passage of the ark, the sign of God's presence, through the land to the site on Mount Zion, chosen as the religious Metropolis of the world, David sees a repetition in the religious realm of the earlier march into and occupation of the country in the birth-time of the nation. His mind runs back to that first victorious advance of God through the desert at the head of His chosen race; to the entrance of the victorious people into the land of Canaan; to the establishment of Zion as the place of His settled worship; and he sees in this second and more illustrious establishment of Zion as the place of God's rest not only the security for the blessedness of his own land, but the promise of a universal dominion, of which the fitful gleams of peace and happiness that they had as a nation under the new monarchy formed but a faint and imperfect foreshadowing.

And then, as he thinks of the splendid issue of this Divine occupation of Mount Zion, and the establishment there of the true worship, he breaks forth into a direct ascription of praise to God. He looks back on the long years of the Divine patience and forbearance; on not only the special times of deliverance, but the day-by-day guardianship and sustenance of God, and as he does so he says:

"Blessed be the Lord, who daily beareth our burden,
Even the God who is our salvation."

¶ In the Authorized Version this verse reads thus: "Blessed be the Lord, who daily loadeth us with benefits," the last two words being in italics, to show that they are not in the original. In point of fact, the Hebrew is equally capable of both interpretations, and may be rendered either, "Blessed be the Lord, who daily burdens us," that is, "with benefits"; or, "Blessed be the Lord, who daily beareth our burden." The great objection to the rendering which has become familiar to us all, "who daily loadeth us *with benefits*," is that these essential words are not in the original, and need to be supplied in order to make out the sense. Whereas, on the other hand, if we adopt the suggested emendation, "who daily beareth our burden," we get a still more beautiful meaning, which requires no forced addition in order to bring it out. There is a still more attractive rendering found in several of the ancient versions: "Blessed be the Lord who daily beareth us."

I.

THE INEVITABLE BURDEN.

Perhaps the most perplexing element in life is the wide sway of the Inevitable. The area of our freedom of choice is so painfully limited that, though we are turned into a capacious garden, stored with an incalculable wealth of flower and fruit, yet we can do so little ourselves, and are of so little account, that we are fain to despise our inheritance and neglect the care of our flower-beds and the watch of the fruit-trees. The life we contrive for ourselves is unexpectedly broken up or overpressed, till it has none of the shape and little of the beauty we intended; indeed, it sometimes seems little more than a central thoroughfare for the irresistible steeds of fate. The youth descries his far-off goal, and with measureless pluck and brightest hope sets out resolved to reach it, but is tripped up before he has travelled many yards; and though he rises, gains his feet and attempts the herculean task a hundred times, it is to find himself nearer indeed, but only to what is now a receding mark. The man of business builds his barns larger in time for them to be burnt by the desolating fire, or sends his boat to sea to be destroyed by the despotism of the storm. Pettiness and weariness eat the heart out of the life of artist and artisan, patriot and poet, and make existence and toil poor and bitter as the apples of Sodom. Thus life not only has its burdens but, in a true and not ignoble sense, it is itself a burden.

1. There is the awful burden of *personal existence.* It is a solemn thing to be able to say "I." And that carries with it this, that, after all sympathy, after all nestling closeness of affection, after the tenderest exhibition of identity of feeling, and of swift godlike readiness to help, each of us lives alone. Like the inhabitants of the islands of the Greek Archipelago, we are able to wave signals to the next island, and sometimes to send a boat with provisions and succour, but we are parted, "with echoing straits between us thrown." Every man, after all, lives alone, and society is like the material things round about us, which are all compressible, because the atoms that compose them are not in actual contact, but separated by slenderer or more substantial films of isolating air. Thus there is even in the sorrows which we can share with our brethren, and in all the burdens which we can help to bear, an element which cannot be imparted. "The heart knoweth its own bitterness"; and neither "stranger" nor other "intermeddleth" with the deepest fountains of "its joy."

¶ Dr. McLaren began to feel more keenly the inevitable solitariness of old age, as one by one his contemporaries left him. Reviewing old days in Lancashire, he said on one occasion, "There were three—Stowell Brown went home; there were two—Charles Williams gone—and I am left alone, it is very solitary." Two of his sisters reached ninety years of age and beyond it, but between 1903 and 1906 they, and two brothers-in-law and a sister-in-law, died. Referring to these family losses, he writes: "I feel as if we were like shipwrecked sailors clinging to the keel of an upturned boat, and seeing one after another lose their hold and sink. But thank God, we shall rise, and not sink when our hands can no longer grasp the seen. Each departure brings us sensibly more face to face with our soon-coming turn. May the gate open a little as we draw nearer it, and give us some beam of the light within. Let us keep nearer to the Lord of life and we shall be ready for our passing into life."[1]

2. Then again there is the burden of *responsibility,* which each has to bear for himself. A dozen soldiers may be turned out to

[1] E. T. McLaren, *Dr. McLaren of Manchester,* 242.

make a firing party to shoot the mutineer; and no man knows who fired the shot, but one man did fire it. And although there may have been companions, it was his rifle that carried the bullet, and his finger that pulled the trigger. We say, "The woman Thou gavest me tempted me, and I did eat." Or we say, "My natural appetites, for which I am not responsible, but Thou who madest me art, drew me aside, and I fell"; or we may say, "It was not I; it was the other." And then there rises up in our hearts a veiled form, and from its majestic lips comes, "Thou art the man"; and our whole being echoes assent—*Mea culpa; mea maxima culpa*—"My fault, my exceeding great fault." No man can bear that burden for me.

¶ Mr. Gladstone sometimes so far yielded to his colleagues as to sanction steps which he thought not the best, and may in this have sometimes erred; yet compromises are unavoidable, for no Cabinet could be kept together if its members did not now and then, in matters not essential, yield to one another. When all the facts of his life come to be known, instances may be disclosed in which he was the victim of his own casuistry or of his deference to Peel's maxim that a minister should not avow a change of view until the time has come to give effect to it. But it will also be made clear that he strove to obey his conscience, that he acted with an ever-present sense of his responsibility to the Almighty, and that he was animated by an unselfish enthusiasm for humanity, enlightenment, and freedom.[1]

3. Closely connected with the burden of responsibility there is another—the burden of the inevitable *consequences of transgression*, not only in the future, when all human bonds of companionship shall be broken, and each man shall "give account of himself to God," but here and now. The effects of our evil deeds come back to roost; and they never make a mistake as to where they should alight. If I have sown, I, and no one else, will gather. No sympathy will prevent to-morrow's headache after to-night's debauch, and nothing that anybody can do will turn the sleuth hounds off the scent. Though they may be slow-footed, they have sure noses and deep-mouthed fangs. "If thou be wise, thou shalt be wise for thyself; but if thou scornest, thou alone shalt bear it."

[1] J. Bryce, *Studies in Contemporary Biography*, 452.

¶ While Farrar dared not set limits to the infinite mercy of an all-merciful God and Father, none ever pointed with sterner finger to the ineluctable Nemesis that attends on sin. "The man who is sold under sin is dead, morally dead, spiritually dead; and such a man is a ghost, far more awful than the soul which was once in a dead body, for he is a body bearing about with him a dead soul. Better, far, far better for him to have cut off the right hand, or plucked out the right eye, than to have been cast as he has been, now in his lifetime—and as he will be cast until he repents, even beyond the grave, into that Gehenna of aeonian fire! It shall purify him, God grant, in due time; but oh! it shall agonize, because he has made himself, as yet, incapable of any other redemption. So that if any youth have wickedly thought in his heart that God is even such an one as himself—that he may break with impunity God's awful commandments, that he may indulge with impunity his own evil lusts, let him recall the sad experience of Solomon, 'Walk in the ways of thine heart, and in the sight of thine eyes; but know thou, that for all these things God will bring thee into judgment.' Let him remember the stern warning of Isaiah, 'Woe unto them that call evil good, and good evil; that put darkness for light, and light for darkness; that put bitter for sweet, and sweet for bitter! Therefore as the fire devoureth the stubble, and the flame consumeth the chaff, so shall their root be as rottenness, and their blossom shall go up as dust: because they have cast away the law of the Lord of hosts, and despised the word of the Holy One of Israel.'"[1]

4. The burdens grow with the growing life of man, so that the more the man has the more he has to carry; the severer the test of what he is in himself, of his conscience and heart, his sympathy and will, his faith and love. The boy strong, agile, without work and without want, is as free from care as a frisky kitten. The man solitary, without friend or home or responsibility, carries all his cares under his hat, and the thinner his life, the less there is of anxiety. But the father of a family is the bond of the house, the support of wife and children, and must bear himself erect under the cares of the home, of business, of parish, and of State. Add life, and you add care. Enlarge your world, and you increase your burdens. All strong emotions, all really great ideas, outleap our individual life, and carry us to the larger, deeper, fuller life of the world. Therefore the greatest life is the most burdened,

[1] R. Farrar, *Life of Dean Farrar*, 269.

and the saintliest soul feels the mystery and greatness of human
life most of all.   To the Greek, life is sunshine and joy; beauty
swims in upon the soul; his spirit is glad and he carries no care;
but the Hebrew, with his stern, inexorable righteousness, his
awful sense of stewardship, his solemn knowledge of a "covenant
with the Eternal," cries out for deliverance from the taint of guilt
and the burden of perplexity; and of all the Hebrews it is the
man of widest culture, maturest thought, and loftiest aspiration
who exclaims, "O wretched man that I am! who shall deliver me
from this body of death?"

¶ Who can tell us of the power which events possess—
whether they issue from us, or whether we owe our being to
them?   Do we attract them, or are we attracted by them?   Do
we mould them, or do they mould us?   Are they always unerring in their course?   Why do they come to us like the bee to the
hive, like the dove to the cote; and where do they find a resting-
place when we are not there to meet them?   Whence is it that
they come to us; and why are they shaped in our image, as
though they were our brothers?   Are their workings in the past
or in the future; and are the more powerful of them those that
are no longer, or those that are not yet?   Is it to-day or to-
morrow that moulds us?   Do we not all spend the greater part
of our lives under the shadow of an event that has not yet come
to pass?   I have noticed the same grave gestures, the footsteps
that seemed to tend towards a goal that was all too near, the pre-
sentiments that chilled the blood, the fixed, immovable look—I
have noticed all these in the men, even, whose end was to come
about by accident, the men on whom death would suddenly seize
from without.   And yet were they as eager as their brethren,
who bore the seeds of death within them.   Their faces were the
same.   To them, too, life was fraught with more seriousness than
to those who were to live their full span.   The same careful,
silent watchfulness marked their actions.   They had no time to
lose; they had to be in readiness at the same hour; so completely
had this event, which no prophet could have foretold, become the
very life of their life.[1]

> Here in our little island-home we bide
>   Our few brief years—the years that we possess.
> Beyond, the Infinite on every side
>   Holds what no man may know, though all may guess.

[1] M. Maeterlinck, *The Treasure of the Humble*, 51.

Earth, that is next to nothing in the sum
  Of things created—a brief mote in space,
With all her aeons past and yet to come.
  How we miscalculate our size—our place!

Yet are we men—details of the design,
  Set to our course, like circling sun and star;
Mortal, infinitesimal, yet divine
  Of that divine which made us what we are.

And yet this world, this microscopic ball,
  This cast-up grain of sand upon the shore,
This trivial shred and atom of the ALL,
  Is still our Trust, that we must answer for.

A lighthouse in the Infinite, with lamps
  That we must trim and feed until we die;
A lonely outpost of the unseen camps
  That we must keep, although we know not why.

Maker of all! Enough that Thou hast given
  This tempered mind, this brain without a flaw,
Enough for me to strive, as I have striven,
  To make them serve their purpose and Thy law.[1]

II.

The Burden-Bearer.

The Psalmist employs here that name of God which most strongly expresses the idea of supremacy and dominion. Rule and dignity are the predominant ideas in the word "Lord," as, indeed, the English reader feels in hearing it; and then, side by side with that, there lies the thought that the Highest, the Ruler of all, whose absolute authority stretches over all mankind, stoops to this low and servile office, and becomes the burden-bearer for all the pilgrims who put their trust in Him. This blending together of the two ideas of dignity and condescension to lowly offices of help and furtherance is made even more emphatic if we glance back at the context of the psalm. For there is no

---

[1] Ada Cambridge, *The Hand in the Dark*, 12.

place in Scripture in which there is flashed before the mind of the singer a grander picture of the magnificence and the glory of God than that which glitters and flames in the previous verses. The majestic greatness of God described in its earlier part seems purposely intended to heighten our sense of the wonder and blessedness of this God stooping from heaven to take on Himself the burdens which rest on His children on the earth.

And if we look deeper, this is not a case of contrast. It is not that there are sharply opposed to each other these two things, the gentleness and the greatness, the condescension and the magnificence, but that the former is the direct result of the latter; and it is just because He is Lord, and has dominion over all, that, therefore, He bears the burdens of all. For the responsibilities of the Creator are in proportion to His greatness, and He who has made man has thereby made it necessary that He should, if we will let Him, be Burden-bearer and our Servant. The highest must be the lowest, and just because God is high over all, therefore is He the Supporter and Sustainer of all. So we may learn the true meaning of elevation of all sorts, and from the example of the loftiest may draw the lesson for our more insignificant varieties of height, that the higher we are, the more we are bound to stoop, and that men are then likest God, when their elevation suggests to them responsibility, and when he that is chiefest becomes the servant.

1. *God takes our burdens upon Himself.*—There are burdens that men can help us with, but the heaviest burdens are those they cannot touch. "The heart knoweth its own bitterness." The burden of a hidden grief, of a besetting sin, of a lifelong trial of disease or of sorrow through the wrong-doing of others— men may not help much here. But God can and does help. He enters into the very life of those whom He teaches to trust Him. It is not they themselves who do the good things and speak the kind words and think the holy thoughts that go to the upbuilding of their spiritual house. It is God. He "worketh in you both to will and to do of his good pleasure." And so of the care that is cast upon Him. He bears it as He bears the sin. He is in the burdened soul, and so, though the outward and visible trial be unremoved, yet God bears it, for the Divine strength is in the

heart. God infuses His own power into the soul, until the downward pressure is no longer felt, and the burden is known to be
effectually "cast upon the Lord."

¶ The word redemption, all the past which it implies, all the
future which it points to, has for me a wonderful charm. I
cannot separate the idea of deliverance from the idea of God, or
ever think of man as blessed except as he enters into God's redeeming purpose, and labours to make others free. The bondage
of circumstances, of the world, but chiefly of self, has at times
seemed to me quite intolerable, the more because it takes away all
one's energy to throw it off, and then the difficulty of escaping to
God! of *asking* to have the weight taken away! Oh there is
infinite comfort in the thought that He hears all our cries for
rescue, and is Himself the Author and Finisher of it.[1]

2. *God's help is continual.*—He *daily* beareth our burden. He
will not suffer us, if we are guided by His teaching and Spirit, to
think of Him as simply transcending our life, living above it, and
out of it, and looking on it as from a distance; He assures us that
He shares it, is in it, and through and over and under all; in it
always; Himself bearing the burdens of it, not now and again, at
far-separated intervals and in the special crises of our experience;
but "daily"—"Blessed be the Lord, who daily beareth our
burden." It is the monotonous daily pressure of the same weight,
in the same wearying way, that slays the hope in us and makes
us sigh for the wings of a dove to bear us away to some place of
freedom and rest; and it is exactly that "daily" hour-by-hour
burden God Himself carries for us, and with us, and so sustains
us and trains us. Like some river that runs by the wayside and
ever cheers the traveller on the dusty path with its music, and
offers its waters to cool his thirsty lips, so, day by day, in the slow
iteration of our lingering sorrows, and in the monotonous recurrence of our habitual duties, there is with us the ever-present help
of the Ancient of Days, who measures out daily strength for the
daily load, and never sends the one without proffering the other.

¶ In feudal times the peasantry used to build their little
cottages beneath the shadow of their lord's castle-walls so that in
time of need they could easily take refuge within the stronghold,
and so that by their very proximity to their master's dwelling he
might be reminded that they cast upon him the burden of their

---

[1] *Life of Frederick Denison Maurice,* i. 520.

safe-keeping. So may we build the frail house of life beneath the shadow of the Almighty, that in the day of sore need we may surely find the way into the secret of His presence.

> Never a battle with wrong for the right,
> Never a contest that He doth not fight,
> Lifting above us His banner so white;
> Moment by moment we're kept in His sight.

> Never a trial and He is not there,
> Never a burden that He doth not bear,
> Never a sorrow that He doth not share,
> Moment by moment we're under His care.[1]

3. *God bears our burden by sharing it.*—A physical burden is one thing, a spiritual another, and there is no such literal transference in the moral realm as to make the spirit oblivious of the existence of such a thing as a burden at all. But in this they are alike, that those who help can help only on condition of themselves undergoing the pressure from which they release others. If you want to relieve any one of trouble, you must bear it yourself. Only so can spiritual release be secured. You give blessing at the price of feeling pain. As has been well said, "There is no bearing of a moral burden without feeling it to be a burden." And if God bears our burdens, then the pressure and the pain of them become His. Our trouble becomes His trouble, and our sorrow His sorrow. "In all their afflictions he was afflicted."

¶ If any one still insist that it seems irreverence, if not blasphemy, to speak of a suffering God, or to ascribe in any way pain or unhappiness to the Ever-Blessed, then, let me add, it may in some measure meet his difficulty to reflect that all moral suffering contains or carries with it what may be called an element of compensation, in virtue of which it is transmuted into a deeper joy. . . . And if this be so, then surely what we must find in Christ as the God-man is, not a being who stript or emptied Himself of His essential divinity in order to share in the weakness and suffering of humanity, but a manifestation of God in all the plenitude of the Divine Nature; and the whole life of the Man of Sorrows—His earthly lowliness, His mortal weakness, grief, and sorrow, His loneliness and forsakenness, His drinking of the cup of suffering to the very dregs, yea, in His very crucifixion and

---

[1] P. C. Ainsworth, *A Thornless World*, 159.

death—must be to us the disclosure of an ineffable joy triumphing over sorrow, of a Divine bliss in sacrifice which is the last, highest revelation of the nature of God.[1]

4. *It is not the burden, but the burden-bearer, that God sustains.* —It is not the heavy sorrow, but the bleeding heart that He takes into His strong keeping. And here we may notice the significant rendering of this text found in some of the most ancient versions: "Blessed be the Lord, who daily beareth us." So we can give God our burden only by giving Him our life. At this point the figure of a burden fails to represent accurately the toil and trouble of life, unless we remember it is a burden that cannot be laid down. It is bound to our shoulders by the cords of many necessities, Divine and human, and the answer to our prayer for help does not come in a loosening of these cords, but in inward refreshment of spirit. So the exhortation to us to cast our burden on the Lord and this promise of His sustaining grace do not speak to us of an occasional expedient to which the more trying experiences of life may drive us, but of the true relation of our life to God day by day.

¶ A father sitting in his study, sent his little boy upstairs to fetch a book that had been forgotten. The boy was long gone, and after a time the father thought he heard the sound of sobbing on the stairs. He went out, and at the top of the staircase he saw his son crying bitterly, with the great book he had tried to lift and carried so far, lying at his feet. "Oh, father!" the lad cried, "I cannot carry it, it is too heavy for me!" In a moment the father ran up the stairs, and stooping down, took up both the little lad and the book in his strong arms, and carried them down to the room below. Before he reached it, the child's tears were all dried up, and he was leaning on his father's arm, the burden and the trouble gone.[2]

5. *When God thus bears our burden the burden itself becomes a blessing.*—It carries him that carries it. It is like the wings of a bird; it is like the sails of a ship. In many lands the habit prevails, especially amongst the women, of carrying heavy loads on their heads; and all travellers tell us that the practice gives a dignity and a grace to the carriage, and a freedom and a swing to the gait, which nothing else will do. Depend upon it, that so

[1] John Caird. [2] G. S. Barrett, *Musings for Quiet Hours*, 29.

much of our burdens of work and weariness as is left to us, after we have cast them upon Him, is intended to strengthen and ennoble us.

¶ The bearing of God has been likened to a father carrying his child, to an eagle taking her young upon her wings, to the shepherd with the lamb in his bosom. But no shepherd, nor mother-bird, nor human father ever bore as the Lord bears. For He bears from within, as the soul lifts and bears the body. The Lord and His own are one. "To me," says he who knew it best, " to me to live is Christ." . . . It is not the sight of a visible leader, though the Gospels have made the sight imperishable, it is not the sound of Another's Voice, though that Voice shall peal to the end of time, that Christians only feel. It is something within themselves; another self—purer, happier, victorious. Not as a voice or example, futile enough to the dying, but as a new soul, is Christ in men.[1]

¶ The hindrances that baffle or overwhelm us, the small annoyances that rob our days of zest and sweetness, the body's perpetual chafing tyranny, in all these we are facing universal conditions, and bidden to realize a universal being. An infinitesimal fraction of the burden that God bears is on our shoulders —but we are not bearing it alone. This spiritual toil is no degrading punishment laid on us merely for our sins, but the measure of our sonship. Infinite patience seems often to be all that is asked of us. But patience is Godlike—patience is love submitting, and enduring, transmuting poison to sweetness in the life, as surely as enthusiasm is love conquering and striving, and flowing out towards God and man. Nor can we draw distinctions concerning their relative value to God.[2]

> The bonds that press and fetter,
> That chafe the soul and fret her,
> What man can know them better,
>   O brother men, than I ?
>
> And yet, my burden bearing,
> The five wounds ever wearing,—
> I too in my despairing
>   Have seen Him as I say ;—
> Gross darkness all around Him
> Enwrapt Him and enwound Him,—
> O late at night I found Him
>   And lost Him in the day !

[1] George Adam Smith.   [2] May Kendall.

Yet bolder grown and braver
At sight of one to save her
My soul no more shall waver,
   With wings no longer furled,—
But cut with one decision
From doubt and men's derision
That sweet and vanished vision
   Shall follow thro' the world.[1]

[1] F. W. H. Myers, *A Vision.*

A Sun and a Shield.

LITERATURE.

Davies (D.), *Talks with Men, Women and Children,* v. 145.

Foxell (W. J.), *God's Garden,* 142.

Kirkpatrick (A. F.), *The Book of Psalms* (Cambridge Bible), 509.

Maclaren (A.), *The Book of Psalms* (Expositor's Bible), ii. 449.

Morrison (G. H.), *The Unlighted Lustre,* 65.

Peabody (F. G.), *Mornings in the College Chapel,* ii. 127.

Pearce (J.), *The Alabaster Box,* 96.

Pearse (M. G.), *The God of Our Pleasures,* 49.

Spurgeon (C. H.); *Metropolitan Tabernacle Pulpit,* xxviii. (1882), No. 1659.

Voysey (C.), *Sermons,* xi. (1888), No. 20.

Wiseman (N.), *Children's Sermons,* 36.

Christian World Pulpit, xxiv. 332 (H. W. Beecher).

A Sun and a Shield.

The Lord God is a sun and a shield.—Ps. lxxxiv. 11.

An ancient legend tells that Abraham, in his untaught devoutness and yearning reverence. took the sun for his God until he observed the setting of its beams in the west. In the absence of authentic revelation, it is no more strange that reflective and reverential minds should exclaim, in the presence of a world of light, " The sun is our God," than that the Heaven-instructed Hebrew singer, dwelling in the light of God's countenance, should declare, " The Lord God is a sun "; for a more fitting material symbol of God than the sun it would be difficult to find, whether we consider the vastness of it, the glory of it, or the beneficence of it. Hidden by its very glory! So far off, yet finding out our distant world and bathing it in its genial warmth, breathing about it a new hope! So mighty, yet so gentle! Stooping not only to the lowest and least forms of life, but ministering to its hidden and shapeless beginnings.

Could there be a more felicitous and apposite representation of Him of whom an Apostle wrote: " God is light, and in him is no darkness at all "? As the sun opens the gates of day, floods the world with light, gives it without stint to palace or cottage, to peasant and prince, and enables us to discern a thousand pleasing objects, so God shines into our lives and gives us power to see a thousand moral glories. The secret of seeing is not in us. God is the great revealer. We are the organs favoured with the holy visions. We can see only what He is pleased to show us. But He is not slow to reveal Himself to our understanding, nor is the light inadequate. No nook or corner of our being need go unirradiated. If we open the life to God as we open the eye to the sun, we shall no longer be children of the darkness. " For God, who commanded the light to shine out of darkness, hath shined in our hearts, to give the light of the knowledge of the glory of God in the face of Jesus Christ."

¶ Nowhere else in the Old Testament is Jehovah directly called a sun, though the ideas conveyed by the metaphor are frequent. Cp. Ps. xxvii. i; Isa. x. 17, lx. 19, 20; Mal. iv. 2. Perhaps the prevalence of sun-worship in the East led to the avoidance of so natural and significant a metaphor. Even here the oldest Versions either had a different reading or shrank from a literal rendering. The LXX and Theodotion have: "For the Lord God loveth mercy and truth." The Targ. paraphrases: "For the Lord God is like a high wall and a strong shield," reading *shemesh* (=sun), but taking it in the sense of "battlement" (R.V. "pinnacles"), which it has in Isa. liv. 12. The Syr. gives: "Our sustainer and our helper." Only the later Greek Versions render the Massoretic text literally.[1]

¶ In his Hibbert Lectures on the Religion of the Babylonians Professor Sayce quotes a hymn to Samas the Sun-god, beginning:

O Sun-god, king of heaven and earth, director of things above and below,
O Sun-god, thou that clothest the dead with life, delivered by thy hands,
Judge unbribed, director of mankind,
Supreme is the mercy of him who is the lord over difficulty,
Bidding the child and offspring come forth, light of the world,
Creator of all thy universe, the Sun-god art thou.

¶ Another time Napoleon breaks out [in conversation with Gourgaud]: "Were I obliged to have a religion, I would worship the sun—the source of all life—the real God of the earth."[2]

I heard a Saint cry to the Sun—"Be dim.
Why shouldst thou rule on high with boastful ray,
Till fools adore thee as the God of Day,
Robbing thy Master's honour due to Him?"
But the sun-spirit, thro' each radiant limb
Translucent as a living ember coal,
Glowed. At the anger of the seraph soul
His golden orb trembled from boss to rim.

Then made he answer as a dove that sings,
"God's glory is my glory, and my praise
Only His praising. They, who kneel to me,
See thro' the waving of my orient wings
A choir of stars with voices like the sea,
Singing hosanna in the heavenly ways."[3]

[1] A. F. Kirkpatrick, *The Book of Psalms*, 509.
[2] Lord Rosebery, *Napoleon: The Last Phase*, 171.   [3] Lord De Tabley.

I.

GOD IS A SUN.

1. The sun is the centre of power in the system where it stands. There is nothing that can hold out against it. All planets are obliged to own their allegiance to it. They march to its music. They cannot wander or get out of the path which its power prescribes for them. The sun is the governor of the planetary kingdom—central, uncontradicted, unwasting, unexhausted and inexhaustible, steadfast, going forth for ever and for ever. So there is a sublime centre in that higher creation, in conscious human life. In the realm of intelligence, in the realm of righteousness or morality, in the great superior realm of mind, there is a central power. Amidst all the apparent detonations and explosions and miscarriages of minor human life upon this sphere there is, nevertheless, a great central influence that is holding mankind to their career, to their general orbit. The government of God in its extensiveness, in its patient perseverance, in its power universal, could not be more fitly represented than by this symbolization of the sun itself. The universality of God—"omnipresence," as it is called—is a thing somewhat difficult to be understood, as all things that reach toward or are born of the infinite are to finite intelligence; nevertheless, the outreaching of the sun is everywhere. Both of the poles recognize its presence. The equator never abandons the light and warmth of the sun. Wherever the earth and all its luminaries may travel, and wherever the satellites of the sun may go, there is its power. There is no thunder, no utterance in it. It is silent, but it is there.

¶ Fénelon had many friends affectionately attached to him, in Versailles, Paris, and other parts of France; but in his banishment he saw them but very seldom. Many of them were persons of eminent piety. "Let us all dwell," he says in one of his letters, "in our only Centre, where we continually meet, and are all one and the same thing. We are very near, though we see not one another; whereas others, who even live in the same house, yet live at a great distance. God reunites all, and brings together the remotest points of distance in the hearts that are united to Him.

I am for nothing but unity; that unity which binds all the parts to the centre. That which is not in unity is in separation; and separation implies a plurality of interests, self in each too much fondled. When self is destroyed, the soul reunites in God; those who are united in God are not far from each other. This is the consolation which I have in your absence, and which enables me to bear this affliction patiently, however long it may continue." [1]

2. Another idea is suggested by the sun. Many of us have been oppressed by the thought of a distant God; we sometimes have thought of Him as far away, as having His throne in the remote heaven of heavens. But if the sun can have its being ninety million miles away, and yet can fall with such power as to heat a continent, and with such exquisite nicety as to make the rosebud redden, why should it seem a thing incredible to us that the Creator who fashioned that glorious lamp should dwell apart immeasurably far, yet touch and turn and bless and save humanity? He takes up the isles as a very little thing—the nations before Him are as nothing. Yet He knows the way that I take; He understands my thought; He will not quench the smoking flax nor break the bruised reed. Powerful, yet very far away; thoughtful and tender, though hidden in the distance.

¶ God is the God of *all*, and yet He is *my* God. At the same moment He pervades heaven and earth, takes charge of the sustenance, progress, and growing happiness of the unbounded creation, and He is present with me, as intent upon my character, actions, wants, trials, joys, and hopes, as if I were the sole object of His love. [2]

3. God is a sun: that is infinity of blessing. No man among us can conceive the measure of the light and heat of the sun. They are beyond conception great. Light and heat have been continually streaming forth throughout many ages, yet all that has come forth of it is far less than that which still remains. For all practical purposes the light and heat of the sun are infinite; and certainly in God all blessedness is absolutely infinite. There is no measuring it. We are lost. We can only say, "Oh, the depths of the love and goodness of God!" In being heirs of God we possess all in all. There is no bound to our blessedness in God. Further, if God be called a sun, it is to let us know

[1] T. C. Upham, *Life of Madame Guyon*, 455.   [2] W. E. Channing.

that we have obtained an immutability of blessedness, for He is "the Father of lights with whom is no variableness, neither shadow of turning." God is not love to-day and hate to-morrow; He saith, "I am God, I change not." There are said to be spots in the sun which diminish the light and heat which we receive; but there are no such spots in God; He shines on with the boundless fulness of His infinite love toward His people in Christ Jesus. "This God is our God for ever and ever." If we were to live as long as Methuselah, we should find His love and power and wisdom to be the same, and we might confidently count upon being blessed thereby. What treasures of mercy do we possess in being able to say, "O God, thou art my God"! We have the source of mercy, the infinity of mercy, and the immutability of mercy to be our own.

¶ What is the glory of the sun? Is it its power, its energy, or is it not the way in which it finds out things one by one and gives itself away to them? I have watched the sun rising amidst the mountains, crowning them with gold and robing them with purple, until they stood like lords-in-waiting arrayed for the coming of their king, and it has seemed in keeping with the sun's greatness. But little by little it rose higher, and now it covered the fir trees with glory, and now it lit up the moss of the rock. Still higher rose the sun, and then it reached the meadows, and every tiny grass blade caught its warmth and energy, and every flower had its golden cup filled to the brim. And lower still it went down, to the seeds that were buried in darkness, and whispered to them of hope, and put new strength into them. Think if I could tell the tiny flower how far off the sun is, how many myriads of miles away, how great it is, how splendid in its majesty. "Surely," the flower would say, "it can never stoop to me, or find me out, or care for me, or minister to my want!" Ah, but it does; it gives itself to the flower with such tenderness and thoroughness as if there were not another in the round world. Surely this is the glory of our God. We think of Him in the greatness of His power. We sing of Him, "Who is like unto thee . . . glorious in holiness, fearful in praises, doing wonders?" But is not this His glory, that He comes to us away by ourselves, one by one, and gives Himself to us separately, stooping to the lowest, reaching to the farthest off, finding out the most hidden? The sun is not going to put to shame the ingenuity of our Father's love.[1]

[1] M. G. Pearse, *The God of our Pleasures*, 56.

Behold the sun, that seemed but now
  Enthroned overhead,
Beginning to decline below
  The globe whereon we tread;
And he, whom yet we look upon
  With comfort and delight,
Will quite depart from hence anon,
  And leave us to the night.

Thus time, unheeded, steals away
  The life which nature gave;
Thus are our bodies every day
  Declining to the grave;
Thus from us all our pleasures fly
  Whereon we set our heart;
And when the night of death draws nigh
  Thus will they all depart.

Lord! though the sun forsake our sight,
  And mortal hopes are vain,
Let still Thine everlasting light
  Within our souls remain;
And in the nights of our distress
  Vouchsafe those rays divine,
Which from the Sun of Righteousness
  For ever brightly shine![1]

4. Without a favourable medium and a suitable object, the
sunlight can do little. All the sunlight of all time cannot
illumine a man who is blind. The suns of all the seasons can
avail nothing for the dead. There must be the faculty to receive
the light and to respond to it. The sun cannot give life, it can
only develop it. It cannot transform the nature. But He who
is the Light of the World is also the Lord and Giver of life. See
Him by whom grace and truth come to us. See Him as He
bends over the couch of the dead maiden, and, taking her by the
hand, says, "Maiden, arise." See Him as He lays those fingers
on the blind man's eyes and says, "Be opened." In Him the
blessed grace of forgiveness is ours. His coming is in relation to
our sins—His very name is Jesus, for He shall save His people
from their sins. "The wages of sin is death; but the gift of God

[1] George Wither.

is eternal life through Jesus Christ our Lord." He gives to us a new nature whose instinct it is to know God and to serve Him. He will give grace. And we have to receive that grace, and avail ourselves of it. The golden sun shall in vain pour its beauty where the plough has not turned the furrow and the seed-corn has not been flung. Man's work is to avail himself of the sun and to adapt himself to its times and seasons. And even so it is with God's grace. It cannot avail him anything who does not receive it and respond to it. "As many as received him, to them gave he power to become the sons of God."

¶ Richard Jefferies is closely akin to Wordsworth in his overpowering consciousness of the life in nature. This consciousness is the strongest force in him, so that at times he is almost submerged by it, and he loses the sense of outward things. In this condition of trance the sense of time vanishes; there is, he asserts, no such thing, no past, or future, only now, which is eternity. In *The Story of my Heart,* a rhapsody of mystic experience and aspiration, he describes in detail several such moments of exaltation or trance. He seems to be peculiarly sensitive to sunshine. As the moon typifies to Keats the eternal essence in all things, so to Jefferies the sun seems to be the physical expression or symbol of the central Force of the world, and it is through gazing on sunlight that he most often enters into the trance state.[1]

¶ Francis Thompson in his "Orient Ode" seems to worship the Sun, but it is because he finds Christ in that symbol:

> Lo, of thy Magians I the least
> Haste with my gold, my incenses and myrrhs,
> To thy desired epiphany, from the spiced
> Regions and odorous of Song's traded East.
> Thou, for the life of all that live
> The victim daily born and sacrificed;
> To whom the pinion of this longing verse
> Beats but with fire which first thyself did give,
> To thee, O Sun—or is't, perchance, to Christ?[2]

5. The heat and light of the sun come to this world through the surrounding atmosphere. Without the envelope of closely clinging air that engirdles this globe like some diaphanous garment, the heat of the sun and all the light of it would fall in-

[1] C. F. E. Spurgeon, *Mysticism in English Literature,* 68.
[2] E. Meynell, *The Life of Francis Thompson* (1913), 210.

effectually on the earth. When we climb a mountain we get nearer the sun; would one not naturally think that it ought to get hotter there? As a matter of fact it gets colder as we rise till we reach the peaks that are robed with perpetual snow. The reason is that we are piercing through that air which wraps and enwraps this little earth of ours. It is the atmosphere that mediates the sun, that catches and stores and distributes the heat. Were there no air, but only empty space, then the greenest valley would be like Mont Blanc, and the tropics would be ice-bound in a perpetual winter, though the sun in itself were as fiery-hot as ever.

May we not make use of this mystery of nature to illumin-ate a kindred mystery of grace? It is one of the ways of God to grant His blessings through an intermediary. You say that the sun is the source of heat and light; why then should anything be intruded between earth and sun? One can only answer, So the Creator works—without that mediating element all is lost. You say that God is the source of love and blessing; why should anything intervene betwixt God and man? One can only answer that it is the way of heaven to grant its richest blessing through a mediator. How often men and women have said, "I do not feel any need of Christ or Calvary. I believe in God, I reverence and worship God; but the sacrifice and the atonement just confuse me. They appear to be outside of me altogether; I cannot make them real to my heart." But through every sphere of God's activity runs the great principle of media-tion. The presence of Christ is like the air, making available for our need the love of God. Remove the atmosphere, and the sun will still shine in heaven. Take away Jesus, and God will still be love. Banish the air, and the sun will not lose its heat. Banish the Christ, and God will not lose His power. But with the air gone, the glory of the sun will never so fall as to bless our little world, and with Jesus banished, the mercy and love of God may stream on other realms but not on ours. Christ is the mediator of the better covenant. He stands—the vital breath—'twixt God and us. Through Him the sunshine of heaven's love can reach us, and in the rays of that sunshine we are blessed.

¶ What was said with truth of Bishop Fraser of Manchester was, in a less direct and practical way, true of Stanley: "He was daily bringing down light from Heaven into the life of other people." No one could long come in contact with Stanley without feeling that he was walking in the light, and without being affected by its radiation. It was this background that gave dignity to his simplicity of character, that preserved the spiritual elements of his nature from materialism, that gilded his social intercourse with a tenderness, an unobtrusiveness, a sincerity, an evenness of temper, and a consideration for others, that permeated, purified, and strengthened the society in which he moved.[1]

II.

GOD IS A SHIELD.

To the Psalmist God was not only a Sun radiating forth good but also a Shield protecting from evil—the source not only of life and joy but also of security. As the Sun, God may be considered as dwelling in inaccessible light; whilst as a Shield He may be regarded as so protecting His people that they cannot be approached. Life may be looked upon as a battle-field, on which we have protection from God, if we are on His side; for the battle is His. By the figure of a shield, this verse is connected with ver. 9 : "Behold, O God our shield, and look upon the face of thine anointed."

¶ The ancient warrior bore strapped on his arm a shield of brass or of wood covered with leather, armed with which he rushed into battle and turned death aside. In modern warfare the shield is quite unserviceable; it hangs with bows and arrows in the museum of ancient armour. But, as Parker says, " No word ever becomes obsolete which has once deeply touched the heart of humanity. The shield will always be a weapon of spiritual warfare; God will never cease to be a shield to all them that trust in Him." The believer's defence is complete; before and behind, on the right hand and on the left, he is beset by the protective power of God. This was a favourite thought of Luther's, whose famous spiritual battle-song opens with the words:

A safe stronghold our God is still,
A trusty shield and weapon.

"What will you do," Luther was asked, "if the Duke, your protector, should no longer harbour you?" "I will take my shelter," he answered, "under the broad shield of Almighty God."

[1] R. E. Prothero, *Life of Dean Stanley*, ii. 23.

Modern nations, with their immense armies and fleets, are apt
to forget how insecure they are without that Divine protection.
Foolish are they if they "put their trust in reeking tube and iron
shard." He who spread His shield over Abraham and his little
Hebrew army must equally be the "Lord of the far-flung battle
line." He is the ultimate safeguard of all national greatness, and
no weapon formed against Him shall prosper.[1]

1. The Lord is to us first a sun and then a shield. Remember
how David puts it elsewhere: "The Lord is my light and my
salvation." Light first, salvation next. He does not save us in
the dark, neither does he shield us in the dark. He gives enough
sunlight to let us see the danger so that we may appreciate the
defence. We are not to shut our eyes and so find safety, but we
are to see the evil and hide ourselves. Ought we not to be very
grateful to God that He so orders our affairs? Ours is not a
blind faith, receiving an unknown salvation from evils which are
unperceived; this would be a poor form of life at best. No, the
favour received is valued because its necessity is perceived. The
heavenly Sun lights up our souls, and makes us see our ruin and
lie down in the dust of self-despair; and then it is that grace
brings forth the shield which covers us, so that we are no more
afraid, but rejoice in the glorious Lord as the God of our salvation.

¶ Most people in their religious experience think of God as
a shield. He stands between them and the storm. They hide
beneath the shadow of His wings. It is the religion of special
Providence and of Divine interposition. God shields His people
from the burning heat. Religion is a protective system—a very
present help in time of trouble. Some people, on the other hand,
think of God as a sun. When all is bright and cloudless, then they
can believe, but when it storms, then the universe seems Godless. When God is in heaven, all's right with the world. I
remember a comfortable and church-going citizen who was over-
taken by a great domestic sorrow, and said of it, "It never
occurred to me that such a thing could happen." He had grown
so in the habit of living in the sunshine that he was as helpless
as a child in the dark.[2]

2. Look at the text in another way. When the sun shines
upon a man he is made the more conspicuous by it. Suppose a
hostile army to be down in the plain, and a soldier in our ranks is

[1] J. Strachan, *Hebrew Ideals*, i. 74.   [2] F. G. Peabody.

sent upon some errand by his captain. He must pass along the hillside. The sun shines upon him as he tries to make his way among the rocks and trees. Had it been night he could have moved safely, but now we fear that the enemy will surely pick him off; for the sunshine has made him conspicuous. He will have need to be shielded from the many cruel eyes. Christian men are made conspicuous by the very fact of their possessing God's grace. "Ye are the light of the world," and a light must be seen. "A city set on a hill cannot be hid." If God gives light, He means that light to be seen ; and the more light He gives us the more conspicuous we shall be. He is our sun, and He shines upon us ; we reflect His light, and so become ourselves a light ; and in doing so we run necessary risks. The more brightly we shine the more will Satan and the world try to quench our light. This, then, is our comfort. The Lord God, who is a sun to us, will also be a shield to us. Did He not say to Abraham, "Fear not, Abram : I am thy shield, and thy exceeding great reward " ?

¶ By the term *shield* is meant that our salvation, which would otherwise be perilled by countless dangers, is in perfect safety under God's protection. The favour of God in communicating life to us would be far from adequate to the exigencies of our condition, unless at the same time, in the midst of so many dangers, He interposed His power as a buckler to defend us.[1]

¶ Grove mentioned that at some period when Havana was under martial law, a man had been killed in a row in the street. Everybody ran away except an Englishman, who, having nothing to do with the murder, thought there was no occasion to do so, and was, of course, immediately arrested. Some one naturally was found to swear that he was the culprit, and he was sentenced to be shot next morning. The English Consul (Mr. Crawford), hearing what was going on, went in full uniform to the place of execution and claimed the man as a British subject. The officer in charge of the firing party showed his orders, and said he could not give him up. "Very well," said Mr. Crawford, "at least you will not object to my shaking hands with him before he is shot ?" "By no means," was the answer. He then walked up, whipped the Union Jack out of his pocket and threw it round the man. "Now," he said to the officer, "shoot if you dare." The officer applied for instructions to the Governor, and the prisoner's innocence was soon made clear.[2]

[1] Calvin.　　　[2] M. E. Grant Duff, *Notes from a Diary, 1892-5*, i. 126.

The Home of the Soul.

LITERATURE.

Clifford (J.), *Social Worship an Everlasting Necessity*, 26.

Glover (R.), *The Forgotten Resting-place*, 3.

Liddon (H. P.), *Christmastide in St. Paul's*, 240.

Marten (C. H.), *Plain Bible Addresses*, 173.

Myres (W. M.), *Fragments that Remain*, 122.

Rendall (G. H.), *Charterhouse Sermons*, 276.

Richards (W. R.), *For Whom Christ Died*, 141.

Shannon (F. F.), *The Soul's Atlas*, 68.

Spurgeon (C. H.), *New Park Street Pulpit*, i. (1855), No. 46.

Stephen (R.), *Divine and Human Influence*, ii. 255.

Christian Commonwealth, xxxi. (1911) 557 (R. J. Campbell).

Christian World Pulpit, xlvii. 396 (W. Sinclair); lxiv. 419 (E. H. Eland); lxv. 102 (R. Rainy).

The Home of the Soul.

**Lord, thou hast been our dwelling place
In all generations.—Ps. xc. 1.**

The 90th Psalm, says Isaac Taylor, might be cited as perhaps the
most sublime of human compositions, the deepest in feeling, the
loftiest in theologic conception, the most magnificent in its imagery.
True is it in its report of human life as troubled, transitory, and
sinful; true in its conception of the Eternal—the Sovereign
and the Judge, and yet the refuge and the hope of men who,
notwithstanding the most severe trials of their faith, lose not their
confidence in Him, but who, in the firmness of faith, pray for,
as if they were predicting, a near-at-hand season of refreshment.
Wrapped, one might say, in mystery, until the distant day of
revelation should come, there is here conveyed the doctrine of
Immortality; for in this very plaint of the brevity of the life of
man, and of the sadness of these his few years of trouble, and
their brevity, and their gloom, there is brought into contrast the
Divine immutability: and yet it is in terms of a submissive piety:
the thought of a life eternal is here in embryo. No taint is there
in this psalm of the pride and petulance, the half-uttered blasphemy,
the malign disputing or arraignment of the justice or goodness of
God, which have so often shed a venomous colour upon the language
of those who have writhed in anguish, personal or relative. There
are few, probably, among those who have passed through times of
bitter and distracting, woe, or who have stood, the helpless spectators of the miseries of others, that have not fallen into moods of
mind violently in contrast with the devout and hopeful melancholy
which breathes throughout this Ode. Rightly attributed to the
Hebrew lawgiver or not, it bespeaks its remote antiquity, not
merely by the majestic simplicity of its style, but negatively, by
the entire avoidance of those sophisticated turns of thought which
belong to a late—a lost—age, in a people's intellectual and moral

history.   This psalm, undoubtedly, is centuries older than the moralizing of that time, when the Jewish mind had listened to what it could never bring into a true assimilation with its own mind—the abstractions of the Greek Philosophy.[1]

1. There was a tradition among the Jews, although these traditions are not altogether trustworthy, that Moses, the man of God, wrote this psalm or prayer.   And it has always been felt that the psalm seemed to have some special connexion with, or reference to, the experience and the impressions of the children of Israel in the days that they were doomed to wander up and down in the wilderness without being allowed to enter into the Promised Land. And there is much in the psalm that corroborates that view.   It is the psalm of a generation of men who felt themselves to be wasting away under God's wrath, consumed by His anger.   They are spending their years as a tale that is told.   The vanity and emptiness of life are pressed home upon them with great severity. At the same time, it is not a psalm of mere wailing and lamentation.   Very far from it.   There is the exercise of faith in it, not only in the first verse, but in the appeal to God to come and dwell with them as their case requires, and make them experience His mercy.   The cloud is dark that hangs over the congregation, but faith is still, as it were, seeing the bow in the cloud.

2. By whomsoever written, the psalm makes it plain that the writer was thinking and speaking not only for himself, but for all his own people of Israel, if not for the whole race of mankind. These opening words are the Eternal Gospel of the Fatherly Love of God, in which the sons of men can ever find their "home." How precious is that last word, and what a pity that our translators did not adopt it instead of "dwelling place."   Alas! how many there are whose dwelling-place is not a "home."   The Prayer-Book Version is a little better in giving us the word "refuge"; for to most of us home is the best refuge we can find, if not the only one.   It is our retreat after the toils and turmoils of the busy world, our refuge from the strife of tongues, our covert from the scornful rebuke of the proud.   Our home, if it be as God intended it should be, is the place where all that is best

[1] Isaac Taylor, *Spirit of the Hebrew Poetry*, 161.

and sweetest in life is cherished and enjoyed, the one sacred shrine where even the outcast can find love, and the stern, hard heart can also find an opportunity for giving a little love in return. Home is the scene of our keenest anxieties and our bitterest griefs, no less than of our most restful peace and of our highest joys. But in the process of evolving and growing mankind, all things are yet unfinished and imperfect; even our very homes are not full enough of purity and peace and love to satisfy the immortal heart of man. Defect, disturbance, and decay, with all the varied chances of this mortal life, make even the best of homes partial and transient. Our immortal souls want everlasting security, unbroken peace, unalloyed happiness. Nothing less than the Eternal God can be a perfect refuge, a perfect home, for the souls of His children. And in Him is all that the most craving and grasping can possibly desire. God has made us so that nothing shall, nothing can, ever satisfy us but Himself. And when we have found Him, and made Him our real refuge and home, we have gained the Eternal Peace, which the whole world can neither give nor take away.

¶ "Lord, thou hast been our dwelling place in all generations." Beside that venerable and ancient abode, that has stood fresh, strong, incorruptible, and unaffected by the lapse of millenniums, there stands the little transitory canvas tent in which our earthly lives are spent. . . . If I make God my Refuge, I shall get something a great deal better than escape from outward sorrow— namely, an amulet which will turn the outward sorrow into joy. The bitter water will still be given me to drink, but it will be filtered water, out of which God will strain all the poison, though He leaves plenty of the bitterness in it; for bitterness is a tonic. The evil that is in the evil will be taken out of it in the measure in which we make God our Refuge, and all will be "right that seems most wrong," when we recognize it to be "His sweet will."[1]

I.

HOME.

1. Men everywhere have either burrowed under the ground or built above it, and sought to provide some kind of place in which

[1] A. Maclaren, *The God of the Amen*, 166.

they might dwell, and which they call home. Rude and imperfect it often is, made of such materials as they could find to hand, or in such ways as their faculties could devise. Or where civilization and intelligence have advanced or wealth abounded, men have built houses larger, more splendid, and furnished with ample conveniences. But in all, the aim and desire have been to have a place where they could obtain shelter and rest.

The wilderness episode in Israel's life meant that they had no home. They were always moving, moving—all the year, and then another year, for forty years. Never settling down at home, always moving—you might well call such an experience a wilderness. Old Egypt, the land of bondage, had been bad enough; but at least there were homes in Egypt, and it was no wonder if at times the people longed to turn back into Egypt. Homes had been promised in Canaan, but that promise was for the benefit of their children. These adult Israelites through one long forlorn generation must be always moving. And the long-continued homelessness taught them something. For all time to come the memory of that homeless wilderness would make them value the homes that God should give them in Canaan.

¶ Archbishop Leighton died in an inn in 1684 during a visit to London. He had often expressed a wish to die in an inn "because it looks so like a pilgrim's going home, to whom this world is all a pilgrimage."[1]

¶ How passionately the longing could possess Stevenson is familiar to all those who have read the thoughts of home from abroad in *Songs of Travel* and *Vailima Letters*. In a deeper sense, as it concerned the inward life, the same thing is true. Apparently an unresting traveller in the spiritual country, he yet had come to rest upon certain great convictions, in which his spirit had its home. These he expresses often with an evident sense of relief and the comfortable peace of assurance. In the longest journey of all, the lifelong journey, the same shadowy but hospitable and firelit sweetness awaits its close. The Covenanters pass the dark river amid a "storm of harsh and fiercely jubilant noises" which add a tenfold peacefulness to the shores which they had reached. For himself, who does not know the Requiem which, written seven years before his death, was inscribed upon his tombstone at the last:

[1] A. Alexander, in *The Expository Times*, xii. 563.

Under the wide and starry sky,
Dig the grave and let me lie.
Glad did I live and gladly die,
    And I laid me down with a will.
This be the verse you grave for me ;
" Here he lies where he longed to be ;
Home is the sailor, home from sea,
    And the hunter home from the hill."

Such words imply more than they express ; perhaps they mean
more than the speaker knows.   In them we hear echoes of a great
voice that calls home the thinker to faith, the struggler to
achievement, and the dead from dying to a new life.   And so
there is arrival as well as travel, after all.   Indeed the two are
combined in regard to faith, and achievement, and that dimly
seen but beautiful country beyond the grave.   In all these, the
true life is at once making for a land that is very far off, and
yet at the same time it is ever coming home.[1]

Now more the bliss of love is felt,
    Though felt to be the same ;
'Tis still our lives in one to melt,
    Within love's sacred flame :

Each other's joy each to impart,
    Each other's grief to share ;
To look into each other's heart,
    And find all solace there :

To lay the head upon one breast,
    To press one answering hand,
To feel through all the soul's unrest,
    One soul to understand :

To go into the teeming world,
    The striving and the heat,
With knowledge of one tent unfurl'd
    To welcome weary feet :

A shadow in a weary land,
    Where men as wanderers roam :
A shadow where a rock doth stand—
    The shadow of a Home.[2]

[1] John Kelman, *The Faith of Robert Louis Stevenson*, 183.
[2] George J. Romanes.

2. There are places in which men live, calling them homes, but in which there is no comfort, and not even the appearance of it. Poor, wretched dwellings and abodes of poverty, squalor, and suffering, where there is scarce a glow on the hearth to warm, or a morsel on the table to soothe the pangs of hunger. Or there are dwellings of misery and wretchedness from vice and its effects, scenes of brawling, strife, and anger. Or there are abodes where, though there may be earthly abundance and luxuries, there is a moral coldness, a want of sympathy and affection between those who dwell under the same roof; and so with all its comforts, it is a home of misery. But it is not such that we associate with the true idea of home, for the right and good and true home is a place of happiness and comfort.

¶ How can those who do not know Christ and our Father's home in heaven form any idea of them save from what they see in us and our homes? That is the way the heathen learn of Christ and heaven. In Hangchow, China, Mrs. Mattox had been accustomed to invite the little children to her home and make them happy there. Once a Chinese teacher was talking to some of them, and asked, "Where do you want to go when you die— to heaven?" "No," they answered. "To hell?" "No." "Where, then, do you want to go?" "To Mrs. Mattox's house," they replied. They could not imagine anything more heavenly than that.[1]

3. There is no place on earth which is so dear to the heart as home, if the home is such as we usually associate with the name. It is connected with our earliest and happiest resolutions. It is the place round which are twined the most tender and hallowed memories. It is the spot in which are centred our fondest affections, and it contains in it the hopes of all the purity and goodness which are to come hereafter. However humble or lowly, still it is home, a dearer and a sweeter spot than all the world beside. And it is one of the most endearing aspects in which God can be regarded, when He is revealed as the home of His people, as the habitation, "the dwelling and abiding place," of the soul in all time and under every circumstance.

¶ Arriving in New York, after their tour in Canada, the party proceeded by the night train to Washington, where they spent a day driving round and seeing all the chief buildings, and then, two

[1] R. E. Speer, *Men Who were Found Faithful*, 141.

days afterwards, they went on board the "Lucania." My father writes: "Never shall I forget the joy of this morning and the excitement of seeing, as we drove up, the funnels of the grand 'Lucania': I passed through the crowded wharf as on enchanted ground, and stepped on board with a feeling of delight and gratitude reaching almost to ecstasy. Thank God for this trip, for all His mercies, for all the kindness of friends and for the pleasure and instruction of the experience; but oh, the joy of returning to the old country, and to *home*! That swallows up all other gratification in one great rejoicing. When at length I reach the gates of death, may I have the same joy in prospect of the heavenly home!"[1]

¶ As one contemplates Mr. Gladstone's triumphs, one finds oneself recurring in memory to the beautiful background of domestic quiet and stately dignity in which he was as much or more at home than in the public gaze. I can see him now in an old wideawake and cloak—trudging off in the drizzle of an October morning to an early service. I remember how, at Hawarden in 1896, on one of the sad evenings after my father's death, I dined alone with him and one other guest, and with what beautiful consideration he talked quietly on about things in which he thought we should be interested — things that needed neither comment nor response, and all so naturally and easily, that one hardly realized the tender thoughtfulness of it all. And last of all, I remember how I came one evening at a later date to dine at Hawarden, and was shown into a little half-lit ante-room next the dining-room. He was just at the beginning of his last illness, and he was suffering from discomfort and weakness. There on a sofa he sat, side by side with Mrs. Gladstone; they were sitting in silence, hand in hand, like two children, the old warrior and his devoted wife. It seemed almost too sacred a thing to have seen; but it is not too sacred to record, for it seemed the one last perfect trans-figuring touch of love and home.[2]

II.

GOD OUR HOME.

Moses was a homeless man. Early in life he had fled from Pharaoh's court, where he had been brought up. When he lived in Midian as the son-in-law of Jethro, he took part in the wandering life of the desert tribes. When he was called upon to deliver the children of Israel from Egypt, and to be their

---

[1] *The Life of Henry J. Pope*, by his Son, 174.
[2] A. C. Benson, *Along the Road*, 53.

leader and lawgiver, he shared their wanderings for forty years
in the great and terrible wilderness, where they had no fixed
abode. In all their journeys they had before them the prospect
of Canaan, the good land which God was to give them for a
possession. But Moses was not permitted to enter upon that
goodly inheritance. He was to see it from afar from Mount
Pisgah, but he was to die in the wilderness, where "no man
knoweth of his sepulchre unto this day." And so the old man,
who knew no home or lasting abode on earth, finds his home and
refuge in Him. He contrasts the eternity and unchangeableness
of God with the transitory and fleeting circumstances of man.
Thinking of the past generations, he remembered what God was
to Abraham, Isaac, and Jacob, when they had no fixed abode,
but confessed that they were strangers and pilgrims on earth.
And looking to future generations he discerned beyond the earthly
Canaan the city which hath foundations, whose builder and maker
is God. And so, for the homeless man and the homeless people,
faith beheld the promise of a dwelling-place, a home, in the Lord.

> Nay, by no cumulative changeful years,
> For all our bitter harvesting of tears,
> Shalt thou tame man, nor in his breast destroy
> The longing for his home which deadens joy.
> Not blindly in such moments, not in vain,
> The open secret flashes on the brain,
> As if one almost guessed it, almost knew
> Whence we have sailed and voyage whereunto;
> Not vainly, for albeit that hour goes by,
> And the strange letters perish from the sky,
> Yet learn we that a life to us is given
> One with the cosmic spectacles of heaven,—
> Feel the still soul, for all her questionings,
> Parcel and part of sempiternal things;
> For us, for all, one overarching dome,
> One law the order, and one God the home.[1]

1. God is the natural home of the soul. In that home it was
born, from that great Father our spirits came, "trailing clouds of
glory from God, who is our home." To live and dwell in Him,
nurtured by His care, fed by His bounty, watched by His grace,

---

[1] F. W. H. Myers, *The Renewal of Youth.*

guarded by His mercy; to be brought up and kept in His love, and to love Him with our heart and soul, and there and then to find all peace, rest, and blessedness—that is our purpose and our destiny, that the design and blessedness of our existence. And only in Him do we find what we require—protection against temptation, shelter from trials, and refuge from calamity, light in the midst of darkness, warmth to cheer our dulled and deadened hearts, release from the burden of sin, deliverance from the power of passion, food for our hunger, safety from every evil, and rest, quiet, peaceful rest, to our agitated and worn hearts.

¶ When we have been long in a foreign land, associating with strangers or casual acquaintances who have little interest in us, and no love for us; if we have been ill, far away from home and friends, and have had no friendly faces to smile on us, and no sweet, tender sympathy to soothe us, how gladsome it is, after such an experience, to leave that land of exile and strangeness and to sail for home, where we know—

There is an eye will mark
Our coming, and look brighter when we come.

And how cheering and comforting it is for us to know that, though now we are wanderers from home, our home in God still awaits us, the door is ever open to receive us, and the kind, compassionate Father watching for us, eager for our return, and ready to receive us and enfold us in His love, and set us in royal state at His own right hand to partake of His fulness, to be with Him and His dear and loved ones, whose faces will beam on us with tenderness and whose hearts will overflow to us with sympathy and affection; and that out of that home we shall never again go, but be there in infinite joy and glory for evermore. Your soul leaves its house of clay within which it has dwelt here below. Where shall that soul, when it goes, find rest and home?

Here is the house,
Empty and lone;
Where is the home of that which is gone,
Out in the regions of boundless black space,
Floating and floating, no space, no place?
Or did it gather its wealth and remove
To the home up above?
All's still in the house here below,
God grant that the soul that has wandered away,
Be not homeless to-day.

Into Thy house,
　Lord, take us straight,
Lest we be left in the darkness to wait;
Lest we be *lost* in realms without sun,
And wander for ever where mansion is none,
Crying without, "Let us in! Let us in!"
When the feast shall begin,
And the door shall be shut.[1]

2. Home suggests a place where care is thrown aside, while the affections expand themselves freely and fully, and loving looks and kindly words and gentle deeds are the order of the day. When God is said to be the refuge or home of man, it is meant that God offers man His best and tenderest welcome; that in God, and God alone, man finds that which yields perfect repose and satisfaction to all the pure and tender sympathies of his nature. For man's higher or spiritual self the One Eternal Being is what the fireside represents to the heart's affection—a sphere in which man may abandon himself to perfect enjoyment, to that unrestrained delight which accompanies a sense of being among friends, with whom reserve is neither necessary nor possible.

There is a presence moving in that home, anticipating all our wants, cheering us when we are sad, hushing us when we are fretful and impatient, smoothing us when we are ruffled, ministering to us when we are in suffering; and the soul, enfolded in God's great, tender love, finds rest and blessedness. And as it is a home of love, it is one in which there is no coldness or reserve. In the world there is always a certain reserve. There are joys which delight us, but which others cannot care for. There are sorrows, cares, anxieties which trouble us, but in which others have no interest. There are things that we do not tell and cannot tell. Even with our most familiar acquaintances, there are some chambers in our heart kept locked from them. But at home, in a home of love, everything is open, frank, free, natural; we throw off all restraint, unbosom all our heart's cares and troubles; we know we shall get sympathy; we speak to interested ears and loving hearts, whose joys and sorrows are ours. We are not afraid to whisper our secrets. It is to no rude and heartless gaze we expose them. We do not fear ridicule or

---

[1] R. Stephen, *Divine and Human Influence*, ii. 271.

cold indifference. We confide in hearts which love us as they love themselves. And we get relief by others sharing and bearing with us. So the soul finds sympathy in God.

¶ Lord, I have viewed this world over, in which Thou hast set me; I have tried how this and that thing will fit my spirit, and the design of my creation, and can find nothing on which to rest, for nothing here doth itself rest, but such things as please me for a while, in some degree, vanish and flee as shadows from before me. Lo! I come to Thee—the Eternal Being—the Spring of life—the Centre of rest—the Stay of the Creation—the Fulness of all things. I join myself to Thee; with Thee I will lead my life, and spend my days, with whom I aim to dwell for ever, expecting, when my little time is over, to be taken up ere long into Thy eternity.[1]

3. The Old Testament is rich in promises that God will supply the earthly needs of those whose trust is in Him. He fed His people with manna in the wilderness; He satisfieth our mouth with good things (Ps. ciii. 5). He prepareth a table before us in the presence of our enemies (Ps. xxiii. 5). The promise to those who trust in the Lord is that verily they shall be fed (Ps. xxxvii. 3). And the Psalmist records his lifelong experience that he had never "seen the righteous forsaken, nor his seed begging bread" (Ps. xxxvii. 25). And He who gives us our daily bread also satisfies the higher needs of our souls. This blessed fact is fully developed in the New Testament; but even the Old Testament saints record that they panted for God "as the hart panteth after the water brooks" (Ps. xlii. 1); that by Him their "soul shall be satisfied as with marrow and fatness" (Ps. lxiii. 5). "He satisfieth the longing soul, and filleth the hungry soul with goodness" (Ps. cvii. 9). If we make the Lord our habitation, all our wants, spiritual and temporal, will be supplied.

¶ As is a mother to her babe, so is God to us. She makes the children's home—not the two-roomed cottage of the peasant, with the bare walls and scant furniture, nor the many-roomed ducal palace, with its teeming wealth and oppressive luxury; but the love and light, the warm kisses and tender care, the sweet smile and the strong soul of the mother—she, and all that she is, makes "Home, sweet, sweet Home." She is the dwelling-place of the child's heart, the satisfaction of desire, the unfailing

[1] John Howe, *The Vanity of Man as Mortal.*

nourishment of the child's life. What God has made that mother to her child, He Himself is to us men—our asylum of peace, our refuge from passing foes, our dwelling-place and home from age to age.[1]

4. The inviolability of home is the spirit of our English proverb, that a man's house is his castle. And in this sense God is the Home of the soul; the soul finds in the presence of God a protection against the enemies which threaten it with ruin in the rough life of the world. In this sense David cries, " I will love thee, O Lord, my strength. The Lord is my rock, and my fortress and my deliverer; my God, my strength, in whom I will trust; my buckler and the horn of my salvation, and my high tower." Or again, " Be thou my strong rock for an house of defence to save me. For thou art my rock and my fortress." Or, again, " Be thou my strong habitation, whereunto I may continually resort; thou hast given commandment to save me; for thou art my rock and my fortress." Once more, " He that dwelleth in the secret place of the Most High shall abide under the shadow of the Almighty. I will say of the Lord, He is my refuge and my fortress; my God, in whom I will trust. For he shall deliver thee from the snare of the fowler, and from the noisome pestilence. He shall cover thee with his pinions, and under his wings shalt thou take refuge: his truth is a shield and a buckler."[2]

¶ One incident of the voyage to America served as a sharp test to Wesley of his own spiritual condition. Amongst the passengers he found a little group of Moravian exiles, who, by the simplicity and seriousness of their piety, strangely interested him. A storm broke over the ship one evening just as these simple-minded Germans had begun a religious service; Wesley describes what follows: " In the midst of the Psalm wherewith their service began, the sea broke over, split the mainsail in pieces, covered the ship, and poured in between the decks as if the great deep had already swallowed us up. A terrible screaming began amongst the English. The Germans calmly sang on. I asked one of them afterwards, ' Were you not afraid?' He answered, ' I thank God, no.' I asked, ' But were not your women and children afraid?' He replied mildly, ' No; our women and

---

[1] J. Clifford, *Social Worship*, 26.
[2] H. P. Liddon, *Christmastide Sermons*, 243.

children are not afraid to die.' From them I went to their crying, trembling neighbours, and pointed out to them the difference
in the hour of trial between him that feareth God and him that
feareth Him not."[1]

5. The soul that talks to God rises out of a narrow and selfish
individualism into fellowship, not only with the Eternal Creator,
but also with the vast and various family of God in the past,
present, and future. We are dwelling in the same home as our
fathers and brothers and sons. Israel is there in its completeness.
God is the eternal home of the race. " The elders who, through
faith, obtained a good report," in the grey dawn of the world,
dwelt therein. Abraham, Isaac, and Jacob, the founders of Israel,
had long since passed away, but their home was not broken up,
for they still lived in and to God. Indeed, all our dead live in
Him, for He is not the God of dead men, but of living men, for
all live unto Him. Thus we are already all together with the
Lord.

¶ Bunyan's Mr. Fearing was "kept very low, and made his
life burdensome to himself" by fear of death. But as he came
near to his end his fear disappeared, and "he went over at last
not much above wetshod," sending, as his last message to his
friends, the brave words, "Tell them all, it's all right."[2]

[1] W. H. Fitchett, *Wesley and His Century*, 98.
[2] J. Clifford, *Social Worship*, 31.

The Right Use of Time.

Literature.

Darlow (T. H.), *The Upward Calling*, 346.
Gregg (D.), *Our Best Moods*, 339.
Hobhouse (W.), *The Spiritual Standard*, 210.
Hodge (C.), *Princeton Sermons*, 346.
Lee (R.), *Sermons*, 268.
Lefroy (E. C.), *The Christian Ideal*, 102.
Morgan (G. E.), *Dreams and Realities*, 49.
Murray (W. H.), *The Fruits of the Spirit*, 157.
Prothero (G.), *The Armour of Light*, 33.
Smellie (A.), *In the Secret Place*, 396.
Trimmer (R.), *Thirsting for the Living Waters*, 132.
Tyng (S. H.), *The People's Pulpit*, iv. 205.
Christian World Pulpit, lviii. 65 (M. G. Pearse).
Guardian, lxvii. (1912) 418 (J. W. Willink).
Homiletic Review, l. 379 (M. G. Pearse).
Literary Churchman, xxiii. (1877) 540.
National Preacher, xxxiv. 33 (A. Barnes).
Preacher's Magazine, viii. 557 (T. Puddicombe) ; xxii. 67 (J. Edwards).

The Right Use of Time.

So teach us to number our days,
That we may get us an heart of wisdom.—Ps. xc. 12.

1. THIS psalm of man's pilgrimage through all generations has in it, says Ewald, "something unusually arresting, solemn, sinking deep into depths of the Divinity. Moses might well have been seized by these awful thoughts at the close of his wanderings; and the author, whoever he be, is clearly a man grown grey with vast experience, who here takes his stand at the close of his earthly course." The verses of the psalm have become the funeral hymn of Christendom, which every Church recites at the burial of its dead.

The slow, sad experience of life wrought out in the Psalmist a twofold result—he has learned the secret both of detachment and of attachment. This aged pilgrim grows more and more weaned from the world and detached from things trivial and temporal; he stands aloof and absolved from the accidents of existence. But he clings closer and closer still to things unseen and eternal, and is made partaker of their everlastingness. Such should be the effect of a right numbering of the days and years as they escape us—to teach at last that, though the world passeth away, and the lust thereof, yet he who doeth the will of God abideth for ever.

2. But he has learned more than that. He has learned that God is from everlasting to everlasting. It would help to cheer us if we could lay this thought to heart, numbering our days, not merely to realize their brevity, but to realize by contrast the length of God's years. We have but a short time to work, and it is well to remember that, in order that we may be diligent. But God has a whole eternity wherein to work, and it is well to remember that also, so that we may cease from fretfulness and

impatience at the slow progress of the Divine Kingdom. It is by so numbering both our years and God's that we attain to a wise heart.

¶ Time was Napoleon's most precious commodity, and for every stage and state of life he had a routine from which he deviated most unwillingly. In these years his days were spent in the careful husbanding of every hour.[1]

I.

A PRAYER FOR INSTRUCTION.

"Teach us."

1. At first thought it would seem as though we needed not to be instructed on such a subject. It would seem as though man's mortality were so evident that it would be impossible for him to hide it from himself. Nevertheless, he does hide it from himself, and on this account no prayer is more important than the prayer of the text. The demonstration of human mortality is in a hundred generations of the dead. It is in the ground beneath our feet, which is billowy with graves full of the dust which once lived in human forms and spoke and was loved. It is in the long line of the one hundred thousand human lives which every day pass the boundary-line from time into eternity and melt into nothingness before our eyes. It is in every tick of the clock which marks the passage of some immortal soul and declares the death-rate of the world. Yet, humanity at large does not realize the mortality of humanity. So thoroughly unrealized is the mortality of man that the first condition of right living, the fundamental thought of a wise life, is ignored and undreamed of by thousands and thousands.

¶ We can number other men's days and years, and think they will die ere it be long, if we see them sick or sore or cold : but we cannot number our own. When two ships meet on the sea, they which are in one ship think that the other ship doth sail exceedingly fast, but that their ship goeth fair and softly, or rather standeth still, although in truth one ship saileth as fast as the other; so every man thinks that the other post and run and fly

---

[1] W. M. Sloane, *Napoleon Bonaparte*, ii. 253.

to the grave, but that himself standeth stock still, although, indeed, a year with him is no longer than it is with the other.[1]

¶ I remember, in the seminary, a fellow student who had upon the crown of his head a tumour that was constantly growing. The physicians told him that it was impossible, by any effort of human skill, to relieve him. He was waiting the moment when, in its growth, it should at last pierce the hard bone of the skull; and he knew that the moment that should be accomplished, he would fall dead. God has spared him these many years to preach the gospel. But, when others were full of frolic and fun, I noted the serious mirth of that man. He lived in a division of his days. He counted nothing in the future. He finished each day's work when the night came.[2]

2. The uncertainty of human life and the vanity of human wishes have always been the theme of the satirist as well as of the preacher. But satire by itself is no remedy; it can, at best, only point out the disease. In the very fact that nothing is certain about life except its uncertainty, we have a safeguard. We know roughly the limits by which we are circumscribed; we know enough to warn, but not enough to paralyse. Could we look forward with absolute certainty to half a century of health and vigour, we might be carried away even more than we are by the pride of life. Did we know that death awaited us in the near future, our spirits would be dulled, our ardour damped in carrying out legitimate schemes of useful work. As it is, we may construct our averages of life, we may frame our insurance tables for the mass with some approach to accuracy; but we cannot predict the length of an individual life, save when medical skill can anticipate by a little the decree which has already gone forth. It is a merciful dispensation that has so ordered things. God would, indeed, have us to ponder over the mysteries which surround our existence, but not in such a way as to sap the power of action in us.

¶ Herein is the secret, the true alleviation of the burden of to-morrow; not the false and feeble attempt to oppose care by carelessness, to turn from the anxieties and troubles of life to a wild recklessness, assuming only a painful jauntiness which conceals the pain. The true remedy is not forgetfulness, but faith. This is the peace of God which passeth all understanding, which guards the heart and calms the fevered life. To the soul which

---

[1] Henry Smith.   [2] S. H. Tyng.

has this noble courage born of faith no turn of affairs can come amiss. He is not open to the blows of chance. It is not mere resignation: it is glad confidence that all things work together for good to them that love the Lord. "If I should intend Liverpool and land in heaven," said John Howe about a passage from Ireland. If, what then? To John Howe, who knew that the eternal God was his refuge, and underneath were the everlasting arms, what shadow could the future have? Why should he be bowed down by the burden of to-morrow? As his day's, right on till the last sand had run, right on till the last gasp of breath, so would be his strength.[1]

II.

A WISE ENUMERATION.

"Teach us to number our days."

1. What does it mean to "number our days"? Not just to calculate the chances of our own survival in this world—which we may easily gather from the actuarial tables of an insurance company. It means to take the measure of our days as compared with the work to be performed, with the provision to be laid up for eternity, with the preparation to be made for death, with the precaution to be taken against judgment to come. It is to estimate human life by the purposes to which it should be applied, by the eternity to which it must conduct. It means to gauge and test our own career in the light of its moral and spiritual issues. And as God teaches us this, we understand the secret of true wisdom. For wisdom lies in a just estimate of the real value of things. "What shall it profit a man?" remains the final question. As Plato said, in one of his mystical sentences, it is the art of measurement which would save the soul.

2. The Psalmist's petition in effect asks that we shall so mind the things of this world as not to forget their issues; and that we shall so mind the things of eternity as not to forget that they are to be gained through godliness, righteousness, and sobriety in using the things of time. The sublime motive in the distance must not overpower us, so that we shall be rendered unfit for discharging our present duty, small and insignificant though it may be; nor

[1] Hugh Black, *Comfort*, 189.

must we be so engrossed with the present duty as to lose sight of
the grand motive, which redeems from littleness every duty, however small, which is a means to so great an end.

3. The true way to number our days is not so to number them
that they seem to include the result of our lives, but so to number
them that they seem to include simply the beginning of our lives.
They and all they bring are only stepping-stones which lead us
up to the threshold of a nobler life, nobler in its opportunities,
occasions, and the character of its joy. Life is not mere existence,
the coming and the going of breath, and its coming again; life
means all that it includes of feeling and thinking and doing and
growth. And the heavenly life is only the continuing of our
activities and the multiplication of serviceable occasions along
those high levels and stretches of being to the altitude of which
we are lifted by the movement of prior activities, as birds are
lifted by the movement of their wings. The man who numbers
his days rightly, numbers them not as if they ended anything, but
as if they began something. He thinks of them in their termination as bringing him not to an end but to a beginning — a
beginning for which, if rightly used, they prepare and fit him.

¶ "What would you wish to be doing," was the question once
put to a wise man, "if you knew that you were to die the next
minute?" "Just what I am doing now," was his reply, though
he was neither repeating the creed nor telling his religious experience, but, for aught I know, posting his accounts, or talking
merry nonsense with his children round the fire. Nothing that is
worthy of a living man can be unworthy of a dying one; and
whatever is shocking in the last moment, would be disgraceful in
every other.[1]

¶ The family motto of Dr. Doddridge was *Dum vivimus,
vivamus*, which in its primary significance is, to be sure, not very
suitable to a Christian divine; but he paraphrased it thus:—

> Live, while you live, the epicure would say,
> And seize the pleasures of the present day.
> Live, while you live, the sacred preacher cries,
> And give to God each moment as it flies.
> Lord, in my views let both united be,
> I live in pleasure, when I live to Thee.[2]

[1] James Martineau.   [2] *Gentleman's Magazine*, 1786, p. 35.

Life is unutterably dear,
　God makes to-day so fair;
Though heaven is better,—being here
　I long not to be there.

The weights of life are pressing still,
　Not one of them may fall;
Yet such strong joys my spirit fill,
　That I can bear them all.

Though Care and Grief are at my side,
　There would I let them stay,
And still be ever satisfied
　With beautiful To-day![1]

III.

THE UNITS OF LIFE.

"Our days."

1. Notice the writer's unit of computation in measuring life.
He speaks not of years, not even of months or weeks, but of days.
There is something very impressive in such a mode of reckoning.
A year is a long period; and while we may hope for years of life,
be they many or few, the passage of time is not continuously felt
by us. But days—how they rush past and fly away with a
rapidity which on reflection is almost appalling! Even the
heedless man must feel the ebb of life when it comes to be
calculated by days. Yet as we see the winged hours go by, we are
apt to think as lightly of them as if the series would never cease.
We sleep and play and busy ourselves with what we call the
serious business of life without much reference to the rising and
setting of the sun. A day lost, a day half wasted, a day misused,
causes us no poignant regret. We are so confident that many
others are still in store for us. As they have come and gone in
the past, so will they come and go in the future. We must admit,
if we are pressed, that the supply is not absolutely unlimited. An
end will be reached at some indefinite epoch, but not yet—not
yet; and if meanwhile we are careless or prodigal, we anticipate

[1] Charlotte F. B. Rogé.

many opportunities of "making up for lost time "—as if it were
ever possible to make up for lost time!

> Oh, Day, if I squander a wavelet of thee,
> A mite of my twelve hours' treasure,
> The least of thy gazes or glances,
> (Be they grants thou art bound to or gifts above measure)
> One of thy choices or one of thy chances,
> (Be they tasks God imposed thee or freaks at thy pleasure)
> —My Day, if I squander such labour or leisure,
> Then shame fall on Asolo, mischief on me![1]

2. On our maps we have lines to mark the parallels of latitude
—but these lines are only on the map. Crossing the equator or
the tropics you see no score in the water, no line in the sky, to
mark it; the vessel gives no lurch, no call is emitted from the
deep; it is only the man of skill, the pilot or the captain, with his
eye on the signs of heaven, who can tell that an event has
happened, and that a definite portion of the voyage is completed.
And, so far, our life is like a voyage on the open sea, every day
repeating its predecessor—the same watery plain around and the
same blue dome above—each so like the other that you might
fancy the charmed ship was standing still. But it is not so. The
watery plain of to-day is far in advance of the plain of yesterday,
and the blue dome of to-day may be very like its predecessors, but
it is fashioned from quite another sky.

> Their advent is as silent as their going,
> They have no voice nor utter any speech,
> No whispered murmur passes each to each,
> As on the bosom of the years' stream flowing,
> They pass beyond recall, beyond our knowing,
> Farther than sight can pierce or thought can reach,
> Nor shall we ever hear them on Time's beach,
> No matter how the winds of life are blowing.

> They bide their time, they wait the awful warning
> Of that dread day, when hearts and graves unsealing,
> The trumpet's note shall call the sea and sod,
> To yield their secrets to the sun's revealing:
> What voices then shall thrill the Judgment morning,
> As our lost hours shall cry aloud to God?[2]

[1] Browning, *Pippa Passes*.   [2] R. T. W. Duke.

3. Is it because God gives us time so imperceptibly that none of us estimates the full value of time? The individual moment is not looked upon as a precious grain of gold. One could prove this in many ways; but let us be satisfied with one way. Take, as an example, the names of our various methods of getting rid of time. These indicate our undervaluation of time. Notice some of these names: "pastime," *i.e.*, what consumes and uses up the hours easily; "amusement," *i.e.*, what prevents musing or meditation; "diversion," *i.e.*, what turns aside; "entertainment," *i.e.*, what holds in suspense or equilibrium. These words, which are in common use, indicate and reveal a wrong condition of thought and feeling about time. They characterize it as a drug in the market to be got rid of at any price and in any quantity, whereas it is the most precious trust we have.

¶ The illusion haunts us, that a long duration, as a year, a decade, a century, is valuable. But an old French sentence says, "God works in moments,"—"En peu d'heure Dieu labeure." We ask for long life, but 'tis deep life, or grand moments that signify. Let the measure of time be spiritual, not mechanical. Life is unnecessarily long. Moments of insight, of fine personal relation, a smile, a glance—what ample borrowers of eternity they are![1]

Forenoon and afternoon and night,—forenoon
And afternoon and night,—forenoon and—what?
The empty song repeats itself. No more?
Yea, that is life: make this forenoon sublime,
This afternoon a psalm, this night a prayer,
And Time is conquered, and thy crown is won.[2]

IV.

RECKONING WITH A PURPOSE.

"So teach us to number our days, that we may get us an heart of wisdom."

The reckoning must be made with a purpose. Objectless meditations, and laments without a practical outcome, will avail nothing. The result of our counsels must be the attainment of "wisdom," and wisdom does not consist in the mere recognition of a truth, however momentous. It is a small thing to face the

[1] Emerson.   [2] Edward Rowland Sill.

fact of the shortness of human life, and call it an evil not to be avoided by any. The shallowest of heathen philosophies could tell us that. " So teach us to number our days, that we may get us an heart of wisdom."

1. Wisdom is a great word, because the idea it symbolizes is great. It is greater than knowledge, for knowledge symbolizes only what one has received. Knowledge signifies the accumulation of facts, the gathering and retention of information, the reception on the part of our memories of whatever has been discovered. But wisdom represents that finer power, that higher characteristic of mind, which suggests the proper application of facts, the right use of knowledge, the correct direction of our faculties. Knowledge is full of error. The stubble and the chaff lie together in its chambers, and both represent it. But wisdom never errs. It separates the wheat from the chaff. It discards what is worthless, and retains only the valuable. Knowledge represents the results of human industry. Wisdom represents the characteristic of Divinity. He whose heart is applied to wisdom has put himself in such a position that he can think divinely—think as God would think in his place.

¶ Wisdom signifies an acquisition, by means of the soul's faculty of perception, of true knowledge; and the lack of such knowledge is ignorance. The idea, held by many people, that wisdom is a gift bestowed on a few privileged souls is erroneous. Wisdom is open to all, without price or favour. Wisdom, beautiful and divine, represents the highest development of the human soul. There is a path leading from the lowest to the highest, and it is open equally to all. As soon as a man begins to seek for knowledge and truth, he begins to advance out of ignorance and to acquire wisdom. The desire for knowledge and truth is itself an evidence of wisdom.[1]

2. Now wisdom for time and for eternity does not lie in the pursuit of pleasure, not even in the pursuit of happiness, but in the cultivation of a rising life. This is not to say that happiness may never be hoped for or enjoyed when it comes. If we did not desire to be happy, we should be more than human,—or less. But the only way of obtaining happiness is to renounce altogether the pursuit of it. "Seek ye first the kingdom of God and his

[1] R. H. Hodgson, *Glad Tidings*, 42.

righteousness, and all these things"—things which go to make life happy—"shall be added unto you." Self-consecration is the root of all true happiness. It is the one thing that ensures contentment here and hereafter; the one thing that will bring a man peace at the last. Only by losing our life in God can we hope to find it immortalized. Only by a dedication of all that we have, and are, and desire, shall we attain to the perfect existence. This is wisdom and this is happiness.

¶ The third chapter of Dr. Hanna's *Memoir* describes Dr. Chalmers' ordination to his Fifeshire parish of Kilmany, in the Maytime of 1803; but we have to journey on to the eighth chapter and the winter of 1811, before the preacher has any Gospel to proclaim. Through the intervening years Chalmers was more interested in mathematics than in the New Testament, and in his lectures to the students of St. Andrews on chemistry and geology than in the spiritual welfare of his people. "The author of this pamphlet," he wrote in self-defence, "can assert, on the authority of his own experience, that, after the satisfactory discharge of his parish duties, a minister may enjoy five days in the week of uninterrupted leisure for the prosecution of any science in which his taste may dispose him to engage." Years afterwards, in a debate in the Assembly of 1825, he recanted the words and confessed his error amid the deathlike stillness of the House. " I have no reserve in saying that the sentiment was wrong, and that, in the utterance of it, I penned what was most outrageously wrong. Strangely blinded that I was ! What, sir, is the object of mathematical science ? Magnitude, and the proportions of magnitude. But then, sir, I had forgotten two magnitudes. I thought not of the littleness of time ; I recklessly thought not of the greatness of eternity."[1]

3. The end of life is not to live the maximum number of hours in pleasure, but to form a character for all eternity ; and if we want to take stock of loss and gain aright, we must look into our own hearts. We must see what treasure it is to which they are drawn, whether above or below. Let us not scruple to put this to familiar and matter-of-fact tests ; there should be no false dignity about religion. Let us ask ourselves plain questions like these: Has our time been frittered away, in society, in amusement, in the thousand distractions of life—harmless, perhaps, each one taken by itself, but in the aggregate fatal to the usefulness

[1] A. Smellie, *Robert Murray McCheyne*, 13.

and true greatness of life? Has God been crowded out of
our thoughts? Has our hold on the unseen diminished? Have
we become more encrusted with earthly things, till we find it impossible to look up, prayer being more difficult and the thought of
religion more unwelcome? Is our moral courage less? Are we
more afraid to confess God before men, or to protest against
insults which we hear offered to His name? Are we more haunted
by evil thoughts, and less able to resist them? Have we grown
in patience, cheerfulness, humility? Are we more ready to do
the "little, nameless, unremembered acts of kindness," which have
none of the charm of heroism, and remain unknown beyond the
narrowest circle? Has our will grown in strength, so that we
are less at the mercy of "chance desires" and sudden temptations,
more at unity with ourselves, more settled in the drift and direction of our lives? And an answer we can give to these if we take
the trouble—not necessarily the same answer to all, not perhaps
an unqualified answer to many, but still something that will
show us whether we are being carried along by the stream or
making way against it.

¶ The universe is full of miracle and mystery; the darkness
and silence are set for a sign we dare not despise. The pall of
night lifts, leaving us engulphed in the light of immensity under
a tossing heaven of stars. The dawn breaks, but it does not
surprise us, for we have watched from the valley and seen the pale
twilight. Through the wondrous Sabbath of faithful souls, the
long day of rosemary and rue, the light brightens in the East; and
we pass on towards it with quiet feet and opening eyes, bearing
with us all of the redeemed earth that we have made our own,
until we are fulfilled in the sunrise of the great Easter Day, and
the peoples come from north and south and east and west to the
city which lieth foursquare—the Beatific Vision of God.[1]

> Time speeds on his relentless track,
>   And—though we beg on bended knees—
> No prophet's hand for us puts back
>   The shadow ten degrees:
>
> Yet dream we each returning spring,
>   When woods are decked in gold and green,
> The dawning year to us will bring
>   The best that yet has been.

[1] Michael Fairless, *The Roadmender*, 90.

Which is an earnest of the truth
 That when the years have passed away,
We shall receive eternal youth
 And never-ending day.

An angel to each land and clime
 Shall locust-eaten years restore,
And swear by Him who conquered Time
 That Time shall be no more.[1]

[1] Ellen Thorneycroft Fowler, *Love's Argument*, 115.

God's Inner Circle.

LITERATURE.

Broughton (L. G.), *The Soul-Winning Church*, 50.
Butler (H. M.), *University and Other Sermons*, 254.
Darlow (T. H.), *The Upward Calling*, 38.
Edmunds (L.), *Sunday by Sunday*, 193.
Hutton (J. A.), *The Fear of Things*, 45.
Landels (W.), *Until the Day Break*, 24.
Maclaren (A.), *Last Sheaves*, 160.
Norton (J. N.), *Every Sunday*, 257.
Pearson (A.), *The Claims of the Faith*, 64.
Pierson (A. T.), *The Heights of the Gospel*, 63.
Price (A. C.), *Fifty Sermons*, iv. 297 ; viii. 73.
Raleigh (A.), *Rest from Care and Sorrow*, 1.
Spurgeon (C. H.), *Till He Come*, 23.
Watkinson (W. L.), *The Ashes of Roses*, 114.
Christian World, Nov. 10, 1910 (J. H. Jowett).
Christian World Pulpit, lx. 378 (W. Glover) ; lxx. 285 (A. S. Renton) ;
    lxxi. 219 (G. H. Morgan).
Weekly Pulpit, i. 3 (P. T. Forsyth).

GOD'S INNER CIRCLE.

He that dwelleth in the secret place of the Most High
Shall abide under the shadow of the Almighty.—Ps. xci. 1.

THE beauty of the language of this poem fitly corresponds to the grandeur of the thoughts which it conveys. The Psalmist here sings "to one clear harp in divers tones"; and the central thought which he exhibits in its different aspects is that of God's response to man. For every advance on man's part there is an immediate and corresponding advance on God's part. When man goes out to seek God, God meets him more than half-way. When he calls upon God, God will answer him. Loving faith on man's part will be met by faithful love on the part of God. This is in the first verse, of which the whole psalm is an expansion. If man dwells "in the secret place of the Most High," he shall abide "under the shadow of the Almighty." We have here the condition and promise.

¶ In his later years, Calvin's colleague at Geneva was Theodore de Beza (1519–1605), the writer of the metrical version of Psalm lxviii., which was the battle-song of the Huguenots. Taste for the culture of the Renaissance, passion for poetry, worldly success and fame, had weakened the impression of the religious training of his youth. A dangerous illness revived his former feelings. Escaping from the bondage of Egypt, as he called his previous life, he took refuge with Calvin at Geneva. In 1548, when he for the first time attended the service of the Reformed Assembly, the congregation was singing Psalm xci., "Whoso dwelleth under the defence of the Most High shall abide under the shadow of the Almighty." He never forgot the effect of the words. They supported him in all the difficulties of his subsequent life; they conquered his fears, and gave him courage to meet every danger.[1]

¶ "The 91st Psalm is a mountain of strength to all believers"; so General Gordon wrote from Gravesend in 1869, one of the six

---

[1] R. E. Prothero, *The Psalms in Human Life*, 185.

quiet years which he used to speak of as the happiest of his life. Again, thirteen years later, in January 1882, he wrote thus from Mauritius : " I dwell more or less (I wish it were more) under the shadow of the Almighty."

I.

IN THE SECRET PLACE.

1. "He that dwelleth in the secret place of the Most High." We get the clearest idea of the meaning of this phrase by an examination of the different passages in the Psalms where the word here translated "secret place" occurs. Thus in Psalm xxxi. 20, we read : "Thou shalt hide them in the secret of thy presence"; also in Psalm lxxxiii. 3, where another form of the same word occurs, we read of God's "hidden ones." From these and similar passages we find that the word is usually connected with the idea of a fugitive hiding from his pursuers. It calls up before us the picture of a man running away from his enemies. Weary and panting, he knows not where to hide himself, and in his despair he flees to some friend of his and seeks protection, and the friend hides him in a secret place. The fugitive gives his all into the keeping of his friend. He places his life in his friend's hands, and he has now power of life and death over him. So, then, the man who dwells in "the secret place of the Most High" is he who ventures his all upon God. With a sure and steadfast trust, with a simple but unwavering faith, he gives himself, his all, into the keeping of God. He surrenders himself to God, and by that very act he is taken near to God ; he is put in the secret place of the Most High and becomes one of "God's hidden ones." By his act of absolute self-surrender he has attained to that state which the Apostle Paul describes in language very similar to that of the Psalmist—only going a little further than the latter with his imperfect light could go—when he says, "Ye died, and your new life is hid with Christ in God."

¶ We are like vessels which are near a lee shore in the night. The darkness of the open sea is safer for the skilled seaman than the line of the shore. Our safety is to stand out in the bosom of the dark ; it is to press into the mysteries of God. Why is it that our moral nature, even the religious, is too often shallow and poverty-stricken? It is because we do not pursue the growing knowledge of God on our own account. We are religious, or at least we are always in danger of being religious, without spiritual growth, and spiritual growth surely means spiritual insight. We cease to become sensible of spiritual enrichment. We come to a time of life when we are content to say, "I get no secrets from God now." Revelations do not arrive; doors are not opened in Heaven; new vistas of faith do not spread away before the soul. Faith runs on upon the level, and it does not mount, and it does not soar. God becomes by habit a uniform Presence to us. He is not denied. We do not venture to deny Him. I was almost going to say we had not the courage to deny Him. But, at any rate, we do not deny Him. We only disregard Him, like the air and the sky. We do not give our minds seriously and deliberately to realizing Him. We do not pore upon Him until fold after fold removes, and depth after depth opens, and we look into His heart. The secret, the secret of the Most High is not with us.[1]

2. While this is the general idea, it is possible that the immediate figure of "the secret place" may have been borrowed from the arrangements and appointments of the Temple. There was the vast outside world stretching on every side beyond the Temple walls; then the outer courts of the Temple; then the inner chambers and precincts; then the Holy Place with its golden candlestick and table of shewbread; and last of all, the Holy of Holies, the secret place, the mystic abiding-place of the eternal God. And every Jew thought reverently and almost awfully of that secret, silent place where God dwelt between the cherubim. He turned towards it, he worshipped towards it, his desire moved towards it; it was the mysterious centre of his adoration and service. And that arrangement and apportionment of the Temple became to the Psalmist the type and the symbol of human life. Life could be all outside, or it could spend itself in outer courts, on the mere fringe of being, or it could have a secret place where everything found significance and interpretation and value in the mysterious fellowship of God. That seems to be the primary meaning of life "in the secret place"; it is life abandoning the mere outside of things, refusing to dwell in the outer halls and passages of the stately temple of being, and centralizing itself in

[1] P. T. Forsyth.

that mysterious interior of things where " cherubim and seraphim continually do cry, Holy, holy, holy, Lord God Almighty."

¶ The necessity of an inward stillness hath appeared clear to my mind. In true silence strength is renewed, and the mind is weaned from all things, save as they may be enjoyed in the Divine will; and a lowliness in outward living, opposite to worldly honour, becomes truly acceptable to us. In the desire after outward gain the mind is prevented from a perfect attention to the voice of Christ; yet being weaned from all things, except as they may be enjoyed in the Divine will, the pure light shines into the soul. Where the fruits of the spirit which is of this world are brought forth by many who profess to be led by the Spirit of truth, and cloudiness is felt to be gathering over the visible church, the sincere in heart, who abide in true stillness, and are exercised therein before the Lord for His name's sake, have knowledge of Christ in the fellowship of His sufferings; and inward thankfulness is felt at times, that through Divine love our own wisdom is cast out, and that forward, active part in us is subjected, which would rise and do something without the pure leadings of the spirit of Christ.[1]

¶ Don't be too much taken up with excitements social and intellectual. The depths of life are still and ought not to be ruffled by every wanton breeze, else they lose the capacity which they ought to possess of being that centre of rest, and peace, and content, to which we can withdraw when wearied of the world which is too much with us. Life to be worth anything at all must have a moral basis. After all, it is the root of the matter, unless the universe was made in jest.[2]

3. The Church is, in God's idea, a home where we recover from the fatigue of effort, when we take a new hold of high purposes from which our hand had slackened; a place of compensations; a place from which we see our life more truly, for we see more than itself. Here, in this house, we may feel something, some one, even God, in the form and manner of Jesus Christ, coming between us and the things which would dishearten us and work despair. Here we may sit under a shadow, under the shadow of thought and faith. Here we may come under the rebuke and deliverance of high and unworldly considerations; here we may receive the emancipation which comes the moment we adopt the

[1] *The Journal of John Woolman*, 29.
[2] *Memoir of Robert Herbert Story*, 401.

spiritual view and seek not our own will but the will of God. To seek the face of God in worship is the instinct of the soul which has become aware of itself and its surroundings. Life and death are the great preachers. It is they who ring the church bells. That instinct for God, that instinct for the shadow, will never pass away. It may only become perverted and debased. The foundation—which is man's need for God, for guidance, for cleansing, for support, and that again is but God's search for man, God's overtures to man—the foundation standeth sure.

¶ Whatever temple science may build there will always need to be hard by a Gothic chapel for wounded souls.[1]

"A little chamber" built "upon the wall,"
    With stool and table, candlestick and bed,
    Where he might sit, or kneel, or lay his head
At night or sultry noontide: this was all
A prophet's need: but in that chamber small
    What mighty prayers arose, what grace was shed,
    What gifts were given—potent to wake the dead,
And from its viewless flight a soul recall!

And still what miracles of grace are wrought
    In many a lonely chamber with shut door,
Where God our Father is in secret sought,
    And shows Himself in mercy more and more!
Dim upper rooms with God's own glory shine,
And souls are lifted to the life Divine.[2]

4. The secret place is not to be limited to a particular locality, but means nearness to God, the close fellowship into which the soul enters, the inner circle of communion in which the soul realizes vividly the Divine presence. Some may associate such communion with one locality, and some with another, according to their individual experience. But this matters not. The essential thing is the nearness of the soul to God, its entering into His presence with the full consciousness that He graciously regards it, and will hear its prayer and accept its homage, breathing its feelings and desires into His ear, and spreading all its case before Him. His is not that distant and formal inter-course which one man may hold with another when, in the open

[1] F. Paulsen, *Ethics.*   [2] R. Wilton.

and crowded places of the city, they have to restrain themselves because of being exposed to the observation of others; it is that intimate and unrestrained intercourse which friend holds with friend when they meet in privacy, where no other eye sees or ear hears, and each communicates to the other not the things which are open to public observation, but the secret and hidden feelings of the heart. Reverently, although freely and confidently, does the worshipper in the secret place speak to God as a child to its father, giving expression to all his feelings, whatsoever they may be.

¶ "Fellowship with the living God," says Andrew Bonar in his graphic little sketch of Samuel Rutherford, "is a little distinguishing feature in the holiness given by the Holy Ghost. . . . Rutherford could sometimes say, 'I have been so near Him, that I have said I take instruments (documents by way of attestation) that this is the Lord,' and he could from experience declare, 'I dare avouch, the saints know not the length and largeness of the sweet earnest, and of the sweet green sheaves before the harvest, that might be had on this side of the water, if we only took more pains.' . . . All this," adds Bonar suggestively, "is from the pen of a man who was a metaphysician, a controversialist, a leader in the Church, and learned in ancient scholastic lore."

> Where is that secret place of the Most High?
> And who is He? Where shall we look for Him
> That dwelleth there? Between the cherubim,
> That o'er the seat of grace, with constant eye,
> And outspread wing, brood everlastingly?
> Or shall we seek that deeper meaning dim,
> And as we may, walk, flutter, soar, and swim,
> From deep to deep of the void, fathomless sky?
> Oh! seek not there the secret of the Lord
> In what hath been, or what may never be;
> But seek the shadow of the mystic word—
> The shadow of a truth thou canst not see:
> There build thy nest, and, like a nestling bird,
> Find all thy safety in thy secrecy.[1]

5. How are we to maintain our life of fellowship with God? How are we to dwell in the Secret Place? The Psalmist doubtless would find guidance in the ways and ministries of the Temple.

[1] Hartley Coleridge.

(1) *The spirit of reverence* must be cherished. There was to be no tramping in the sacred courts. He was to move quietly, as in the presence of something august and unspeakable. And that is the very first requisite if we would dwell in the secret place— the reverent spirit and the reverent step. The man who strides through life with flippant tramp will never get beyond the outer courts. He may "get on," he will never "get in"; he may find here and there an empty shell, he will never find "the pearl of great price." Irreverence can never open the gate into the secret place.

(2) The second thing requisite in the Temple ministry to any one who sought the fellowship of the secret place was *the spirit of sacrifice.* No man was permitted to come empty-handed in his movements towards the secret place. "Bring an offering, and come into his courts." And in that Temple-ministry the Psalmist would recognize another of the essential requisites if he would dwell in the secret place. That offering meant that a man must surrender all that he possesses, of gifts and goods, to his quest of the central things of life. For there is this strange thing about the strait gate which opens into the secret place: it is too strait for the man who brings nothing; it is abundantly wide for the man who brings his all. No man deserves the hallowed intimacies of life, the holy tabernacle of the Most High, who does not bring upon the errand all that he is, and all that he has. Life's crown demands life's all.

(3) And other Temple-ministries in which the Psalmist would find principles of guidance would be the requirement of *prayer* and *praise.* "Sing unto the Lord a new song." Such was to be one of the exercises of those who sought the grace and favour of the holy place. They were to come wearing the garment of praise. And therefore the Psalmist knew that praise was to be one of the means by which he was to possess the intimacies of the secret place. And praise is still one of the ministries by which we reach the central heart of things, the hallowed abode where we come to share "the secret of the Lord." And praise is not fawning upon God, flattering Him, piling up words of empty eulogy; it is the hallowed contemplation of the greatness of God, and the grateful appreciation of the goodness of God. And with praise there goes prayer—the recognition of our dependence upon

the Highest, the fellowship of desire, the humble speech which co-operates in the reception and distribution of grace.

¶ "I passed my time in great peace, content to spend the remainder of my life there, if such should be the will of God. I employed part of my time in writing religious songs. I, and my maid La Gautière, who was with me in prison, committed them to heart as fast as I made them. Together we sang praises to Thee, O our God! It sometimes seemed to me as if I were a little bird whom the Lord had placed in a cage, and that I had nothing to do now but to sing. The joy of my heart gave a brightness to the objects around me. The stones of my prison looked in my eyes like rubies. I esteemed them more than all the gaudy brilliancies of a vain world. My heart was full of that joy which Thou givest to them who love Thee in the midst of their greatest crosses." [1]

> Let praise devote thy work and skill employ
> Thy whole mind, and thy heart be lost in joy.
> Well-doing bringeth pride, this constant thought
> Humility, that thy best done is naught.
> Man doeth nothing well, be it great or small,
> Save to praise God; but that hath saved all:
> For God requires no more than thou hast done,
> And takes thy work to bless it for His own. [2]

¶ The wise man will act like the bee, and he will fly out in order to settle with care, intelligence, and prudence on all the gifts and on all the sweetness which he has experienced, and on all the good which God has done to him; and through the rays of the sun and his own inward observation he will experience a multitude of consolations and blessings. And he will not rest on any flower of all these gifts, but, laden with gratitude and praise, he will fly back again toward the home in which he longs to dwell and rest for evermore with God. [3]

II.

UNDER HIS SHADOW.

The man who commits himself to God, and dwells in Him, has this promise, that he will abide under the shadow of the Almighty. There are two names of God used in the text, "The

---

[1] Madame Guyon, in *Life*, by T. C. Upham.   [2] R. Bridges.
[3] M. Maeterlinck, *Ruysbroeck and the Mystics*, 130.

Most High" and "The Almighty"; and when we remember the
deep religious significance which the different names of God had
for the Hebrew, and the careful way in which they are used
throughout the whole of the Old Testament, so that in general
it is true that that name of God is used which alone serves to
indicate the particular aspect of God's character or government
upon which the writer wished to lay stress; when we remember
this, we are justified in looking for a meaning in the distinction
between the two names of God used here. The man to whom the
promise is made seeks to dwell in the secret place of "the Most
High." He seeks to be near God as the "Most High" God, the
God of surpassing excellence. He desires the company of Him
who is "Most High" because He is most holy. The character
which he contemplates in God is not so much His power as His
holiness. He desires to be near God, not because of what God
can do for him, but because of what God is; it is in the thought
of God's goodness that he rests secure. It is the holiness of
Jehovah that attracts him; it is the beauty of the Lord his God
that he would behold continually. To the man who thus disin-
terestedly seeks after Him God will reveal Himself in the character
of the Almighty. The power of the Almighty shall be round about
him. "Because he hath set his love upon me, therefore will I deliver him; I will set him on high, because he hath known my name."
This man is to "abide under the shadow of the Almighty."

¶ This wonderful Psalm has always been a favourite with the
Mystic and the Quietist. For it expresses what we may call the
Beatitude of the Inner Circle. Most religions have distinguished
carefully between the rank and file of the faithful, and that select
company of initiates who taste the hidden wisdom and have access
to the secret shrine. From the nature of the case some such
distinction exists even in the Kingdom of Heaven. Christ Himself allowed a difference between "His own friends" and those
many disciples who are servants still. Only we must never forget
on what this difference depends. The Father, who is Lord of
heaven and earth, has seen good to hide His secrets from the wise
and prudent, and to reveal them unto babes. While from the
inmost sanctuary of Christian experience a Voice cries continually,
"Whosoever will let him come freely—if he be content to come
as a little child."[1]

[1] T. H. Darlow, *The Upward Calling*, 38.

1. What does the Psalmist mean by "abiding under the shadow"? Does he mean to say that the shadow of the Almighty rests on the secret place? At first sight it would seem so, but such a conclusion would not be in harmony with the trend of thought throughout the Psalm. What he appears really to teach is that, when a man regularly communes with God in secret, then, wherever he goes, the shadow of the Almighty shall rest upon him, and in times of trial and danger shall shelter and protect him. As the pillar of cloud by day and the pillar of fire by night went before the children of Israel, and was both a guide and a shelter to them, so the shadow of the Almighty shall ever rest upon those who dwell in the secret place of the Most High. A shadow is produced when some object intercepts the light. Here it re-presents God placing Himself in front of the sun, to screen His people from heat. The sun shall not smite them by day, nor the moon by night.

¶ The last poems of Miss Havergal are published with the title, *Under His Shadow*, and the preface gives the reason for the name. She said, "I should like the title to be, *Under His Shadow*. I seem to see four pictures by that: under the shadow of a rock in a weary plain; under the shadow of a tree; closer still, under the shadow of His wing; nearest and closest, in the shadow of His hand. Surely that hand must be the pierced hand, that may oftentimes press us sorely, and yet evermore encircling, upholding, and shadowing." [1]

2. Now it is one thing to be touched by the shadow of the Almighty, another to abide within that shadow. One has not lived long, or has lived only on the surface, who has never for a moment been *touched* by the shadow of God. It may have fallen upon us in one or other of several experiences. It may have come to us in some reverse of fortune, in some change in our prospects. Or it may have come to us in some bodily illness or the threaten-ing of some illness. Or it may have come to us, as so much with regard to the unseen world comes to us all, in the great silence of a bereavement. But there is probably not one of adult years who has not had at least one experience which has touched him to the quick and has brought him for the time being face to face with God. And yet, if we are strict with ourselves, we shall have

[1] C. H. Spurgeon, *Till He Come*, 23.

to confess that as the trouble eased the high seriousness which it brought began to pass away, so that probably not one of us has worked out into our life and character the holy intentions which we proposed to ourselves on a certain day when our heart was sore. We have lost from ourselves a certain dignity, a certain superiority to the world which was ours in days that we can still recall, when some suspense was keeping our heart open, when in some precious concern of our life we were depending utterly upon God for something. To be touched—that is the work of God, the work of life upon us; whereas to *abide* requires the consent of our will. In order to abide it needs that the whole man, who knows that in the personal crisis God was singling him out, shall live henceforth by the wisdom and calling of that hour. It needs that he shall depart from all the iniquity which the light of that holy hour revealed to him.

¶ The original meaning of the word here translated "abide" is "to wrap up in a garment for warmth and rest during the cool of the night." The reflexive form of the verb is here used: "He that dwelleth in the secret place of the Most High shall wrap himself round in the shadow of the God of Might." Nearness to God is to be to him as the garment which the traveller wraps around him as he goes to sleep in the desert, when the chills of night descend. God's immediate presence is to be wrapped round about him for his protection.[1]

3. God's protection does not mean exemption from outward calamities. But there is an evil in the calamity that will never come near the man who is sheltered under God's wing. The physical external event may be entirely the same to him as to another who is not covered with His feathers. Here are two partners in a business; the one is a Christian man, and the other is not. A common disaster overwhelms them. They become bankrupts. Is insolvency the same to the one as it is to the other? Here are two men on board a ship, the one putting his trust in God, the other thinking it all nonsense to trust anything but himself. They are both drowned. Is drowning the same to the two? As their corpses lie side by side, you may say of the one, but only of the one, "There shall no evil befall thee, neither shall any

[1] A. S. Renton.

plague come nigh thy dwelling." For the protection that is granted to faith is to be understood only by faith.

¶ "If you believe in God," wrote Robert Louis Stevenson, "where is there any more room for terror? If you are sure that God, in the long-run, means kindness by you, you should be happy." Fighting a losing battle with death, he wrote: "The tragedy of things works itself out blacker and blacker. Does it shake my cast-iron faith? I cannot say that it does. I believe in an ultimate decency of things; aye, and if I woke in hell, should still believe it." Let us thank God for the faith of that high and brave soldier of suffering, going up and down the earth in quest of health, and singing as he went:

> If to feel in the ink of the slough,
> And sink of the mire,
> Veins of glory and fire
> Run through and transpierce and transpire,
> And a secret purpose of glory in every part,
> And the answering glory of battle fill my heart;
> To thrill with the joy of girded men,
> To go on forever and fail and go on again,
> And be mauled to the earth and arise,
> And contend for the shade of a word and a thing not
>   seen with the eyes:
> With the half of a broken hope for a pillow at night;
> That somehow the right is the right
> And the smooth shall bloom from the rough:
> Lord, if that were enough?

4. But the promise is absolutely true in a far higher region —the region of spiritual defence. For no man who lies under the shadow of God, and has his heart filled with the continual consciousness of that Presence, is likely to fall before the assaults of evil that tempt him away from God; and the defence which He gives in that region is yet more magnificently impregnable than the defence which He gives against external evils. For, as the New Testament teaches us, we are kept from sin, not by any outward breastplate or armour, not even by the Divine wing lying above us to cover us, but by the indwelling Christ in our hearts. His Spirit within us makes us "free from the law of sin and death," and conquerors over all temptations. Every step taken into a higher, holier life secures a completer immunity from the power

of evil. Virtually there is no temptation to those who climb high
enough; they still suffer the trial of their faith and principle,
but they have no evil thought, no affinity with evil; it exercises
over them no fascination; it is to them as though it were not.
Never deal with temptation on low utilitarian grounds of health,
reputation, or interest. If you have a vice, convict it at Sinai;
arraign it at the bar of the Judgment Day; make it ashamed of
itself at the feet of Christ; blind it with heaven; scorch it with
hell; take it into the upper air where it cannot get its breath, and
choke it.

> And chok'st thou not him in the upper air
> His strength he will still on the earth repair.

¶ Migratory birds invisible to the eye have been detected by
the telescope crossing the disc of the sun six miles above the earth.
They have found one of the secret places of the Most High; far
above the earth, invisible to the human eye, hidden in the light,
they were delightfully safe from the fear of evil. Thus it is with
the soul that soars into the heavenly places; no arrow can reach
it, no fowler betray it, no creature of prey make it afraid: it
abides in the shadow of the Almighty.[1]

> How good it is, when weaned from all beside,
> With God alone the soul is satisfied,
>   Deep hidden in His heart!
> How good it is, redeemed, and washed, and shriven,
> To dwell, a cloistered soul, with Christ in heaven,
>   Joined, never more to part!
> How good the heart's still chamber thus to close
>   On all but God alone—
> There in the sweetness of His love repose,
>   His love unknown!
> All else for ever lost—forgotten all
>   That else can be;
> In rapture undisturbed, O Lord, to fall
>   And worship Thee.[2]

[1] W. L. Watkinson, *The Ashes of Roses*, 117.
[2] Frances Bevan, *Hymns of Ter Steegen*, 36.

STRENGTH AND BEAUTY.

LITERATURE.

Goodwin (H.), *Parish Sermons*, iv. 95.

Holden (J. S.), *Life's Flood-Tide*, 172.

Kirkpatrick (A. F.), *The Book of Psalms* (Cambridge Bible), 577.

Maclaren (A.), *The Book of Psalms* (Expositor's Bible), iii. 55.

Purves (G. T.), *Faith and Life*, 177.

Simpson (A. L.), *The Near and the Far View*, 219.

Wilson (F. R.), *The Supreme Service*, 15.

Wirgman (A. T.), *The Spirit of Liberty*, 104.

Christian World Pulpit, xlviii. 180 (F. L. Goodspeed); liii. 157 (C. S. Horne); lxii. 238 (W. J. K. Little); lxx. 23 (J. Waddell); lxxiv. 147 (F. Tite).

Churchman's Pulpit : Harvest Thanksgiving and Choir Festivals, Pt. 99, p. 399 (G. A. Poole).

STRENGTH AND BEAUTY.

Strength and beauty are in his sanctuary.—Ps. xcvi. 6.

THE Psalmist, in that lyrical outburst of adoration from which the
text is taken, professes to have discovered two qualities which
are revealed in combination in the character of God, and which,
such is the suggestion, He will Himself communicate to devout,
worshipful, and aspiring souls. These two qualities are strength
and beauty. Neither quality is of itself uncommon; it is their
combination that is so rare. Somehow in this world the strong
is not usually the beautiful, and the beautiful is not the strong.
We think of the beautiful in nature as the fragile, the delicate,
the evanescent. We think of the strong, and with its massive
solidity it is difficult to associate any thought of grace and loveliness. But this psalm was a hymn for the Temple; and if it be
true, as we suppose, that there yet remained many of the glorious
pillars which adorned that magnificent structure, it is conceivable
that they suggested to the Psalmist's mind this rare combination
of qualities. For these pillars of the Temple were of radiant
marble, stately and splendid in themselves, and with the added
decoration of capitals nobly carved in all manners of exquisite
device. And not the pillars alone, but the whole majestic pile
itself, was it not the standing witness to the truth that the God
whom it represented to men was at once strong and beautiful?
For its durability and solidity was equalled only by its magnificence; the strength of its stone by the beauty of its colouring and
the glory of its decoration. The architects of that ancient cathedral
seem to have derived their ideas from nature; and to have seen
that He who laid the enduring foundations of the earth decorated
the world which He made with the gold of the crocus, the crimson
of the field-lily, or the blue of the gentian and the harebell; and
they built for Him a fane which, like the world He built for them,

was strong and beautiful, massive, but full of delicate colour.   As was this temple of their God, so was the God of the Temple—in His Divine Being they felt there must be this glorious combination of strength and beauty.

¶ If it was Solomon's temple of which the Hebrew writer of this psalm spoke, we can imagine some of the features which he must have had in mind.   The immense blocks of stone, of which the foundation was composed, and the great Lebanon cedars which were brought by Hiram, king of Tyre, explain the reference to the strength of the building.   Though not large, it was a solid, massive structure, built to last through ages, while the foundations themselves rested on imperishable rock.   And then the resources of art were exhausted to make it beautiful as well as strong.   The interior was overlaid with pure gold, on which were carved figures of cherubim and palm trees and flowers.   All the utensils of worship were of the same costly metal and elaborately ornamented; while precious stones gleamed amid the gold and Tyrian tapestries hung on every side.   The wealthiest of kings lavished his riches; the most skilled artificers taxed their art; the adventurous mariners laid tribute upon distant lands to make beautiful the Temple of Jehovah.   It thus seemed to combine the two elements of architectural perfection—strength and beauty.[1]

I.

STRENGTH.

1. It is better that a building should be strong than that it should be ornamental.   And the same is true of character also. Ornament, moreover, ought to accompany strength.   It is not good art to put into a building a useless feature merely because it is beautiful.   The true artist will beautify the useful.   The practical purpose will be first.   So a character which aims only to be beautiful is not to be admired.   It merely becomes bric-à-brac.   It has the taint of cosmetics.   The man who is absorbed in the mere adornment of his character is not much beyond the man who is absorbed in the adornment of his body.   No, beauty must be superimposed upon strength.   The practical usefulness and moral power of life are to be the first things sought.   Then you

[1] G. T. Purves, *Faith and Life*, 177.

have something worth adorning. It is the hard stone that takes the best polish. It is the strong, earnest character that may be made the most beautiful.

¶ In the life of Archbishop Temple we read: "He stands out from amongst the men of his day, a notable figure, unlike others, cast in a larger mould, nobler than most, more self-reliant, more absolutely incapable of doing anything mean or of acting from self-interested motives; he worked harder and longer; he was more unworldly; he grasped more firmly the substance of life; he was a greater man; but a man nevertheless, working with and for his fellows, compelling the admiration of all, but winning most love from those who knew best the man's heart within him. To the elders who are left he is a great memory, and as they look back and realize to what extent they lived in him they fancy that life now lies behind them. But it was a real life which they shared, and it still remains; for it belonged to the eternal world, and is of those things 'which cannot be moved.' Even its methods will last long; they had always about them something of the enduring spirit of the man. And thus the life points onward and has a meaning for those who are young. The air of perpetual spring blows round the old man's grave: the memory speaks reality and hope, and these are the memories which live."[1] Yet to those who knew him best his strength was not more notable than the depth and tenderness of his affections.

2. Some foolish people associate religion with weakness. Perhaps some weak Christians are responsible for this. But there is nothing weak about true religion. The man who lays hold upon God is strong. "Strong in the Lord, and in the power of his might." There is nothing weak about faith. It can remove mountains; it can carry men through fire and water, and has inspired the noblest heroism that the world has ever seen. There is nothing weak about truth or righteousness. Falseness is weak; unrighteousness is weak. But to be really good is to be strong. In the Bible weakness is not pitied but condemned, and the watchword to believers over and over again is "Be strong!" The great essential of Christian character is strength—strength to overcome evil and to labour for the good of others.

¶ In February, 1865, Dr. Punshon delivered in Exeter Hall his famous lecture on William Wilberforce, the thoroughness of whose religious decision was thus referred to: "With the

---

[1] *Frederick Temple, Archbishop of Canterbury*, ii. 711.

accidents of birth and station in his favour, with youth upon
his side, fortune at his feet, and fame and power within the
grasp of his outstretched hand—when life was in its summer,
and he was compassed, so to speak, with its gladness, and music,
and flowers—with everything at hand which it is deemed the
most costly to surrender—he stepped forth in the sight of the
world, for which his name had already a charm, took the crown of
his manhood, and laid it humbly at the feet of Christ. I can see
in the act a courage of that sort which is the truest and rarest,
but which is, notwithstanding, within the reach of you all. The
true idea of power is not embodied in Hercules or Samson, brute
forces with brute appetites, takers of strong cities, but slaves to
their own passion. Nor is it in the brave soldier who can storm
a fortress at the point of the bayonet, but who yields his manhood to the enticements of sinners, and hides the faith which the
scoffer's sneer has made him frightened to avow. The real power
is there when a man has mastered himself, when he has trampled
upon the craven and the shameful in all their disguises, and when,
ready on all fit occasions to bear himself worthily among his
fellows and 'give the world assurance of a man,' he dares to say
to that world, the while it scorns and slanders him, 'I will not
serve thy gods, nor worship the golden image which thou hast set
up.'"[1]

3. A man who loves and trusts God cannot but be a strong
character. He will not be easily moved by any temptation. He
will not be unduly anxious about the future. He will be in no
hurry. He will have the calm assurance that, be the present
mysteries what they may, all is going well. And he will feel that
his life is inseparably linked with the Highest One Himself.
"Love is strong as death," says the old writer; and if we see
instances of the love of man to man in which this is true, much
more is it true that in proportion as a human soul loves God will
it be firm against evil and strong for all good. The mighty
granite masses out of which we quarry the material for our great
buildings were once in a fluid, molten state, but they have
crystallized into the hardest of rocks. So will belief in God and
Christ, and love to God in Christ, crystallize a soul into the
strongest of characters.

¶ Unwearied in their efforts to prevent Luther's appearance,
the papal ambassadors had at last succeeded in procuring an

[1] F. W. Macdonald, *Life of W. Morley Punshon*, 229.

Imperial edict for the delivery and burning of Luther's books. This was practically a condemnation in advance, and seemed to render Luther's presence unnecessary; but the Emperor tried to steer between the two parties by saying that Luther was summoned only for the purpose of having him recant. At Weimar this edict reached him, and its intention was immediately seen. The Imperial herald, who was favourably disposed to Luther, asked whether he would proceed. Only for a brief moment did he tremble; but quickly regaining his self-possession, he answered: "Yes. I will proceed, and entrust myself to the Emperor's protection," thus foiling the plan of his adversaries to have him condemned for contumacy in disobeying the summons. Worn out and sick, he wrote to Spalatin from Frankfort: "Christ lives; and we shall enter Worms, though all the gates of Hell and powers of the air be unwilling." [1]

II.

BEAUTY.

1. The next thing is beauty. Some Christians are content with the strength, and care little for the beauty, of the Christian life. They are stern in their adhesion to principle, careless of the lesser charities of life, apt to be harsh in their condemnation of error and sin. Every one knows their worth, believes in their honesty, would trust implicitly to their integrity. But they do not win love by their gracious bearing, their kind words, their charitable construction of men and things. In a word, they have the strength, but they lack something of the beauty of the Christian character. We have always the practical, hard-headed people with us (like Dickens' " Mr. Gradgrind "), who say, " Never mind about the beautiful, give us the useful, the durable," and who would regard all ornamentation as useless and extravagant. But God has a ministry both for strength and for beauty. He made not only things great but things beautiful. " O, worship the Lord in the beauty of holiness," says the Psalmist, and we must remember there is also a holiness of beauty. In the fabric and services of the sanctuary nothing is too beautiful or too good for God. " Jerry-building " and cheap fittings are out of place here. God

[1] H. E. Jacobs, *Martin Luther*, 184.

should have the best of workmanship, the loveliest of music, and the perfection of reverence and order.

¶ If you behold the sky with its peerless blue, the meadow with its emerald green, the grain-field with its yellow gold, the lake with its silver white, you will see that beauty has been wrought into all the patterns of nature. What skilled artist can put another touch upon the rainbow, or mix colours that will heighten the beauty of the transfigured cloud-land? The spring in its fresh green, the winter in its robes of pearl, the cataract, the crystal spray, the pearly dew, the ocean all aglow with phosphorescence, every wavelet flashing and sparkling as it caps and breaks, the towering mountains, with their ceaseless lights and shadows, the jewelled sphere of night, the glorious transparency of day, the sunset glories God has hidden beneath the surface of the roughest shell—all these declare with a thousand voices that God loves beauty as well as strength.[1]

2. We must have the strength first, and beauty afterward. It is disaster to reverse this order—to try to get beauty and then have strength. The magnificent Brooklyn Bridge, when viewed at a distance, is a beautiful poem. But the beauty is dependent on the strength of mighty abutments which reach down far below the river bed and take hold of the foundations of the earth. In everything, both artistic and moral, strength is the stalk; beauty is the flower that blooms on it.

¶ The great porch of Solomon's temple was upheld by two famous pillars of bronze, cast and adorned by the most skilful workmen of the day. Those massive pillars, called Jachin and Boaz, have been described and discussed in a thousand books, and have been the cause of endless speculation. The Biblical description closes with this suggestive sentence, "on the top of the pillars was lily work." The columns that supported ended in tracery that adorned. The strength that upheld blossomed out into grace and beauty at the top. In our day there is a great desire for the lily work without the pillars, a vain longing for the graces of life and the beauties of character without the supporting power of truth and duty. There are thousands of men who would like the virtues of the fathers, but who do not want the faith which made them virtuous. They would like to have reproduced in their life the qualities of soul which marked the early Christians, the Reformers, and the Puritans; but not their sturdy

[1] F. L. Goodspeed.

faith, not their tenacity of conviction, not their majestic conscience or their tremendous hold on things unseen. They want the simplicity and affection of the Waldenses, but not their faith in God; the audacity and fearlessness of John Knox and Oliver Cromwell, without their vivid sense of the Divine Presence; the morality of John Robinson and Miles Standish, without their heroic creed; the integrity of Washington and Lincoln, without their trust in a sustaining and overruling God. Mothers are anxious that their daughters should shine in every social accomplishment; that their sons should be men of talent and of skill; that their homes should be beautiful with music and art and all kindly grace. But they are not so solicitous about the solid foundations of character.

III.

Strength and Beauty.

"Know ye not," says the Apostle, "that ye are the temple of God, and that the Spirit of God dwelleth in you?" The sanctuary of God is a human soul that is governed and moulded by God. Such a soul is His temple. Of this it is true that strength and beauty are in His sanctuary. In other words, a true Christian character is the realization of the highest ideal of what a man should be.

1. A noble character must contain in high degree, and in right proportions, just those two elements of which the text speaks — strength and beauty. There must be strength of character. You cannot make a house out of sand, because the particles do not cohere to one another. Neither can you make a worthy character out of irresolution, vacillation, doubt, fear, instability. A true man must have ruling convictions, concentration and constancy of purpose, firmness in the right as he sees it, power to endure reverses, positive purposes and ideas. These make a strong character. A true man must also have these elements of strength adorned by gentler virtues. Manliness is not mere strength. There must be refinement of feeling, humanity, and benevolence, gentleness and patience. These make character beautiful. And the two elements must combine

in right proportion. A merely strong character is as one-sided and imperfect as a pugilist is an abnormal specimen of physical manhood. A merely gentle, loving character is often pitiably weak and unpractical. A true man is strong in his convictions, but gentle in his judgments; constant of purpose, but gentle to the weak and mindful of others' rights; positive but humble; energetic but meek. This is the ideal which Christianity has taught the world.

¶ God has room in His Church for both strength and beauty. Is there not a parable in the fact that Jubal, the inventor of music, and Tubal-cain, the first blacksmith, were brothers? When Tubal-cain set up the first smithy he was starting an industry which has been of great use in the world; but when Jubal struck chords of music from his first primitive harp, he laid succeeding generations of men under no less obligation.[1]

¶ The finest and most impressive effects are often produced by the combination of things that are unlike each other. The painter recognizes this principle when he brings his darkest shadows to heighten the effect of his clearest lights, or contrasts the peaceful life of some humble cottage home with the stately magnificence of the stern mountains that surround it. The architect appeals to the same principle when he crowns his columns with beautiful capitals, and relieves the massive masonry of his walls with delicate tracery. The massive wall and the marble column suggest the thought of strength; while the delicate carvings and the sculptured friezes appeal to the sense of beauty. The thought which lies deep in the artist's mind, and to which he strives to give expression in his work, is that there is a natural alliance between strength and beauty. He is not satisfied with the stern severity of mere strength, nor does he allow the idea of beauty to exclude all other thoughts. But he endeavours to clothe and crown strong things with beauty, and to support beautiful things by strength.

2. Strong characters are not rare, and beautiful characters are not rare; but characters that are both strong and beautiful are rare. It is so difficult to be firm and not to be hard, to be inflexibly just and not to be cold, to have the solid virtues that make for strength, and with them the soft and gracious qualities that command our love. Some men and women have the decorative virtues—they are full of generosity, noble impulse, charity

[1] F. R. Wilson, *The Supreme Service*, 17.

and magnanimity, and enthusiasm; but they have not with these the strength of mind and will that can resist the "taking" and popular tendency if it be forbidden by sound principles of justice and of practical common sense. Some people, on the other hand, have only the fundamental qualities—they are just, but they cannot be generous; honest, but never liberal; truthful, but never merciful. They have principle, but they have never yielded to a wise enthusiasm, or been moved out of their slow, plodding habit by some sacred zeal for a great and good cause. The world yields to the strong men; it admires them, it honours them; but it does not love them. They command its respect, but they do not engage its affection. On the other hand, the world's heart is drawn out to the beautiful lives, but it discovers to its pain that it must not lean upon them. They cannot be trusted in our hours of real trial and perplexity. What they gain in heart they seem to lose in head; and we grow conscious that they are tender and generous and kind, but they are not wise. Of how few is it true that they are not only strong but beautiful, not only beautiful but strong!

¶ All the strong things in nature are beautiful; all the beautiful things are exhibitions of strength. David speaks of the "strength of the hills" which is "his also." We feel the power and appropriateness of the words as we look up to the mountains. But do we not speak with equal truth of the beauty of the hills, clad in exquisite verdure, or flushed with the light that is "new every morning"; delicate flowers and tender ferns nestling in the shelter of their crags, and purple rocks reflecting the sunsets of a thousand years? Take the strongest thing that nature yields, and we shall find that its strength is the cradle of an exquisite and unfathomable beauty. Take the most beautiful thing, and we shall find that its beauty is in closest alliance with immeasurable strength. The dewdrop that glitters on the roseleaf—we all know the perfection of its beauty; but how little do we understand the mystery of the strength by which its beauty is secured! That little drop of water is composed of elements which are held together by electric forces sufficient to form a flash of lightning that would rend the rocks of the mountain or blast the stoutest oak of the forest. All that mighty thunder of power lies sleeping in the crystal sphere of a tiny dewdrop.

¶ Florence Nightingale had that " excellent thing in woman "— a gentle voice. Lady Lovelace in her poem spoke of her friend's "soft, silvery voice"; but it could command, as well as charm, unless indeed it were the charm that commanded. "She scolds sergeants and orderlies all day long," wrote Mr. Bracebridge to her parents (Nov. 20); "you would be astonished to see how fierce she is grown." That was written, of course, in fun; but there was always a note of calm authority in her voice. A Crimean veteran recalled her passing his bed with some doctors, who were saying, "It can't be done," and her replying quietly, "It must be done." "I seem to hear her saying it," writes one who knew her well; "there seemed to be no appeal from her quiet, conclusive manner."[1]

3. In Jesus Christ strength and beauty appear as nowhere else among men. He is the ideal man. His character contains every element of strength—profound knowledge, constant faith, ability to suffer for the truth, composure in the face of an assailing world. Yet His character contains also every element of beauty. He is tender as a woman, devoted in His love of man, humble and meek, gentle and patient too. Each quality exists in accurate proportion in Him; so that we may say, without hesitation and after the closest examination, that the architecture of Christ's character is absolutely perfect.

¶ The mediæval conception of our Saviour, as meek, and suffering, and patient, and gentle above all others, is true though incomplete. He was "strong Son of God" also. It was the boldness of Peter and John that reminded men of their courageous Master. How constantly in His life do we see strength and beauty, in perfect balance and poise, shining forth from His acts and words! In the garden of agony, faced by cruel and murderous men, He stands erect, calmly repeating to His enemies, "I have told you that I am he"—there is strength; but mark the tender beauty of what follows: "If ye seek me, let these go their way"—solicitude for His faint-hearted followers mingling with His fortitude. As one has truly said: "The eyes that wept beside the grave of Lazarus were eyes that were like a flame of fire." By His strength and beauty, combined with perfect symmetry in one holy character, Jesus endlessly attracts. His charm is not like that of any other. "Thou hast conquered, O Galilean," for Thou art strong and Thou art fair, Thou art chiefest among ten thousand, Captain of the Lord's hosts, and Thou art altogether lovely, beautiful beyond compare.[2]

[1] Sir Edward Cook, *The Life of Florence Nightingale*, i. 186.
[2] J. Waddell.

A rose, a lily, and the Face of Christ
  Have all our hearts sufficed:
For He is Rose of Sharon nobly born,
  Our Rose without a thorn;
And He is Lily of the Valley, He
  Most sweet in purity.
But when we come to name Him as He is,
  Godhead, Perfection, Bliss,
All tongues fall silent, while pure hearts alone
  Complete their orison.[1]

[1] Christina G. Rossetti, *Christ our All in All.*

LIGHT AND GLADNESS.

LITERATURE.

Carroll (B. H.), *Sermons*, 340.
Christopherson (H.), *Sermons*, 30.
Halsey (J.), in *Jesus in the Cornfield*, 143.
Jerdan (C.), *Gospel Milk and Honey*, 311.
Landels (W.), *Until the Day Break*, 125.
Learmount (J.), *Fifty-two Sundays with the Children*, 92.
Miller (J. R.), *A Help for Common Days*, 91.
Spurgeon (C. H.), *Metropolitan Tabernacle Pulpit*, xiv. (1868), No. 836.
Stubbs (W.), in *Oxford University Sermons*, 318.
Voysey (C.), *Sermons*, x. (1887), No. 20 ; xii. (1889), No. 22.
Wilson (S. L.), *Helpful Words for Daily Life*, 384.
Christian World Pulpit, lxxviii. 33 (R. J. Campbell).

LIGHT AND GLADNESS.

Light is sown for the righteous,
And gladness for the upright in heart.—Ps. xcvii. 11.

THE peculiar metaphor employed in this passage is somewhat arrestive because of the form in which it is expressed. This way of putting things is quite different from ordinary language; we do not commonly speak of sowing light and gladness in the same fashion as we sow grain in the spring-time with the expectation of an autumn harvest. The figure is so striking that we are at once compelled to pause and ask what this writer has in mind. To say the least of it, the suggestion is very beautiful. Imagine a husbandman sowing rays of light in the ploughed fields instead of the ordinary corn and flower seed! Why, the very idea is full of spiritual suggestion, and sets us on the track of high and holy things. Perhaps it is for this reason that the Revisers have allowed it to stand, although, as has frequently been pointed out, the translation is not literally correct. If we have a mind to be pedantically accurate we might render the text thus: "Light has arisen—or, is scattered—for the righteous, and gladness for the upright in heart." It is almost identical in form with Ps. cxii. 4, "Unto the upright there ariseth light in the darkness." This reduces the sentiment to a much more commonplace category, for, of course, it means no more than an allusion to the phenomenon of sunrise, a figure in which there is nothing so very remarkable or out of the common. But somehow one thinks the Authorized translators have got nearer the original meaning of this utterance than a mere prosaic literalism could have done. It is true poetry to say that light is sown for the righteous, and there is nothing fantastic about it.

¶ Milton, in *Paradise Lost*, wrote these words about the sunbeams and the dew: "Morn advancing sowed the earth with orient pearl." And when, with this thought in our minds, we look up on a winter night to the starry sky, does that not seem like an immense concave field sown all over with light ?[1]

I.

SOWN LIGHT.

1. It is no merely fanciful use of the words, "light is sown," to suggest that, in a literal sense, light has been sown for our harvesting in those vast buried forests which constitute our coal-fields, and are the source of nearly all our artificial light and heat. The sunbeams that streamed through long millenniums upon our planet were absorbed by those giant ferns and conifers that flourished in what geologists call the Carboniferous period, and were afterwards submerged and overlaid with other deposits; and after having been imprisoned in the depths and the darkness for long ages, like seed in the soil, the light of those beams is now breaking forth once more for the illumination and service of man.

¶ George Stephenson, the inventor of the locomotive engine, was once standing with Dean Buckland, the famous geologist, and others upon the terrace of Sir Robert Peel's mansion at Drayton Manor, when a railway train flashed along in the distance, throwing behind it a long trail of white steam. "Now, Dr. Buckland," said Stephenson, "can you tell me what is the power that is driving that train?" "Well," said the Dean, "I suppose it is one of your big engines." "But what drives the engine?" "Oh, very likely a canny Newcastle driver." "What do you say to the light of the sun?" "How can that be?" asked the Dean. "It is nothing else," replied the engineer; "it is light bottled up in the earth for tens of thousands of years and now, after being buried in the earth for long ages in the fields of coal, the latent light is again brought forth and liberated; made to work, as in that engine, for great motive purposes." That answer was itself a flash of illumination to the mind of the man of science, and there is more meaning in it than even Buckland or Stephenson himself ever dreamed. For, since that day, not only has light produced by the combustion of coal gas become the chief means of artificial illumination to all civilized nations, but mineral oils derived from the same source are also largely used, and it is the pent-up force of the sunbeam locked up in the coal

[1] C. Jerdan.

that drives our motor-cars, and, transformed into heat, generates the power which we transmute again into light in the form of the electric beam. Hundreds of thousands of years ago the light was sown, and now the harvest is being reaped.[1]

2. A seed is a germ. When, therefore, we say that God has sown the light for us, we mean that He gives us our blessings in germ, not in full form—that they come to us, not developed into completeness of beauty, but as seeds which we must plant, waiting, sometimes waiting long, for them to grow into loveliness. A seed does not disclose all the beauty of the life that is folded up within it. We see only a little brown and unsightly hull which gives no prophecy of anything so beautiful as springs from it when it has been planted. These facts in nature have their analogies in the seeds of spiritual blessing which God sows for us. The blessing does not appear: what does appear is often unlovely in its form, giving in itself no promise of good. Yet it is a seed carrying in it the potency of life and the possibilities of great blessing. Every duty that comes to our hand in the common days is a seed of light which God has sown for us. Some seeds are dark and rough as we look upon them; so there are duties that have in them no promise of joy or pleasure as they first present themselves to us. They look hard and repulsive, and we shrink from doing them, but every one knows that there is in the faithful doing of every duty a strange secret of joy; and the harder the duty, the fuller and the richer is the sense of gladness that follows its performance.

> God's angels drop like grains of gold
>   Our duties 'midst life's shining sands,
> And from them, one by one, we mould
>   Our own bright crown with patient hands.
> From dust and dross we gather them;
>   We toil and stoop for love's sweet sake
>   To find each worthy act a gem
>   In glory's kingly diadem
> Which we may daily richer make.

¶ It has been said that faith in God and belief in immortality were Browning's sources of inspiration. It is not possible to say that of all our poets—perhaps not of any in the same degree as of

[1] J. Halsey.

him. One other great poet of the Victorian age, Tennyson, may be very properly described as a religious poet. He, too, treats of the eternal mysteries of God and the universe, and the awful problems of life and death; but where Tennyson whispers, or speaks with bated breath, Browning sends forth a clear, distinct, ringing voice—where the former " faintly trusts," the latter avows a confidence which nought can disturb, and which inspires faith in the more timid and halting of his fellows around him. What Browning makes the Pope say in "The Ring and the Book," he might have said of himself with perfect truthfulness :

> Never I miss footing in the maze,
> No,—I have light nor fear the dark at all.[1]

3. This figure of light sown implies something hidden and long waited for, yet certain at last; even as the seed is buried in the soil, and " the husbandman hath long patience until he receive the early and the latter rain," and finally, the assured fruition of his labour. The sower does not doubt the harvest because he has to wait weary months for it. He knows that in due season he shall reap if he faint not. And so the Psalmist would have us believe that the certainty of the coming light is as great as that of the present darkness, and that if our calamities are inevitable, our consolations are assured. " Weeping may endure for a night, but joy cometh in the morning."

The seed which is cast into the soil does not immediately yield the harvest. The waiting is the price we have to pay for the hundredfold increase. It cannot be reaped yet. But it is sown, and will yet grow and ripen. God's hand has prepared the soil and cast the seed, and His care and culture secure an abundant harvest. It is sown, and is growing under His eye. Those dark clouds that overshadow sometimes drop down fatness on it. Those storms that are so trying strengthen it. And God's love, like genial sunshine, is promoting its continual growth. It is sown, and will be reaped before long. Fear not; rather look beyond.

> Lift up thine eyes beyond the night
>   Of life's dark setting; blossoms of to-day
> Shall break in flower to-morrow.
>   This year's light sucked into every spray
> Is food for summer blossoms yet to be.

[1] J. Flew, *Studies in Browning*, 7.

¶ The rays of the sun are streaming across ninety-six million miles of space every day in the year, and every hour in the day. Some of them are turned into planetary energy at once; others pass down into darkness and silence in the earth and there remain; or they may spring up immediately in the form of vegetation, which by and by becomes a coal mine or a petroleum well. After the lapse of ages, it may be, that stored-up light, scattered so lavishly upon the earth's surface so long ago, is discovered and brought into use once more. We drive our looms and illuminate our houses with it. We call it by a variety of names, according to the service we manage to draw from it. In the form of electricity we make it flash our thoughts from continent to continent across intervening oceans. In another form, it will carry a floating city, like a modern mammoth Atlantic liner, from the old world to the new. In others, it shines forth as beauty and splendour in the complex and manifold achievements of art and science. What untold wonders are being wrought every day by the bringing forth of the stored-up light of the sun! They constitute the harvest of that which was sown long before we who profit by the blessing were born to inherit it.[1]

4. God has sown His holy light in the field of His *Word*. The sacred writings are full of hidden light—the light of truth, holiness, and joy; and this light the Holy Spirit shows to the devout and diligent student. Every gospel promise is a star, shining in the dark night of time; and the Bible is a " book of stars." Light is sown also in the field of Divine *Providence*. Everything that God allows to happen to His people is right: this is so, even when darkness wraps them round for a season. " We know that all things work together for good to them that love God." And light is sown especially in the field of *human hearts*. The Spirit of God scatters in this soil seeds of living light— knowledge and purity and gladness. " The fruit of the Spirit is love, joy, peace, longsuffering, gentleness, goodness, faith, meekness, temperance."

¶ I have been deep in my study of the ways of God in heathen religions. The past of mankind does not now seem a black ocean covered with fog and storm, and wrecks drifting everywhere, but a long wake of light crosses it coming from the light that lighteth every man in the world, the Pharos of humanity—the Spirit of

[1] R. J. Campbell.

God. In that gleam, the nations have steered their barks and made towards haven. He hath not left Himself without a witness.[1]

¶ I have been thinking especially of those prayers which are most legitimate and most surely answered—prayers for help to resist temptation, for strength in the performance of duty, for the lifting of despondency, and for all the way in which men are raised above themselves and out of weakness are made strong. In such cases as these it does not often happen that the supplicant is conscious of any direct intervention of God. He will indeed rise from his knees in a calmer frame of mind; the habit of prayer, and the trustfulness which goes with such a habit, cannot fail of their effect in quieting for the time the troubled spirit. The humble Christian does not look for more than this; but he waits awhile, and the crisis passes. He does not know what has happened; but in some strange way the difficulties that seemed to beset him have vanished; the problem that seemed so unmanageable is solved; the thing that seemed so impossible is done.[2]

II.

Sown Gladness.

"Light and gladness"! What a wonderful conception of the future portion of the righteous does the Psalmist here give us! The two words, as is customary in the parallelism of Hebrew poetry, mean almost the same thing. The one is figurative, the other literal. The word "gladness" itself teaches us most emphatically that joy is the portion of the righteous—exuberant, exultant joy—joy which beams in the eye, and lights up the countenance, and gives buoyancy to the frame, and is heard in the jubilant tones of the voice, and which yet has its seat deep among the springs of feeling—in the very heart's core. Gladness! It is joy, full, deep, and placid, like a lake which knows no ebb, and is sheltered from every agitating storm, and yet like a lake whose calm waters ripple under the gentle breeze, and flash with bright scintillations in the rays of the summer's sun, with singing birds around pouring out their melody, and flowers shedding fragrance

---

[1] *Life of Charles Loring Brace*, 458.
[2] W. Sanday, in *The Expository Times*, xxiv. (1913) 440.

on the air, and beautifying all the scene. Gladness! It is the
laughter of the heart, when, full of enjoyment to overflowing, it
ripples over in spontaneous expression, more cheerful than the
laughter of childhood at play, serene as a summer evening sky.
Gladness! Surprising revelations — expectation more than
realized; fears dispelled and dangers escaped; sorrows changed
into joys; all perils passed, all apprehensions hushed; satisfy-
ing bliss already possessed, higher bliss anticipated! All this is
included in this portion of the righteous.

1. This gladness will be accompanied by, and no doubt partially
spring from, the revelation of things that are wrapped in darkness
now. It will be no small element in the joy of the righteous that
many of the mysteries which perplex them will be unravelled.
God's ways, which now seem to us mysterious, and which try the
faith and patience of His people, will not always be so unfathomable as they are now; they will present themselves in a very
different aspect when His chosen have reached the end of their
course, and begin to see as they are seen, and to know as they are
known. " Unto the upright there ariseth light in the darkness."
And we cannot but believe that their hearts will be gladdened by
the surprisingly new light in which the most trying dispensations
appear, and by the lifting up of the veil from the great and
glorious purposes which they were designed to promote. There
may still be room for the exercise of faith. But, largely, faith
will give place to sight, and hope to realization. And in their
clearer understanding of the Divine method, and their better
acquaintance with its glorious issues, they will find no small
portion of their joy. The gladness of brighter and ever-increasing
light will be theirs for ever.

¶ The missing qualities in Wesley's religious state at this
time [before his conversion] are sufficiently obvious. It utterly
lacked the element of joy. Religion is meant to have for the
spiritual landscape the office of sunshine, but in Wesley's spiritual
sky at this time there burned no Divine light, whether of certainty
or of hope. He imagined he could distil the rich wine of spiritual
gladness out of mechanical religious exercises; but he found himself, to his own distress, and in his own words, "dull, flat, and
unaffected in the use of the most solemn ordinances." Fear, too,
like a shadow, haunted his mind: fear that he was not accepted

before God; fear that he might lose what grace he had; fear both of life and of death.[1]

2. God is the God of gladness, as well as the God of terror. And this needs special emphasizing for some who would limit His interest to the graver things of life—sorrow, affliction, mourning. It is true, beautifully true, that He is the *Consolatio afflictorum*, the real, genuine Refuge for thousands who are burdened and heavy laden; but it is also true that He presides over the pleasures of His people. Is not the average Englishman's conception of God that of a stern, stiff Being, more or less confined to certain times and places, associated chiefly with stiff-backed pews, but having very little, if anything, to do with the pleasures or the gladder side of daily life? This—though it has its good side—is a view we want to review and revise. We want to get back to the old, happy conception of the Psalmist: "Thou art about my path and about my being, and spiest out *all* my ways." And worse still: some of us keep this gladsome view of God outside even our religion. The Hundredth Psalm has a line which runs in the old metrical version,

"Him serve with *mirth*, His praise forth tell,"

which is often sung as if the words were,

"Him serve with *fear*."

The change is a bad one. Fear has its part to play in life, but here it spoils the whole idea of the hymn, and is out of harmony with the verse in the Psalm from which the thought is borrowed: "Serve the Lord with *gladness*, and come before his presence with a song." Let us get back to the original as soon as we can in thought, word, and deed.

¶ Froude reminds us how bright and happy and even humorous were the great heroes of the Reformation—Luther, Calvin, and Knox; and yet they lived in times when there was far more to lament and to be ashamed of even than in ours; they fought a battle for light and truth and liberty under far heavier discouragements than we have to bear, and yet they were among the happiest of men. And why? Because they were doing something, they were not idle and sentimental spectators of the foul state of things around them, but every day and all day they were active in trying to overthrow them; they were for ever fighting against the lies

[1] W. H. Fitchett, *Wesley and His Century*, 82.

and baseness and follies and superstitions on every hand and
therefore they were not morbid or melancholy; they knew that
God was on their side and therefore their true hearts were glad.
Difficulties did not daunt them; wounds did not disable them;
reproaches, curses, mortal danger did not even damp their spirits
or lower the temperature of their joy. Amidst the Egyptian
darkness, the darkness which might be felt, as we are told, the
children of Israel had light in their dwellings. True or not as
a matter of history, it is grandly true that wherever there is
righteous work for God there is light in the mind and soul,
wherever there is fidelity there is joyful gladness.[1]

¶ Many a man gets little credit for his indomitable good cheer,
because it is supposed that this is but his natural inclination.
But a virtue is still a virtue, even though it be congenial; and
those who have diligently kept their lamp of joy alight are not
the least worthy of God's faithful ones. As for Stevenson, he
deliberately drew upon and encouraged all the available sources
of gladness. He carried with him into manhood, not only the
glee that comes from physical vitality, and the sense of the
world's opulence, but also the spirit of the Lantern-bearer, who
carefully kept alive his inner light. His natural optimism is
unquestionable, but it should be remembered that he needed it all,
and that, if his strenuous choice of it had flagged, pessimism would
not have been far to seek. It is a great and potent secret, that
of fostering our own peculiar enthusiasm as a sacred flame.
Regard yourself, as you face the simplest duty of to-morrow, as
tending within your soul's temple the fires of God, and you shall
find the bright parable true. Both these sources, the outward
and the inward, were largely drawn upon by Stevenson.[2]

III.

THE REAPERS OF LIGHT AND GLADNESS.

God's light is sown for all mankind, but only "the righteous"
can find it; His gladness waits at the door of every soul, but it
never enters save to "the upright in heart." But who are "the
righteous" who are thus favoured, and what does it mean to
be "upright in heart"? What Jesus meant by righteousness
was substantially what the great prophets of the Old Testament

[1] C. Voysey.
[2] J. Kelman, *The Faith of Robert Louis Stevenson*, 250.

had meant before Him when they protested against idolatry. He meant motive rather than deed; He meant that equality of mind and heart whereby a man loses sight of self-interest in the desire to help and succour his fellow-creatures. From this standpoint it is clear that the more righteous a man becomes the less will he think about it; he will cease to be self-conscious; he will just go on giving himself quietly and simply without asking whether he is to be rewarded or not.

No sooner does a man become absorbed in some great impersonal achievement, ceasing to care what may or may not happen to himself in the process, than he begins to find that life discloses new and vaster meaning; and he knows more of true blessedness than he ever knew before. He may be quite willing to forgo everything in the shape of reward, but it is part of the very law of universal being that he cannot do so. The less he thinks about reward the more certainly will the highest kind of reward pour in upon him. He cannot be wretched; life forbids it. He may have to go down into the darkness for a brief hour, but it is only to bring up the everlasting light; he may wrestle awhile in Gethsemane, but it is only a stage in the ascent to the gladness beyond the cross. Who will gainsay the truth of this? It is the eternal paradox which faces every generation, and challenges every individual experience as though it had never been known before. It lies at the heart of all religion, and reaches its highest expression in the life and death of our Lord Jesus Christ Himself.

1. While it is true of all good men in every creed that light springs up in their hearts, and joyful gladness is ever the sweet handmaid of sincerity, yet it is especially true that God often rewards an intense desire for righteousness with clearer views of His own righteousness and more light to shine upon us from His love. We have been faithful to some obligation or trust, and so God in His mercy has revealed to us more light to shine on His dealings with mankind, and has blessed us with the joy of knowing more of His infinite fidelity and trustworthiness. Or we have been more than usually kind, merciful, and generous in our dealings with others, and then God has shown us more and more of His inexhaustible kindness, mercy, and generosity unto all. Or

we have had to make some daring sacrifice of worldly advantage, some loss of position or friends rather than be false to ourselves and our convictions, and then God has revealed to us the delight that He takes in a brave man and in moral courage, and He puts a joy and liveliness into our whole nature which the chances of fortune cannot steal and the frowns of the world cannot crush.

¶ I know but one way in which a man who craves the light and cannot find it may come forth from his agony of doubt scathless; it is by holding fast to those things which are certain still—the grand, simple landmarks of morality. In the darkest hour through which a human soul can pass, whatever else is doubtful, this at least is certain. If there be no God and no future state, yet, even then, it is better to be generous than selfish, better to be chaste than licentious, better to be true than false, better to be brave than to be a coward. Blessed beyond all earthly blessedness is the man who, in the tempestuous darkness of the soul, has dared to hold fast to these venerable landmarks. Thrice blessed is he who, when all is drear and cheerless within and without, when his teachers terrify him, and his friends shrink from him, has obstinately clung to moral good. Thrice blessed, because *his* night shall pass into clear, bright day.[1]

2. "Light is sown for the righteous," because only the righteous can perceive and rejoice in the light. There are certain rays in the spectrum that are invisible to us, simply because our optic nerve is not sufficiently sensitive to respond to the rapidity of their vibrations. There are new colours awaiting those who can bring new eyes to them. So much of the joy in our life depends on our capacity to see the Divine purpose and meaning in the things that befall us. The comfort is there, but we cannot take it. We are like Hagar in the wilderness, wretched with thirst, while the fountain is there flashing back the sunlight before our blinded eyes.

¶ There is a shining light ahead, and Evangelist points Christian to that. Every soul of man can see at least *some* light of hope ahead, shining in the direction of the God or Christ or ideal which is as yet obscure. It may be but the light of some possible duty, some sense of honour, some belief in life, some vague trust in the future. The point is not that the light is full, or even comprehensible. If it be clear enough to flee towards,

[1] F. W. Robertson, *Lectures, Addresses, and Literary Remains*, 49.

that is enough. For, here as elsewhere, "solvitur ambulando." What is wanted is directed motion towards the light; the rest will follow. So it comes to pass that one may be on the road to Christ when one cannot as yet see Him.[1]

> He that walks it only thirsting
> For the right, and learns to deaden
> Love of self, before his journey closes,
> He shall find the stubborn thistle bursting
> Into glossy purples, which outredden
> All voluptuous garden-roses. . . .
> He, that ever following her commands
> On with toil of heart and knees and hands,
> Thro' the long gorge to the far light has won
> His path upward, and prevail'd,
> Shall find the toppling crags of Duty scaled
> Are close upon the shining table-lands,
> To which our God Himself is moon and sun.[2]

3. If a man is to reap light, he must sow light. Every one of us makes his own future. If we would have the capacity for light hereafter, we must cultivate it now. There is a tendency in light to beget light, just as there is a tendency in the seed to bring forth thirty to a hundredfold. Believe and walk in the light you have, and it shall grow from more to more unto noon-day splendour. If in the darkness a man, loving the light, sow the seeds of light, further illumination shall come to him hereafter.

¶ "Curses come home to roost," says the proverb. No less do gentle speech and kindly acts come back to nestle softly in our hearts. Faber, the Roman Catholic poet, sings how he caught up a little child and kissed it and gave it new joy in the sense of having made a new friend. And then he adds:

> I am a happier and a richer man,
> Since I have sown this new joy in the earth:
> 'Tis no small thing for us to reap stray mirth,
> In every sunny wayside where we can.
> It is a joy to me to be a joy,
> Which may in the most lowly heart take root;
> And it is gladness to that little boy
> To look out for me at the mountain foot.

[1] J. Kelman, *The Road*, i. 9. [2] Tennyson.

ALL HIS BENEFITS.

LITERATURE.

Brooke (S. A.), *Christ in Modern Life*, 351.
    „   „   *The Gospel of Joy*, 67.
    „   „   *The Ship of the Soul*, 16.
Brown (A. G.), in *The People's Pulpit*, No. 20.
  „ (C. G.), *The Word of Life*, 141.
Campbell (J. M.), *Grow Old Along with Me*, 19.
Cross (J.), *Knight-Banneret*, 292.
Drummond (H.), *The Ideal Life*, 145.
Hall (F. O.), *Soul and Body*, 73.
Hutton (J. A.), *The Soul's Triumphant Way*, 23.
Iverach (J.), *The Other Side of Greatness*, 119.
Macmillan (H.), *The Ministry of Nature*, 321.
Matheson (G.), *Leaves for Quiet Hours*, 213.
Miller (J.), *Sermons Literary and Scientific*, i. 270.
Morrison (G. H.), *The Oldest Trade in the World*, 103.
Myres (W. M.), *Fragments that Remain*, 89.
New (C.), *The Baptism of the Spirit*, 278.
Owen (J.), *The Renewal of Youth*, 1.
Pearce (J.), *The Alabaster Box*, 141.
Price (A. C.), *Fifty Sermons*, vii. 17.
Robinson (W. V.), *Angel Voices*, 137.
Selby (T. G.), *The Unheeding God*, 216.
Spurgeon (C. H.), *Metropolitan Tabernacle Pulpit*, xviii. (1872), No.
        1078; xxv. (1879), No. 1492; xlix. (1903), No. 2860.
     „   „ *Evening by Evening*, 152.
Voysey (C.), *Sermons*, xviii. (1895), No. 34 ; xxv. (1902), No. 44 ; xxvii.
    (1904), No. 10.
Christian World Pulpit, xxvii. 161 (M. G. Pearse) ; xxxvi. 218 (A. B.
    Bruce) ; xlix. 72 (J. Stalker) ; lxxv. 59 (J. Birch).
Contemporary Pulpit, 1st Ser., viii. 10 (A. Whyte) ; ix. 175 (A. Saphir).
Weekly Pulpit, i. 582 (D. Dann).

103.

ALL HIS BENEFITS.

Bless the Lord, O my soul ;
And all that is within me, bless his holy name.
Bless the Lord, O my soul,
And forget not all his benefits :
Who forgiveth all thine iniquities ;
Who healeth all thy diseases ;
Who redeemeth thy life from destruction ;
Who crowneth thee with lovingkindness and tender mercies:
Who satisfieth thy mouth with good things ;
So that thy youth is renewed like the eagle.—Ps. ciii. 1-5.

THIS psalm, with which we are all familiar from our childhood, shines in the firmament of Scripture as a star of the first magnitude. It is a song of praise, yet not the praise of an angel, but the praise of one who has been redeemed from sin and from destruction, and who has experienced that grace which, although sin abounds unto death, doth much more abound unto eternal life. It is the song of a saint, yet not of a glorified saint, but of one who is still working in the lowly valley of this our earthly pilgrimage, and who has to contend with suffering, with sin, and to experience the chastening hand of his Heavenly Father. And therefore it is that this psalm, after beginning upon the lofty mountain heights of God's greatness and goodness, in which all is bright and strong and eternal, descends into the valley where the path is always narrow and often full of darkness and danger and sadness. But as the Psalmist lives by faith, and as he is saved by faith, so he is also saved by hope ; and after having described all the sadness and all the afflictions and conflicts of this our earthly pilgrimage, he shows that even at this present time he is a member of that heavenly and everlasting Kingdom of which the throne of God is the centre, and where the angels, who are bright and strong, are his fellow-worshippers, and in which all the works which God has made will finally be subservient to

285

His glory and be irradiated with His beauty. And thus he rises again, praising and magnifying the Lord and knowing that his own individual soul shall, in that vast and comprehensive Kingdom, for evermore be conscious of the life and of the glory of the Most High.

I.

BLESS THE LORD.

1. To praise God, to bless God, is only the response to the blessing which God has given us. God speaks, and the echo is praise. God blesses us and the response is that we bless God. And those five verses of praise in Psalm ciii. are nothing but the answer of the believing heart to the benediction of Aaron, which God commanded should be continually laid upon the people. The Lord who is the God of salvation; the Lord, who has revealed His Holy Name as Redeemer; the Lord who, by His Spirit, imparts what the Father of love gives, what the filial love reveals—this is the Lord who is the object of the believer's praise. For to praise God means nothing else than to behold God and to delight in Him as the God of our salvation. Singing may be the expression of praise, may be the helpful accompaniment of praise, but praise is in the spirit who dwells upon God, who sees the wonderful manifestation of God in His Son Jesus Christ, and the wonderful salvation and treasures of good things stored up in His beloved Son.

¶ We commonly begin our prayers with a request that God will bless *us*; the Psalmist begins his prayer by calling on his soul to bless *God*! The eye of the heart is generally directed first to its own desires; the eye of the Psalmist's heart is directed first to the desires of God! It is a startling feature of prayer, a feature seldom looked at. We think of prayer as a mount where man stands to receive the Divine blessing. We do not often think of it as also a mount where God stands to receive the human blessing. Yet this latter is the thought here. Nay, is it not the thought of our Lord Himself? I have often meditated on these words of Jesus, "Seek ye first the kingdom of God and his righteousness"! I take them to mean: Seek ye first the welfare of God, the establishment of His Kingdom, the reign of His righteousness!

Before you yield to self-pity, before you count the number of the things you want, consider what things are still wanting to *Him*! Consider the spheres of life to which His Kingdom has not yet spread, consider the human hearts to which His righteousness has not yet penetrated! Let your spirit say, "Bless the Lord." Let the blessing upon God be your morning wish. It is not your *power* He asks, but your wish. Your benediction cannot sway the forces of the Universe; your Father can do that without prayer. But it is the prayer itself that is dear to Him, the desire of your heart for *His* heart's joy, the cry of your spirit for His crowning, the longing of your soul for the triumph of His love. Evermore give Him this bread![1]

¶ If we want to know what it is to praise God, let us remember such a chapter as the first chapter of the Epistle to the Ephesians, where Paul blesses God who has blessed him with all spiritual blessings in heavenly places in Christ, and where he sees before him the whole counsel and purpose of the Divine election, of the wonderful, perfect, and complete channel of the purposes of God in the redemption which is in the blood of Jesus, and the wonderful object and purpose of the Divine grace, that we, united with Christ, should through all ages show forth the wonderful love of God. That is to praise God, when we see God and when we appropriate God as He has manifested Himself to us in Christ Jesus. And it is only by the light which comes from above, and by the wonderful operation of the Holy Ghost, that it is so wrought in the heart of the Christian, although it may be in silence, that his soul magnifieth the Lord and his spirit rejoiceth in God his Saviour.[2]

2. "Bless the Lord, O my soul; and all that is within me, bless his holy name." The Psalmist desires to bless God with all that is within him. He who succeeds in doing this offers to God an eloquent worship. Eloquence means speaking out, letting the whole soul find utterance. And the Psalm before us supplies us with a choice sample of the kind of worship made by David. In this Psalm, mind, heart, conscience, imagination, all come into play. The whole inner man speaks rightfully, thoughtfully, devoutly, musically, pathetically; and, as was to be expected, God is praised to some purpose.

¶ The metrical version of the Psalm puts us in possession of the fuller meaning of this verse:

[1] G. Matheson, *Leaves for Quiet Hours*, 213.   [2] A. Saphir.

> O thou my soul, bless God the Lord;
> And all that in me is
> *Be stirred up* his holy name
> To magnify and bless.

How truly and with what fine knowledge of the soul of every spiritual man has this rendering caught the real point of that verse! And it is not this once only that the metrical psalm selects and emphasizes some word which we did not quite realize in the prose version. Here and there it may be that to our modish and sophisticated ears the psalms in metre may fail as poetry; but they never fail in spiritual discernment. They always take hold of the point, of the real business of the prose text. They always recognize the matters which really concern our souls; so that again and again the metrical psalm serves as a kind of commentary upon the prose, developing the finer sentiments, bringing out of the text certain beauties which we might never have become aware of, though we recognize them at once the moment they are set out for us. You see what I mean in this particular instance. The prose reads: "Bless the Lord, O my soul; and all that is within me, bless his holy name." We might read those words again and again, feeling in each case that it is merely a devout utterance of the soul, having nothing individual or characteristic about it. But how the metrical version cuts down to the root of the idea! What a distinction, what a precise meaning, the metrical form gives to the prayer!

> O thou my soul, bless God the Lord;
> And all that in me is
> Be stirred up his holy name
> To magnify and bless.

It was pure spiritual genius to bring out that idea of "stirring up" all that is within our souls.[1]

II.

FORGET NOT.

If we would rightly praise God, we must keep ourselves from forgetfulness. Moses warns against this vice when he says: "Beware lest thou forget the Lord thy God, in not keeping his commandments, and his judgments and his statutes, which I

[1] J. A. Hutton, *The Soul's Triumphant Way*, 23.

command thee this day, lest when thou hast eaten and art full, and hast built goodly houses, and dwelt therein; and when thy herds and thy flocks multiply, and thy silver and thy gold is multiplied, and all that thou hast is multiplied; then thine heart be lifted up, and thou forget the Lord thy God, which brought thee forth out of the land of Egypt, out of the house of bondage." In the Prophets the sad complaint re-echoes from the Lord's mouth: "Ye are they that forget my holy mountain."

¶ One of the first stories I recall from my childhood was a story of the evil of forgetting God. I remember the very spot on which it was told to me. I feel the warm grasp of the hand which had hold of mine at the time. I see once more the little seaport town stretching up from the river mouth, with its straggling "fisher town" at one extremity, and at the other its rows of well-built streets and its town hall and academy. On this occasion we were standing on a high bank looking down on the beautiful shore at our feet. Across the tiny harbour, and along the shore on the other side of the river, is a very different scene. What one sees there is a dreary waste of sand. No grass grows there, no trees shadow it, no house stands upon it. It is a place forsaken and desolate. It has been a desolation longer than the oldest inhabitant can remember. But it was not always desolate. It was once a fair estate, rich in cornfields and orchards. A stately mansion stood in the midst of it, and children played in the orchards, and reapers reaped the corn. But the lords of that fair estate were an evil race. They oppressed the poor, they despised religion, they did not remember God. They loved pleasure more than God, and the pleasures they loved were evil. To make an open show of their evil ways they turned the day of the Lord into a day of rioting and drunkenness. And this evil went on a long while. It went on till the long-suffering of God came to an end. And then upon a Sunday evening, and in the harvest-time, when the corn was whitening for the reaper, the riot and wickedness had come to a height. The evil lord and his evil guests were feasting in the hall of the splendid house. And on that very evening there came a sudden darkness and stillness into the heavens, and out of the darkness a wind, and out of the wind a tempest; and, as if that tempest had been a living creature, it lifted the sand from the shore in great whirls and clouds and filled the air with it, and dropped it down in blinding, suffocating showers on all those fields of corn, and on that mansion, and on the evil-doers within. And the fair estate, with all its beautiful gardens and fields, became a widespread heap of sand and a desolation, as it is to this day.[1]

III.

ALL HIS BENEFITS.

Of the benefits that David enumerates the first three are all negative: He forgives our sin, He heals the consequences of our sin, our diseases, He delivers us from destruction, the wages of our sin. But in the forgiveness of sin and in the healing of our diseases, in the deliverance from the devil and from everlasting hell, God gives Himself, He gives the whole fulness of His love, He elevates the soul into the very highest spiritual life; and therefore, the Psalmist continues, he who has been thus delivered out of destruction is a king, he is crowned with lovingkindness and with tender mercies, he is enriched and satisfied with good things; and not merely outwardly enriched, but there is a life given him which is unfading, the youth of which is perennial, continually renewing itself by the very strength of God.

1. The Psalmist sets himself to count up the benefits he has received from God. He has not proceeded very far when he finds himself to be engaged in an impossible task. He finds he cannot count the blessings he has received in a single day, how then can he number the blessings of a week, of a month, of a year, of the years of his life? He might as well try to count the number of the stars or the grains of sand on the seashore. It cannot be done.

¶ St. Francis, dining one day on broken bread, with a large stone for table, cried out to his companion: "O brother Masseo, we are not worthy so great a treasure." When he had repeated these words several times, his companion answered: "Father, how can you talk of treasure where there is so much poverty, and indeed a lack of all things? For we have neither cloth nor knife, nor dish, nor table, nor house; neither have we servant nor maid to wait upon us." Then said St. Francis: "And this is why I look upon it as a great treasure, because man has no hand in it, but all has been given us by Divine Providence, as we clearly see

[1] Alexander McLeod.

in this bread of charity, in this beautiful table of stone, in this clear fountain." [1]

¶ I was walking along one winter's night, hurrying towards home, with my little maiden at my side. Said she, "Father, I am going to count the stars." "Very well," I said; "go on." By and by I heard her counting—"Two hundred and twenty-three, two hundred and twenty-four, two hundred and twenty-five. Oh! dear," she said, "I had no idea there were so many." Ah! dear friends, I sometimes say in my soul, "Now, Master, I am going to count Thy benefits." I am like the little maiden. Soon my heart sighs—sighs not with sorrow, but burdened with such goodness, and I say within myself, "Ah! I had no idea that there were so many." [2]

2. But if he cannot remember them all, he may at least try not to forget them all. He may try to remember some of them. But this also is a hard task. For memory is weak, and the blessings are many and manifold. How can he help himself not to forget? How shall he help himself to remember those benefits which he values most highly? He sets himself to find helps to memory, helps not to forget. So he falls upon a plan which he finds to be most helpful, and which others ever since have found to be so. He takes those benefits which he desires not to forget, and he ties them up in bundles. And then, to make sure that he will not forget them, the Psalmist shapes the bundles of God's benefits into a song. A song is the easiest thing of all to remember. So he shapes them into a song, which people can sing by the wayside as they journey, can carry with them to their work, and brood over in their hours of leisure.

¶ By tying the benefits up in bundles, and by shaping them into a song, the Psalmist earned for himself the undying gratitude of future generations. Specially has he earned for himself our gratitude, for he gave us a song which we sing in Scotland to-day, and have sung for more than three hundred years, when our religious emotions are at their highest and their best. We sing this song when the feeling of consecration has been renewed, widened, and deepened by communion with God at His table. I never was at a communion-time at which this song has not been sung, and no other song could do justice to the feelings of gratitude

[1] E. Meynell, *The Life of Francis Thompson* (1913), 283.
[2] M. G. Pearse.

of the Lord's people. So we sing, "Bless the Lord, O my soul, and forget not all his benefits: who forgiveth, who healeth, who redeemeth, who crowneth, and who satisfieth."[1]

i.

Forgiveness.

"Who forgiveth all thine iniquities."

Note how the Psalmist begins. He begins with iniquity. Where else could a sinful man begin? The most needful of all things for a sinful man is to get rid of his sin. So the Psalmist begins here. This beginning is not peculiar to him, it is the common note of the Bible. In fact, we here come across one of the distinctive peculiarities of the Bible. We may read other literatures and never come across the notion of sin in them. Crimes, blunders, mistakes, miseries enough one may find, but sin as estrangement from a holy personal God who loves man and would serve him one never finds. But in the Bible we are face to face with sin from first to last. One chapter and a bit of another are given to the story of the making of the world and the making of man, and then the story of the entrance of sin is told, and the reader is kept face to face with sin in every part of it. In the gospel story we read at the outset: "Thou shalt call his name Jesus: for he shall save his people from their sins"; and in John almost the first word about Him is, "Behold the Lamb of God, which taketh away the sin of the world." It is characteristic of the Bible to keep its reader face to face with sin and its consequences, till he is stirred up to the effort to get rid of it.

¶ Sometimes in business a man will say: "There is a limit to everything. I have trusted such an one, and he has deceived me. I have forgiven him much, but now he has crossed the score, and I will have no more dealings with him." But it is only when men, in their own estimation, have got over that score that the heavenly business begins. Some minister comes from somewhere, to preach some day, and preaches the forgiveness of sins, and that is the beginning of the business; and at length the man finds Heaven for himself, and can say: "He forgiveth all mine iniquities."[2]

[1] James Iverach, *The Other Side of Greatness*, 121.   [2] A. Whyte.

ii.

Healing.

"Who healeth all thy diseases."

Once a prophet said, "From the sole of the foot even unto the head there is no soundness in it; but wounds, and bruises, and putrefying sores." When we read these words, we are inclined to say they are Oriental figures of speech, exaggerated metaphors. If our spiritual vision were as keen as that of the prophet, we should find that he was speaking what he knew. Sin then makes disease, and God's relation to disease is described as that of healing. In the Scriptures this relation is described so fully that it gives a distinctive name for God—Jehovah the Healer. He not only forgives sin, He also so deals with the results of sin that He removes every trace of sin. He heals all our diseases.

¶ The nineteenth century produced three famous persons in this country who contributed more than any of their contemporaries to the relief of human suffering in disease : Simpson, the introducer of chloroform; Lister, the inventor of antiseptic surgery; and Florence Nightingale, the founder of modern nursing. The second of the great discoveries completed the beneficent work of the first. The third development — the creation of nursing as a trained profession—has co-operated powerfully with the other two, and would have been beneficent even if the use of anæsthetics and antiseptics had not been discovered. The contribution of Florence Nightingale to the healing art was less than that of either Simpson or Lister; but perhaps, from its wider range, it has saved as many lives, and relieved as much, if not so acute, suffering as either of the other two.[1]

iii.

Redemption.

"Who redeemeth thy life from destruction."

That is, God preserves the life that He saves. Here is first a life forfeited. That life is then saved by forgiveness. Then there is a life imperilled by disease, and saved by God's healing. But that life is in a thousand dangers. Many seek after the

---

[1] Sir Edward Cook, *The Life of Florence Nightingale*, i. 439.

young child—the Christ within us—to destroy it. But God "redeemeth thy life from destruction." How often God has saved some of us from impending ruin, He alone knows.

¶ In my native town of Stirling workmen were blasting the castle rock near where it abuts upon a wall that lies open to the street. The train was laid and lit, and an explosion was momentarily expected. Suddenly, trotting round the great wall of cliff, came a little child going straight to where the match burned. The men shouted. That was mercy. But by their very shouting they alarmed and bewildered the poor little thing. By this time the mother also had come round. In a moment she saw the danger, opened wide her arms, and cried from her very heart, "Come to me, my darling." That was tender mercy; and instantly, with eager, pattering feet, the little thing ran back and away, and stopped not until she was clasped in her mother's bosom. Not a moment too soon, as the roar of the shattered rock told.[1]

¶ I remember one who had been for a long time drifting towards an evil act which was certain to do more harm to others than to himself, but who had not as yet determined on flinging friends, society, work, good repute, his past and future, and God Himself, to the winds. The one thing that kept him back was a remnant of belief in God, in One beyond humanity, beyond the world's laws of convention and morality. Nothing else was left, for he had, in the desire for this wrong thing, passed beyond caring whether the whole world went against him, whether he injured others or not. He was as ready to destroy all the use of his own life as he was careless of the use of the lives of others. But he felt a slow and steady pull against him. He said to himself, "This is God, though I know Him not." At last, however, he determined to have his way. One day the loneliness and longing had been too great to be borne, and when night came he went down his garden resolved on the evil thing. "This night," he said, "I will take the plunge." But as he went he heard the distant barking of a dog in the village; the moon rose above a dark yew tree at the end of the garden, and he was abruptly stopped in the midst of the pathway. Something seemed to touch him as with a finger, and to push him back. It was not till afterwards that he analysed the feeling, and knew that the rising of the moon over the yew tree and the barking of the dog in the distance had brought back to him an hour in his childhood, when in the dusk he had sat with his mother, after his father's

[1] A. Grosart.

death, in the same garden, and had heard her say—" When thou passest through the waters, I will be with thee; and through the rivers, they shall not overflow thee." It was this slight touch that saved him from wrong which would have broken more lives than his own. It was God speaking; but it would have been as nothing to him, had he not kept his little grain of faith in God alive, the dim consciousness that there was One who cared for him, who had interest that he should conquer righteousness. Next day, he left his home, travelled and won his battle; and his action redeemed not only his own but another's life.[1]

¶ There is an old poem which bears the curious title of "Strife in Heaven," the idea of which is something like this. The poet supposes himself to be walking in the streets of the New Jerusalem, when he comes to a crowd of saints engaged in a very earnest discussion. He draws near and listens. The question they are discussing is which of them is the greatest monument of God's saving grace. After a long debate, in which each states his case separately, and each claims to have been by far the most wonderful trophy of God's love in all the multitude of the redeemed, it is finally agreed to settle the matter by a vote. Vote after vote is taken, and the list of competition is gradually reduced until only two remain. These are allowed to state their case again, and the company stand ready to join in the final vote. The first to speak is a very old man. He begins by saying that it is a mere waste of time to go any further; it is absolutely impossible that God's grace could have done more for any man in heaven than for him. He tells again how he had led a most wicked and vicious life—a life filled up with every conceivable indulgence, and marred with every crime. He has been a thief, a liar, a blasphemer, a drunkard, and a murderer. On his death-bed, at the eleventh hour, Christ came to him and he was forgiven. The other is also an old man, who says, in a few words, that he was brought to Christ when he was a boy. He had led a quiet and uneventful life, and had looked forward to heaven as long as he could remember. The vote is taken; and, of course, you would say it results in favour of the first. But no, the votes are all given to the *last*. We might have thought, perhaps, that the one who led the reckless, godless life—he who had lied, thieved, blasphemed, murdered; he who was saved by the skin of his teeth, just a moment before it might have been too late—had the most to thank God for. But the old poet knew the deeper truth. It required great grace verily to pluck that withered brand from the

[1] S. A. Brooke, *The Ship of the Soul*, 23.

burning. It required depths, absolutely fathomless depths, of mercy to forgive that veteran in sin at the close of all those guilty years. But it required more grace to keep that other life from guilt through all those tempted years. It required more grace to save him from the sins of his youth and keep his Christian boyhood pure, to steer him scathless through the tempted years of riper manhood, to crown his days with usefulness, and his old age with patience and hope. Both started in life together; to one grace came at the end, to the other at the beginning. The first was saved from the guilt of sin, the second from the power of sin as well. The first was saved from dying in sin. But he who became a Christian in his boyhood was saved from living in sin. The one required just one great act of love at the close of life; the other had a life full of love—it was a greater salvation by far. His soul was forgiven like the other, but his life was redeemed from destruction.[1]

iv.

Crowning.

"Who crowneth thee with lovingkindness and tender mercies."

So far the Psalmist has been thinking of God's action as it is defined in relation to sin. Now his thoughts take a grander flight, and he thinks of the Divine action when sin is taken out of the way, and no longer presents a barrier to the fellowship between God and His people. His words take on a finer meaning, and mould themselves into a more musical form. For he tries to represent the intercourse between God and the children of God, when sin is removed from between them. "Who crowneth thee with lovingkindness and tender mercies." These words are about the most musical and pathetic in the whole Bible, and they are as fine in meaning as they are in form.

¶ God puts honour upon the brow of a forgiven man. He does not merely forgive, and that in a formal way, but, when He forgives, He crowns. He crowns me with the title of " son," and He places the coronet of heirship upon my head, for "if children, then heirs; heirs of God, and joint-heirs with Jesus Christ." Sweet picture this. Observe that it is not a crown of merit, for "He crowneth thee with lovingkindness and tender *mercies*." This is the only crown that I can consent to wear.[2]

[1] H. Drummond, *The Ideal Life*, 149.   [2] A. G. Brown.

1. *Lovingkindness.*—Note how the translators of the Psalm
have been constrained to tie two English words together in order
to set forth the meaning of the original.   These translators of the
Bible were poets as well as scholars.   They took the two words
" love " and " kindness " and tied them together in order to shut
out the weaker meanings of both, and from the union of them set
forth a higher and better meaning than either alone could express.
Love has always been recognized to be the strongest and best
thing in the world of life, and in recent years it has come to
even larger recognition.   It really holds society together, is at the
basis of family life, is the motive power of the highest activities
of mankind.   But while love is so and acts so, it may partake of
the weakness or the selfishness of human nature.   It may become
fierce, jealous, regardless of the interest of the person who is its
object.   It may look at the person merely as belonging to itself,
and fiercely insist on exclusive possession.   No doubt ideal love
would labour, toil, and spend itself for the good of the person
loved.   But all love is not ideal, and it may have more ferocity
than kindness in it.   So this fierce side of love is shut out, and
only the ideal side is kept, and kept by uniting it with kindness.
But kindness is apt to be weak, injudicious, and foolish.   It is the
kindness, perhaps, of a fond young mother who gives the baby
whatever it desires, cloys it with sweets, or gives it unwholesome
food because the child likes it, or, as George MacDonald suggests,
gives the child a lighted candle because it cries for it.   This
foolish side of kindness is shut out by tying it to the firmer,
wiser fact of love.   So united, kindness becomes lovingkindness,
and the two become, in their union, something higher and better
than either of the two elements contained in it, when these are
taken by themselves.

¶ Another young friend writes: " From such an array of
beautiful characteristics as is called up by his name it is hard to
choose the greatest, but his ' loving-kindness ' is the outstanding
trait that not only those who knew him best, but those who came
only casually into contact with him, will remember with tenderness.   How he loved every one, especially ' those who were of
the household of faith ' !   How eagerly would he seek out, even
when on holiday, the brother-minister, superannuated by affliction
from active work, to encourage and help him by his sympathy, to
cheer him with his humour and his jollity, to stimulate him with

his wide and varying interests! And in what good stead that wonderful fund of quiet humour stood him through the days of pain and weakness and weariness through which God's veteran passed, and from which he is now released! One revered him as a saint, but loved him as a man, a man who radiated such love as compelled a willing love in return."[1]

¶ It is twenty-five years since I first had my attention drawn to this clause. I went to college then, and one day a minister gave me a tract, and told me, " Take that and read it, and when you bring it back, tell me what you think of it." He said to me —and he proved a sound prophet—" I may not live to see it, but you will see it. The lad that spoke these words—his name will be heard wherever the English language is spoken,"—the name was Charles Spurgeon. It was a discourse on this word—" He crowneth me with lovingkindness and tender mercies." He had never been to college, and had taken none of your envied degrees that seem to stamp a man as a Master of Divinity. My friend said: " I may not live to see it, but you will." A young man in his teens, not far up in the offices yet, Spurgeon was under twenty-one when he preached a sermon that made my old friend prophetic. " When God takes a man's head out of the dust "— said this young fledgling Puritan preacher—" He crowns it with a crown that is so heavy with His grace and goodness that he could not wear it were it not lined with the sweet velvet of His lovingkindness." Not a classic figure perhaps, but Spurgeon's figure is graven on my memory while many a classic figure has faded away. Many a costly gift, given carelessly with lavish abundance, you have nearly forgotten : but one gift, given many years ago, you remember still. It was only a cup of cold water, perhaps, but given with a hand and with a look of lovingkindness. And when God crowns us with such love as this, when He smiles upon us, no wonder that it gladdens the heart so that a man never forgets it.[2]

2. *Tender mercies.*—Mercy in itself is one of the grandest things in human nature. It is not mere feeling, it is feeling in action. It is not mere sympathy or pity, it is sympathy made alive and active. It is not pity, it is pity going forth into action, to bind up the broken-hearted, to comfort the sorrowful, to make the widow's heart to sing for joy. But tender mercy is even more than mercy, great and good though the exercise be. It is

---

[1] *Love and Life : The Story of J. Denholm Brash* (1913), 179.
[2] Alexander Whyte.

mercy exercised in the most tender way. For mercy may be exercised in such a way as to wound the feelings of the person to whom you are merciful. You may intend to help your friend who has fallen into misfortune. He may have been blameworthy, his misfortune may have arisen from his want of thought, from his recklessness, or even from wrong-doing. You intend to help him, but you are annoyed with his conduct; you insist on showing him how foolish he was, how reckless was his conduct, how unprincipled was his motive, until he almost feels that he would be without the help if he could be free from the scolding. Or you are merciful to the person who asks you for help, but you fling the penny to him across the street. It is possible in this way to undo all the effects of a merciful action by the ungracious way in which it is done. Mercy according to our text is exercised tenderly. You help your friend, or come to the assistance of those who are in poverty and need, in such a way as to bind up their wounds, to cheer them, and to give them courage to begin the battle of life anew, though life heretofore has been all a failure. For the mercy which man shows to man interprets for man the tender mercies of God. After that interview with you, during which you entered into the sorrow of your friend sympathetically and tenderly, gave him of your wisdom, of your experience, of your means, he goes forth to the work of life again with a new outlook, with a firmer resolution to do well. He says to himself, "It is a good, kind world after all, and there are good, kind people in it. I must show myself worthy to live in so good a world, and worthy of the help I have received." So tender mercies help, but they help in such a way as to bind up the broken-hearted, and to open a door of hope for those who have failed, and to give them courage to lift them above the feeling of despair.

¶ Stern and unflinching in his denunciation of drunkenness, Ernest Wilberforce was tenderness itself in his dealings with the individual sinner. Few cases are more distressing or more difficult to deal with than those where a clergyman has fallen into habits of intemperance. The Bishop's correspondence in one of them is lying before me as I write, marked throughout by the strong sense of justness and fairness which ever characterized him, yet compassionate and considerate, so far as consideration was possible. The facts were clear, and the unfortunate gentleman was induced to vacate his office without the scandal of judicial proceedings. But there were features which induced the Bishop to hope that, under happier auspices, he might yet do good and useful work in his chosen calling. Without any effort at minimizing the sad story, he succeeded in inducing an experienced parish priest in another diocese to give the transgressor a fresh start. The good Samaritan had no cause to regret his charity, and in writing to the Bishop he congratulated the clergy of Northumberland in having one set over them to whom they could appeal with perfect confidence in the hour of need. "If ever," he wrote, "I should be in a fix, I shall wish for such a friend as your Lordship."[1]

v.

Satisfaction.

"Who satisfieth thy mouth with good things; so that
thy youth is renewed like the eagle."

1. The word "crowneth" suggests something external, something coming to us from without, and after the crowning there may conceivably be some wants unsupplied, some needs of man which have not been met. But the note of Christianity is that no human needs are left unsatisfied. "My God shall supply all your need." Satisfied with good, so that every need shall be met—this is the promise.

¶ The thirst of the mind for truth, the thirst of the will and conscience for guidance, and the thirst of the heart for life are satisfied through Him who is the Way, and the Truth, and the Life. If there were needs which He could not or would not satisfy, He would have told us of them.[2]

2. The Psalmist felt, as we often feel, that he had emerged from the very gulf of destruction; that he had been, as it were, against his will, rescued from moral suicide; that all his life had been redeemed by God. Therefore he burst out into joy and thanksgiving! He who had been through grave sorrows; who had known sin, disease, even destruction; who might have cursed life and shrieked at what men call Fate; cries out in unfeigned

---

[1] J. B. Atlay, *Bishop Ernest Wilberforce*, 162.
[2] James Iverach, *The Other Side of Greatness*, 133.

and mistakable rapture—it is a very outburst of song—"Bless the Lord, O my soul; and all that is within me, bless his holy name. Bless the Lord, O my soul, and forget not all his benefits." And in realizing this joyful victory of the moral and spiritual powers; in the resurrection of his spiritual being into strength; in the leaving behind him in its own grave of all that was dead in his past; in the great cry of his heart as he looked back—"I am not there, I am risen"—his youth was renewed like the eagle's! It was a great triumph; for his best life came back in a higher and a stronger way, with now but little chance of failure. He could again, like the eagle, look upon the sun, and love the upper ranges of the sky; again soar, but with steadier beat of wing than in youth; again possess the freedom he loved before disease and destruction had enslaved his plumes; again breathe the breath of immortal love; again in conscious union with God hear the great spheres "in measured motion draw after the heavenly tune." And certainty was now with this victory, for he had known and found the Father of his spirit. The waters of his new life arose out of the fountain Life of God Himself, and he knew whence they came. There was now a source as well as a goal for his ideals, hopes, efforts, for the beauty he loved, and for universal joy. It was the Almighty Love and Life of loveliness Himself who was now in him—a personal friend, redeemer, strengthener, exalter; who crowned him with lovingkindness and tender mercies. This is the true resurrection; this is the triumph of life.

¶ The brilliant Princess Anastasia Malsoff (the Nancy Malsoff of the Russian Court) was one of those led to Christ by the Maréchale, with whom she kept up a close friendship during the rest of her life. One of the Princess's letters is peculiarly interesting: "I will see the Emperor in these days," she writes, "and I will seek strength to speak to him. You see, my darling, speaking is not enough, one must in such a case pour out one's soul and feel that a superior force guides one and speaks for one." It turned out as she hoped. One night she was at the Palace in St. Petersburg. After dinner the Czar came and seated himself beside her. Soon they were deep in intimate conversation. She began telling him what her new-found friend in Paris had done for her. She talked wisely as he listened attentively. At length he said: "But, Nancy, *you* have always been good, always right." "No," she answered; "till now I have never known the Christ.

She has made Him real to me, brought Him near to me, and He has become what He never was before—my personal Friend." [1]

¶ "I shall be sorry," says Eckhart, the German mystic, "if I am not younger to-morrow than I am to-day—that is, a step nearer to the source whence I came." And Swedenborg tells us that when heaven was opened to him he found that the oldest angels seemed to be the youngest.

'Tis said there is a fount in Flower Land,—
De Leon found it,—where Old Age away
Throws weary mind and heart, and fresh as day
Springs from the dark and joins Aurora's band:
This tale, transformed by some skilled trouvère's wand
From the old myth in a Greek poet's lay,
Rests on no truth. Change bodies as Time may,
Souls do not change, though heavy be his hand.
Who of us needs this fount? What soul is old?
Age is a mask,—in heart we grow more young,
For in our winters we talk most of spring;
And as we near, slow-tottering, God's safe fold,
Youth's loved ones gather nearer:—though among
The seeming dead, youth's songs more clear they sing. [2]

[1] J. Strahan, *The Maréchale* (1913), 184.
[2] Maurice Francis Egan.

The Father's Pity.

LITERATURE.

Buckland (A. R.), *Text Studies for a Year*, 143

Clifford (J.), *The Gospel of Gladness*, 17.

Conn (J.), *The Fulness of Time*, 1.

Dykes (J. O.), *Sermons*, 138.

Fleming (A. G.), *Silver Wings*, 26.

McLeod (M. J.), *Heavenly Harmonies*, 99.

Murray (W. H.), *The Fruits of the Spirit*, 397.

Pierce (C. C.), *The Hunger of the Heart for Faith*, 59.

Selby (T. G.), *The God of the Frail*, 2.

Spurgeon (C. H.), *Metropolitan Tabernacle Pulpit*, xvi. (1870), No. 941.

Vaughan (J.), *Sermons* (Brighton Pulpit), vii. (1868), No. 678.

Walters (F.), in *Sermons by Unitarian Ministers*, 53.

Christian World Pulpit, xxx. 230 (J. Baillie); xxxii. 376 (F. Ferguson); xxxviii. 188 (D. Hobbs); lx. 376 (E. Griffith-Jones); lxi. 251 (J. Ritson).

Church Pulpit Year Book, 1909, p. 153.

THE FATHER'S PITY.

Like as a father pitieth his children,
So the Lord pitieth them that fear him.
For he knoweth our frame;
He remembereth that we are dust.—Ps. ciii. 13, 14.

1. "LIKE as a father." The history of religion shows that it has not been easy for men to think of God in that extremely simple and human fashion; and yet, to Christians, no other way of thinking appears so obvious or so natural. It met us in our childhood, grew into the thinking of our youth, and has swayed the conceptions we have formed of that august and invincible power that works for righteousness and peace for evermore. We lisped it in our earliest hymns. It had a place in the first prayers we offered at our mother's knee. It was set out in many winsome forms in the Sunday school; and when we realized something of the joy of the Divine pardon, we felt more deeply than ever the entire appropriateness and unsurpassed charm of the poet's words. God is like a father. It saturates the Christian atmosphere. It is shaping the thought and the life of the world.

And yet it is a matter of historic fact that men were thinking and inquiring for ages before they were able to interpret God in the terms of human fatherhood. Groping after God, if haply they might find Him, they sought their symbols first of all in the many-leaved picture book of nature, and said, God is like the sun, shining in its strength, and filling the world with its radiance. The moon is His symbol as it casts its light on the path of the pilgrim in the night. "God is like the rock," they exclaimed; "His work is perfect." He abides amid the storms and stress of life, stable as the everlasting hills.

Quite late in history did men come to the human in their quest for the terms in which they might express God; and when they reached this point, they seized at first only upon the more arresting qualities of the animal in man, and said, "God is like Hercules" in the invincible strength with which He crushes the evils in the world, and makes an end of them.   Later still, Plato advanced to the suggestion that God was like a "geometer," a thinker and fashioner, full of ideas and ideals; and, latest of all, in one of the youngest portions of the Old Testament, not in Genesis, not in any part of the Pentateuch, but in this wonderful and most gracious lyric, the 103rd Psalm, possibly one of the last contributions of Hebrew Psalmody, the seer surpasses all the great historical religions, and pictures God to us as a pitiful, compassionate, sin-forgiving, and soul-healing Father, and thus supplies the basis for the most true, most worthy, and most inspiring conception of God.

¶ There was once a group of friends standing at the house door, gazing in wonder at an eclipse.   It was a cloudless night; and, as they saw the shadow of the earth gliding so punctually over the face of the brilliant moon, a solemn emotion of awe fell upon every mind, and in absolute silence they watched the magnificent phenomenon.   Everything connected with their daily lives seemed for a season to be forgotten; they were citizens of infinitude; all their thoughts were swept into the regions of immensity.   But suddenly the silence was broken by a cry from the nursery where a child had been laid to sleep.   In that company, how soon you could tell who was the mother; in a moment she had left the scene, had rushed upstairs, and was clasping the baby in her embrace!   What were the wonders of nature compared to the needs of a suffering child?   More sacred than the music of the spheres was that feeble appeal for pity; more powerful than the sweet influence of the Pleiades was the attraction of love which at once absorbed that woman's soul. Then was she most like God, not when she was exalted into amazement at the marvels of the sky, but when she was soothing pain and chasing fear by tenderness and pity.[1]

2. In depicting the milder and kindlier aspect of God's character the Old Testament writers make pity the ground quality on which everything is based.   With the Psalm writers it is a standing description of God on this side of His nature that He is "gracious and full of compassion."   His compassion for the perishable life and oppressed state of Israel is expressly assigned

[1] F. Walters.

by the prophets as His reason for "redeeming" His people and forgiving their rebellions with long-suffering mercy. When He withdraws locusts from the wasted fields of Palestine, it is because He pities His people's sufferings. The repentant city of Nineveh is spared because its helpless myriads touched in God's great heart such ruth as Jonah had for his withering gourd. And after Jerusalem's fall, the patriot-poet who mourned so exquisitely over its ruin finds the explanation of all disaster in these plaintive, half-reproachful words, "Thou hast not pitied." It reads as if the Almighty's long-suffering patience with men, His gracious kindness to His people, His relenting, even His mercy in pardoning sin, were all felt by these old Hebrews to root themselves in that beautiful sentiment of compassion with which a Being so immense and self-contained in blessedness must look down on the fragile and sorrowful creatures whose origin, whose habitation, and whose end are all of them in the dust.

¶ "Pity lies at the core of all the great religions." The chapters of the Koran, all of them, begin with these words: "In the name of God, the compassionate, the merciful." The vast religion of Buddha numbers five hundred million votaries, and pity is the keynote to it all.[1]

3. The sense of God's fatherly compassion grows out of man's deepest experience. The Psalmist is face to face with his own life, and with the life of Israel. He looks back in his history, and counts up the "benefits" he has received from the Lord: forgiveness and healing, solace and renewal, quickening and uplift. He is swayed by the spirit of praise and adoration and love; and out of his own growing affection there leaps up irresistibly this thought of God. It must be so. The God who meets his sin with such pity and pardon, bears with his errors and guilty ignorance so patiently, must have the heart of a father. These are the gifts of love. They reveal wisdom, intelligence, adaptation of means to an end, but chiefly they show the same sort of care for the soul of man as a loving father shows for his child; they disclose the Divine heart. God forgives as a father does the mistakes and follies and sins of his son. He delivers from peril, He crowns with loving-kindness and tenderness. He satisfies

[1] M. J. McLeod, *Heavenly Harmonies for Earthly Living*, 99.

the soaring desires of the spirit; He renews the springs of life. "Like as a father pitieth his children, so the Lord pitieth them that fear him."

But the most vital element in the Psalmist's experience iş the forgiveness of his sins. It is to that he recurs again and again. God forgives as only a father-heart in its fullest flow of pity and compassion can forgive. For it is not easy to forgive. Brothers have been known to pursue one another in a spirit of retaliation for years, and some fathers and mothers have shown hardness of heart towards their own offspring; but God forgives with a generosity and completeness which show that no father has a love so large as His.

> Who is a pardoning God like Thee,
> Or who has grace so rich and free!

It seems impossible to exaggerate in describing it. Listen to the singer as, with soul bursting with thankfulness, he says, God does chide—but not always; nor does He keep His anger for ever. Take your measuring-glass and look up into the heavens. Let your gaze reach out to the farthest depths of the infinite blue, soar and still soar, and still you do not reach the boundaries of His forgiving love: "He hath not dealt with us after our sins; nor rewarded us according to our iniquities. For as the heaven is high above the earth, so great is his mercy toward them that fear him."

¶ Years ago when death came to me first and took a child, the anguish was great. Watching her while she lay dying, I learnt for the first time what is meant by the words, "Like as a father pitieth his children." Only so could I be taught the pity of God. And I learnt too, at the same time, what God must feel at the loss of His children. What are all these passionate affections but parables of Divine things? Shall God suffer and not we?[1]

> My little Son, who look'd from thoughtful eyes
> And moved and spoke in quiet grown-up wise,
> Having my law the seventh time disobey'd,
> I struck him, and dismiss'd
> With hard words and unkiss'd,
> His Mother, who was patient, being dead.

[1] *Life of R. W. Dale of Birmingham,* 621.

Then, fearing lest his grief should hinder sleep,
I visited his bed,
But found him slumbering deep,
With darken'd eyelids, and their lashes yet
From his late sobbing wet.
And I, with moan,
Kissing away his tears, left others of my own;
For on a table drawn beside his head,
He had put, within his reach,
A box of counters, and a red-vein'd stone,
A piece of glass abraded by the beach
And six or seven shells,
A bottle with bluebells
And two French copper coins, ranged there with careful art,
To comfort his sad heart.
So when that night I pray'd
To God, I wept, and said:
Ah, when at last we lie with tranced breath,
Not vexing Thee in death,
And Thou rememberest of what toys
We made our joys,
How weakly understood,
Thy great commanded good,
Then, fatherly not less
Than I whom Thou hast moulded from the clay,
Thou'lt leave Thy wrath, and say,
"I will be sorry for their childishness."[1]

4. The New Testament discloses the fact that the pity of God
is the sympathy of One who associates Himself with us and under-
takes for us. When we speak of the Incarnation we think of the
Divine in the human. But there is another side to that great
truth. There is the human in the Divine—what Robertson of
Brighton used to call the humanity of Deity, and what the late
Principal Edwards of Bala called "the humanity of God." That
is something which makes Him one with us, so that He identifies
Himself with us, and, in a word, pities us. Now nobody resents
that kind of pity, the pity of a genuine sympathy, which makes a
man suffer because you suffer and compels him so to identify
himself with you as to enter into your experience. That comes
to you like balm; there is healing in it. It stands by your

[1] Coventry Patmore, *The Unknown Eros.*

side; it puts its arms around you, so to speak, and in quivering tones says: "My brother, my sister, my child, this misfortune touches us both, for you are bone of my bone, and flesh of my flesh. Because you suffer I must suffer. In the name of our common humanity, in the name of God, let us try to help each other." That is pity. That is the pity of God; for that is the pity of love.

What is the meaning of Gethsemane and the cross but this, that the Son of God by virtue of His identification with us in His humanity entered sympathetically into the sin and suffering of the world? Not that He shared our sin by actual transgression, for He knew no sin; but as a father shares the sin and shame and suffering of his child, so the Lord Jesus shared our sin and shame and suffering. "Himself bare our sins in his own body on the tree." "He was wounded for our transgressions, he was bruised for our iniquities." He who knew no sin "was made sin for us." How otherwise could He have made atonement for us? And what is the teaching of the parable of the Prodigal Son in this regard? How did the father pity his wandering boy? He yearned for him when he was away in the far country; he knew well what it all meant—the degradation, the undying stain, the suffering. And for every pang in the heart of the son there was an answering pang in the heart of the father. And how did the pity express itself? While the son was yet a great way off the father saw him, and had compassion on him, and ran to meet him. Ah! pity does not think of its dignity. The pity of some people could never get beyond a walk; it is too often on stilts. The father's pity made him run; he ran and fell on his neck and kissed him. And that is the pity of God; that is how it is unfolded in the story of redemption.

¶ A chord which has been once set in unison with another vibrates (they say) when its fellow is sharply struck. God has set His heart through human suffering into perpetual concord with human hearts. Strike them, and the heart of God quivers for fellowship. If this is compassion, it is so in a more literal sense than when we use the word as a mere synonym for pity. It is sympathy, in the Greek and New Testament sense; it is, as our version has it, being "touched" with the same feeling. It is the remembrance of His own human past which stirs within the soul of Christ, when, now, from His high seat, He sees what mortal men endure.[1]

[1] J. O. Dykes.

5. The Psalmist says that man's weakness makes a sure appeal to the Father's heart. "For he knoweth our frame; he remembereth that we are dust." Dust is a synonym for frailty. While the mountains stand fast for generations, the dust into which they are slowly worn has no abiding place. The winds toss it, carrying its unresisting particles whithersoever they will. And the stuff out of which we are fashioned is just as unstable and never at one stay. Our lives are of slenderer fibre than unspun silk, brittle as threads of fine-drawn glass, breath-breakable as the texture that holds together only in a vacuum. The Psalmist goes on to speak of death, reminding us that man is like a flower of the field which, untended by human care, unscreened by human device, unwarmed by human art, shrivels at the first sign of change and the first moan of desert wind, and dies neglected and forlorn. Through the entire round of his days he is ever matching and measuring his puny capacities against the strong. Death, which draws the curtain over his cold, inert, baffled clay, is but the last phase in that ever-recurring spectacle of impotence. And yet man draws the Almighty God down to his help; and, marvellous to say, man draws God by reason of his very frailty. Of the sum of that human life over which He bends I am but a thousand-millionth part, and yet "the Lord thinketh upon me," who "am poor and needy"—thinketh of me the more closely for that very reason.

¶ In his essay on "The Sublime and Beautiful," Burke points out the fact that we always associate physical smallness with the idea of beauty, and he supports his rule by reminding us that in every known language terms of endearment are diminutives. Is not the reason for this common note in the taste and speech of mankind that the hearts of the strong and the chivalrous are captured by the very weakness which solicits defence? When we are called upon to play the part of providence to the helpless we experience a mysterious satisfaction which influences our æsthetic judgment, and the helpless grow beautiful in our eyes. And does not this peculiarity in human nature give us the clue to a mystery in the heart of God? When He made man He put Divine qualities into a slender framework, filled up with delicate clay, because to such beings the deepest secret of His tenderness could be spoken.[1]

[1] T. G. Selby.

¶ Will you say to a mother, Why do you waste such love on that poor child? Do you not see that he is a cripple, has curvature of the spine, always will be a cripple? See the little fellow creeping on his hands and knees! The doctor says that he can never be strong; always will be a source of anxiety to you; most likely never will be able to walk. Why worry so over him? What good will he ever be? Ah, if you spoke thus, she would give you a look that would shrivel you.

> My silent boy, I hold thee to my breast,
>   Just as I did when thou wast newly born.
> It may be sinful, but I love thee best,
>   And kiss thy lips the longest night and morn.
> Oh, thou art dear to me beyond all others,
>   And when I breathe my trust and bend my knee
> For blessing on thy sisters and thy brothers,
>   God seems the nighest when I pray for thee.[1]

6. God's intimate knowledge of our weakness is the sure pledge of tender parental treatment. It is certain that a very great part of the harshness of judgment which passes among men is the result of imperfect knowledge. You do not know the man you are speaking about; you do not know the natural infirmities, the bodily hindrances, the constitutional causes which affect the person whom you are blaming. You cannot take into your calculation all the circumstances, all the pressure, all the temptation. You cannot read his motives, you cannot dip into the secret processes going on in that man's mind. If you could see all this, your feelings would be very different, and your sentiments would be reversed.

Now, of all upon earth, a parent can best estimate these things in his own child. Has he not watched him from the first passages of his dawning life? Has he not seen the moulding of his frame? Has he not become intimate with the secret framework of his being? Can he not take a more comprehensive view of him than any other man can? And this pity flowing from parental knowledge is the shadow of that love of God. He sees what no other eye sees, and His calculations include all the extenuating circumstances—the health, the position, the conflict, the effort, the struggle, the sorrow, the penitence. "He knows"

[1] M. J. McLeod, *Heavenly Harmonies for Earthly Living*, 110.

and—blessed be God for the kind word, a word very rarely known to us—" He remembers." And so pity is the child of knowledge. " Like as a father pitieth his children, so the Lord pitieth them that fear him. For he knoweth our frame; he remembereth that we are dust."

> Not as one blind and deaf to our beseeching,
>   Neither forgetful that we are but dust,
> Not as from heavens too high for our upreaching.
>   Coldly sublime, intolerably just :—
>
> Nay but Thou knewest us, Lord Christ Thou knowest,
>   Well Thou rememberest our feeble frame,
> Thou canst conceive our highest and our lowest,
>   Pulses of nobleness and aches of shame.
>
> Therefore have pity!—not that we accuse Thee,
>   Curse Thee and die and charge Thee with our woe;
> Not thro' Thy fault, O Holy One, we lose Thee,
>   Nay, but our own,—yet hast Thou made us so!
>
> Then tho' our foul and limitless transgression
>   Grows with our growing, with our breath began,
> Raise Thou the arms of endless intercession.
>   Jesus, divinest when Thou most art man![1]

7. The Psalmist based the pity of our Heavenly Father on His special knowledge of our frame—such knowledge as only the Framer of it can possess. But to know man's frame, to know what is in man, even to search and try with Divine inspection the heart and spirit of a man, is after all something less intimate and perfect than to be a man. To learn a child's lessons, feel a youth's passions, think a man's thoughts; to be actually tempted to evil as men are tempted, and find out by trial how hard it is for them to be good; to undergo the moral probation and discipline peculiar to a human creature, impossible to the Creator; this must give— or, if we are to think about the subject at all, it must be supposed by us to have given—to the Son of God a fresh acquaintance with human experience, of quite another sort from the omniscience of the creating Father. At all events, who can help feeling this,

[1] F. W. H. Myers, *Saint Paul.*

that, if it is possible for any one to know us, understand us, and do us justice, Jesus Christ is that One; since, as our Maker, He both knows what He made us fit to be and to do and, as our Fellow-Man, has learned through what hindrances and temptations we have become what we are?

¶ An obelisk, originally brought from Egypt, stands in the piazza of St. Peter's at Rome. It was put into its present position in the sixteenth century. It weighs a little short of a million pounds, and required the strength of eight hundred men, one hundred and fifty horses, and forty-six cranes, to lift it on to its pedestal. The crowds who witnessed the feat were forbidden to speak under pain of death. As the ropes were tugged by hosts of workmen, and the huge obelisk slowly reared itself like a waking giant, the movement suddenly stopped and the ropes threatened to give way. The huge mass was about to fall crashing upon the pavement. An old sailor in the crowd, familiar with the humours of ropes and the methods of treating them, broke the silence and cried, "Pour water on the ropes!" The advice was quickly followed, the ropes tightened, and the obelisk slowly rose again and settled securely upon its base. In our past life how often have strain, tension, and peril come to us! The ties by which we were knit to goodness, to truth, to purity, to faith, were sorely tested, and seemed ready to snap and plunge us into ruin. Some temptation arose out of all proportion to the staying power of our trust in God, some shock fraught with impending disaster to the character, some partial alienation from right paths threatening to strand our lives in uselessness. But the eye of infinite wisdom was watching, and God remembered the weakness of the flesh. From within the unseen there came a voice that saved us, and the peril was overpast. The strain eased off, character strengthened itself to the emergency, and we were kept in the plane of our providential lot. And through this wise, watchful pity of our infirmities we come to find ourselves with a place in the living temple, monuments of the gentleness, the sympathy, and the upholding power of the God who pities the frail. In the moments which show most our weakness the Lord remembers that we are but dust, and fortifies us against the strains and hazards which belong to our earthly course.[1]

8. Who are they that experience this pity of God? What does the text say? "Like as a father pitieth his children, so the

---

[1] T. G. Selby, *The God of the Frail*, 14.

Lord pitieth them that fear him." The same expression occurs in the eleventh verse: "As the heaven is high above the earth, so great is his mercy toward them that fear him." And again in the seventeenth verse: "The mercy of the Lord is from everlasting to everlasting upon them that fear him." Now, let us not imagine for a moment that God does not yearn with compassion over men who are utterly reckless, men who are breaking through God's law, and treading the path that leadeth to destruction. God pities them; but, then, observe, they are indifferent to Him; and if we are indifferent to any one, we do not care for that one's pity, we have no wish for his compassion. God's compassion goes forth upon all men, but all men cannot receive it, and do not receive it. It is not the idea of terror that is conveyed by this word "fear." We do not crave mercy from a tyrant; we demand justice from him. If one might translate this word "fear" one should do so by two words—"reverential love." We can receive real sympathy only from those we love with reverence. When we are bearing a great trial, when we are going through our testing time, when we are bowing under a heavy sorrow, who are the men and women from whom we seek sympathy or pity? It may be we seek for the companionship of but one—only one—for whom our love is deep and reverent.

¶ Bunyan in his long treatise *On the Fear of God* deals with the matter of "right fear" very fully. "Take heed," he says in that treatise, "of hardening thy heart at any time against convictions of judgments. I bid you before to beware of a hard heart, now I bid you beware of hardening your soft heart. The fear of the Lord is the pulse of the soul. Pulses that beat are the best signs of life; but the worst show that life is present. Intermitting pulses are dangerous. David and Peter had an intermitting pulse in reference to this fear." Christian is no coward, and the adjective *right* is emphatic when he speaks of right fear. The word fear has two senses, according as it relates to dangerous or to sublime things. In the one connexion it is a sense of danger; in the other it is the faculty of reverence, the habit of wonder, the continued power of awe and admiration. Christian's analysis of it includes both these senses. (1) It rises in the conviction of sin—not (it will be observed) in the approach of punishment, but in the horror of sin itself, as a thing to be abhorred apart from its consequences. (2) It leads to a laying hold on Christ for salvation—in which the sense of danger and the faculty of reverence are combined. (3) It begets in the soul a great reverence for God.[1]

¶ Among the children of God, while there is always that fearful and bowed apprehension of His majesty, and that sacred dread of all offence to Him, which is called the Fear of God, yet of real and essential fear there is not any, but clinging of confidence to Him as their Rock, Fortress, and Deliverer; and perfect love, and casting out of fear; so that it is not possible that, while the mind is rightly bent on Him, there should be dread of anything either earthly or supernatural; and the more dreadful seems the height of His majesty, the less fear they feel that dwell in the shadow of it ("Of whom shall I be afraid"), so that they are as David was, "devoted to His fear"; whereas, on the other hand, those who, if they may help it, never conceive of God, but thrust away all thought and memory of Him, and in His real terribleness and omnipresence fear Him not nor know Him, yet are by real, acute, piercing, and ignoble fear, haunted for evermore.[2]

[1] John Kelman, *The Road*, ii. 162.
[2] Ruskin, *Modern Painters*, ii. ch. xiv. (*Works*, iv. 199).

THE DAY'S WORK.

LITERATURE.

Bain (J. A. K.), *For Heart and Life*, 357.

Boyd (A. K. H.), *The Graver Thoughts of a Country Parson*, ii. 144.

Brooks (P.), *Seeking Life*, 331.

Brown (J. B.), *The Christian Policy of Life*, 108.

Clarke (J. E.), *Common-Life Sermons*, 94.

Dewhurst (F. E.), *The Investment of Truth*, 157.

Dix (M.), *Christ at the Door of the Heart*, 65.

Hood (P.), *Dark Sayings on a Harp*, 69.

Hunter (J.), *De Profundis Clamavi*, 227.

Lambert (J. C.), *The Christian Workman*, 1.

Newman (J. H.), *Sermons on Subjects of the Day*, 395.

Prothero (R. E.), *The Psalms in Human Life*, 315.

Smith (G. A.), *The Forgiveness of Sins*, 89.

Christian World Pulpit, xli. 56 (G. A. Smith) ; xlii. 8 (T. Young); lxx. 139 (H. M'Gahie) ; lxxvii. 309 (H. S. Holland).

Church of England Pulpit, xlix. 309 (J. White); lix. 197 (B. S. Tupholme).

Church Times, May 6, 1910 (H. S. Holland).

Literary Churchman, xxxii. 316 (J. L. Spencer).

104

The Day's Work.

Man goeth forth unto his work
And to his labour until the evening.—Ps. civ. 23.

THE psalm from which the text is taken is one of the most complete and impressive pictures of the universe to be found in ancient literature, and it breathes the very spirit of the Hebrew race. It has been called the Psalm of the Cosmos. It moves through all creation, and begins and ends with praise. Like all the highest reaches of the human imagination, it lays hold of the inner and deeper truth of things, and suggests much more than literary description can convey. He was not a man of knowledge in the modern sense, this Hebrew poet, although the wide sweep of his thought seems to speak of some contact with foreign culture; but he was at home in that knowledge of God which is Eternal Life. No careful reader of the psalm will fail to see that it follows mainly the order and sequence of the story of the beginnings of things with which our Bible opens—a story which in its groupings of the creative action into progressive stages dimly anticipates our modern idea of development: yet the psalm is no mere copy of that story. The story of Genesis is the record of a past and finished creation: the psalm is a picture of a continuous, ever-proceeding creation—a kind of prophecy of the genesis of science. All the work of the ancient record we see going on before our eyes: the wondrous week of Divine activity is every week, and its six great days are repeated in all the days. In the psalm, as in the Book of Genesis, we see life moving on in the same ordered and stately way to the same goal; rising up in slow and steady grandeur to man, and in man reaching its summit and crown. The going forth of man is the highest point in the vast, ascending movement—the end or goal of life on its material side. In this psalm, until we reach this verse, God is represented as working alone, causing the grass to grow and giving to the wild beasts their food; but man goeth forth—goeth forth a self-conscious, self-acting being, a distinct person, a sovereign soul with power to shape the course of his own life and activity. And this going forth of man is not only the summing-up and end of a creation, but the beginning of a new creation. However closely he may be allied to what is beneath him, he belongs to another order. Because he thinks and wills and loves, he is kindred to the Infinite Mind and Will and Heart—kindred to God; not only a creature formed and sustained by the Creator's power, but a son of God, and therefore more to God than vast worlds and blazing suns.

¶ In the Psalms, Alexander von Humboldt recognized an epitome of scientific progress, a summary of the laws which govern the universe. "A single Psalm, the 104th," he writes, "may be said to present a picture of the entire Cosmos. We are astonished to see, within the compass of a poem of such small dimension, the universe, the heavens and the earth, thus drawn with a few grand strokes."[1]

¶ In the 104th Psalm the inspired poet gives us a magnificent picture of the movement and march of a living world. The clouds roll on like the swift chariots of God; the winds are winged creatures; the springs of water run among the hills; the grass is growing, the sap circling through the cedars, the birds building their nests among the branches; the moon keeps her seasons; the sun rises and sets, the beasts of the forest creep forth in search of their food; the ships are sailing upon the great and wide sea. And of man, set in the midst of this vast, busy scene, the Psalmist says, "Man goeth forth unto his work and to his labour until the evening." There is a beauty and pathos in these words which makes them smite upon the heart like the fingers of a skilled player upon his instrument, a beauty and pathos which is due essentially to their truthfulness to human experience, turning them, all simple as they are, into the solemn refrain of the Psalm of Life.[2]

[1] R. E. Prothero, *The Psalms in Human Life*, 315.
J. C. Lambert, *The Christian Workman*, 18.

I.

Work as a Law of Man's Life.

1. To the vast majority of men and women work is a law, first
of all, in the sense that it is a positive necessity of their daily
existence. We must eat to live, and we must work to eat; that
is what the law comes to in its ultimate physical form.

¶ In one of his poems Arthur Hugh Clough gives us a realistic
picture of morning in the city :—

> Labourers settling
> Slowly to work, in their limbs the lingering sweetness of
> slumber;
> Humble market-carts coming in, bringing in not only
> Flowers, fruit, farm-store, but sounds and sights of the country
> Dwelling yet on the sense of the dreamy drivers; soon after,
> Half-awake servant-maids unfastening drowsy shutters
> Up at the windows, or down letting in the air by the doorway.

No early stroller through the streets has failed to observe with
interest this awaking of a great city from its slumbers, this re-
application of itself to all its manifold tasks and toils. And if he
seeks an explanation of it all, the reason at bottom undoubtedly
is that in no other way than by arising and working can human
beings earn their daily bread. A little further on in Clough's
poem, we get a glimpse of the secret spring which drives the huge
machine, as we read of the

> Little child bringing breakfast to "father," that sits on the
> timber
> There by the scaffolding; see, she waits for the can beside
> him.[1]

2. But it is not merely in this lower sense that work must be
conceived of as the universal law of human life, a sense determined
by the relations in which we stand to the forces of Nature on the
one hand, and the social order on the other. Work is the proof
that man offers of his manhood. This is his law of relationship
to the complex universe. He works. He creates a world for
himself. He makes his own environment. He does not merely
accept from Nature his range of opportunity. He does not merely

[1] J. C. Lambert.

find her useful for his purposes, and rest satisfied with the food he can capture from her, or the shelter that she suggests. He sets to work to bring about what he will require. He takes up what she gives him, and out of its materials he contrives, fashions, invents, improves, thinks, reasons, imagines, and toils until he has brought into existence a whole creation of things that were not there before. His life is his own in the sense that his head and hands and heart have produced it. It could not come into existence but by the sweat of his brow. And as he began, so he continues. He is ever at work. He is ever bettering, correcting, enlarging. Ever a worker! Ever a creator! Ever a builder! Ever labouring to win a fuller result! Ever sowing in tears that he may reap in joy! Ever hoping to wring a richer spoil out of the rugged soil! Ever dreaming of a finer reward, ever foreseeing a better day; ever spending and being spent; ever giving himself away for a vision still denied him, of a hope still deferred! Ever on his pilgrim way, with his eyes set on far horizons! Ever warring with a stubborn earth which must be purged of thorn or thistle in order to correspond with his strong desire! So man down all the ages, amid the awful silence of a nature that waits around him in expectation, "goeth forth to his work and to his labour."

¶ It has been well said—said by a poet—that labour is at once the symbol of man's punishment and the secret of man's happiness. And it has been well said too that the gospel does not abolish labour, but gives it a new and nobler aspect. "The gospel abolishes labour much in the same way as it abolished death : it leaves the thing, but it changes its nature."[1]

¶ There are three things to which a man is born—labour, and sorrow, and joy. Each of these three things has its baseness and its nobleness. There is base labour, and noble labour. There is base sorrow, and noble sorrow. There is base joy, and noble joy. But you must not think to avoid the corruption of these things by doing without the things themselves. Nor can any life be right that has not all three. Labour without joy is base. Labour without sorrow is base. Sorrow without labour is base. Joy without labour is base.[2]

¶ When Charles Lamb was released for life from his daily drudgery of desk-work at the India Office, he felt himself the

[1] A. K. H. Boyd, *The Graver Thoughts of a Country Parson*, ii. 148.
[2] Ruskin, *Time and Tide*, v. § 21.

happiest of men. "I would not go back to my prison," he said to a friend, "ten years longer, for ten thousand pounds." He also wrote in the same ecstatic mood to Bernard Barton: "I have scarce steadiness of head to compose a letter," he said; "I am free! free as air! I will live another fifty years. Would I could sell you some of my leisure! Positively the best thing a man can do is—nothing; and next to that, perhaps good works." Two years—two long and tedious years—passed; and Charles Lamb's feelings had undergone an entire change. He now discovered that official, even humdrum work—"the daily round, the common task"—had been good for him, though he knew it not. Time had formerly been his friend; it had now become his enemy. To Bernard Barton he again wrote: "I assure you, no work is worse than overwork; the mind preys on itself—the most unwholesome of food. I have ceased to care for almost anything. . . . Never did the waters of heaven pour down upon a forlorner head. What I can do, and overdo, is to walk. I am a sanguinary murderer of time. But the oracle is silent."[1]

3. Work, then, is the significance of our manhood. We are those who present themselves to the earth in the eye of God as workers. We create a world of our own—the world of human society. We build a city, we organize a fellowship, we produce a wealth, which were not there until we called them into existence out of the resources and materials supplied us by God in nature. And every one contributes to this work, every one is a worker, who spends a continuous and rational effort in creating, or sustaining, or fulfilling, or enriching, the social fabric that man has fashioned for himself. All who contribute by head, or hand, or heart, to the common endeavour have found and verified their manhood; they have justified themselves as members of that humanity which for ever goes forth to its work and to its labour. And, reversely, those who play no such part at all, who have no intelligible function to fulfil, who bring no contribution, who have discovered no rational purpose for which to labour, and no special use for their heads or their hands, and no end that they can serve, and can see no reason why they should not be idle if they choose, and leisured when they like, and live to please themselves—such, the workless, have failed their manhood; they have betrayed humanity.

[1] S. Smiles, *Character*, 98.

¶ On a passenger ship the officers and crew keep the watches day and night, and busy themselves continually with the working and the safety of the vessel; while the passengers, looking upon the voyage as a mere holiday, amuse themselves on deck by day, and lie down in their berths at night, without any sense of responsibility. But on board ship every one knows that the positions and relations of passengers and crew are of a special and temporary kind, due to the specialization of social function through the division of labour, and that they justify themselves by that very fact. When Jack gets ashore, it is his turn for a holiday; while yonder lounging passenger in the deck-chair will have to put on his harness again as soon as the vessel reaches port, and work all the harder because of the respite he is now enjoying. What is natural and proper, for the time being, on board of an ocean liner is neither natural nor tolerable on the voyage of life. Here all are sharers in a common duty and responsibility. No one has any prescriptive right to enter himself in the ship's books as a mere cabin-passenger. In some capacity or other every one is morally bound to take a part in the working of the vessel; and, from the point of view of social obligation, those who refuse to do so are no better than malingerers or mutineers.[1]

¶ Indolence is one name of many for the abstraction of Francis's mind and the inactivities of his body. He was not of the stuff to " break ice in his basin by candle-light," and no doves fluttered against his lodging window to wake him in summer, but he was not indolent in the struggle against indolence. Not a lifetime of mornings spent in bed killed the desire to be up and doing. In the trembling hand of his last months he wrote out in big capitals on pages torn from exercise-books such texts as were calculated to frighten him into his clothes. "Thou wilt not lie a-bed when the last trump blows"; "Thy sleep with the worms will be long enough," and so on. They were ineffectual. His was a long series of broken trysts—trysts with the sunrise, trysts with Sunday Mass, obligatory but impossible; trysts with friends. Whether it was indolence or, as he explained it, an unsurmountable series of detaining accidents, it is certain that he, captain of his soul, was not captain of his hours. They played him false at every stroke of the clock, mutinied with such cunning that he would keep an appointment in all good faith six hours after it was past. Dismayed, he would emerge from his room upon a household preparing for dinner, when he had lain listening to sounds he thought betokened breakfast. He was

[1] J. C. Lambert.

always behindhand with punctual eve, and in trouble with strict noon.[1]

II.

WORK AS A HIGH CALLING OF GOD.

1. We ought to think of our work as an expression of our personal life—to think of it as the means granted to us to give body and coherence and aim to the great universe-forces. And then, if in our imagination we can identify these universe-forces with the wisdom and love of God, the One who with us lives and works, we shall be able to rise to the point of view which Christ took—that point of view which becomes both light and inspiration: "My Father worketh continuously, and so do I." That is the highest reach of the human spirit—to conceive of one's work as a part of the Divine activity itself. The daily life, with its tasks and occupations, its duties and its cares, its problems to solve, its burdens to carry, its beauty to appreciate and enjoy—all these become an echo and reflection of what the infinite activity itself is. Viewed in this light

> The trivial round, the common task,
> Would furnish all we ought to ask—
> Room to deny ourselves; a road
> To bring us daily nearer God.

¶ "Ask me," she wrote, "to do something for your sake, something difficult, and you will see that I shall do it *regularly*, which is for me the most difficult thing of all." Let those who reproach themselves for a desultoriness, seemingly incurable, take heart again from the example of Florence Nightingale! No self-reproach recurs more often in her private outpourings at this time than that of irregularity and even sloth. She found it difficult to rise early in the morning; she prayed and wrestled to be delivered from desultory thoughts, from idle dreaming, from scrappiness in unselfish work. She wrestled and she won. When her capacities had found full scope in congenial work, nothing was more fixed and noteworthy in her life and work than regularity, precision, and persistence.[2]

¶ No author of modern times has striven more earnestly or impressively than George Eliot to inculcate a law of duty which

---

[1] E. Meynell, *The Life of Francis Thompson* (1913), 32.
[2] Sir Edward Cook, *The Life of Florence Nightingale*, i. 40.

rests simply upon our human and social relations, and is independent of the great spiritual sanctions of the Christian faith. The late Mr. F. W. H. Myers, in one of his essays, tells how at Cambridge he walked with her once in the Fellows' Garden of Trinity, and how she, "taking as her text the three words which have been used so often as the inspiring trumpet-calls of man—the words God, Immortality, Duty—pronounced, with terrible earnestness, how inconceivable was the first, how unbelievable the second, and yet how peremptory and absolute the third. Never, perhaps, had sterner accents affirmed the sovereignty of impersonal and unrecompensing law. I listened, and night fell; her grave majestic countenance turned towards me like a Sibyl's in the gloom; it was as though she withdrew from my grasp, one by one, the two scrolls of promise, and left me the third scroll only, awful with inevitable fate. And when we stood at length and parted, amid that columnar circuit of the forest trees, beneath the last twilight of starless skies, I seemed to be gazing, like Titus at Jerusalem, on vacant seats and empty halls—on a sanctuary with no Presence to hallow it, and heaven left lonely of a God." [1]

¶ Carlyle preached the gospel of work as the panacea for human ills. But he did so with the air of a parent who is mixing a disagreeable medicine for a child, and is insisting on its wholesome effects in order to take away attention from its nauseousness. To Morris work was a sheer joy. It has been said that he picked out only those forms of work that were attractive. It would be truer to say that whatever work he undertook he made attractive. It was a joy to him, because he imported beauty into it. When his spirits flagged, it meant, not that he was tired, but that his insatiable energies cried out for even more. [2]

2. Work and labour have changed indeed since the Psalmist pictured man in the fields, on the hillside, rising with the sun, to go out to his work on the soil until the fading twilight sent him peacefully home again. Now labour stays not with the dying day. No evening sets in its quiet limit. On and on through the night its vast mechanism clangs and roars. On and on through the night the loaded trains groan and shriek; the furnaces blaze on in the deep holds of the liners that press on untiringly through the black waters. Labour means no longer the slow pacing of ploughing oxen, the long watch of the creeping sheep along the folds. It means now the storm and stress of tumultuous cities,

[1] J. C. Lambert.   [2] A. G. Rickett, *William Morris*, 24.

the haste of quivering looms, the heat of rushing wheels, the shout of hurrying multitudes, and the rush of crowded streets. Yes! But all this is still humanity at work. It is man achieving his purpose. It is man fulfilling his Divine prerogative. It is man building himself a city. By his labour, tremendous in its volume and energy and force, he comes to himself. He discloses his powers. He reveals his elemental character. He creates a new world. He proclaims himself a man, he discharges his obligations to God. He fulfils his high calling.

¶ Woe to us if we let our work lose the inspiration that comes from knowing that we do it for our Heavenly Father and not for ourselves! We stand in danger of letting that knowledge go, because work so absorbs us and enchains us by its own sheer power; but yet we know that that slavery to work which we are aware is growing in ourselves is not the highest or most noble type of life as we behold it in other men. We know that the man to whom work is really sanctifying and helpful is the man who has God behind his work; who is able to retire out of the fret and hurry of his work into the calmness and peace of Deity, and come out again into his labour full of the exalted certainties of the redemption of Christ and the love of God: to make work sweet and fresh and interesting and spiritual by doing it not for himself, not for itself, but for the Saviour in whom he lives.[1]

¶ In Millet's "Angelus" we see the toil-worn peasants, who have been bending over the ground through the long afternoon, standing up from their work to think reverently and prayerfully of God, as the notes of the evening bell come floating over the fields from the dim church tower. The pious men of Israel continually heard a Divine monition, as clear and sweet as the sound of the Angelus-bell, reminding them that life's labours were part of a godly service, and that the eyes of the Lord were upon them in the midst of the common occupations of each returning day.[2]

III.

Work as Fellowship with God.

1. St. Paul more than once in his Epistles describes himself and his companions in service and sacrifice as fellow-workers with

---

[1] Phillips Brooks, *Seeking Life*, 347.   [2] J. C. Lambert.

God. The words speak of conscious and voluntary co-operation, of willing and intelligent oneness of purpose and effort, with the will and work of God. In creating and perfecting His world, in getting His will done on earth as it is in heaven, God has made Himself dependent upon the help and fidelity of His human children. And the more we understand of the nature of God and the range of His working, the more shall we realize the extent to which it is possible for man to have a share in doing God's work. Our Lord's teaching about the Fatherhood of God and His personal care for every detail of every life has thrown a new light both on the nature of human work and on the spirit in which it may be done. Since all the trivialities of life and the petty drudgeries are steps in the progress towards one end, there is no sphere of human activity which is excluded from contributing towards the realization of the Divine purpose for the comfort and good of man.

All service ranks the same with God.

And there is no labourer, however humble, who may not be inspired at his toil by the child's proud consciousness that he is helping his Father. Under all circumstances he is called to co-operate with God in the service of man.

¶ Her devotion and her power of work were prodigious. " I work in the wards all day," she said, " and write all night"; and this was hardly exaggeration. Miss Nightingale has been known, said General Bentinck, to pass eight hours on her knees dressing wounds and administering comfort. There were times when she stood for twenty hours at a stretch, apportioning quarters, distributing stores, directing the labours of her staff, or assisting at the painful operations where her presence might soothe or support. She had, said Mr. Osborne, " an utter disregard of contagion. I have known her spend hours over men dying of cholera or fever. The more awful to every sense, any particular case, especially if it was that of a dying man, the more certainly might her slight form be seen bending over him, administering to his ease by every means in her power, and seldom quitting his side till death released him." [1]

¶ You remember George Eliot's fine poem on the famous violin-maker of Cremona and its lesson :

[1] Sir Edward Cook, *The Life of Florence Nightingale*, i. 234.

> . . . Not God Himself can make man's best
> Without best men to help Him. . . .
>   'Tis God gives skill,
> But not without men's hands: He could not make
> Antonio Stradivari's violins
> Without Antonio.

It is a bold saying, but true. We have a work to do in the world which God cannot do, which we must do, or it will be left undone. Only as we co-operate with Him, can His will be done on earth as in heaven.[1]

2. The Divine power in the world is not an abstract, impersonal energy. God is in the world creating and perfecting, His power and spirit dwelling in and working through industrious, righteous, faithful, beneficent lives. The unit of power in the world is not God isolated from man, and not man isolated from God; but God and man united, working purposely and continuously together; God quickening and inspiring man, and man opening his life to be a part of the Divine life of the world. The religion of Jesus Christ represents this union of man and God in purpose and work. Man works with God: God inspires man. "My Father," said Jesus, "works continuously and I work. The works I do are not Mine, but the Father's who sent Me. I do what I see My Father doing. And as the Father sent Me so send I you. The glory He has given to Me I give to you—that we may all be one, doing the same thing, working the same work."

¶ We have all been tired in our time, one may presume; we have toiled in business, or in some ambitious course, or in the perfecting of some accomplishment, or even in the mastery of some game or the pursuit of some amusement, till we were utterly wearied: how many of us have so toiled in love? How many of us have been wearied and worn with some labour to which we set ourselves for God's sake? This is what the Apostle has in view in his phrase "labour of love," and, strange as it may appear, it is one of the things for which he gives God thanks. But is he not right? Is it not a thing to evoke gratitude and joy, that God counts us worthy to be fellow-labourers with Him in the manifold works which love imposes?[2]

[1] John Hunter, *De Profundis Clamavi*, 238.
[2] J. Denney, *The Epistles to the Thessalonians*, 29.

Ah! brothers, let us work our work, for love
Of what the God in us prevails to do!
And if, when all is done, the unanswering void
And silence weigh upon our souls, remember
The music of a lonely heart may help
How many lonely hearts unknown to him!
The seeming void and silence are aware
With audience august, invisible,
Who yield thank-offering, encouragement,
And strong co-operation; the dim deep
Is awful with the God in whom we move,
Who moulds to consummation where we fail,
And saith, "Well done!" to every faithful deed,
Who in Himself will full accomplish all.[1]

3. If work is ever to win its honour, it will be from out of
the name of Jesus Christ our Lord. He was Himself the ideal
worker. He lived in the spirit of work, aware of the task set
Him—lived to do the will of Him that sent Him; conscious of
the strain of the allotted limit—the twelve hours of the working
day into which all the work must be crowded before the night
fall, in which no man can work; living ever among men as one
that worketh; straining under the yoke as He felt the terrible
pressure of His task; straitened until it was accomplished;
consecrated to the work of glorifying the Father by doing the
work which He gave Him to do; yielding Himself to death as
soon as He could pronounce that work to have been done faithfully and could say over it, "It is finished."

¶ The highest soul this world has seen was a mechanic by
trade. Behind His year and a half as a teacher lay long years in
which He toiled in wood, "making ploughs and yokes," as one of
the earliest Fathers says. And that was a preaching mightier
perhaps than His mightiest word. It was the inauguration of
labour's day. It was the shifting of the basis of esteem. In the
age into which He came, work of that kind was under taboo.
The Greek, the Roman, thought it an occupation for slaves. And
for long ages after, that continued the current view. It was
endorsed by official Christianity. The Pope in the splendour of
his Court forgot the tradition of the Carpenter. To-day we are
beginning once more to remember it. The Redeemer of our soul

---

[1] Roden Noel, *Collected Poems*, 354.

is becoming the Redeemer of our economics, of our social state.
The age-long blindness is passing away.[1]

Lord of the breeze, the rolling tide,
    The rivers rushing to the sea,
The clouds that through the azure glide,—
    Well works the hand that works with Thee.

How finely toil, from morn till eve,
    Thy ministers of light and shade;
How fair a web the sunbeams weave
    Of waving grass and blossoms made!

O Thou that madest earth and man
    That man should make an earth more fair,
Give us to see Thy larger plan
    And Thy creative joy to share.

Had we but eyes, and hands of skill,
    Had we but love, our work would be
Wisely begun, and bettered still,
    Till all were perfected by Thee.

Work Thou with us, that what is wrought
    May bring to earth diviner days,
While in the higher realms of thought
    A temple glorious we raise.[2]

IV.

WORK AND REST.

The strangest thing about work is the way in which all men
praise it, and yet all men try to get away from it. There is no
subject so popular as the blessedness of work. There is no theory
so universal as that of the wretchedness of not being compelled to
work. There is no man who does not feel a certain excited sense
of admiration, a certain satisfaction, a certain comfort that things
are right, when he stands where men are working their hardest,
where trade is roaring or the great hammers are deafening you

[1] J. Brierley, *Life and the Ideal*, 24.
[2] W. G. Tarrant, *Songs Devout*, 48.

as they clang upon the iron. Everywhere work and the approval of work! and yet everywhere the desire to get away from work! Everywhere what all these men we see are toiling for is to make such an accumulation of money that they shall not have to toil any longer. Now, this double sense, this value of work and impatience with work as they exist together, seems to be the crude expression in men's minds of the conviction that work is good, that men degenerate and rust without it, and yet that work is at its best and brings its best results, is most honourable and most useful, only when it is aiming at something beyond itself. Everybody will bear witness that this is the healthiest feeling about any work that we have to do; satisfaction and pleasure in doing it, but expectation of having it done some day and graduating from it into some higher state which we think of as rest.

1. If we look to the arrangements of nature for indications of what man's life is meant to be, we see at once that, bravely as she has provided for his work, she has not thought of him only as a working being. She has set her morning sun in the sky to tempt—nay, to summon—him forth to his work and to his labour, to make him ashamed of himself if he loiters and shirks at home; but she has limited her daylight, she has given her sun only his appointed hours, and the labour and work are always to be only "until the evening." Rest as truly as work is written in her constitution. Rest, then as much as work is an element of life.

¶ After a very hard day's work,—during which he had confirmed candidates, preached at the re-opening of a church, spoken two or three times, and done much beside in a manner which perhaps no person but himself could have accomplished,—Bishop Wilberforce returned in the evening to Turvey, where he was staying. A small party had been invited to meet him at dinner, and there was some bright and pleasant conversation. When the time came for retiring into the drawing-room, the Bishop, who looked a little fatigued, said to me: "There is nothing which makes me more absolutely disgusted with myself than feeling tired when evening comes. What business have I to be tired? nothing gives me any comfort at all but that verse in the Psalms,—'Man goeth forth to his work and to his labour until the evening'; and so, I suppose that, when evening comes, he may rest."[1]

[1] J. W. Burgon, *Lives of Twelve Good Men*, ii. 39.

2. Man goes out to his work, to his labour, only with one
softening clause in the agreement—"until the evening." There
are limits set; there are reliefs permitted and contrived; there
are moments for slackening, for recreation, for repose. Not
unbroken this labour; not monotonously blind this work. No,
fixed times, ordered signals, ordained closes!

> Sunset and evening star,
> And one clear call for me.

Man knows the signs. He is not left forgotten or unconsidered.
He can calculate when the strain will be off.

> Twilight and evening bell,
> And after that the dark.

So, in kindly, successive periods, he turns to the rest that he has
earned. "He goeth forth to his work" with the friendly sense
in his heart that it will not last for ever. It will end in the quiet
hour when the sun goes down.

¶ When in the beginning God said: Let there be Light, and
there was Light, Light did not spring into undivided empire, but
was ordained to rule alternately with darkness. Day and night
abide for ever. What was the reason, so far as man is concerned,
for this curbing and restriction of so free an element as Light?
The readiest reason seems to be—for our relief and rest. But that
is not half the reason. Our light is broken up and shortened, not
only in order to afford us intervals of rest, but also to bestow upon
us intensity; not only to relieve our faculties from the strain of
life, but also to strain and stimulate them ever more keenly.
According to Christ Himself the night cometh when no man can
work, not merely that man may hope for release beneath its
shelter, but that he may work while it is called to-day. Had
there been no interval, since first upon the tones of God's word
Light rippled across the face of the deep—had the Sun been
created to stand still in the midst of the heavens, then indeed one
might say there would have been no progress for man. Let your
imagination strike Night out of the world, and you need not begin
to speculate on the iron frames men should have required to bear
the unrelieved strain, for it is tolerably certain that, without the
urgency and discipline which a limited day brings upon our life,
we should never have been stimulated to enough of toil to make
us weary. Night, which has been called the Liberator of the
Slave, is far more the task-mistress of the free—a task-mistress
who does not scourge nor drive us in panic, but who startles our

sluggishness, rallies our wandering thoughts, develops our instincts of order, reduces our impulsiveness to methods, incites us to our very best, and only then crowns her beneficence by rewarding our obedience with rest.   In short, Night, while she is nature's mercy on our weakness, is nature's purest discipline for our strength.[1]

3. The daily drawing of the curtain between man and his active labours represents and continually reminds us of the need of the internal as well as the external in our lives.   It brings up to us our need, by bringing up to us our opportunity, of meditation, of contemplation.   For active life is always tending to become shallow.   It is always forgetting its motives, forgetting its principles, forgetting what it is so busy for, and settling itself into superficial habits.   So God shuts us out from our work and bids us daily think what the heart of our work is, what we are doing it for.   If this is the meaning of the evening—and no man sees the daylight sink away and the shadows gather without sensitively feeling some such meaning in it—then surely we need it.

¶ It is hard to see how, were it not for the continually repeated, daily stoppages of work, we could remember, as we need to remember, the great close of work which is coming to every one of us and may be very near.   I picture to myself a world without an evening, a world with an unsetting daylight, and with men who never tired at their tasks ; and it seems as if death in a world like that would be so much more terrible and mysterious than it is now ; when once a day, for many years, we have learned that work was not meant to last always, and have had to drop our tools as if in practice and rehearsal for the great darkness when we are to let them go for ever.[2]

> " And is the twilight closing fast ?
>   (I hear the night-breeze wild);
> And is the long week's work all done ? "
>   " Thy work is done, my child."
>
> " Must I not rise at dawn of day ?
>   (The night-breeze swells so wild);
> And must I not resume my toil ? "
>   " No ! nevermore, my child."

[1] George Adam Smith, *The Forgiveness of Sins*, 92.
[2] Phillips Brooks, *Seeking Life*, 348.

" And may I sleep through all the dark ?
   (The wind to-night is wild);
And may I rest tired head and feet ? "
   " Thou mayest rest, my child."

" And may I fold my feeble hands ?
   (Hush! breezes sad and wild);
And may I close these wearied lids ? "
   " Yes, close thine eyes, my child."

" Oh, passing sweet these closing hours !
   And sweet the night-breeze mild,
And the Sabbath-day that cometh fast ! "
   " The Eternal Day, my child."

" The night is gone, clear breaks the dawn,
   It rises soft and mild;
Dear Lord! I see Thee face to face ! "
   " Yes! face to face, my child."

LEANNESS OF SOUL.

LITERATURE.

Banks (L. A.), *David and his Friends*, 212.

Dinwoodie (J.), *Outline Studies*, 157.

Eyton (R.), *The Search for God*, 88.

Holden (J. S.), *Life's Flood-Tide*, 35.

Jeffs (H.), *The Art of Exposition*, 133.

Jellett (H.), *Sermons on Special and Festival Occasions*, 115.

Maclaren (A.), *The Book of Psalms* (Expositor's Bible), iii. 139.

Murphy (J. B. C.), *The Service of the Master*, 160.

Parker (J.), *The City Temple*, i. 147.

Perowne (J. J. S.), *The Book of Psalms*, ii. 223.

Spurgeon (C. H.), *The Treasury of David*, v. 77, 97.

Voysey (C.), *Sermons*, ix. (1886), No. 47.

Wordsworth (C.), *Christian Boyhood at a Public School*, ii. 189.

LEANNESS OF SOUL.

And he gave them their request;
But sent leanness into their soul.—Ps. cvi. 15.

1. THE history of God's past is a record of continuous mercies,
the history of man's is one of as continuous sin. The memory
of the former quickened the Psalmist into his sunny song of
thankfulness in the previous psalm; that of the latter moves
him to the confessions in this one. The two psalms are comple-
ments of each other, and are connected not only as being both
retrospective, but by the identity of their beginnings and the
difference of their points of view. The parts of the early history
dealt with in the one are lightly touched or altogether omitted in
the other. The key-note of Psalm cv. is, "Remember his mighty
deeds"; that of Psalm cvi. is, "They forgot his mighty deeds."

2. After an introduction in some measure like that in Psalm cv.,
the Psalmist plunges into his theme, and draws out the long, sad
story of Israel's faithlessness, of which he recounts seven instances
during the wilderness sojourn. One is the lusting for flesh food
—an evil traced to forgetfulness of God's doings, to which is
added impatient disinclination to wait the unfolding of His counsel
or plan. These evils cropped up with strange celerity. The
memory of benefits was transient, as if they had been written on
the blown sands of the desert. "They hasted; they forgot his
works." Of how many of us that has to be said! We remember
pain and sorrow longer than joy and pleasure. It is always difficult
to bridle desires and be still until God discloses His purposes.
We are all apt to try to force His hand open, and to impose our
wishes on Him, rather than to let His will mould us. So, on
forgetfulness and impatience there followed then, as there follow
still, eager longings after material good and a tempting of God,
who is "tempted" when unbelief demands proofs of His power,

instead of waiting patiently for Him. In Num. xi. 33 Jehovah is said to have smitten the people "with a very great plague." The psalm specifies more particularly the nature of the stroke by calling it "leanness" or "wasting sickness," which invaded the life of the sinners. The words are true in a deeper sense, though not so meant. For whoever sets his hot desires in self-willed fashion on material good, and succeeds in securing their gratification, gains with the satiety of his lower sense the loss of a shrivelled spiritual nature. Full-fed flesh makes starved souls.

I.

DESIRE AND ITS GRATIFICATION.

1. The words of the text have a wider scope than as a reference to an incident in Israelitish history. They tell a sad story indeed, written in the annals of God's ancient people, but they call up stories innumerable in the lives of men for whose example the story was written, but who have failed to profit by it, and to whose lives there may be appended the same legend, "He gave them their request; but sent leanness into their soul." And if we are like the Israelites, if we forget all that God has done for the promotion of our happiness here, all that He has done to fit us for a higher state of being hereafter; if we will not wait for His counsel, wait for a time when we shall no longer see His dealings darkly reflected to us in an imperfect mirror, but clear before us in the pure atmosphere of heaven; and if, instead of patiently bearing with the conditions of our pilgrim life, we murmur because we cannot have all our wishes gratified, and are dissatisfied with the restraints under which we may be placed, is it incredible that God should punish us, as He did them, by granting us the things upon which we have set our hearts?

2. It is certain that God does not always interfere to keep us from sin, for that would frustrate His purpose in wishing us to grow good by experience, to grow good by first hating evil and then loving the good so that we may follow and do the good from a free choice. He will help us if we earnestly desire it, but not otherwise; for that would be forcing instead of drawing and

winning our wills to His. By the discipline of experience God often lets us have our own way, permits us to gain what we desire, sometimes honourably, at other times dishonourably, through the mazes of meanness and even of crime. Some desires are in themselves perfectly innocent and lawful, others vicious and unlawful. But under the discipline of God the gratification of desires quite lawful in themselves sometimes leads to our moral and spiritual injury.

¶ God recognizes and respects, at all times, His gift to man of freewill. God does not, for example, force grace upon the soul. He does not even, in some cases, reveal Himself except to those who seek Him. He points out to us indeed the right way. "Walk in this way," He says, "and it shall be your glory and your joy." But He does not say, "Walk in it, you shall and must." And, in like manner, if God sees that our hearts are set upon something which we have said we must have, at all costs, He says, "You shall have it—but the consequences of your choice be upon your own head!" There is much insight and teaching in the old fable of Midas, King of Phrygia, who prayed that everything he touched might turn to gold. But his wish, when it was granted, proved a fatal one, for his very food turned into gold also, and soon he was starving.[1]

¶ It is well to pray that God should put into our minds good desires, and that we should use our wills to keep ourselves from dwelling too much upon small and pitiful desires, for the fear is that they will be abundantly gratified. And thus when the time comes for recollection, it is a very wonderful thing to look back over life, and see how eagerly gracious God has been to us. He knows very well that we cannot learn the paltry value of the things we desire, if they are withheld from us, but only if they are granted to us; and thus we have no reason to doubt His fatherly intention, because He does so much dispose life to please us. And we need not take it for granted that He will lead us by harsh and provocative discipline, though when He grants our desire, He sometimes sends leanness withal into our soul.[2]

3. It does not follow that all pleasure or attainment of desire is highly dangerous, if not pernicious, and that the welfare of the soul is incompatible with physical enjoyment. All these conclusions are false. The mischief arising from gratification is

---

[1] J. B. C. Murphy, *The Service of the Master*, 165.
[2] A. C. Benson, *Joyous Gard* (1913), 91.

caused only by the undue importance which is attached to it, and
not by the gratification itself, so long as it is lawful. The
righteous and loving God, we may be sure, does not grudge us any
one of our pleasures, is not moved with malignity or envy, that
He should seek to revenge Himself for our pleasure by smiting
our souls with the curse of leanness. But He knows the infinite
value of the soul and the necessity for its being properly
nourished and in full vigour, and He must teach us by experience
how immensely more valuable the soul is and how far more
needful it is for us to have our souls in health than to have any
earthly desires satisfied. He did so teach those poets of old
who said " The law of thy mouth is better unto me than thousands
of gold and silver." " I have esteemed the words of his mouth
more than my necessary food." "Thou art my God, my bliss.
My welfare is nothing without thee." It is to bring us into this
state that, whenever we set our hearts too much upon our own
gratification, our souls are made to suffer for it.

¶ A man may have before him only the attainment of a
perfectly honourable and legitimate ambition. Let such an one,
in the Name of God, go on, and prosper. But if it so be that God
is banished from that man's life because of his ambition—if he
begin to say that he has "no time" for prayer, for the reading of
God's Word, for meditation upon holy things, no time for preparation for Holy Communion—then let him tremble also. He will
get his desire, it may be, but what will that avail him if, when he
has won the prize, it suddenly lose all its value in his eyes and
bring him no real satisfaction ; if there shall spring up within him
the consciousness of a never-dying, ever-increasing hunger—a
hunger of the soul—a gnawing, a restlessness, a craving, which
God, and God alone, can satisfy and soothe ? And what is all
this but fulness of body and leanness of soul ? [1]

4. Mark where the judgment of God falls. It falls on the
highest nature—it falls on the soul! The man on whom God's
disapprobation rests, withers at his very root. His mental power
declines, his moral nature shrivels ; he goes down in the volume
and quality of his being. Think of a lean soul! No compass,
no grandeur, no tenderness of manhood! A lean soul, narrow,
stunted, withered, sapless, blind, deaf, idiotic! The man would
have his prize ; he would set up his own wisdom ; he would be as

[1] J. B. C. Murphy, *The Service of the Master*, 167.

God unto himself; and now look at him, and see how hunger-bitten and ghastly is his dishonoured soul. We know the horror, the ghastliness, of external emaciation brought about by illness, when man or woman becomes literally skin and bone. What a suggestion such a sight conveys of the possibilities of inward emaciation! Beneath the sleek, prosperous, well-fed, comfortable appearance, what if there be, hidden from men but open before God, a horrible emaciation in a man's real self-leanness of soul!

¶ You have heard of the white ant that commits such terrible devastations in wooden buildings in some portions of the globe. That little insect will insert itself into the largest wooden structure that men can put up, and in course of time it will eat away the whole of it, leaving nothing but the thinnest outer shell; the building will look as if nothing had befallen it; the shape will be unaltered; but put your finger upon it, or bring the slightest pressure to bear upon it, and you will find that it is no longer solid, but a hollow and useless outline. Is there not a more terrible power that enters into the inner nature of man, and utterly consumes all that is strong and noble and beautiful in his soul?[1]

II.

THE LOWER SATISFACTION.

1. Of how many is it true that the attainment of wealth and the gratification of ambition have not satisfied an ever-increasing longing for more, and that the happiness which they were expected to secure is ever marred by a leanness that enters into the soul. Moral and spiritual decline often follows the too eager pursuit of earthly things. "They that will be rich," says the Apostle, "fall into temptation and a snare, and into many foolish and hurtful lusts, which drown men in destruction and perdition." How must it be in this money-loving age with the many whose whole souls are filled with this fatal desire, and how terrible is the spiritual leanness of a soul from which the love of money has wholly driven out the love of God! So far as our outward circumstances are concerned, our fullest request may have been granted. We may have estates, titles, honours; men may wait for our word, and follow our guidance in all secular speculations and engage-

[1] Joseph Parker.

ments; and yet it may be said of us, "In thy lifetime thou
receivedst thy good things"—so, with the request on the one
hand answered to the utmost, we have on the other a soul that
has been dwarfed almost up to the point of extinction.

¶ There is a deep lesson to be read in a strange picture by
Burne Jones, called "The Depths of the Sea." A mermaid, beautiful in face, but hideously repellent in her scaly train, has flung
her arms around a youth, and is dragging him down through the
green waters to her cave. In her face is the intense malignity
of cruel triumph and cruel scorn; in the youth's face is the agony
of frustration and of death. And the motto below is, "Habes
totâ quod mente petisti, Infelix !"—" Thou hast what thou sought-
est with all thy soul, unhappy one." Oh that it were in my
power to preach to all young men a sermon of meaning so intense
as that picture! The mermaid, like the Siren of mythology, like
the strange woman of the Proverbs, is the harlot Sense. She is
the type of carnal temptation, ending in disillusion, shame, anguish,
death. It is the meaning of the saying of the rabbis, "The demons
come to us smiling and beautiful: when they have done their
work, they drop their mask." It is the meaning of Solomon:
"But he knoweth not that the dead are there, and that her guests
are in the depths of hell." God has granted to that youth his
heart's desire, and sent leanness withal into his bones. He has
got what he passionately longed for, and it is—death ![1]

¶ "But sent leanness into their soul." Ah, that "but"! It
embittered all. The meat was poison to them when it came
without a blessing: whatever it might do in fattening the body,
it was poor stuff when it made the soul lean. If we must know
scantiness, may God grant it may not be scantiness of soul: yet
this is a common attendant upon worldly prosperity. When
wealth grows with many a man his worldly estate is fatter, but
his soul's state is leaner. To gain silver and lose gold is a poor
increase; but to win for the body and lose for the soul is far
worse. How earnestly might Israel have unprayed her prayers
had she known what would come with their answer! The prayers
of lust will have to be wept over. We fret and fume till we have
our desire, and then we have to fret still more because the attainment of it ends in bitter disappointment.[2]

2. We must guard against the mistake—into which we may
so easily fall—of applying the text and the lessons to be drawn

[1] F. W. Farrar, *Social and Present Day Questions*, 174.
[2] C. H. Spurgeon.

from it only to the rich and prosperous, whereas it applies to them in exactly the same sense as it applies to every one, whether he be rich or poor, who is in the state of earnest desire for some earthly good or who is in the state of satisfied desire, a contentment wholly derived from possession or gratification. And this experience is to be met with in all classes, among all sorts and conditions of men. The Israelites, of whom the words of the text were spoken, were certainly not among the rich, but at the time were poor and afflicted—or thought themselves so— and were therefore all the more in danger of the ill effects of full gratification.

¶ There are business men in our city to-day who have schemed for a future which, if analysed, would disclose nothing but a careful regard for personal and domestic comfort. I can give you the brief programme of such men: it runs after this fashion— country, garden, quietness, out-door amusements. They are at perfect liberty to leave the city, to abandon the poor, to get away from all that is fœtid, noisome, and otherwise offensive; but let them beware lest, in reaching this supposed heaven, they find that they have gone in the wrong direction, and that where they expected heaven to begin they find that they have only reached the outward edge of earth.[1]

¶ There is a German folk story of a very poor charcoal burner who had a kind heart and was always doing good turns to people. He often wished that he were rich that he might help still more. One day in the forest a wicked-looking gnome appeared and told him he would make him rich on one condition. He must exchange his heart of flesh for a wonderful mechanical stone heart that the gnome had made and kept in his workshop in a cave underneath the forest. The poor man did not like the condition, but was tempted and consented to the bargain. He was cast into a deep sleep and when he awoke the exchange had been effected and he felt the stone heart working within him with perfect regularity, but it was cold, very cold. When he got back to the village everybody noticed the change. He was harsh, overbearing, a changed man; riches came to him; everything he touched turned to gold, but the richer he grew, the colder seemed the heart, and when old age crept upon him he longed to be poor again and have back his warm human heart. That is a modern way of saying that the man got his request, but leanness came to his soul.[2]

[1] Joseph Parker.   [2] H. Jeffs.

III.

The Higher Satisfaction.

1. How are we to avoid the creeping over us of this insidious disease—leanness of soul? The Apostle shall answer:—" Set your affections on things above." We conquer by the force and direction of desire. Desire is, in the moral world, like the law of gravitation in the natural world—it determines man's relations to beings and objects around him. Desire is the raw material of goodness or wickedness, and thus it has everything to do with the formation of character. There is no power like it. Hence the importance attached in the Bible to strong wishes: " Ask, and ye shall have "; " Seek, and ye shall find "; " Knock, and it shall be opened unto you." Wishes are in truth prayers. We do not pray only when we utter conscious prayers. Every time we wish for anything, our Father understands our wishes.

2. The great lesson, then, which we have to learn from this text is to say from the heart, with trembling yet earnest love, " Not my will but thine be done." That is the lesson ; but where is the school in which it can be learned? The school is called Calvary. There is no other school in which this lesson is taught. Men may try to reason themselves into it ; men may try by fine philosophy to come to a point of resignation that shall yield them high advantages ; but all their labour will be in vain. We must be slain on the Saviour's cross ; we must enter fully into the pain which our Saviour endured ; our hands and our feet must be nailed to the accursed yet blessed tree ; the very last desire of our selfishness must be extinguished, and then shall we come into the joy and the infinite peace of walking with God. Whither are our desires tending? In which direction are they bearing us, upwards or downwards? Are we letting ourselves drift towards some crisis which is the culmination of a gradual deterioration, and which may leave us with what we want (or think that we want), at the cost of everything which makes life worth living? Is desire more and more concentrated on the material, the sensuous? Is some accomplishment or some passing interest utterly possessing us, and are we becoming lean within—without faith, without

sympathy, without self-respect, without generosity, letting others
minister to us without giving aught in return? If so, it may be
well to look on to the end. A day and hour will come when desire
will be manifested; when the true, deep-seated desire of each soul
will be seen. Now there are restraints that hinder its manifestation; there are all sorts of considerations and motives which are
keeping us back and causing us to hide our real desires. Then
every man's true aim and object, as well as every man's work, will
be manifested; each one, freed from constraint, will turn to his
own way. The lips of the Judge need not open to pronounce any
sentence. He but lifts off each constraining law, each limiting
infirmity, each instrument of education, and the result speaks for
itself. Each soul, by its own inner tendency, seeks its own place.
Father and son, brother and brother, sister and sister, wife and
husband, each with the old habitual restraints lifted off them,
turn to their own place—the one goes by an inner power to the
right, the other to the left. It needs no angel to guide or urge
them on. Each one turns to his own desire, to fulness or leanness,
to heaven or hell.

"He will fulfil the desire of them that fear him." "Delight
thyself also in the Lord; and he shall give thee the desires of
thine heart." "O rest in the Lord, and wait patiently for him;
and he will give thee thine heart's desire." It is true we have to
wait; it is true that we have to find our way to rest often through
many very humbling disappointments; but because the mouth of
the Lord hath spoken, we may be sure that the denial of our
prayers is one of the Divine blessings which fall to our lot, and
that when we perish in the outward man the inward man is
blessed with the renewal which will be consummated in the
imperishable and unmingled bliss of heaven. Let us dare to
desire, to wish, to ask for as our chief good, to be like Christ; to
have reproduced within us that loveliness of character, that
tenderness of sympathy, that strength of endurance, that calmness under suffering, that patient self-possession which characterized Him. We cannot see in His life anything but beauty. Let
us dare to wish, to long, to pray, to struggle to be like Him,
and He will give us our desire, and send fulness undreamt of—
the fulness of love, and faith, and strength, and patience—into our
inmost soul.

¶ Goodness and happiness are not one yet; and their conflict oscillates through the centuries from asceticism on the one side to riot on the other, and from Puritanism to Stuart licence. This ever-recurring oscillation indicates a beautiful truth laid bare by our Lord. James Hinton devoted almost all his books to this conflict of goodness and happiness, and pointed out that our Lord had solved their conflict. The human heart desires happiness, and, at the same time, righteousness. A most wholesome thing it is to desire happiness. A heart that does not desire happiness is one with which I should be very sorry to have much to do. Happiness is a legitimate and a God-implanted desire, of which men and women need never be ashamed provided they link it to goodness. But the linking of it to goodness is only to be done by using self for others' good. That is what Hinton points out as the sum of our Lord's teaching for this life, and the conditions which are to be perfect conditions here we may assume to be entrance conditions of the life which is to come.[1]

The awakening swan grows tired at last
   Of weltering pastures where he feeds;
With wings and feet behind him cast,
   He cleaves the labyrinth of the reeds.

He arches out his sparkling plumes,
   He wades and plunges, till he finds
Beneath his breast the azure glooms
   Where the great river brims and winds.

Then, with white sails set to the breeze,
   The current cold about his feet,
He fares to those Hesperides
   Where morning and his comrades meet.

Nor—since within his kindling veins
   A livelier ichor stirs at last—
Regrets the gross and juicy stains,
   The saps and savours of the past;

But through the august and solemn void
   Of misty waters holds his way,
By some ecstatic thirst decoyed
   Towards raptures of the radiant day.

[1] *The Life of William Denny*, 319.

So sails the soul, and cannot rest,
  Inglorious, in the marsh of peace,
But leaves the good, to seek the best,
  Though all its calms and comforts cease,—

Though what it seems to hold be lost,
  Though that grow far which once was nigh,—
By torturing hope in anguish tossed,
  The awakened soul must sail or die.[1]

[1] Edmund Gosse, *In Russet and Silver.*

A VOLUNTEER ARMY.

LITERATURE.

Ball (C. J.), *Testimonies to Christ*, 209.

Critchley (G.), *When the Angels have gone Away*, 163.

Duff (R. S.), *Pleasant Places*, 120.

Henderson (A.), *Sermons*, 9.

Macgregor (W. M.), *Jesus Christ the Son of God*, 52.

Maclaren (A.), *Sermons Preached in Manchester*, iii. 321.

Meyer (F. B.), *Christian Living*, 62.

Morrison (G. H.), *Flood-Tide*, 282.

Price (A. C.), *Fifty Sermons*, vii. 129.

Spurgeon (C. H.), *New Park Street Pulpit*, ii. No. 74.

„ „ *Metropolitan Tabernacle Pulpit*, xlvii. (1901), No. 2724.

Tipple (S. A.), *Days of Old*, 200.

Vaughan (J.), *Sermons to Children*, i. 132.

„ „ *Sermons* (Brighton Pulpit), xxv. (1884), No. 1291.

110

A VOLUNTEER ARMY.

Thy people offer themselves willingly in the day of thy power:
In the beauties of holiness, from the womb of the morning,
Thou hast the dew of thy youth.—Ps. cx. 3.

1. THIS psalm was composed by some patriotic Hebrew poet on
the sallying forth of the king to war, to whom he hears Jehovah
promising support and success in the coming campaign, and sees
in imagination Jehovah Himself accompanying the king as his
chariot rolled away, driving with him, seated by his side, to the
battle. Fired by this vision, he pictures him triumphantly
victorious over his foes, their power shattered, and the field
heaped with their dead bodies; while he describes the enthusiasm
of the people for the sovereign and his cause, the readiness with
which they flock to follow him on his march to the frontier, the
great multitude eager to put themselves at his disposal for the
fray; and the splendid appearance of the troops, in their glittering
armour, like priests clad in sacred vestments, or victims decked
for the sacrifice, innumerable and brilliant as dew-drops from the
womb of morning, and fresh as dew in comprising all the fine
youth, all the young blood and vigour of the land.

But in the course of time the psalm came to be read as a
prophetic description of what should be achieved by the future
Messiah of whom the nation dreamt; to whom, indeed, would be
the gathering of the people; who would prove the champion of
Israel's redemption, and of whose Kingdom and dominion there
would be no end, His name enduring for ever, His name continuing as long as the sun throughout all generations.

¶ This was a favourite psalm of Luther's. "The 110th," he
says, "is very fine. It describes the kingdom and priesthood of
Jesus Christ, and declares Him to be the King of all things and
the intercessor for all men; to whom all things have been remitted

by His Father, and who has compassion on us all. 'Tis a noble psalm; if I were well, I would endeavour to make a Commentary upon it." [1]

2. In accordance with the warlike tone of the whole psalm, the subjects of the monarch are described as an army. The military metaphor comes out more clearly when we attach the true meaning to the words, " in the day of thy power": Calvin translates, " at the time of the assembling of their army "—" au jour des montres," " in the day of the review." And the meaning is, " Thy subjects shall be ready in the day when thou dost muster thy forces, and set them in array for the war."

I.

PATRIOTS.

"Thy people offer themselves willingly in the day of thy power."

1. The subjects of the King are true patriots. There are no mercenaries in these ranks, no pressed men. The soldiers are all volunteers.

There are two kinds of submission and service. There is submission because you cannot help it, and there is submission because you like it. There is a sullen bowing down beneath the weight of a hand which you are too feeble to resist, and there is a glad surrender to a love which it would be a pain not to obey. Some of us feel that we are shut in by immense and sovereign power which we cannot oppose. And yet, like some raging rebel in a dungeon, or some fluttering bird in a cage, we beat ourselves all bruised and bloody against the bars in vain attempts at liberty, alternating with fits of cowed apathy as we slink into a corner of our cell. Some of us, however, feel that we are enclosed on every side by that mighty hand which none can resist, and from which we would not stray if we could; and we joyfully hide beneath its shelter, and gladly obey when it points. Constrained obedience is no obedience. Unless there be the glad surrender of the will and heart, there is no surrender at all.

[1] R. E. Prothero, *The Psalms in Human Life*, 122.

God does not want compulsory submission. He does not care to rule over people who are only crushed down by greater power. He does not count that those serve who sullenly acquiesce because they dare not oppose. Christ seeks for no pressed men in His ranks. Whosoever does not enlist joyfully is not reckoned as His.

¶ An ironic historian sets side by side Frederick the Great's account of the performance of his troops in one battle and a home letter of a recruit engaged in it. "Never," says Frederick, "have my troops done such marvels in point of gallantry, never since it has been my honour to lead them." And the soldier tells his squalid story, of men driven into battle with blows from sergeants' canes, skulking, when they could, behind walls, and taking the opportunity of passing through a vineyard to desert in scores. Frederick won many battles, but he won them in spite of a detestable system, and this poet finds a promise of triumph for his King in the glad loyalty with which He inspires His soldiers.[1]

2. The soldiers are not only volunteers; they are animated by a spirit of self-surrender and sacrifice. The word here rendered "willing" is employed throughout the Levitical law for "freewill offerings." It is a striking word in the Hebrew. We have a similar idea in Ps. lxviii. 9, where we are told that God has poured forth a refreshing rain for His inheritance because it is weary. And as we receive the refreshing rain of God's Holy Spirit from heaven, in order that we may become a river pouring out His riches, so the real meaning of the Hebrew is this, "Thy people shall become a freewill offering in the day of thy power." It is in that host as it was in the army whose heroic self-devotion was chanted by Deborah under her palm tree—"The people willingly offered themselves." Hence came courage, devotion, victory. With their lives in their hands they flung themselves on the foe, and nothing could stand against the onset of men who recked not of themselves.

For there is this one grand thing even about the devilry of war—the transcendent self-abnegation with which, however poor and unworthy may be the cause, a man casts himself away, "what time the foeman's line is broke." The poorest, most vulgar, most animal natures rise for a moment into something like nobility, as

[1] W. M. Macgregor, *Jesus Christ the Son of God*, 59.

the surge of the strong emotion lifts them to that height of heroism. Life is then most glorious when it is given away for a great cause. That sacrifice is the one noble and chivalrous element which gives interest to war, the one thing that can be disentangled from its hideous associations, and can be transferred to higher regions of life. That spirit of lofty consecration and utter self-forgetfulness must be ours, if we would be Christ's soldiers. Our obedience will then be glad when we feel the force of, and yield to, that gentle persuasive entreaty, "I beseech you therefore, brethren, by the mercies of God, that ye present your bodies a living sacrifice."

¶ "I raised such men," said Cromwell, "as had the fear of God before them, as made some conscience of what they did; and from that day forward, I must say they were never beaten."

¶ To be true to himself, to renounce nothing which he knew to be good and yet bring all things captive to the obedience of Christ, was the problem before him. He hesitated long before he could believe that such a solution was possible. His heart was with this rich, attractive world of human life, in the multiplicity and wealth of its illustrations, until it was revealed to him that it assumed a richer but a holier aspect when seen in the light of God. But to this end, he must submit his will to the Divine will in the spirit of absolute obedience. Here the struggle was deep and prolonged. It was a moral struggle mainly, not primarily intellectual or emotional. He feared that he should lose something in sacrificing his own will to God's will. How the gulf was bridged he could not tell. He wrote down as one of the first of the texts on which he should preach, "Thy people shall be willing in the day of thy power," with the comment that "willingness is the first Christian step." Thus the conversion of Phillips Brooks becomes a representative process of his age. So far as the age has been great, through science or through literature, its greatness passed into his soul. The weakness of his age, its sentimentalism, its fatalism, he overcame in himself when he made the absolute surrender of his will to God. All that he had hitherto loved and cherished as the highest, instead of being lost, was given back to him in fuller measure. To the standard he had now raised there rallied great convictions and blessed experiences, the sense of the unity of life, the harmony of the whole creation, the consciousness of joy in being alive, the conviction that heaven is the goal of earth.[1]

[1] *Phillips Brooks: Memories of his Life*, by A. V. G. Allen, 82.

II.

PATRIOT-PRIESTS.

"In the beauties of holiness."

The phrase "in the beauty of holiness" is frequently used for the sacerdotal garments, the holy festal attire of the priests of the Lord. So the soldiers are priests as well as patriots.

1. The King and Leader is Himself a Priest of God's making, another Melchizedek. In different ages of the world there have been men in whom a certain native priestliness has been apparent, men born to bring others into the secrets of God, and seeming to need no introduction or furtherance themselves; men who, in the Scots phrase, are "far ben," for they always, with unveiled face, see God. It is their task to make the hidden things apprehensible to those who belong to the rough world outside. And God's King, when He comes, will be a priest of that kind, whose priesthood is a matter of native endowment and not of human ordination.

The mediæval emperor was a deacon in the Roman Church, just as the pope, on his side, was a great secular prince. In Israel, too, the king had something of priestly rank. But here is no such fictitious dignity. "Thou art a priest of my making," says God, "another Melchizedek." Professor Davidson comments on the picture which is given us of Melchizedek—without father, without mother, without descent. "He passes over the stage a king, a priest, living; that sight of him is all we ever get. He is like a portrait having always the same qualities, presenting always the same aspect, looking down on us always with the same eyes, which turn and follow us wherever we may stand—always royal, always priestly, always individual, and neither receiving nor imparting what he is, but being all in virtue of himself."

The conquering King whom the psalm hymns is a Priest for ever; and He is followed by an army of priests. The soldiers are gathered in the day of the muster, with high courage and willing devotion, ready to fling away their lives; but they are clad not in mail, but in priestly robes, like those who wait before the altar rather than like those who plunge into the fight, like those who compassed

Jericho with the ark for their standard and the trumpets for all their weapons. We can scarcely fail to remember the words which echo these and interpret them. The armies which were in heaven followed Him on white horses, clothed in fine linen, white and clean.

Christina Rossetti comments on the strangeness of such armour against cut of sword and thrust of spear. But the suggestion is that the soldiers have one heart with their Leader, and are great in consecration like Himself. They go out after Him where hard blows are struck, where there is turmoil and shouting and the burden of the weary day, but they go as priests. That warfare which belongs to the extension of the Kingdom of God calls for services which may often be sordid and ugly and painful; but when they are rightly rendered they are as sacred and as acceptable as any incense offering in the dim seclusion of a temple. The one priestly sacrifice worth speaking of which men can render is the offering of a heart given willingly to the Divine service: and the cause is sure to prevail which can count on volunteers of that complexion.

¶ Dr. Butler, Master of Trinity College, Cambridge, writing of Keith-Falconer, who had been one of his pupils at Harrow, says: "I do not think our dear friend and I had any further communication with each other till the end of last year (1886), when I received from him at Davos-Platz a most kind letter of congratulation on my appointment to the Mastership of Trinity. He told me also of the plan which he had formed for going to Aden, and there employing his knowledge of Arabic for missionary purposes. The result of this generous enterprise we know but too well. The work was scarcely begun before it reached its earthly end. To those who believe in the abiding results of devotion to the cause and the Person of Christ, his short life will not seem a failure. His image will remain fresh in the hearts of many as of a man exceptionally noble and exceptionally winning, recalling to them their own highest visions of unselfish service to God and man, and helping them to hold fast the truth that in the spiritual world nothing but self-sacrifice is permanently fruitful, and that the seed of a truly Christian life is never quickened except it die." [1]

2. The priestly attire suggests that the great power which we are to wield in our Christian warfare is character. Purity of

[1] R. Sinker, *Memorials of the Hon. Ion Keith-Falconer*, 23.

heart and life, transparent simple goodness, manifest in men's sight—these will arm us against dangers, and these will bring our brethren glad captives to our Lord. We serve Him best, and advance His Kingdom most, when the habit of our souls is that righteousness with which He invests our nakedness. Be like your Lord, and as His soldiers you will conquer, and as His priests you will win some to His love and fear. Nothing else will avail without that. Without that dress no man finds a place in the ranks.

¶ "I have known many a man," says Thoreau, "who pretended to be a Christian; but it was ridiculous, for he had no genius for it." This poet was persuaded that his King would go far because of the temper of the people. "They offer themselves willingly; in holy, beautiful garments they come, fresh, young, countless like dew at the dawn." [1]

¶ Turn your energies towards your moral cultivation. In doing so you will accumulate imperishable riches. All that your worldly care can bring will be the doubtful possession of riches of doubtful value. In the possession of the moral wealth of a noble and disciplined character, you possess that which can neither wither nor be stolen. What we have we must leave at the threshold of the grave. What we are goes with us into the other world. Riches will drop from our dying hand into the grasp of others. Character passes with us into the presence of God. Character is everything. This, rather than worldly riches, is the true end of life. The perfecting of this is the true purpose of God in life. [2]

¶ Few things tell on character more surely and precisely than the goal on which the heart is set and the temper in which that goal is sought. And certainly the Christian character, as it appears in Christ-like lives, does not look at all as though it had been formed and fostered and determined by a mercenary attention to a selfish aim. For the faculties and the capacity that grow in those who try to be true to Christ in daily life are strikingly ill-suited for the opportunities of enjoyment which might be imagined in a heaven of selfishness. Christians do not grow in the capacity for selfish pleasure, nor attain an exceptional power of relishing to the utmost a separate and individual gratification. The faculty which they develop is the faculty of self-denial; of glad, unhindered self-forgetfulness for others' sake; of delighting in goodness and eliciting what is best in others; of simple, cheerful, unclouded self-surrender. These, and such as these, are the

[1] W. M. Macgregor.   [2] Bishop Boyd Carpenter.

powers that accrue to those who choose the Christian life; and it is strange if the way along which they are acquired is a way of self-seeking; strange if, in striving towards a paradise of selfish pleasure, there is formed a character which would be as wretched there as a selfish character in the heaven of the saints. Surely it is a very different sort of aim and quest that is betrayed in the development of the Christian character and in the lines on which it presses forward; its preparation through the discipline of this life is for something else than what is here called pleasure or success; the faculties that are strengthened with its strength must have a work surpassing all our thoughts, and the capacity it brings can never be satisfied with aught that is created. For, in truth, the Christian character prophesies of this—that God has made us for Himself; and that there is neither rest, nor goal, nor joy for man, save in His love.[1]

III.

PATRIOT-PRIESTS IN PERPETUAL YOUTH.

"From the womb of the morning, thou hast the dew of thy youth."

Alexander Henderson, expounding this passage, says: "The words are somewhat obscure even to the learned ear, but look to the 133rd Psalm, and there ye will see a place to help to clear them. Always (however) observe here, 'from the womb of the morning, thou hast the dew of thy youth,' that as in a May morning, when there is no extremity of heat, the dew falls so thick that all the fields are covered with it, and it falls in such a secret manner that none sees it fall, so the Lord, in the day of His power, He shall multiply His people, and He shall multiply them in a secret manner; so that it is marvellous to the world, that once there should seem to be so few or none of them, and then incontinent He should make them to be through all estates."

1. The "dew of thy youth" has often been understood to mean the fresh youthful energy attributed by the psalm to the Priest-King. It has been suggested that the historical setting of the psalm is to be found in the Maccabean period. The heroic Judas had fallen in battle. Only one Maccabee remained, an

---

[1] Francis Paget, *Studies in the Christian Character.*

elder brother, Simon, who had been passed over till this time—
a great man and a wise one, it would seem, who had deliberately
and unselfishly stood aside while his younger brethren had been
doing their mighty work. He had been their lieutenant, counsellor,
helper in every way. "The father of them all" was the affection-
ate title which he bore among them; the organizer and statesman
of the valiant band; one of those strong, keen, silent souls who
are content to work in obscurity, so that the grand object is
obtained, but who often have more real power than those who
stand glittering in the front. But now his time was come—come
when he was apparently more than sixty years of age. He rose
to the occasion; he took the critical and dangerous place. He
went up to Jerusalem, stood among the excited and trembling
multitude, and said: "Ye yourselves know what great things I
and my brethren and my father's house have done for the laws
and the sanctuary. You know the battles and troubles we have
seen, by reason whereof all my brethren are slain for Israel's sake,
and I am left alone. Now therefore, be it far from me that I
should spare mine own life in any time of trouble, for I am no
better than my brethren. I will defend my nation and the
sanctuary, and our wives and our children, though all the heathen
be gathered together to destroy us for very malice."

The people gazed upon the grand old man. They watched his
kindling eye, his martial bearing; they saw the fires of a still
youthful spirit burning in the aged frame, and they answered with
a loud voice, "Thou shalt be our leader. Fight thou our battles,
and whatsoever thou commandest us, we will do." Then they
brought him into the temple, clothed him in the sacred robes,
placed the tiara upon his head, and saluted him as the great
Priest-King of Israel: and it may be that this 110th Psalm
preserves the memory of the coronation anthem sung at that
service in the temple when the old man with the brave young
heart inside him stood before the awestruck multitudes and took
the perilous honour of the lofty place. A joy-shout of the people
finds its echo in the text, "From the breaking of the morning,
thou hast the dew of thy youth"; that is to say, "Though aged, it
is upon thee still."

¶ Certain leaders in their young days have led their troops to
battle, and, by the loudness of their voice, and the strength of

their bodies, have inspired their men with courage; but the old warrior hath his hair sown with grey; he begins to be decrepit, and no longer can lead men to battle. It is not so with Jesus Christ. He has still the dew of His youth. The same Christ who led His troops to battle in His early youth leads them now. The arm which smote the sinner with His word smites now; it is as unpalsied as it was before. The eye which looked upon His friends with gladness, and upon His foemen with a glance most stern and high—that same eye is regarding us now, undimmed, like that of Moses. He has the dew of His youth.[1]

¶ As I witness the energies of nature, I feel that the heart that fashioned it was young. There is no sign of age about creation. There is no trace of the weariness of years. It is inspired with an abounding energy that tells me of a fresh and youthful mind. Christ may have lived from everlasting ages before the moment of creation came; but the eternal morning was still upon His brow when He conceived and bodied out the world. There are the powers of youth in it. There are the energies of opening life. "Thou hast the dew of thy youth."[2]

2. We may however take "youth" to be a collective noun, equivalent to young men. In that case the army is described as a host of young warriors, led forth in their fresh strength and countless numbers and gleaming beauty, like the dew of the morning. Did you never see the dew-drops glistening on the earth? and did you never ask, "Whence came these? How came they here so infinite in number, so lavishly scattered everywhere, so pure and brilliant?" Nature whispered the answer, "They came from the womb of the morning." So God's people will come forth as noiselessly, as mysteriously, as divinely, as if they came "from the womb of the morning," like the dew-drops. Science has laboured to discover the origin of dew, and perhaps has guessed it, but to the Eastern, one of the greatest riddles was, Out of whose womb came the dew? Who is the mother of those pearly drops? Now, so will God's people come mysteriously. Again, the dew-drops—who made them? Do kings and princes rise up and hold their sceptres, and bid the clouds shed tears, or affright them to weeping by the beating of the drum? Do armies march to the battle to force the sky to give up its treasure, and scatter its diamonds lavishly? No; God speaks; He whispers in

---

[1] C. H. Spurgeon.　　　　[2] G. H. Morrison, *Flood-Tide*, 286.

the ears of nature, and it weeps for joy at the glad news that the morning is coming. God does it; there is no apparent agency employed, no thunder, no lightning; God has done it. That is how God's people shall be saved; they come forth from the "womb of the morning"; divinely called, divinely brought, divinely blessed, divinely numbered, divinely scattered over the entire surface of the globe, divinely refreshing to the world, they proceed from the "womb of the morning."

¶ When you go out, delighted, into the dew of the morning, have you ever considered why it is so rich upon the grass;—why it is not upon the trees? It is partly on the trees, but yet your memory of it will be always chiefly of its gleam upon the lawn. On many trees you will find there is none at all. I cannot follow out here the many inquiries connected with this subject, but, broadly remember the branched trees are fed chiefly by rain,—the unbranched ones by dew, visible or invisible; that is to say, at all events by moisture which they can gather for themselves out of the air; or else by streams and springs. Hence the division of the verse of the song of Moses: "My doctrine shall drop as the rain; my speech shall distil as the dew: as the small rain upon the tender herb, and as the showers upon the grass." [1]

¶ Until I heard from my friend Mr. Tyrwhitt of the cold felt at night in camping on Sinai, I could not understand how deep the feeling of the Arab, no less than the Greek, must have been respecting the Divine gift of the dew,—nor with what sense of thankfulness for miraculous blessing the question of Job would be uttered, "The hoary frost of heaven, who hath gendered it?" Then compare the first words of the blessing of Isaac: "God give thee of the dew of heaven, and of the fatness of earth"; and, again, the first words of the song of Moses: "Give ear, oh ye heavens,—for my speech shall distil as the dew"; and you will see at once why this heavenly food (manna) was made to shine clear in the desert, like an enduring of its dew;—Divine remaining for continual need. Frozen, as the Alpine snow—pure for ever.[2]

3. The soldiers of this King retain their youth. He who has fellowship with God, and lives in the constant reception of the supernatural life and grace which come from Jesus Christ, possesses the secret of perpetual youth. The world ages us, time and physical changes tell on us all, and the strength which belongs

[1] Ruskin, *Proserpina*, i. chap. iii. § 22.
[2] Ruskin, *Deucalion*, i. chap. vii. § 12.

to the life of nature ebbs away; but the life eternal is subject to
no laws of decay and owes nothing to the external world. So we
may be ever young in heart and spirit. It is possible for a man
to carry the freshness, the buoyancy, the elastic cheerfulness, the
joyful hope of his earliest days, right on through the monotony of
middle-aged maturity, and even into old age shadowed by the long
reflection of the tombs which the setting sun casts over the path.
It is possible for us to grow younger as we grow older, because we
drink more full draughts of the fountain of life, and so to have
to say at the last, "Thou hast kept the good wine until now."
"Even the youths shall faint and be weary, and the young men
shall utterly fall. But they that wait upon the Lord shall renew
their strength." If we live near Christ, and draw our life from
Him, then we may blend the hopes of youth with the experience
and memory of age; be at once calm and joyous, wise and strong,
preserving the blessedness of each stage of life into that which
follows, and thus at last possessing the sweetness and the good of
all at once. We may not only bear fruit in old age, but have
buds, blossoms, and fruit—the varying product and adornment
of every stage of life united in our characters.

A man is not old, however hoary and bent, who is conversing,
as Emerson says, with what is above him, with the religious eye
looking upward, and abandoned the while with delight to the
inspirations flowing in from all sides. A man is not old in
whom the faculty of imagination is undecayed, who throbs with
sympathy as eager and strong as ever for whatsoever is just and
lovely and pure and true; whose mind, still responsive and aspiring, is fully open to new thoughts and new ideas, and cherishes
dreams of the ideal; upon whom no weight of custom or of habit
lies so heavily that he cannot move out of grooves under the
direction of some felt better way, or who carries with him the
optimism which, without hiding its face from the dark and ugly
facts of existence, can front them smilingly, and sing its song in
defiance of them, because of faith in humanity and trust in the
divine purpose of the Universe. A man is not old, who is at one
with Michael Angelo when, just before he died on the verge of
ninety, he carved an allegorical figure, and inscribed on it in large
letters, "Still learning," or whose heart echoes Robert Browning,
when he sang:

Grow old along with me!
The best is yet to be,
The last of life, for which the first was made:
Our times are in His hand
Who saith "A whole I planned,
Youth shows but half; trust God: see all nor be afraid!"

¶ 1st December 1895. A pleasant party at York House. The conversation straying to Watts, Miss Lawless, who was sitting on one side of me, mentioned that he had said to her: "I think I am quite accurate in telling you that I saw the sun rise every day last summer," and Mrs. Tyrrell, who was sitting on my other side, told us that he had said to her: "I am seventy-eight, and I hope still to do my best work."[1]

4. The soldier of the cross should exercise in the world a gracious refreshing influence, like the dew. The dew, formed in the silence of the darkness while men sleep, falling as willingly on a bit of dead wood as anywhere, hanging its pearls on every poor spike of grass, and dressing everything on which it lies with strange beauty, each separate globule tiny and evanescent, but each flashing back the light, and each a perfect sphere, feeble one by one, but united mighty to make the pastures of the wilderness rejoice—so, created in silence by an unseen influence, feeble when taken in detail but strong in their myriads, glad to occupy the lowliest place, and each "bright with something of celestial light," Christian men and women are to be in the midst of many people as dew from the Lord.

¶ The personal influence of Henry Bradshaw (the librarian at Cambridge University) was extraordinary. It was not gained by any arts, nor did he ever manifest the slightest wish to interfere or to exercise influence. One just knew him to be a man of guileless life, laborious, high-principled, incapable of any sort of meanness or malice. To love is to understand everything, says the French proverb. It is not easy really to improve people by scolding them or lecturing them, but if one knows that a generous, unsuspicious, high-minded man has a real affection for one, it is impossible not to be restrained by the thought from acting in a way that he would disapprove. Bradshaw's influence over the men he knew was stronger than the influence of any other man at Cambridge. But his affection was sisterly—if one can use the

[1] M. E. Grant Duff, *Notes from a Diary, 1892-95*, ii. 290.

word—rather than paternal. He was fond of little demonstra-
tions of affection, would pat and stroke one's hand as he talked,
and yet there was never the least shadow of sentimentality about
it. I have never heard any one suggest that there was anything
weak or unmanly about his tenderness. It was preserved from
that by his critical judgment, his excellent sense, his power of
saying the most incisive things, and the irony which, however
lambent, had got a very clear cutting edge, and which he was
always ready to use if there was occasion. If any one traded on
the affection of Bradshaw or counted on indulgence, he was sure
to be instantly and kindly snubbed. It was more that there was
an atmosphere of intimacy and confidence in one's relations with
him, which pervaded the time spent in his company as with
fragrant summer air.[1]

¶ When love has made the most of the man himself it over-
flows to bless others. Christ's disciples are not here to be
ministered unto, but to minister. Religion, says Christ, is love,
and love is gentle toward those with hollow eyes and famine-
stricken faces. Love is kindly toward those who have a tragedy
written in the sharpened countenance. Love is patient toward
those who have lost fidelity as a man loses a golden coin ; who
have lost morality as one who flounders in the Alpine drifts.
And this religion of love takes on a thousand modern forms. If
it is not rowing out against the darkness and storm, as did Grace
Darling, to save the shipwrecked, it is going forth to those tossed
upon life's billows, to succour and to save. For love is making
the individual life beautiful, making the home beautiful, and
will at last make the Church and State beautiful. Men will not
bow down to crowned power nor philosophic power nor æsthetic
power ; but in the presence of a great soul, filled with vigour of
inspiration and glowing with love, man will do obeisance. There
is no force upon earth like Divine love in the heart of man, and
at last that force will sweeten and regenerate society.[2]

[1] A. C. Benson, *The Leaves of the Tree*, 225.
[2] N. D. Hillis, *The Investment of Influence*, 274.

THE BROOK IN THE WAY.

LITERATURE.

Chadwick (G. A.), *Pilate's Gift*, 266.
Hanks (W. P.), *The Eternal Witness*, 81.
Hunter (J.), *The Angels of God*, 27.
Jerdan (C.), *Gospel Milk and Honey*, 245.
Jones (J. D.), *The Unfettered Word*, 145.
Norton (J. N.), *Old Paths*, 231.
Piggott (W. C.), *The Imperishable Word*, 190.
Smellie (A.), *Service and Inspiration*, 49.

The Brook in the Way.

He shall drink of the brook in the way:
Therefore shall he lift up the head.—Ps. cx. 7.

1. THIS jubilant and magnificent psalm opens with a passage which was taken possession of by the Apostles, in the name of their Lord, so long ago that it has lost any suggestion of foreignness; and just as some of our older colonies have acquired a look of England overseas, so do we welcome these verses when we come upon them, as if they were an outlying tract of the New Testament. They give a description of the King, set at God's right hand, a Priest for ever, which in itself is great; and yet, in the writer's view, it was only a preparation for something else. These things were spoken of Him that faith might have a chance; for what possessed the poet was not that his King was great and highly favoured, but that a King so great would go far and that of His conquests there would be no end. It is through getting big thoughts of the King that men are prepared to cherish worthier expectations with regard to the Kingdom.

2. The poet first shows the kingship at rest, as it is in its dignity, created and secured by God, and when his heart is full of that he goes on to show the kingship in action. A royalty based upon the will of God, which, indeed, is nothing else than an instrument of that will, cannot but make way; present and future have nothing in them to withstand it, and thus it will go farther and farther, passing out at last beyond the imagination of men. That is the poet's idea, which a rhetorician would have expressed in some resounding phrase; but as an artist this man had no liking for vague words without any picture in them. He wanted men to feel that the King beyond their sight was pushing His conquests still, and he manages that by a quaint touch of imagination. The King, urging on His enemies in their flight,

stops for a moment to drink, and then He passes off the scene with head uplifted, fresh as when the battle-day began.   There He is—the true King, God's gift to men, travelling out beyond our sight, on always vaster enterprises, and without a sign of flagging strength.   That fired the poet's soul, and it should live with us as the scope and outlook of the psalm.

I.

THE IDEAL KING.

1. Who is this King and Captain that the poet celebrates ? The answer must be that we have here not a portrait but an ideal, which embodies the dream of those who trusted that God would give them one day a ruler who should be all that a king can be to men.   The poet follows this warrior priest, this priestly king, to the war ; he sees him winning victory after victory, until the earth seems filled with the slaughtered bodies of his foes. But he grows weary and tired in the conflict ; his tongue cleaves to his mouth for thirst ; his sword well-nigh drops from his hand for sheer weariness as he toils on beneath the fierce glare of the Eastern sun.   And it seems as if he must faint and fall before the full fruits of victory are reaped, when suddenly a little brook of cool and limpid water presents itself to his gaze, and the faint and tired warrior stoops and drinks a long, deep draught, and the clear, cool water brings refreshing and new strength to his exhausted frame, so that, with new vigour and determination, he resumes the pursuit, and makes the victory final and complete. "He shall drink of the brook in the way : therefore shall he lift up the head."

2. This ideal King overthrows all His enemies and wins a lasting dominion because He is God's own partner.   He knows how to conquer.   He is content that His battles should be taken out of His hands, and that the victory when it comes should be God's victory and not His own.   In Him there is no self-assertion or display ; He accepts what God allows and asks no more. Inferior men may be restless, as they take on themselves the burden of the world and its future, striking hotly in defence

of their view of truth, and growing troubled and dejected when that view does not make way. But in the true Master of men there is a superlative trust in God; He suffers His own effort and His own message to pass into the sum of God's providential forces, which are working for new heavens and a new earth. He does not bear the burden of the world anxiously, but leaves it in the strong hands of Him who can sustain it all. Peter speaks of Jesus "sitting at the right hand of God, expecting," which is a word of admonition for all unquiet minds so ludicrously solicitous about the interests and the work of God. But whilst He was still on earth, Jesus suffered God to fight His battles for Him. He tarried for the Lord's leisure. He believed in powers which work slowly and without noise, and He knew the rest of heart of those who wait for God and are content that He should work.

3. "What is to hinder this man from governing?" says Carlyle of the Abbot Samson. "There is in him what far transcends all apprenticeships; in the man himself there exists a model of governing, something to govern by. He has the living ideal of a governor in him." In like fashion the poet sweeps aside the whole mob of kings so called, David and Solomon and their posterity, who in turn had claimed to sit on the throne of Jehovah. He did not mean that kind of thing at all—a merely titular kingship, which had no promise in it. One day there will be born a King, possessing every gift of rule, born to command the wavering hearts of men; and when He comes the first to acknowledge Him will be God, who will make a place in His universe for Him, and raise Him not to where these spectral majesties have sat, these uneasy phantasms which have flitted across the scene, but to where none ever sat before. "Sit at my right hand."

Thus Christ alone answers fully to the description of the conquering King, who is also "a priest for ever after the order of Melchizedek." It is He alone who goes forth at the head of an army numberless as the dewdrops of a summer morn, every soldier in it clothed in holy garments, sweeping His enemies before Him, gaining one victory after another until they are all beneath His feet, and His Kingdom stretches from the river unto the ends of the earth.

4. This King not only sits as partner with the King of
kings, but is content to share the lot of the common soldier.
The Psalmist writes of " his Lord " at the right hand of Jehovah,
that He shall be refreshed along His conquering march, not with
the rich wines of Helbon cooled in the snows of Lebanon, but,
like any private soldier, from the wayside brook. And He shall
need refreshment, having taken His full share of toil. This
contrast between a splendid destiny and the simplest life was
never so true of any as of Jesus Christ. It is this contrast that
moves St. Paul to astonishment in the words, " God sent forth
his Son, born of a woman, born under the law." We have not
a High Priest who cannot be touched with the feeling of our infirmity, but One who was tempted in all points like as we are—weary,
athirst, and faint. For thirty years Jesus lived the frugal and
simple life of a carpenter's son in a quiet village among the hills
of Galilee. His first recorded temptation was to break His
fellowship with us by claiming miraculous supplies, at least of
bread; but this help, which He gave to others, He would not
Himself employ. Never once did Jesus use His special powers
for Himself to make a difference between His life and ours, or
drink of other streams but such as ran by the wayside for all.
His first miracle was to make large supplies of wine for a
marriage feast; but, for His own part, He would sit by the
wayside fountain, waiting, and would ask a lost woman to bestow
on Him a cup of cold water. The fever of His cruel death was
alleviated by the vinegar, the sour wine, of the private soldiers
beneath His cross. Even after His resurrection, when He had
already entered upon that sublime and mysterious life which it
is our highest hope to share, He did not scorn to take of the fish
which they had drawn from the Lake of Galilee, and, again, even
of the cold fish which remained from a former meal.

¶ The troops of Charles the Twelfth, in sore distress and
half inclined to mutiny, brought him a specimen of their bread,
which was hard and sour and black. To their astonishment,
the king ate it with a relish, and quietly answered: " It is not
good bread, but it can be eaten." There was no more thought
of mutiny in that camp; nor will such a leader ever lack men
to follow, to suffer, and to die with him.[1]

[1] G. A. Chadwick, *Pilate's Gift*, 269.

(1) The Son of God became one with us *in taking our nature.*
He did not come to the world robed in cloud and fire and
storm, and attended by an army of angels. Rather, He did
much to conceal His majesty during the time that He lived on
earth. He was born a Jew; and the Hebrew nation was "the
fewest of all peoples"—not one of the great broad streams of
mankind, but as a "brook in the way"; yet the Lord Jesus
drank of that brook. "He took not on him the nature of angels;
but he took on him the seed of Abraham." Without for a
moment ceasing to be God, He stooped to become a babe in the
manger, a humble and inquiring boy growing up a working
carpenter in a country town, then a homeless wayfarer, a
rejected religious teacher, and at last a crucified slave.

(2) Our Great Captain at length bowed His head to *drink
our cup of suffering and sorrow.* That bitter cup was put into
His hand in the garden of Gethsemane, and He did not refuse
to drink it. He did not, as He might have done, use His
almighty power to deliver Himself from His enemies. He gave
Himself up, a weary and unarmed man, to their wicked will.
Out of love for us, and with a view to our redemption, He
allowed Himself to be nailed to the cross. And there He was
"made a curse for us," bearing our sin and shame and doom.

¶ Nothing can have a more tranquillizing effect upon us in
this world than the frequent consideration of the afflictions,
necessities, contempt, calumnies, insults, and humiliations which
our Lord suffered from His birth to His most painful death.
When we contemplate such a weight of bitterness as this, are
we not wrong in giving to the trifling misfortunes which befall
us even the names of adversities and injuries? Are we not
ashamed to ask a share of His Divine patience to help us to
bear such trifles as these, seeing that the smallest modicum of
moderation and humility would suffice to make us bear calmly
the insults offered to us?[1]

¶ Before the apotheosis of the cross, suffering was a curse
from which man fled; now it becomes a purification of the soul,
a sacred trial sent by Eternal Love, a Divine dispensation meant
to sanctify and ennoble us, an acceptable aid to faith, a strange
initiation into happiness. O power of belief!—All remains the
same, and yet all is changed. A new certitude arises to deny

[1] *The Spirit of St. Francis de Sales,* 172.

the apparent and the tangible; it pierces through the mystery of things, it places an invisible Father behind visible nature, it shows us joy shining through tears, and makes of pain the beginning of joy.   And so, for those who have believed, the tomb becomes heaven, and on the funeral pyre of life they sing the hosanna of immortality; a sacred madness has renewed the face of the world for them, and when they wish to explain what they feel, their ecstasy makes them incomprehensible; they speak with tongues.   A wild intoxication of self-sacrifice, contempt for death, the thirst for eternity, the delirium of love—these are what the unalterable gentleness of the Crucified has had power to bring forth.   By His pardon of His executioners, and by that unconquerable sense in Him of an indissoluble union with God, Jesus, on His cross, kindled an inextinguishable fire and revolutionized the world.[1]

Christ's Heart was wrung for me, if mine is sore;
  And if my feet are weary, His have bled;
  He had no place wherein to lay His Head;
If I am burdened, He was burdened more.
The cup I drink, He drank of long before;
  He felt the unuttered anguish which I dread;
  He hungered who the hungry thousands fed,
And thirsted who the world's refreshment bore.
If grief be such a looking-glass as shows
  Christ's Face and man's in some sort made alike,
    Then grief is pleasure with a subtle taste:
    Wherefore should any fret or faint or haste?
Grief is not grievous to a soul that knows
  Christ comes,—and listens for that hour to strike.[2]

II.

THE COMMON BROOK.

" He shall drink of the brook in the way."   It is wonderful to think of the spiritual life of Jesus nourished by the same means of grace as are available for us all.   At every point in Christ's experience there was a sense of obstacle and resistance.   Salvation for Him was every day a task entailing agony.   But always He bore down the resistance, and, welcoming the reliefs that were

---

[1] *Amiel's Journal* (trans. by Mrs. Humphry Ward), 168.
[2] Christina G. Rossetti, *Verses*, 37.

given Him by God, He passed on with lifted head to the burden
and the battle of the new day, sure of Himself, sure of His cause,
very sure of God and victory. "True souls always are hilarious."
Think of Him when the disciples came back from their first
excursion, elated, as small men will be, by their minute successes;
their ministry, one may suppose, had scarcely drawn attention in
the single province of Galilee, and He had taken on Himself the
redemption of the world. But hear His comment, "When you
were away I was watching Satan and he was fallen" (an imperfect
tense followed by an aorist). The most meagre encouragement, the first faint effort of a soul to free itself, spoke home
to His heart, and He drew water with joy out of the wells of
salvation.

We do not find that one innocent pleasure which came "in
the way" to Jesus was sourly or wilfully refused by Him. He
would leave a feast at once, if called by Jairus to a sick-bed; but
He would not refuse the feast of His friends in Bethany, though
He knew that He was reproached for eating and drinking, and
though He felt His death to be so near that the ointment then
poured upon Him would go with Him to His burial. How does
His example affect us? We may have to refuse pleasures because
we are weak, because temptations must be avoided, because we
have no longer any choice except to cripple our life, or, having two
feet, to be cast into hell fire; but this is not a thing to boast of.
Or, like St. Paul, we may deny ourselves for our weak brother's
sake, which is an honour, and a Christ-like thing; but the rule,
apart from special cases, is that the best and truest life is such as
welcomes and is refreshed by all simple pleasures which sparkle
and sing by our life's path, which do not require us to leave the
road of duty that we may drink of them.

¶ Eastern people have a very skilful way of drinking from a
flowing stream without stopping in their running. They throw
the water up into the mouth. An Eastern traveller writes: "In
an excursion across an Arabian desert, some of the Arabs, on
coming to water, rushed to it, and, stooping sufficiently to allow
the right hand to reach the water, they threw it up into their
mouths so dexterously, that I never observed any of the water
to fall upon the breast. I often tried to do it, but never
succeeded."

1. Jesus found refreshment in quiet communion with nature.
In one of his letters Nathaniel Hawthorne speaks about bathing
himself in " the refreshing waters of solitude and open-air nature,"
and there is no season of the year in which we may not find this
source of rest and refreshment for the mind and heart. The
creation may always be our recreation. To be in love with this
beautiful world is to be at the secret source of many a noble
pleasure. To have a mind and heart open to the highest
impressions of the natural universe, to be able to enter into the
life of a summer or a winter day, to enjoy a night of stars, to feel
the beauty of a flower, the grandeur of a storm, the spell of the
wide waters or the high mountains, is to have abundant means of
recovery and renewal always nigh at hand whenever we feel the
need of calling ourselves off for a time from the excitement and
strain of the daily conflict. It is true that nature does not
yield the sympathy which the passionate human heart requires,
but insensibly she helps her lovers to bear their burdens and to
find rest in God. We are quickened and comforted by outward
things more than we know. The sun and moon and stars,
unaffected by our little controversies, rebuke and soothe us as we
gaze on their tranquil glory. The mountains bring peace, and our
fretfulness is carried away by the rushing river at our feet. Not
only in the synagogue did Jesus find refreshment, but in the lilies
of the field, in the sunset sky, among the hills, and by the Lake of
Galilee.

¶ In his suggestive journal, Amiel, describing a country walk
taken when a dark and troubled mood was upon him, thus writes :
" The sunlight, the green leaves, the sky, all whispered to me, ' Be
of good cheer and courage, poor wounded one ! ' " We are all at
times poor wounded ones, needing all the refreshment and healing
we can find. And,

What simple joys from simple sources spring ![1]

By the avenue, on to the mansion,
    There runs a clear stream all the way,
Pursuing my path, I can see it,
    And list to its roundelay ;
        Still gleaming and glancing,
        Still laughing and dancing,
    It carols along all day.

[1] J. Hunter, *The Angels of God*, 32.

In summer its rippling music,
   Delight and refreshing instils,
In winter, by torrent-notes swollen,
   Its songs all the dreariness fills;
     Still leaping and bounding,
     Its echoes resounding,
With rapture my soul it thrills.

And precious my " Brook by the way " is,
   As Homewards I journey along,
New life in His depths I discover,
   New courage I take from His song;
     In gloom and in gladness,
     In sunshine and sadness,
He is my Salvation strong![1]

2. One of the richest streams that water the desert of life is
that of social sympathy and helpfulness, whereby we give and
take of the rich solace of brotherly love. To feel that the world
is a little better for our being, that, when the little light of our
life goes out, it will not have altogether failed to light some other
fire of warmth and helpfulness; that some lives will go onward
a little stronger, and more hopeful, for something we have been,
or said, or even tried to be, this is a brook of consolation which
becomes the more precious the nearer we draw to the isolation of
death. Wretched is the man who has missed this brook of gentle
human ministry in life's way, and recognized too late how much
of his soul's life he has lost in saving it.

              Nor, that time,
When nature had subdued him to herself,
Would he forget those Beings to whose minds
Warm from the labours of benevolence
The world, and human life, appeared a scene
Of kindred loveliness: then he would sigh,
Inly disturbed, to think that others felt
What he must never feel.

¶ George MacDonald says: " To know a man who can be
trusted will do more for one's moral nature than all the books
of divinity that were ever written." The beauty of the outward
world is full of Divine help, but there is more beauty and more

---

[1] T. Crawford, *Horae Serenae*, 71.

inspiration in living excellence than in the fairest natural scenes. Wonderfully refreshing is the heart's speech of the truly wise and good, but more beneficent is the brave thought when it becomes the brave deed, and more life-giving the Divine Word when it is made flesh and dwells among us. How rich the quickening and renewing influences which come from the presence and example of men who lift clearly before us the nobler ideals of life; from the memory of the faithful dead; and from the biographic page—

Bright affluent spirits, breathing but to bless,
Whose presence cheers men's eyes and warms their hearts,
Whose lavish goodness this old world renews,
Like the free sunshine and the liberal air.[1]

¶ There is a mysterious power in sympathy, and I thank God that the stream of sympathy is ever "in the way" of sorrowing souls. I see much sorrow, much pain, much heart-break, but I see also, and I thank God for it, much sympathy. Indeed, I am persuaded we never know what a wealth of sympathy and love there dwells in many a heart until sorrow calls it forth. And how a little sympathy comforts, and cheers, and refreshes the soul. "She did help me," said a poor soul about one who was a veritable angel of mercy. "I felt so much better for her visit." "Well, what did she say to you?" I asked. "Well, she didn't say much, but she sat with me and held my hand." That good woman's sympathy, silent sympathy, was a veritable "brook in the way" to that poor bereaved and lonely soul, and she drank of it and lifted up her head.

3. Another brook may be found in the appointed means of grace. Christ frequently drank of it. "There is a river, the streams whereof shall make glad the city of God, the holy place of the tabernacles of the Most High." We must seek, as our fathers did, the perennial springs of refreshment that are to be found in the private and public ordinances of religion. The excitements and exhaustions of modern life make this duty even more imperative. Industry and enterprise are good; but life is not only action, it is thought and feeling also. We do ourselves the greatest wrong if we allow our activities to crowd meditation and prayer out of our days and to rob us of the secret of rest in God. To have depth and elevation and tranquillity in life, and the aim kept high, and the impulse true and steady, it is absolutely

[1] J. Hunter, *The Angels of God*, 36.

necessary for mind and heart to have constant access to the
Source of inspiration. It is a moral calamity to lose the medi-
tative and worshipful spirit. Reverence, faith, and aspiration
are the springs of noble and fruitful living. Sunday and the
Church stand for our highest life. They invite us to drink of
waters that rise from cool and unpolluted depths. They offer an
opportunity of finding that truest rest and recreation which
come through mental and spiritual quickening and uplifting, and
of verifying the word of prophecy, "They that wait upon the Lord
shall renew their strength."

¶ I know a little chapel in my own native land, away out in
the country, far from village and town. But every Sabbath from
miles around the farmers and farm labourers gather in the little
building to hear the gospel preached. Their lives are hard and
monotonous enough; but they find peace, joy, love, in the little
chapel, and because of what it has been to them they have called
it "Elim." There the name stands graven over the door—Elim,
the place of springing water and shady palm trees. And that
is what the sanctuary always is to the humble worshipper.
Whether it is called by the name or not, it is an Elim to him. I
read in the old Book of one who was sore distressed by the difficulties and troubles of life. They harassed him and well-nigh
drove him to distraction. And it seemed as if the trouble would
crush and overwhelm him, until—notice that—until he went into
the sanctuary, and then the trouble all disappeared and his heart
was filled with the peace of God. "I came to church tired,"
wrote one to me only last week. "I came to church tired, and
not a little soul weary; I left rested, refreshed, strengthened; I
met my Lord there."[1]

4. The brook that truly quenches our thirst issues from the
throne of God. All merely ethical and philanthropic systems lack
power to slake man's thirst, apart from the love of Him who was
Love Incarnate. He, and He alone, it is who makes human life
glad with the rivers of God; who gives us to drink not only of
the "still waters" of His peace, but of the rich renewing wine of
His blood.

Faith that looks up to Him finds "streams in the desert," and
many a brook of consolation and refreshment in the way of life's
sternest conflicts. Of such a faith it is true—

[1] J. D. Jones, *The Elims of Life*, 182.

The stars of midnight shall be dear
To her; and she shall lean her ear
In many a secret place
Where rivulets dance their wayward round,
And beauty born of murmuring sound
Shall pass into her face.

¶ I remember an incident in the biography of a prince in learning, who, alas, was not a little child in the family of God. Once, in a time of depression, John Stuart Mill found comfort in music, until the thought came to him that, the octave having no more than eight tones in it, there must be limitations to the possibilities of melody. Even this spiritual octave of ours, various and marvellous as its messages are, has its limitations. Let us quench our thirst at the Fountainhead.[1]

¶ Augustine tried the broken cisterns and he was thirsty still. "Turned from Thee, the One Good, I lost myself among a multiplicity of things. I wandered into fruitless seed-beds of sorrow, with a proud dejectedness and a restless weariness. I bore about a shattered and bleeding soul, impatient of being borne by me, yet where to repose it I found not." So the eager and often disappointed quest went on, until, under the fig-tree in the garden at Milan, in the year of our Saviour 386, he put on the Lord Jesus Christ, and made no provision for the flesh. Then his lips were opened, and he could sing: "This is the happy life, to rejoice to Thee and of Thee and for Thee; this is it, and there is no other. Too late I learned to know Thee, O Thou Beauty of ancient days, too late I learned to love Thee! Many and great are my infirmities; but Thy medicine is mightier."

5. The use of the brook is to give refreshment and strength to continue the battle. Each age has its own impulse which carries it a little way, but then there is the temptation to relax and to rest in what has been attained, as if that were the measure of the thought of God. But with another age a new call has come and courage to deal with it. Men have not come to the end of the warfare to which Christ has committed them. The gospel has a promise for every creature under heaven; it has an application to every variety of condition; it proves its power in men of every age. "It starts each epoch and each century with renewed ardour and redoubled vigour." The things that have been are the pale shadows of things which are to be. But

[1] A. Smellie, *Service and Inspiration*, 70.

every victory over sin in the present or in the future has its explanation in the greatness of the heart of the Redeemer, who still passes undiscouraged on His way.

At the extreme limit of his vision this poet saw not rest and quiescence, but the King setting forth upon yet greater conquests. We are a laggard race, ever anxious and unready, afraid of what may come, doubtful if righteousness can really win the day; and our chief need is to kindle faith for the world afresh by a better study of the world's King. "He shall not fail nor be discouraged, till he have set judgment in the earth; and the isles shall wait for his law."

¶ I think I have sometimes noticed in you an impatience of mind which you should guard against carefully. Pin this maxim up in your memory—that Nature abhors the credit system, and that we never get anything in life till we have paid for it. Anything good, I mean; evil things we always pay for afterwards, and always when we find it hardest to do it. By paying for them, of course, I mean labouring for them. Tell me how much good solid work a young man has in him, and I will erect a horoscope for him as accurate as Guy Mannering's for young Bertram. Talents are absolutely nothing to a man except he have the faculty of work along with them. They, in fact, turn upon him and worry him, as Actæon's dogs did—you remember the story? Patience and perseverance—these are the sails and the rudder even of genius, without which it is only a wretched hulk upon the waters.[1]

¶ The husbandman sows his seed and toils on, and persistence reaps the harvest. The scholar opens his books and toils on, and persistence reaps fame. The reformer attacks the evil and toils on, and persistence destroys the evil. The force that is constant will always overcome the force that is less constant. Indeed, there never lived a man that came to anything who lacked this quality of pertinacity and adherence. How is it that the mountain-climber reached that summit of 23,000 feet? Plainly by going on and on until his foot was on the last stone and the whole earth was under his feet. The motto of David Livingstone was in these words: "I determined never to stop until I had come to the end and achieved my purpose." When Livingstone's work in Africa was done, the Dark Continent was mapped out and spread fully before the merchants of the world. He crossed Africa four times, and marched for days up to his armpits in

[1] *Letters of James Russell Lowell*, i. 183.

water, endured twenty-seven attacks of fever, was surrounded with enemies on every side, faced mutiny, poisoned arrows, wild beasts, the bite of serpents, but never gave up. By sheer, dogged persistence and faith in God he conquered, acting as if he thought his body was as immortal as his spirit.[1]

¶ By his zeal, constancy, and wisdom, by his mechanical genius and his gift of languages, Mackay had made himself a household word and a power in the whole region of Uganda. His hopefulness and courage never failed him. The misfortunes which overtook the Uganda mission at various times were regarded by timid and fearful souls at home as indications from God that the work there should be abandoned. When Mackay heard of these proposals, he wrote: "Are you joking? If you tell me in earnest that such a suggestion has been made, I only answer, Never! Tell me, ye faint hearts, to whom ye mean to give up the mission? Is it to murderous raiders like Mwanga, or to slave-traders from Zanzibar, or to English and Belgian dealers in rifles and gun-powder, or to German spirit-sellers? All are in the field, and they make no talk of 'giving up' their respective missions!" That was the spirit which burnt in the heart of Mackay to the end of his brief life.[2]

[1] N. D. Hillis, *The Contagion of Character*, 228.
[2] W. G. Berry, *Bishop Hannington*, 180.

What shall I Render?

LITERATURE.

Burrows (H. W.), *Parochial Sermons*, iii. 154.

Ketcham (W. E.), *Thanksgiving Sermons*, 245.

Kirkpatrick (A. F.), *The Book of Psalms* (Cambridge Bible), 690.

Maclaren (A.), *Expositions* : Psalms li.–cxlv., 273.

    ,,   ,, *The Book of Psalms* (Expositor's Bible), iii. 226.

Martin (S.), *Rain upon the Mown Grass*, 273.

Price (A. C.), *Fifty Sermons*, vii. 73.

Rowlands (D.), in *Jesus in the Cornfield*, 173.

Spurgeon (C. H.), *Metropolitan Tabernacle Pulpit*, **xvi.** (1870), No. 910.

Stevens (H.), *Sermon Outlines*, 307.

Tyndall (C. H.), *Object Sermons in Outline*, 162.

Waterston (R.), *Thoughts on the Lord's Supper*, 129.

Watkinson (W. L.), *The Education of the Heart*, 253.

Wilkinson (J. B.), *Mission Sermons*, i. 222.

Christian World Pulpit, xxxii. 394 (R. H. Hadden) ; xxxvi. 396 (P. Mearns) ; lvi. 229 (J. Percival).

Church of England Pulpit, xlviii. 195 (J. Percival).

Examiner, Oct. 5, 1905 (J. H. Jowett).

Homiletic Review, New Ser., xxxix. 29 (T. H. Stockton).

Literary Churchman, xxxviii. (1892) 334 (F. St. J. Corbett).

What shall I Render?

What shall I render unto the Lord
For all his benefits toward me?
I will take the cup of salvation,
And call upon the name of the Lord.
I will pay my vows unto the Lord,
Yea, in the presence of all his people.—Ps. cxvi. 12-14.

1. THE psalm from which this text is taken is a psalm of thanksgiving. It is one of six called the Great Hallel, extending from the 113th to the 118th, which were sung by the Jews at their great festivals, especially at the Passover. It was probably one of these psalms that was sung by our Saviour and His eleven disciples when He instituted His own supper, at the close of His last Passover with them; as we are told in the evangelic story, "When they had sung a hymn, they went out unto the mount of Olives."

2. It appears that the Psalmist, when he wrote this psalm, had been delivered by God out of some mighty trouble. How great that trouble was may be gathered from the telling language in which he describes it. "The sorrows of death compassed me, and the pains of hell gat hold upon me: I found trouble and sorrow." But while in this terrible situation he directed his thoughts heavenward, and looked for help where he had often found help before. Nor did he look in vain; for he says, "Thou hast delivered my soul from death, mine eyes from tears, and my feet from falling." And in the text he communes with his own soul, and considers how he may most effectually prove his gratitude for this timely deliverance. "What shall I render unto the Lord for all his benefits toward me?"

I.

A Bountiful Giver.

1. The Psalmist was not one of those thoughtless and indifferent men who pass through life receiving all, enjoying all,
expecting all, without ever bestowing a thought on the bountiful
Giver. On the contrary, he seems to have been so overwhelmed
by the magnitude and multiplicity of God's benefits that he
scarcely knew how to express his gratitude. The language he
employs is that of a man perplexed, bewildered, overcome, hardly
knowing what to say or how to act. " For all his benefits toward
me "—benefits great, benefits small, benefits temporal, benefits
spiritual; but all benefits unmerited and free. "For all his
benefits;" as they rose before his view, a vast, countless host,
they laid him under a debt of obligation which he could never
hope to discharge.

¶ My father's gift of appreciation was of a most charming
type. The constant repetitions of a blessing never dulled the fine
edge of his gratitude. He had a sunlit bedroom, and every
morning, so my mother tells me, he said, "What a beautiful
bedroom! We must thank God!"[1]

2. Few of us are adequately thankful for the commonplace
blessings which surround us; we take them as a matter of course.
We do not know what it is to be without them; we see no
prospect of being deprived of them. If the world has not gone
very well with us, it has not gone very badly; because we might
have more to complain of, we forget for how much we ought to
be grateful. Let us contemplate, as in the presence of God, all
the proofs that we have experienced of His mercy; the pure
affection that He has inspired, the sins that have been forgiven
us, the snares which we have escaped, the protection we have
received. Let our hearts be touched with the remembrance of all
the precious proofs of His goodness. Add to this the sorrows
that He has sent to sanctify our hearts; for we should look upon
these also as proofs of His love for us. Let gratitude for the
past inspire us with confidence in the future. Let us never

[1] *Love and Life: The Story of J. Denholm Brash* (1913), 156.

distrust Him; let us fear only ourselves and remember that He is the Father of mercies, and the God of all consolation. He sometimes takes away His consolations from us, but His mercy ever remains.

¶ O God, for my existence, my life, my reason; for nurture, protection, guidance, education, civil rights, religion; for Thy gifts to me of grace, nature, worldly good; for redemption, regeneration, instruction in the truth; for my call, recall, yea, many calls all through life; for Thy forbearance, longsuffering, long longsuffering, toward me, even until now; for all good things received, for all successes granted to me, for all good deeds I have been enabled to do; for my parents honest and good, for teachers kind, for benefactors never to be forgotten, for religious intimates so congenial and so helpful, for hearers thoughtful, friends true and sincere, servants faithful; for all who have helped me by their writings, sermons, conversations, prayers, examples, rebukes, and even injuries; for all these, and for all others which I know, and which I know not, open, hidden, remembered, forgotten;—"What shall I render unto the Lord for all his benefits?"[1]

3. Our share of God's benefits may not be as complete as we desire, but perhaps it is much more than we deserve. If we lack this or that benefit, so copiously showered on another, shall we venture to suggest that a greater measure of it would be for our eternal good? His wealth might be my curse; my health might rob him of the necessary discipline of suffering. This man's loneliness is meant to make him introspective and spiritual; that man's adversity will teach him humility and compassion. The Lord knows what is best. And, realizing that, let none of us question or complain. Let us see in the distribution of the commonplace benefits of life, not an erratic or partial bestowal, but a Divine assignment of mercies and blessings. Let gratitude and thankfulness and faith possess our hearts and minds. There are indeed moments in life when we awake to the fact of God's boundless, multitudinous, all-encompassing love, and when we are almost overwhelmed by the thought of it. A devout soul in habitual worship acknowledges much, and even then feels more than is expressed, and finally sees more than is felt. Yet, alas! the goodness of God recognized by us is by far the least part of it.

[1] Bishop Andrewes, *Preces Privatæ.*

There is the goodness we overlook. God's gifts are multiplied like the dewdrops or the snowflakes, and, gliding into life just as silently, are easily undiscerned by careless eyes like ours.

¶ One day in the town of Sonora, in the southern mines of California, after a very heavy rain and freshet, a man was leading his mule-cart up the steep principal street, when his foot struck upon a large stone; he stooped down to remove it, and found it was a solid lump of gold, about twenty-five pounds' weight, which had been exposed by the storm, and many hundreds of people had passed over it daily. So do we daily blindly trample on blessings richer than all the wealth of California. There is the goodness we misconstrue. We count sublime things commonplace, and reckon as losses and disappointments the discipline which brings incorruptible treasure. The "benefits" of God are not the pleasant things merely, but all the things of pain and tears.[1]

4. To perceive and appreciate our benefits necessitates a very refined soul. That is so upon the merely human plane. There are some men who cannot appreciate kindness. They either never see their benefits or they misconstrue them. They are the victims either of dulness or of pride, and both these foul spirits make this kind of appreciation impossible. But this spiritual numbness is even more apparent in our relationship to God. We receive multitudes of benefits, but we do not see the Divine mark upon their foreheads. We take them in, but they are not revealed to us as the King's bounty. It is amazing how fine is the perception of other souls! They never open their eyes without seeing the presence of the hosts of God. "The mountains are full of horses and chariots." Having nothing, they yet possess all things.

¶ It has been my lot to pay frequent visits to a man who had cancer in the throat. I have watched the awful advances of the insidious and inevitable disease. I have heard the manly voice sink into whispers, and then entirely cease. And yet when speech was silenced there was a light in the face like the radiant noon. He would take his pen in hand, and write a catalogue of the mercies by which he was beset, and in the contemplation of the multitude he almost forgot his calamity and pain. What an eye he had for the benefits of the Lord! I went into another house which had been suddenly plunged in the darkness of bereavement. The hale and genial father was taken away in

<hr>

[1] W. L. Watkinson, *The Education of the Heart*, 253.

a day, and the happy united family rudely broken up. And yet as soon as I opened the door, and met the sorrowing widow, these were the first words that leapt to her lips: "How good God has been!" Even in the night-time she had been counting the stars, and in the awful pangs of bereavement she had felt the amazing consolations of Christ. What an eye she had for the benefits of the Lord![1]

II.

A GRATEFUL RECIPIENT.

1. As his grateful heart thinks of all God's benefits to him, the Psalmist feels at once the impulse to requite and the impossibility of doing so. With a kind of glad despair he asks the question that ever springs to thankful lips, and, having nothing to give, recognizes the only possible return to God to be the acceptance of the brimming chalice which His goodness commends to his thirst. The great thought, then, which lies here is that we best requite God by thankfully taking what He gives. The Psalmist asks what he can render, and he answers that he will further take! And this is the very essence of true gratitude. The best return we can make for a gift of God is to take a higher gift. Have we thanked Him for our daily bread? Then the best return we can make is to take the bread of life. Have we thanked Him for our sleep? Then the best return we can make is to take His gift of rest and peace. Have we thanked Him for our health? Then the best return we can make is to seek His gift of holiness. "I will take the finest thing upon the Lord's table! He has given me this gift, now I will take a bigger gift!" We do an ill thing to our Lord if we are profuse about His secondary gifts and leave His best upon the table. "My joy I give unto you." Have we taken that yet? "My peace I give unto you." Have we taken that yet? "Glories upon glories hath our God prepared." And the first element in all praise and worship is to take the richer gifts the Lord is offering unto us.

2. Do we not feel that all the beauty and bloom of a gift is gone if the giver hopes to receive as much again? Do we not feel that it is all gone if the receiver thinks of repaying it in any

[1] J. H. Jowett.

coin but that of the heart? Love gives because it delights in giving. It gives that it may express itself and may bless the recipient. If there be any thought of return, it is only the return of love. That is how God gives; and we requite Him by taking rather than by giving, not merely because He needs nothing, and we have nothing which is not His. If that were all, it might be as true of an almighty tyrant, and might be so used as to forbid all worship before the gloomy presence, to give reverence and love to whom were as impertinent as the grossest offerings of savage idolaters. But the motive of His giving to us is the deepest reason why our best recompense to Him is our thankful reception of His mercies.

3. The key-note of the highest and happiest life is thankfulness. Thankfulness means personal communion with God; a perpetual longing to do His will, an absorbing anxiety not to offend Him. Thankfulness involves a passionate love for the human race, a deep sense of responsibility for our brothers and sisters in God's royal family, active endeavours to allay the ills around us. Thankfulness necessitates the strengthening and refreshing of our immortal souls by every grace and every agency we can command. So be thankful! The years that we are here are few and fitful. It is worth taking some trouble to make them fragrant and interesting. They may be so if we will. Life is full of opportunities; it is for us prayerfully, profitably, thankfully, to use them. They may not lead us to all that we hope for; they may not open upon realities we have long sighed after; they may not help us to gratify material aspirations; but they will always point us to avenues of gratitude and thankfulness, to possibilities of effort and goodness. And though there be vouchsafed to us nothing more glorious—as men count glory—than the elementary endowments, the ordinary mercies, the commonplace benefits of life; though fame and wealth and honour never cluster round our names, none the less—nay, all the more—may we lie down at last in peace and quietly commend our souls to Him who gave them, to do for them and with them what He thinks wisest and best in the harvest of the hereafter.

¶ There was an expression which Samuel Rutherford constantly used—a "drowned debtor to God's mercy." He meant that he was over head and ears in debt to God: he could not tell how deep his obligations were, so he just called himself "a drowned debtor" to the lovingkindness and the mercy of his God.

¶ The question in the text recalls a well-known incident in the life of a famous soldier, who also became a famous Christian— Colonel James Gardiner. One night, when he was little thinking of Divine things, but on the contrary had made an appointment of the most vicious kind, he was waiting for the appointed hour, when he saw, or thought he saw, before him in the room wherein he sat alone, a visible representation of the Lord Jesus Christ upon the cross, and he was impressed, as if a voice had said to him to this effect—"O sinner, I did all this for thee; what hast thou done for Me?" The vision and the words he heard were the means of Colonel Gardiner's conversion. The words quoted, it may be added, suggested Frances Ridley Havergal's well-known hymn beginning:—

> I gave My life for thee,
>   My precious blood I shed,
> That thou might'st ransom'd be,
>   And quicken'd from the dead.
> I gave My life for thee;
>   What hast thou given for Me?

Miss Havergal was staying with a German divine, in whose study was a picture of our crucified Saviour, beneath which was placed the motto: "I did this for thee; what hast thou done for Me?" She had come in weary, and, sitting down in front of the picture, the Saviour's eyes seemed to rest upon her. She read the motto, and the lines of her hymn flashed upon her, and she at once wrote them in pencil on a scrap of paper. Looking them over she thought them so poor that she tossed them on the fire, but they fell out untouched. Some months afterwards she showed them to her father, who encouraged her to preserve them, and he wrote the tune "Baca" specially for them. The hymn was published in *Good Words*, and becoming a favourite soon found its way into the hymn-books of the Christian Church.[1]

III.

A CONSECRATED LIFE.

1. God bestows so many blessings upon us that we can in one sense of the word return absolutely nothing to Him for His gifts.

[1] Canon J. Duncan, *Popular Hymns*, 215.

The Psalmist's words imply this: I can bring Thee no great gift, I can lay no priceless offering at Thy feet, I have nothing that is not already Thine own, for all has come from Thee. I will take the cup of salvation. I will accept Thy bounteous mercy with a thankful heart. I will seek to link all my life to Thee. This thought helps us to meet a very common temptation. A man may realize something of the goodness of God. He may say to himself: "If I had very large means like some men, how much I would try to do in return! I would build a stately cathedral for the service of God, a noble house of prayer for all time. I would endow a hospital to minister to human suffering. I would put the highest education within the reach of the poorest man. But I have so little income, it scarcely overlaps my own pressing wants." Then, because he cannot do great things, he sinks back and does nothing at all. He would reform an empire, but does not order his own house. He dreams of cleansing a city, but never sweeps before his own door. The Psalmist teaches us the true lesson, and shows us what we may all do. We may give ourselves first of all, and then the avenues of service will open out before us according to His will.

¶ Any dreams which she may have harboured of literary distinction, she had put resolutely away from her. "Oh God," she had written in her diary at Cairo, "Thou puttest into my heart this great desire to devote myself to the sick and sorrowful. I offer it to Thee. Do with it what is for Thy service."[1]

2. Taking the cup of salvation, in its simple, full meaning, expresses the pledging of our personality to God, the consecration of ourselves to His service. We recognize Him as Redeemer, Deliverer, and Friend, and acknowledge ourselves His in life and death. Our trustful heart, our acquiescent will, our obedient life, our whole personality must be surrendered in the power of love. Christ Himself gave us not only the ritual of an ordinance, but the pattern for our lives, when He " took the cup and gave thanks." And now for us common joys become sacraments, enjoyment becomes worship, and the cup which holds the bitter or the sweet skilfully mingled for our lives becomes the cup of blessing and salvation drunk in remembrance of Him. If we carried that spirit

[1] Sir Edward Cook, *The Life of Florence Nightingale*, i. 95.

with us into all our small duties, sorrows, and gladnesses, how different they would all seem!

¶ "Salvation" can scarcely be taken in its highest meaning in our text, both because the whole tone of the psalm fixes its reference to lower blessings, and because the word is in the plural in the Hebrew. "The cup of salvations" expresses, by that plural form, the fulness and variety of the manifold and multiform deliverances which God had wrought and was working for the Psalmist. His whole lot in life appears to him as a cup full of tender goodness, loving faithfulness, delivering grace. It runs over with Divine acts of help and sustenance.[1]

3. Many cups may be offered us as we go through life. We may for the moment be dazzled by the gemmed and sparkling cup of earthly pleasure, or the cup of worldly aims and ambitions. Let us put them aside. Let each one say, "I will take the cup of salvation." I will accept and use all God's offered mercy. The chalice of redeeming love shall be my chiefest treasure. I will take it—I will seek to be God's true child, the grateful son of so loving a Father. I will endeavour in all things to do His will, hoping to be guided ever by His grace and shielded ever by His protecting care.

¶ There is an old legend of an enchanted cup filled with poison, and put treacherously into a king's hand. He made the sign of the Cross and named the name of God over it, and it shivered in his grasp. Do you take that name of the Lord as a test? Name Him over many a cup of which you are eager to drink, and the glittering fragments will lie at your feet, and the poison be spilled on the ground. What you cannot lift before His pure eyes and think of Him while you enjoy is not for you. Friendships, schemes, plans, ambitions, amusements, speculations, studies, loves, businesses—can you call on the name of the Lord while you put these cups to your lips? If not, fling them behind you, for they are full of poison which, for all its sugared sweetness, at the last will "bite like a serpent and sting like an adder."[2]

[1] A. Maclaren.   [2] *Ibid.*

IV.

A Vow and its Fulfilment.

When the cords of death compassed the Psalmist (ver. 3), he had made a strong and secret vow. He said to himself, "If I get over this I will live a more pronounced life unto the Lord." "If I get my strength back, I will use it for the King." "If I get out of this darkness, I will take a lamp and light the feet of other men." And now he is better again, and he sets about redeeming his vow. The midnight vow was redeemed in the morning. As soon as he was out of the peril he remembered his covenant. "Now!" There must be no delay. In this sphere delays are attended with infinite peril. We may trifle with anything rather than with a fresh and tender vow. Well begun is half done. And he will also surround the redemption of his vow with publicity. He will do something publicly which will strongly proclaim him on God's side, and tell to all men that he has given his devotion to Him. And that must be our way. The vow we made in secret must be performed openly. We must do something to indicate that we have passed through a great experience, and that we are remembering the benefits of the Lord. We can speak His name to another. We can write some gracious letter to a friend. We can attach ourselves publicly to the Master's Church. We can commit ourselves openly and outwardly as professed followers of the King. And wherever we are, throughout all our life, we must continue to pay our vows. In joy, in sorrow, in the valley, on the mount, the vow must perpetually be redeemed. And if that be our part, fervent and unbroken, the Lord's part will also endure. He will continually be pouring His benefits upon us, and we shall grow in riches with every passing day.

¶ Hugh Miller, in his letters, gives an interesting account of his experience. He thought he was falling into consumption—that stone-cutter's tuberculosis was settling upon his lungs—and, realizing that death might not be far away, he thought of living a new and better life. He had always piqued himself on being true to his word. If he passed his word to a fellow-workman, no man could ever say that he had broken it, even if it was a promise given to an idiot boy that passed his time around the shed. To him the promise was sacred and most honourably kept. Well, why not pass his word to God, why not give a promise to the Almighty, and then in his native honesty begin a life of holiness and love ? Fascinated with the idea, he gave his solemn vow,—alas ! only to break it and befool himself, and clothe his soul with shame. He, so honest before men, so staunch and upright and true, found out he was little better than a bankrupt and a liar in the presence of the living God. This led to a humbling exercise of soul, and a truer knowledge of grace. The lesson is a valuable one, and we are slow to learn it. Our cold dead vows, apart from God, are nothing.[1]

[1] R. Waterston, *Thoughts on the Lord's Supper*, 136.

THE DAY WHICH THE LORD MADE.

LITERATURE.

Beveridge (W.), *Theological Works*, iii. 418.

Blackley (T.), *Practical Sermons*, i. 82.

Church (R. W.), *Village Sermons*, ii. 142.

Cottam (S. E.), *New Sermons for a New Century*, 117.

Frank (M.), *Sermons*, ii. 112.

Fuller (M.), *The Lord's Day*, 109.

Hall (R.), *Works*, v. 380.

Hutton (R. E.), *The Crown of Christ*, ii. 7.

Kuegele (F.), *Country Sermons*, New Ser., v. 1.

Liddon (H. P.), *Easter in St. Paul's*, 169.

Maclaren (A.), *The Book of Psalms* (Expositor's Bible), iii. 232.

Mills (B. R. V.), *The Marks of the Church*, 224.

Newman (J. H.), *Parochial and Plain Sermons*, vi. 94.

Simcox (W. H.), *The Cessation of Prophecy*, 310.

Spurgeon (C. H.), *Metropolitan Tabernacle Pulpit*, **xxiv.** (1878), No. 1420.

Strong (A. H.), *Miscellanies*, ii. 219.

Vaughan (J.), *Sermons* (Brighton Pulpit), New Ser., xi. (1875), No. 948.

Wilkinson (J. B.), *Mission Sermons*, i. 176.

Christian World Pulpit, **xi.** 314 (R. Glover); **xxxv.** 276 (Canon Rowsell).

The Day which the Lord made.

This is the day which the Lord hath made;
We will rejoice and be glad in it.—Ps. cxviii. 24.

THIS is unmistakably a psalm for use in the Temple worship, and was probably meant to be sung antiphonally, on some day of national rejoicing indicated in the text. A general concurrence of opinion points to the period of the restoration from Babylon as its date, but different events connected with that restoration have been selected. The psalm implies the completion of the Temple, and therefore shuts out any point prior to that. Delitzsch fixes on the dedication of the Temple as the occasion; but the view is still more probable which supposes that it was sung on the great celebration of the Feast of Tabernacles, recorded in Neh. viii. 14–18. In later times ver. 25 was the festal cry raised while the altar of burnt-offering was solemnly compassed, once on each of the first six days of the Feast of Tabernacles, and seven times on the seventh.

1. Apparently the psalm falls into two halves, of which the former half (vv. 1–16) seems to have been sung as a processional hymn while approaching the sanctuary, and the latter (vv. 17–29), partly at the Temple gates, partly by a chorus of priests within, and partly by the procession when it had entered. Verses 22, 23, 24 probably belong to the priestly chorus. They set forth the great truth made manifest by restored Israel's presence in the rebuilt Temple. The metaphor is suggested by the incidents connected with the rebuilding. The "stone" is obviously Israel, weak, contemptible, but now once more laid as the very foundation stone of God's house in the world. The broad truth taught by its history is that God lays as the basis of His building, *i.e.*, uses for the execution of His purposes, that which the wisdom of man despises and tosses aside.

2. The general truth contained here is that of St. Paul's great saying, "God chose the weak things of the world, that he might put to shame the things that are strong." It is a law which finds its highest exemplification in the foundation for God's true temple, other than which can no man lay. Israel is not only a figure of Christ; there is an organic unity between Him and them. Whatever, therefore, is true of Israel in a lower sense is true in its highest sense of Christ. If Israel is the rejected stone made the head of the corner, this is far truer of Him who was indeed rejected of men, but chosen of God and precious, the corner stone of the one great living temple of the redeemed.

The text is best regarded as the continuation of the choral praise in vv. 22, 23. "The day" is that of the festival now in progress, the joyful culmination of God's manifold deliverances. It is a day in which joy is duty, and no heart has a right to be too heavy to leap for gladness. Private sorrows enough many of the jubilant worshippers no doubt had, but the sight of the Stone laid as the head of the corner should bring joy even to such. If sadness was ingratitude and almost treason then, what sorrow should now be so dense that it cannot be pierced by the Light which lighteth every man?

3. In our Lord's time the whole of this psalm was applied to the Messiah by the Jewish interpreters. Christ was the Stone, refused by the builders of Israel, but afterwards made the Head of the corner. His was the welcome, "Blessed is he that cometh in the name of the Lord"; to Him was addressed the prayer, "Hosanna, save, I pray," as on Palm Sunday, by the Jewish multitude. Thus it was very natural for the Christian Church to find in the words, "This is the day which the Lord hath made; we will rejoice and be glad in it," an application to our Lord Jesus Christ. What was the day in Christ's life which He made His own, beyond all others? Not His birthday; for that meant His entrance on a life of sorrows. Not His ascension day; for that was the closing scene of a triumph already achieved. Not His transfiguration day; it was a momentary flash of glory in a career of pain. Not the day of His crucifixion; it was a great day for a ruined world, but for Him it marked the lowest stage of humiliation and of woe. The day of days in the life of

Christ was the day of His resurrection. It reflected a new glory on the day of His birth. It witnessed a triumph of which the ascension was but a completion. It was to the transfiguration what the sunrise is to the earliest dawn. It poured a flood of light and meaning on Calvary itself; and showed that what took place there was not simply the death-scene of an innocent Sufferer, but a sacrifice which would have power with God to the end of time.

Something of this kind is what was felt by the early Christians about Easter Day; and as it was the greatest day in the life of Jesus Christ, so for them it was the greatest day in the whole year. It was the day of days; it was the Lord's Own Day. Every Lord's Day in the year was a weekly feast of Christ's rising from the dead; on Easter Day, the force and meaning of all these Lord's Days were gathered into one consummate expression of joy and praise. " This is the day which the Lord hath made; we will rejoice and be glad in it."

¶ The song of the angels, the voice at the baptism, the agony in the garden, the sublime anguish of Calvary, would have been inexplicable without the light which was reflected back upon them by the angels at the open tomb on the morning of the resurrection. Such a nature and such a life were not formed and fashioned within the narrow limits of time and space; they brought infinity and immortality within the confines of the world. Alone among men, Christ has visibly put on immortality; but that sublime truth does not rest on the resurrection; it rests on the very structure of man's nature and life. Neither is comprehensible without it; neither is ever complete in itself; both affirm its reality and predict its fuller disclosure. The risen Christ does not stand solitary in a vast circle of unopened graves; He is the visible witness to the sublime truth that the grave has no victory and death no sting; for life and immortality are one and the same.[1]

> Oh, had I lived in that great day,
>   How had its glory new
> Fill'd earth and heaven, and caught away
>   My ravish'd spirit too!
>
> No thoughts that to the world belong
>   Had stood against the wave
> Of love which set so deep and strong
>   From Christ's then open grave.

[1] H. W. Mabie, *The Life of the Spirit*, 360.

No cloister-floor of humid stone
Had been too cold for me;
For me no Eastern desert lone
Had been too far to flee.[1]

I.

A Day of Victory.

The joy of Easter is inspired by the hope which the day of our Lord's resurrection warrants and quickens. What is this hope, and how does it spring from our Saviour's rising again from the dead? The great hope which the resurrection sets before us is the completeness of our life after death.

1. The difficulty of believing in a future life is due, not to the reason, but to the imagination as controlled by the senses. Who of us has not made this discovery, in some one of those dark hours which sooner or later visit every human life? Who of us has not stood by the open coffin, and felt himself, or marked how others feel, the terrific empire of sense in the presence of death? The form which was once full of life, quivering with expressiveness, with thought, with feeling, now lies before us cold and motionless, like a plaster cast of its former self. Perhaps the traces of what must follow are already discernible; and forthwith the imagination surrenders itself, like a docile pupil, to the guidance of the senses, and ends by proclaiming the victory of death; a victory too clear, too complete, too unquestionable, to allow reason or revelation to raise their voices in favour of any sort of life that can possibly survive it.

2. Now it was to deal with this specific difficulty that our Lord willed to die, and then, by a literal bodily resurrection, to rise from the grave. He would grapple with the imperious urgency of the senses and the imagination on their own ground. He would beat down by an act, palpable to the senses, and attested by evidence which should warrant its reality for all time, the tyrant power which sought to shut out from man the hope of an

---

[1] Matthew Arnold, *Elegiac Poems.*

immortal life. When the disciples saw that the Risen Being before them was their Lord; when they noted His pierced hands, His feet, His side; when they conversed with Him, ate with Him, listened to Him, followed Him much as of old; then they knew that the Master who had been killed upon the cross by a protracted agony, and committed to the grave as a bleeding and mangled corpse, had really risen from death, and had opened a new era of hope for the human race. And for us, in a distant age, this fact that Christ rose from death is not less full of precious hope and joy than for our first forefathers in the faith. For the early Christians the resurrection was practically Christianity, nay, the whole of Christianity, in so far as Christianity as a whole rested on it as the proof-fact of its having come from heaven. This is what the first Christians felt: of the truth of their faith "God had given an assurance unto all men, in that he had raised Jesus from the dead." Therefore did the resurrection inspire them with such fervent joy.

¶ If it belong to man to rejoice when some great General has fought his country's enemies, and beaten them and led their chiefs captives; if on such occasions our bells ring, and our cities are decked with garlands, and flags wave, and there are feastings and banquetings,

> And the tumult of their acclaim is rolled
> Through the open gates of the city afar,
> To the shepherd who watcheth the evening star,

if a nation joys in the return of the triumphant General, and hearts are warmed all through the length and breadth of the land at the news, as by electric sympathy, and all agree to make holiday, because now the yoke of the invader has been broken, and they feel themselves free—and hearth, and home, and wife, and child, and all that they hold dear is rescued out of peril, and the possession secured to them—how much more surely ought the Christian to be glad and rejoice on each recurrence of Easter? For it is the anniversary of the Lord's Victory. He comes to us as the Captain of our Salvation, comes amongst us fresh from combat, "with dyed garments from Bozrah," "treading in the greatness of his strength"; He comes, leading the Invader a prisoner, leading captivity captive.[1]

[1] R. D. B. Rawnsley.

II.

A DAY OF REJOICING.

1. The joy of Easter is the joy of a great certainty. The resurrection of our Saviour is the fact which makes an intelligent Christian certain of the truth of his creed. The Apostles entered on their work with one conviction, prominent beyond all others. It was that the truth of Christianity, and its claim upon the minds and hearts of men, depended mainly upon the fact of the resurrection of Christ from the dead. Within a few weeks of the occurrence, and amidst a population passionately interested in denying the truth of what they said, they took every opportunity of virtually saying, "Christianity is true; it is true because Christ has risen from death." They could not have ventured to do this unless they had been sure of the fact upon which they were so ready to risk everything, even life itself; sure, with that sort of certainty which comes from actual experience.

¶ To my mind, the spiritual miracle of the Crucifixion was an infinitely greater miracle than the physical miracle of the Resurrection—a much more impressive evidence of the actual mingling of the Divine with the human. It is strange that a world which can accept heartily the one should find it so difficult, and in some cases so impossible, to accept the other. This implies, I think, that what it does accept it accepts without any true insight into the wonder and majesty of the personal manifestation the reality of which it professes to recognize. Certainly ours is a superstitious age, though superstitious rather in the excess of its respect for the physical energies of the universe, than in the excess of its respect for the spiritual.[1]

2. It is always very difficult to realize any great joy or great sorrow. We cannot realize it by wishing to do so. What brings joys and sorrows of this world home to us is their circumstances and accompaniments. When a friend dies, we cannot at first believe him taken from us; we cannot believe ourselves to be in any new place when we are just come to it. When we are told a thing, we assent to it, we do not doubt it, but we do not feel it to be true, we do not understand it as a fact which must take up a position

[1] R. H. Hutton, *Aspects of Religious and Scientific Thought*, 163.

or station in our thoughts, and must be acted from and acted towards, must be dealt with as existing: that is, we do not realize it. It cannot be denied that we have much to do, very much, before we rise to the understanding of our new nature and its privileges, and learn to rejoice and be glad in the day which the Lord hath made; "the eyes of your understanding being enlightened that ye may know what is the hope of his calling, and what the riches of the glory of his inheritance in the saints, and what is the exceeding greatness of his power to us-ward who believe, according to the working of his mighty power, which he wrought in Christ, when he raised him from the dead, and set him at his own right hand in the heavenly places."

¶ Unbelief once wrote at the entrance of a cemetery the word "Fuerunt," "They have been." Faith always writes over the gate of a churchyard, "I am the Resurrection and the Life." To unbelief the dead are but memories; memories of beings who have ceased to be. To faith the dead are living, working, praying friends, whom nothing but the dulness of sense hides from sight.[1]

3. The joy of Easter is the joy of a great reaction: a reaction from anxiety and sorrow. So it was at the time of Christ's resurrection. The Apostles had been crushed by the sufferings and death of Jesus Christ. They had trusted that it was "he which should have redeemed Israel." Their disappointment, their despondency, their anguish were exactly proportioned to their earlier hopes. When He was in His grave, all seemed over; and when He appeared, first to one, and then to another, on the day of His resurrection, they could not keep their feelings of welcome and delight—traversed though these were by a sense of wondering awe—within anything like bounds. It was a change from darkness to light, from fear to hope, from death to endless life, for the world at large. Those who first felt it, and rejoiced, are long since gathered to their rest; but others came after them, to whom it was just as really a cause of joy as to the women who were early at the tomb; and to us at this present time, separated by nineteen hundred years from the Apostles and followers of the risen Son of God, His rising again is quite as much a matter to encourage us to triumphant faith, to comfort us in trouble and in death, as it was to them.

[1] H. P. Liddon, *Easter in St. Paul's*, 178

¶ Finding that one of his children had been greatly shocked and overcome by the first sight of death, he tenderly endeavoured to remove the feeling which had been awakened, and opening a Bible, pointed to the words, "Then cometh Simon Peter following him, and went into the sepulchre, and seeth the linen clothes lie, and the napkin, that was about his head, not lying with the linen clothes, but wrapped together in a place by itself." Nothing, he said, to his mind, afforded us such comfort when shrinking from the outward accompaniments of death,—the grave, the grave-clothes, the loneliness,—as the thought that all these had been around our Lord Himself, round Him who died, and is now alive for evermore.[1]

4. The joy of Easter is the holy joy of quiet triumph, of hymns of victory and exulting faith. The Lord is risen! What more can the glad Church of the redeemed say? She can only repeat it again and again with multiplied Alleluias. Words seem out of place, for the joy of the Church is too deep to express itself in the ordinary language of the world—and yet it is to the world that she brings the glad tidings of the victory of her Lord. No wonder then that the earth is glad and beautiful in this foregleam of the coming day, when He shall fulfil His promise, "Behold, I make all things new." Even in the order of nature there is nothing but joy and the coming of new life in the spring-time of the world. The very air is full of the songs of the birds, and fragrant with the first fresh scents of the forests and meadows, as they clothe themselves again with foliage and verdure after the long days of wintry gloom, decay and death.

> See the world's beauty budding forth anew,
> Shows with the Lord His gifts returning too!
> The earth with flowers is deck'd, the sky serene;
> The heavenly portals glow with brighter sheen.
> The greenwood-leaves, the flowering meadows tell
> Of Christ, triumphant over gloomy hell.
> Hail! Festal Day! for evermore ador'd,
> Wherein God conquer'd hell, and upward soar'd.

¶ Be sure there is a unity of Law in the universe, and if in that which we call the natural world there is one consistent thought producing one consistent fact, the same thought holds

[1] A. P. Stanley, *Life of Thomas Arnold*, D.D., i. 219.

good in the world of Man; and the life which we possess when we
die—the life which is in thought, feeling, will, and the rest—will
frame for itself, as quickly, as individually, as eagerly, a new form
as the seed in spring has done when we see its twofold arrow
cleave the ground. This will be the resurrection, and of the great
law of which this is the outcome, the result of which we see in
Nature, in all things—the result of which we do not see in Man—
for its result in us is wrought after death—the resurrection of
Christ is the only known result in humanity. The life in
Christ took new form when His earthly body died, and the fact
that it had done so was revealed to His disciples. They knew
He was alive again, and had a new and living form—that on the
death of His mortal body, an immortal form became His own.
He was not unclothed, but clothed upon. Properly speaking, that
is no miracle, if miracle be defined as the violation or transcending
of law. It is, in my mind, that which always takes place in the
other world when we die; shown to us in this world for once, that
we might know it. It is not a reversion, it is a revelation, of law;
it is not apart from our knowledge, it is the declarations that the
same idea that rules the growth of life in the world of Nature
rules its growth in the world of Man. The resurrection of the
body is the renewing of form.[1]

> The yearly miracle of spring,
>   Of budding tree and blooming flower,
> Which Nature's feathered laureates sing
>   In my cold ear from hour to hour,
>
> Spreads all its wonders round my feet;
>   And every wakeful sense is fed
> On thoughts that o'er and o'er repeat,
>   " The Resurrection of the Dead ! "
>
> If these half vital things have force
>   To break the spell which winter weaves,
> To wake, and clothe the wrinkled corse
>   In the full life of shining leaves;
>
> Shall I sit down in vague despair,
>   And marvel if the nobler soul
> We laid in earth shall ever dare
>   To wake to life, and backward roll

[1] Stopford A. Brooke.

The sealing stone, and striding out,
Claim its eternity, and head
Creation once again, and shout,
"The Resurrection of the Dead"?[1]

III.

A Day of Remembrance.

1. Christ's resurrection has not become less important by the passage of years; its virtue is not diminished, its grace and power are not worn out. If Christ had indeed risen this very morning, His resurrection would not be in reality of more concern to us than it is now. Christ is risen—risen never to die again, to be for ever that which He was the first moment when He conquered death. He is there above, the Saviour who could not be kept in captivity by the grave; the very same who spoke to Mary Magdalene, and reproved the doubting Thomas, and talked on the way to Emmaus, and broke bread on the sea-shore. And what was true of Him then is true now; what could be said of Him then can be said now; what He did then for those who loved Him and believed Him, He can do now; what they felt towards Him—the rejoicing and the glorying trust, and the conquering comfort and strength—it is ours to choose whether we shall not feel it too. The Light which broke on men on that third day, shines as brightly on all believing hearts now as it did on St. Peter and St. John, not a mere remembrance of past glory and gladness, but an unfailing and uninterrupted spring of present hope and strength. And it will shine long after we are gone, to cheer the hearts and raise the joy of our children, and of all the unborn generations to the end of the world.

¶ It is the one inspiring element of Christianity that it throws us in boundless hope upon the future, and forbids us to dwell in the poisonous shadows of the past. A new and better growth is before us, a fresher, a diviner, a more enthusiastic life awaits us. We are to wake up satisfied in the likeness of Christ, the ever young Humanity. Therefore, "forgetting those things which are behind," let us "press forward to the mark of the prize of our high calling in Christ Jesus."[2]

[1] George Henry Boker, *The Book of the Dead*, 147.   [2] Stopford A. Brooke.

The women sought the tomb at dawn of day,
  And as they went they wept and made their moan:
" His sepulchre is guarded by a stone,
And who for us shall roll the stone away ? "
But lo !—an Angel, robed in white array,
  Had rent the rock and sat thereon alone.
"Fear not," said he; " the Lord hath overthrown
The power of Death: I show you where He lay."
We echo oftentimes that cry of old:
  Huge stumbling-blocks confront us whilst we wait
    And wonder, weeping, who will help afford:
But as we question sorrowing, behold !
  The stone is rolled away, though it is great,
    And on it sits the Angel of the Lord.[1]

2. The resurrection of Christ was to His early followers a call,
a call louder than that of the trumpet on Mount Sinai, to newness
of life and newness of hope. It called men of old when it was
first preached; it calls men still, now that its remembrance never
ceases among us. It calls aloud to newness of life, it calls on the
sinner and the careless to arise from the death of sin to the life of
righteousness; it cries aloud, "Awake thou that sleepest, and
arise from the dead, and Christ shall give thee light." We know
how it made St. Paul cry out, "If ye then be risen with Christ,
seek those things which are above, where Christ sitteth on the
right hand of God." "In that he died, he died unto sin once:
but in that he liveth, he liveth unto God. Likewise reckon ye
also yourselves to be dead indeed unto sin, but alive unto God
through Jesus Christ our Lord." These were the feelings, these
were the thoughts, which came into the minds of the first
believers in Christ. They felt how much they had to do with the
resurrection. It had weaned them from sin; it strengthened
them, day by day, in all holiness and love. The resurrection had
changed everything to them, and they lived as men to whom this
world had become nothing except a place to live in holily, where
they might love and serve their brethren, and wait patiently God's
will, till their call came to that world and home which was to be
for ever. Christ's resurrection calls us also not only to begin a
new life, but to go on with it, with renewed zeal and carefulness,
if by His grace we have begun it. It reminds us once more how

[1] Ellen Thorneycroft Fowler, *Verses, Wise or Otherwise*, 197.

mighty to save, how unwearied to uphold and help, is He whom
we have for our Leader and Guide through life. He, if we are
trusting Him, is One who has broken the bands of death, who is
in truth the Watcher of our way, and the Director of our steps;
He is One who has endured and conquered—endured all and
conquered all—to lend us of His strength, to feed our faintness
with His renewed life, to show us of that truth and light which
He has won for men. We have only to go to Him for it. We
have only to go straight forward in the way of obedience and
holiness, and we need not fear that we shall fail.

3. There may still be for each of us many anxieties, many
sorrows, many bitter disappointments and griefs in life; for God
does not promise tranquillity, but quite the opposite. Yet in spite
of all this there will be joy in God, and peace, and rest, through
the abiding union with Him who is "our peace." As we conquer
sin we grow in likeness to Jesus Christ; and as we become like
Him we share, through an ever-growing closeness of union, the
joy, the peace, and the brightness of the resurrection life. "I will
see you again, and your heart shall rejoice, and your joy no man
taketh from you." As children say to themselves, "This is the
spring," or "This is the sea," trying to grasp the thought and not
let it go; as travellers in a foreign land say, "This is that great
city," or "This is that famous building," knowing it has a long
history through centuries, and vexed with themselves that they
know so little about it; so let us say, This is the Day of Days,
the Royal Day, the Lord's Day. This is the day on which Christ
rose from the dead; the day which brought us salvation. It is
a day which has made us greater than we know. It is our Day
of Rest, the true Sabbath. We have had enough of weariness,
and dreariness, and listlessness, and sorrow, and remorse. We
have had enough of this troublesome world. We have had
enough of its noise and din. Noise is its best music. But now
there is a stillness that speaks. We know how strange the
feeling is of perfect silence after continued sound. Such is our
blessedness now. Calm and serene days have begun; and Christ
is heard in them, and His still small voice, because the world
speaks not. Let us only put off the world, and we put on
Christ. The receding from one is an approach to the other.

May we grow in grace, and in the knowledge of our Lord and Saviour, season after season, year after year, till He takes to Himself, first one, then another, in the order He thinks fit, to be separated from each other for a little while, to be united together for ever, in the Kingdom of His Father and our Father, His God and our God.

¶ When one says, "Lord, I believe," in Jesus' sense, he means that he trusts—a very different thing. Jesus' physical Resurrection, in the same way, is a question that can be decided only by evidence, and is within the province of reason. His spiritual Resurrection is a drama of the soul, and a matter of faith. When I declare my belief that on the third day Jesus rose, I am really yielding to evidence. When I am crucified with Christ, buried with Christ, and rise to newness of life in Christ, I am believing after the very sense of Jesus.[1]

[1] John Watson, *The Mind of the Master.*

The Clean Path.

LITERATURE.

Cox (S.), *The Bird's Nest*, 131.

Cumming (J. E.), in *Convention Addresses delivered at Bridge of Allan*, 1895, p. 59.

Griffin (E. D.), *Plain Practical Sermons*, ii. 465.

Hopps (J. P.), *Sermons of Love and Life*, 65.

Leitch (R.), *The Light of the Gentiles*, 157.

Maclaren (A.), *Expositions*: Psalms li.–cxlv., 281.

Murphy (J. B. C.), *The Service of the Master*, 9.

Norton (J. N.), *Warning and Teaching*, 140.

Simeon (C.), *Works*, vi. 302.

Smith (W. C.), *Sermons*, 146.

Voysey (C.), *Sermons*, xxi. (1898), No. 22.

Wiseman (N.), *Children's Sermons*, 205.

Christian World Pulpit, xii. 198 (A. P. Peabody); **xxiv.** 90 (H. W. Beecher); **xxix.** 315 (H. W. Beecher).

Church Pulpit Year Book, 1911, p. 271.

Preacher's Magazine, iv. 272 (J. Feather).

THE CLEAN PATH.

**Wherewithal shall a young man cleanse his way?
By taking heed thereto according to thy word.—Ps. cxix. 9.**

1. IT is a great matter to know what is the right question to put, and how to put it rightly. The secrets of nature disclose themselves to the man who knows how to question her properly; for he is already on the line of its solution when he sees clearly what the exact problem is. So also in any discussion, he who can lay aside all extraneous and irrelevant matter, and put his finger on the real point at issue, has already half won the battle; for our errors mainly arise from our mixing up of what is essential with subordinate points, the settlement of which is of no vital consequence. It is the same in the affairs of practical life. There, too, it is all-important to put clearly before our minds what is the supreme question we have to deal with as moral and responsible beings. Our character will depend on the answer to that, but the answer will not be difficult if we put the question rightly. Here we are, for a few short years, in a world of struggle and conflict, having duties to ourselves and to each other and to God, having also various endowments and various temptations. What is the line of thought which should press on each of us as the supreme matter for our most serious consideration? What is the question which every young man should put to himself as he looks out on the troubled sea of life with which he has to battle, and where he may make shipwreck if he take not heed?

2. The question of our text, "Wherewithal shall a young man cleanse his way?" if not absolutely the foremost, is yet among the weightiest thoughts which we should be laying to heart. There are, no doubt, still graver questions which we will do well to put to ourselves. What is the chief end of

man? What is that by failing to achieve which we shall lose the very object of our existence? Or, again, What shall a man do to be saved? or yet further, Wherewithal shall a young man cleanse his heart? These are points of still greater moment, and carry deeper results than the question of the Psalmist here. At bottom, no doubt, he had in view the cleansing of the heart as well as of the way; for his was no shallow spirit, that cared only for mere outside behaviour. The Psalmist knew that we must begin by purifying the fountain if the stream is to be made pure. But the question, as he formally puts it, points to our actions rather than our desires and affections, and so far it is defective. Still, any young man who shall put before him the cleansing of his way as the aim which he must specially strive to reach, will surely make a very much worthier life for himself than they do who start in the race careless whether the way they take be miry or clean.

I.

An Anxious Question.

"Wherewithal shall a young man cleanse his way?"

There are many questions about the future with which it is natural for young people to occupy themselves; and it is to be feared that the most of them ask more anxiously "How shall I *make* my way?" than "How shall I *cleanse* my way?" It is needful carefully to ponder the questions: "How shall I get on in the world—be happy, fortunate?" and the like. But there is another and more important question: "How shall I *cleanse* my way?" For purity is the best thing; and to be good is a wiser as well as a nobler object of ambition than any other.

1. The question of the Psalmist broadly stated is this, Can a man live, in all respects and in all his paths, a pure and beautiful life? and can all his ways be clean? We know well how much the question involves; we know also what the answer means; but we can answer without hesitation—as an ideal, Yes. A man can go into the world, and take his part in all natural and

necessary engagements, and yet have, all through, a cleansed way. He may go into business, become a politician, enjoy pleasure, and build up a home, without inevitable stain, without wading to his object through dishonour ; and is not this just what we want, to make all life what it ought to be ? If the way of business were clean, if the ways of pleasure were clean, if the sanctities of domestic life were all kept unsullied, what a world it would be ! What would become of fraud, and over-reaching, and plotting, and treachery, and strife, and the sickening suspicions of one another that now half choke human love and threaten to starve or poison the charities of life ? We all know what would become of these things. They would die away as naturally as the mists before the advance of day. And why should it not be ? Why should not a man begin life with the deep conviction that his may be a cleansed way ?

2. But when the Psalmist speaks of *cleansing* our way, he implies that, at some points at least, our way has led us through the mire. The picture in his mind was of this sort. There stood before him a young man who had not long set out on the journey of life and who yet, to his own deep surprise and disgust, found many stains of travel already upon him. He had not meant to go wrong; as yet, perhaps, he has not gone very far wrong. And yet, where did all this filth come from ? And how is it to be got rid of ? And if, at the very outset of the journey, he has wandered into by-paths which have left these ugly stains upon him, what will he be like when he reaches the end of his journey ? How can he hope to keep a right course, and to present himself, without spot, before God at the last ? In short, how is he to make his way clean, and to keep it clean ?

3. There are in our lives no isolated acts, but only *ways*. The wrong of which we say, "Only this once, and it shall never be repeated," provokes its own repetition, starts us in its own direction. The violation of truth or integrity, with the expectation and purpose of retrieving it speedily, involves us in a labyrinth, in which we lose our way, and may never find our way back. The laws of sobriety or purity once transgressed, we have not the power which we previously thought we had to retrace our

PS. XXV.–CXIX.—27

steps. We meant an act; we have found a way—a precipitous way, too, on which we gain momentum with every step. A way has a direction, and leads some whither. A way is continuous; and, if we are in it, we are advancing in it. A way differs in its direction from other ways, and diverges more and more from them the farther one travels upon it. There is hardly any error so perilous as that of imagining that there can be isolated acts or states of mind. Every present has its closely affiliated future. Every deed, every reverie, every thought, is a cause. We are moving on in character, as in years. We are not to-day what we were a week ago. We are advancing either in holiness or in unholiness.

¶ Nature moves physically towards perfection, and morally there must be the same unseen but necessary motion. For if the Darwinian theory be true, the law of natural selection applies to all the moral history of mankind, as well as to the physical. Evil must die ultimately as the weaker element in the struggle with the good. The slow consent of the world's history is in the direction of moral goodness, as its physical development is ever toward higher forms. This progress, of course, does not necessarily embrace any particular form of life or especial race. A given race may die, or may remain stagnant. The development goes on with some new variety or form of life. Such a "current of things towards righteousness," or towards physical perfection, is slow, almost imperceptible. It is like the silent motion of the stars of heaven through eternity towards one centre of the universe. But if once the theory of development be accepted and this fact be admitted, what higher evidence can be demanded of a benevolent and perfect Creator than a current of all things towards the best, a drift towards perfection, a silent, august, secular movement of all beings and forms of life, all thought and morals, all history and events towards the completely good and perfect ?[1]

¶ Perhaps the present generation has heard more than enough about progress. Talk of that kind is an affectation that was always unprofitable, and has now become stale. Real progress needs no trumpeting. It announces itself like the flowing stream, which brawls only among the barren rocks, and is most felt as a beneficent agency that is penetrating and vitalizing in those parts where friction and noise are reduced to a minimum. True advancement is humble, earnest, practical. It is single-minded,

[1] *The Life of Charles Loring Brace*, 302.

simple-hearted devotion, ever growing in intelligence, to those grand objects which are dear to Christ and the angels, and the over-shadowing grandeur of which makes obtruding self-consciousness impossible. The Apostles advanced by forsaking the tradition of men and cleaving unto the word of the Lord, that they might do for the world what could be done in no other way. Luther advanced by bringing men up to the simple record of the New Testament, that they might find a firm footing as they passed into eternity and faced the awful facts of life and destiny. We can advance in the present day only as we come nearer to Jesus Christ, and bring others with us.[1]

¶ The poet sings—

Our lives must climb from hope to hope,
And realize our longing,

but it is not often that the record of a man's progress towards a pronounced condition of spiritual exaltation is one of uninterrupted climbing. There are usually some prominent milestones that mark momentous crises in the journey, frequently some definite boundary to which one can point and say, This is where such a one first dedicated himself to the service of God and of his fellows. But with Quintin Hogg one can trace the ever-mounting path back to his earliest days until it is lost in the pure innocence that is God's birth-gift to every little child. There is no apparent genesis of conviction, of dedication. From a child upward he seems to have been imbued with a sense of service owed to a Wonderful Benefactor, and though of course there must have been times of struggle and of darkness, they were principally of a mental rather than of a spiritual character, causing no interruption of his self-appointed labours and leaving no contemporary external indications of their presence.[2]

II.

A SIMPLE ANSWER.

"By taking heed."

1. The answer, like the question of the text, is not perhaps the supremely best, but it is nevertheless very true, and needful to be borne in mind. We should begin by asking, "Wherewithal shall I cleanse my heart?" and the reply to that is, "If any man be in

---

[1] James Stark, *John Murker of Banff*, 54.
[2] E. M. Hogg, *Quintin Hogg*, 35.

Christ he is a new creature"—renewed in the spirit of his mind after the likeness of Christ. But, allowing that, for the practical uses of life, nothing better could be said to one than this, Take heed to your ways, and direct them according to the Word of God

For not a little of the evil of this world arises from the heedlessness of youth. We did not mean to do wrong. Very few do, at least in the beginning. There may be some who have from the first perverse and evil natures, wholly indisposed to go the right way. But on the whole these are not the common staple of human creatures. Most youths are not wishful to do wrong, but would rather, if it did not cost very much trouble, do right in the main. But they do not think as strenuously about it as they should. They are not very watchful of their conduct, or careful to guide it aright; and so they fall into a snare. It is this heedlessness, this inconsiderateness, which does not weigh seriously the step we are going to take, and the consequences it may involve— this is the beginning of many a downward course. "Oh," we say, "I did not think; I did not mean any wrong," and we are fain to consider that a sufficient excuse. But it is not a sufficient excuse. We ought to think. God has given us a power of "seeing before and after" that we may direct our steps aright; and it will not serve our purpose that we did not use that power, but blundered into the mire which we should clearly have avoided. The foremost duty of a man is to think what he is about.

¶ The best made road wants looking after if it is to be kept in repair. What would become of a railway that had no surfacemen and platelayers going along the line and noticing whether anything was amiss? I remember once seeing a bit of an old Roman road; the lava rocks were there, but for want of care, here a young sapling had grown up between two of them and had driven them apart, there were many split by the frost; here was a great ugly gap full of mud, and the whole thing ended in a jungle. How shall a man keep his road in repair? "By taking heed thereto." Things that are left to go anyhow in this world have a strange knack of going one how. You do not need anything else than negligence to ensure that things will come to grief.[1]

¶ One of the greatest of living Englishmen sums up the whole teaching of Goethe, the wisest German of the nineteenth century, in the brief citation: "Gedenke, zu leben," which means literally,

[1] A. Maclaren.

"Think, to live." Carlyle translates, "Think of living." But you will all get hold of its meaning if I say that what it comes to is this: " If you would live rightly and well, you must *think—* think how it is best to live." So that, you see, two of the wisest men of our own time are of one mind with the Psalmist who lived between two and three thousand years before them. He says, " If you would walk in pure and noble ways of life, *think* of your ways."[1]

2. If we examine our self-consciousness, we shall find that it is never as to the qualities of actions that we feel doubt or hesitation. The questions which perplex us, and which it is unspeakably dangerous for a young person to begin to ask, are such as these: How far may I go in a wrong direction, and yet be sure to go no farther? Is there any harm in a slight compromise of principle? Can I not with ultimate safety trespass once, or a little way, on forbidden ground? Can I not try the first pleasant, attractive steps on a way which I am determined on no account to pursue farther? May I not go as far in the wrong as others are going, without reproach and without fear? Is there not some redeeming grace in companionship, so that I may venture with others a little farther than I would be willing to go alone? May not my conscience, under careful home-training and choice home-examples, have become more rigid and scrupulous than is befitting or manly in one who has emerged into comparative freedom? In these questions are the beginnings of evil—the first, it may be, fatal steps in miry ways.

¶ If you once allow yourself to fall into a habit of evil of whatever kind, the idea that you are helpless, that you are made so, that it is your nature, will very speedily creep in and try to lay hold of your mind. Whether it be a sin of passion or of temper, which comes only at times, leaving you free to live a right and perhaps even a religious life in the intervals, and returning with a sort of easy victory in the hour of temptation, making your falls all the more miserable by their contrast with your happier and better moments; or some of those palsies of the soul which seem to benumb the will—sloth for instance, or selfishness; or again, a petty fault which mars all your life without seeming ever to stain it deeply, making you ashamed, and justly ashamed, that you should find a difficulty in overcoming such a trifle; in

[1] S. Cox, *The Bird's Nest,* 136.

such cases, over and above the temptation to the sin itself, there
soon comes the added temptation to treat it as hopeless, to give
up in despair, to reconcile yourself to your enemy, and say that
you are made so, and cannot do otherwise. And this is indeed no
trifling addition. The one chance of escape from habitual sin is
never to intermit the struggle: do that, and you are quite sure to
conquer; some better opportunity for getting power over the
temptation presents itself; or the temptation seems to go away
of itself, you do not know how; or it returns less and less
frequently, till it returns no more; its going may be in one way
or in another; but persevere in the battle, and go it surely will.
Thus ere now have Christians overcome bodily temptations, to
some men the severest trials of all; thus have Christians tamed
down unruly temper; thus have they conquered pride and
vanity; thus have they taught themselves to be true.[1]

3. But it is not in man to direct his steps aright. Therefore
God has bestowed on us what should be "a lamp unto our feet,
and a light unto our path." It is something to be heedful and to
walk warily, for we are beset on all hands by snares and temptations. But that is not enough. For besides these dangers that
encompass us without, we have other perils to face in the shape
of false ideals, mistaken views of what a man should be and do.
Therefore the Psalmist reminds us that we can cleanse our ways
only by taking heed to them according to God's Word. He
meant, of course, the Law of the Lord as it had been made known
to Israel of old. That was to be their practical guide in the
path of duty in his day. It was not merely a doctrine they were
to believe, but a commandment they must obey. And a noble
law it was, of brave and manly and self-denying virtue, leading
them up the steep heights of arduous duty to the fellowship of
Israel's God. Yet, good and precious though it was, quickening
the soul to a higher life than the rest of the world dreamt of, we
have now a surer word and a fairer example to direct us, a more
potent inspiration also urging us to higher and holier attainments.
Think of the Perfect Man, the model of holy beauty, who is in
all things our example, who teaches how to be rich in poverty, how
to be wise though unlearned, how to bear wrong meekly, how to be
true and faithful and brave with all the world against Him, and
how to forget Himself in the love He bore to all.

[1] Archbishop Temple.

¶ In St. Peter the love of God is shown in Christian example. A plain and simple mind, fixed on plain duties, finding in the great law of right a supreme satisfaction, St. Peter seems to think of our Lord chiefly as showing us what we ought to be and do, and sent by the infinite love of God for that purpose. Do Christians find their duty hard ? "Even hereunto were ye called: because Christ also suffered for us, leaving us an example, that ye should follow his steps: who did no sin, neither was guile found in his mouth: who, when he was reviled, reviled not again; when he suffered, he threatened not; but committed himself to him that judgeth righteously: who his own self bare our sins in his own body on the tree, that we, being dead to sins, should live unto righteousness: by whose stripes ye were healed." Or, again, are Christians persecuted? They are reminded that "Christ also hath once suffered for sins, the just for the unjust." And so throughout his writings St. Peter ever seems to think of God's love as upholding a man in doing what it is right to do, in bearing what it is right to bear, and of Christ's life as the assurance of that love.[1]

4. In Christ, who is the Incarnate Word, we have an all-sufficient Guide on our way through life. A guide of conduct must be plain—and whatever doubts and difficulties there may be about the doctrines of Christianity there is none about its morality. A guide of conduct must be decisive—and there is no faltering in the utterance of the Book as to right and wrong. A guide of conduct must be capable of application to the wide diversities of character, age, circumstance—and the morality of the New Testament especially, and of the Old in a measure, secures that, because it does not trouble itself about minute details, but deals with large principles. A guide for morals must be far in advance of the followers, and it has taken generations and centuries to work into men's consciences, and to work out in men's practice, a *portion* of the morality of that Book. If the world kept the commandments of the New Testament, the world would be in the millennium; and all the sin and crime, and ninety-nine-hundredths of all the sorrow, of earth would have vanished like an ugly dream.

¶ I never saw a useful Christian who was not a student of the Bible. If a man neglect his Bible, he may pray and ask God

[1] Archbishop Temple.

to use him in His work, but God cannot make use of him, for there is not much for the Holy Ghost to work upon. We cannot overcome Satan with our *feelings*. The reason why some people have such bitter experience is that they try to overcome the devil by their feelings and experiences. Christ overcame Satan by the *Word*.[1]

5. The fatal defect of all attempts at keeping our heart by our own watchfulness is that keeper and kept are one and the same, and so there may be mutiny in the garrison, and the very forces that ought to subdue the rebellion may have gone over to the rebels. We want a power outside of us to steady us. We want another motive to be brought to bear upon our conduct, and upon our convictions and our will, mightier than any that now influence them; and we get that if we will yield ourselves to the love that has come down from heaven to save us, and says to us, "If ye love me, keep my commandments." We want, for keeping ourselves and cleansing our way, reinforcements to our own inward vigour, and we shall get these if we will trust to Jesus Christ, who will breathe into us the spirit of His own life, which will make us "free from the law of sin and death." We want, if our path is to be cleansed, forgiveness for a past path, which is in some measure stained and foul, as well as strength for the future, to deliver us from the dreadful influence of the habit of evil. And we get all these in the blood of Jesus Christ which cleanses from all sin.

¶ How are we to be made holy? God has made full provision for it. There is wonderful provision laid down in the Word for our sanctification. First of all there is the blood of Jesus Christ which cleanseth from all sin. There is power in it to cleanse even the young man's heart. Secondly, there is the washing with the Word. You remember the Lord said to His disciples, "Now, ye are clean through the word which I have spoken unto you." Thirdly, there is the keeping power of Christ Himself. "I know whom I have believed, and am persuaded that he is able to keep that which I have committed unto him against that day." The power of Christ to keep is another part of the provision that God has made to keep us holy. Then there is the Holy Spirit of God, whose special office on earth is to do this work of sanctification through Christ. The blood of Jesus Christ; the Word of the

[1] D. L. Moody.

living God; the keeping power of Christ; the sanctifying power
of the Holy Ghost. What a provision is this![1]

Four letters that a child may trace!
  Yet men who read may feel a thrill
From powers that know not time nor space,
  Vibrations of the eternal will—
With body and mind and soul respond
To "Love" and all that lies beyond.

On truth's wide sea, thought's tiny skiff
  Goes dancing far beyond our speech,
Yet thought is but a hieroglyph
  Of boundless worlds it cannot reach:
We label our poor idols "God,"
And map with logic heavens untrod.

Music and beauty, life and art—
  Regalia of the Presence hid—
Command our worship, move our heart,
  Write "Love" on every coffin-lid:
But infinite—beyond, above—
The hope within that one word "Love."[2]

[1] J. Elder Cumming.   [2] Annie Matheson, *Maytime Songs*, 59.

THE WONDROUS LAW.

LITERATURE.

Flint (R.), *Sermons and Addresses*, 133.
Harper (F.), *Nine Sermons*, 31.
Ker (J.), *Sermons*, i. 29.
Matheson (G.), *Messages of Hope*, 241.
Salmond (C. A.), *For Days of Youth*, 346.
Voysey (C.), *Sermons*, vi. (1883), No. 44 ; xix. (1896), No. 16 ; xxvi. (1903), No. 22.
Whincup (D. W.), *The Training of Life*, 21.
British Weekly Pulpit, iii. 401 (W. Sanday).
Treasury (New York), xx. 722.

The Wondrous Law.

Open thou mine eyes, that I may behold
Wondrous things out of thy law.—Ps. cxix. 18.

This is a very uncommon idea—that wonder should be the result of intellectual development or the "opening of the eyes." The prevailing notion is the reverse—that wonder belongs to the primitive age alike of the individual and of the race. We say colloquially, "I opened my eyes in astonishment"; the Psalmist's expression is the converse, "I became astonished by opening my eyes." What the Psalmist says is that the marvels of life escape us by reason of our ignorance. His prayer is just the contrary of the common prayer. The common prayer is, "Make me a simple child again that I may feel the mystery of all things and bow with reverence before them." But the Psalmist says, "Emancipate me from the ignorance of childhood, for it is only when I shall see with the eyes of a man that I shall behold the mystery, the marvel, the unfathomable depth, of that ocean on whose bosom I live and move and have my being."

¶ Do we find that the sense of wonder belongs to children? Not so. The sense of mystery is precisely what a child does not feel. He asks many questions; but he will accept the crudest answers as quite adequate explanations. He has not a consciousness of limitation. He has a feeling of power beyond his strength; he will put out his hand to catch the moon. He does not at an early date inquire where he came from. He does not ask who made a watch or who made the sun. To him the watch and the sun are both alive—moving by their own strength, upheld by their own power. His eyes are not opened, and therefore his wonder is not awake. To wake his wonder you must unbar the door of his mind. The mystery comes with his experience—not with the want of it. I do not read that man marvelled in Eden; I do that they marvelled in Galilee. Eden was as wonderful as Galilee; but the eyes were not opened. Knowledge is the parent of mystery. Experience is the forerunner of reverence. Only they who have let down the pitcher can utter the cry, "The well is deep." [1]

¶ Mr. Morley, in his *Life of Gladstone,* speaking of his entrance into college life at Oxford, says: "It was from Gladstone's introduction into this enchanted and inspiring world that we recognize the beginning of the wonderful course which was to show how great a thing the life of a man may be made." So with Christian. Here, in the Interpreter's House, his spiritual experiences really begin. He is no longer in the outer circle of the world's empty life; he has come within the circle of God's direct purposes and protecting power. Dangers he will have to meet, trials of faith and courage; the Hill of Difficulty, the Valley of Humiliation, the Castle of Giant Despair, the struggle with Apollyon—all this is before him. But he is on the pilgrim-road to Zion. There is the sweet companionship; there are the wonders by the way—the Interpreter's House, the Cross where the burden is removed, the Palace Beautiful, the sight of the Delectable Mountains, the River of the Water of Life. So whatever might be the difficulties, Christian was on enchanted ground. He was near to God. He was on the path whose end was heaven. The wicket gate admits him to the rich field of Christian experience: the only experience that has any lasting value. [2]

I.

1. The sense of wonder is one of our most useful emotions. The mind cannot remain long in a state of monotony without something like pain, or if it does, it is a sign of the low level to which it has sunk. It has a craving after what is fresh, and God has provided for this in the form of the world. He has made the works of nature pass before us with a perpetually diversified face. He has created summer and winter, and so ordered the sun that it has probably never set with the same look since man first saw it. Those works of nature are constantly turning up new subjects of thought and study, and will do so, during the world's existence; while, at the same time, the world itself is weaving an ever-shifting and many-coloured web of history. In all this there is a stimulus to man to lead him to look and think.

¶ Not by "mathesis," not by deduction, or construction, not by measuring, or searching, canst thou find out God, but only by the

[1] G. Matheson, *Messages of Hope*, 242.
[2] D. W. Whincup, *The Training of Life*, 21.

faithful cry from the roadside of the world as He passes—"Open thou mine eyes, that I may behold wondrous things out of thy law." In that prayer you have literally expressed to you, not in any wise as we too carelessly assume metaphorically, the two functions of the exercised senses, of which you have so often, I fear incredulously, heard me affirm the necessary connexion—the discerning of what is beautiful and of what is right. "Wondrous things out of thy law." Wondrous, not as to the uneducated senses they are in terror, but wondrous to the educated senses in gentleness and delight ; so that while to the modern demonstrator of the laws of Nature they become mysterious as dreadful in their tyranny, to the ancient perceiver of the laws of Heaven they became lovely no less than wondrous : in the tenderness and the voice of the Borgo Allegri, at the feet of the Mother of Christ, was joy no less of allegiance than wonder—"Oh, how love I thy law."[1]

2. Wonder rises into admiration as we contemplate things that are grand and beautiful. There is a chord in the human heart to which the beautiful and sublime respond, whether these appear in the material or in the spiritual world. If we could only take men away for a little out of the dull, dead round, and from the corroding and often debasing things that draw them down in their common life, there are objects such as these appealing to them daily and hourly, and asking them if they have not a soul. Rich sunsets and moonlit skies are there, only requiring eyes to see them, and acts of self-devotion and heroism are being performed, and lives of patient suffering led, under our sight, which are as capable of thrilling us as anything recorded in history.

¶ At a later time the Maréchale delivered addresses in other cities of France—such as Nîmes, Marseilles, Havre, Rouen, Lyons —and she was everywhere astonished to find that the French, who seem the most thoughtless, are yet among the most thoughtful people in the world. The result of such Conférences as these cannot be tabulated. For one thing, they made the Maréchale more than ever a mother-confessor and spiritual director. The thoughts of many hearts were revealed to her at private interviews of which no record was kept, and in letters, one of which may be given:—

"Your marvellous faith, your simple and powerful eloquence so deeply moved me that I cannot but thank you. I thank you

[1] Ruskin, *Schools of Art in Florence*, § 90 (*Works*, xxiii. 250).

as an artist, as a sincere admirer of beautiful work, of great characters; I thank you as a man blasé, sceptical, benumbed and deadened. As a child I adored Jesus, and now, after having thought much and suffered infinite pains which you cannot understand, I have said adieu to faith and also adieu to hope! I have become one of those you call sceptics. Ah! do not say 'terrible' sceptic, but unfortunate, pitiable, unhappy sceptic. You are, Madame, a great, beautiful, generous heart, and if ever earnest good wishes have been worth anything, I have cherished them for you, your work, and those who fight by your side. You will believe me, an unbeliever, who envies you, admires you, and ideally loves you."[1]

3. Wonder and admiration deepen into awe as we realize the mystery of life. A reflective mind can take but a very few steps in thinking till it comes upon this. It is not so much that there are things unknown around us as that there are things *unknowable*, that there is an infinite and a mystery in the universe which we cannot now penetrate, and which may for ever stretch beyond us. The tokens of man's highest nature lie not in his being able to comprehend but in his ability to feel that there are things which he cannot comprehend, and which he yet feels to be true and real, before which he is compelled to fall down in reverent awe. It is here, above all, that man comes into contact with religion, with a God, with an eternity; and he in whom there is little sense of wonder, or in whom it has been blunted and degraded, will have a proportionately feeble impression of these grand subjects which the soul can feel to be real but can never fully grasp.

¶ I can call my Father a brave man (ein Tapferer). Man's face he did not fear; God he always feared: his Reverence, I think, was considerably mixed with Fear. Yet not slavish Fear; rather Awe, as of unutterable Depths of Silence, through which flickered a trembling Hope. How he used to speak of Death (especially in late years) or rather to be silent, and *look* of it! There was no feeling in him here that he cared to hide: he trembled at the really terrible; the mock-terrible he cared nought for.—That last act of his Life; when in the last agony, with the thick ghastly vapours of Death rising round him to choke him, he burst through and called with a man's voice on the great God to have mercy on him: that was like the epitome and concluding

[1] James Strahan, *The Maréchale* (1913), 123.

summary of his whole Life. God gave him strength to wrestle with the King of Terrors, as it were even then to prevail. All his strength came from God, and ever sought new nourishment there. God be thanked for it.[1]

II.

1. There is nothing so wonderful as God's law; indeed, it may justly be said to include in itself all that is most wonderful— all that truly merits our admiration—all that will really reward our curiosity. For what is it? The Psalmist here was not thinking merely of the law given to Moses or of the words written in any book, however sacred. He was not thinking of spoken words or written characters, but of eternal realities. He was an earnest man, and his mind sought to be in contact with truth itself; he was a pious man, and his heart longed for nothing less or lower than communion with the living God. He felt himself in the Divine presence, and he felt that the Divine law was within and around him. The Bible tells us much about the law of God, but it is only by a figure of speech that we call it the law of God or even that it contains the law of God. In the Bible and other books we have the statements of God's laws, but these laws themselves are far too real to be in any book.

2. It is the law of God that keeps the stars in their courses, regulates the movements of the seas and the revolutions of the earth, develops the plant and organizes the animal, works in our instincts and guides our reason, marks out the path of humanity and determines the rise and fall, the weal and woe, of nations, and measures out to virtue and vice their due rewards in time and eternity. It is not truly separable from God Himself, but is the whole of the modes in which He manifests His power, and wisdom, and goodness in the universe,—the whole of the ways in which He operates through matter and spirit, in creation, providence, and redemption, as Father and King and Judge. Hence it is that we say it is not only most wonderful but includes in itself all that is wonderful. The wonders of physical nature, of the human soul and human history, and of redeeming love and grace, are all wonders of that law of God which the Psalmist longed and prayed

[1] Carlyle, *Reminiscences*, i. 10.

to behold—that law which ruleth alike in what is least and in what is greatest, to which all things in heaven and earth do homage, the seat of which is the bosom of the Eternal, the voice of which is the harmony of the universe.

¶ I read in the Bible that God has "set his glory in the heavens," but in merely reading this I do not see that glory; it is only to be seen by "considering the heavens, which are the work of God's fingers; the moon and the stars, which he has ordained." This terrible law—"the wages of sin is death "—has been published in the Bible, but it does not exist and work in the Bible; it exists and works in the lives of sinful beings like you and me, and if we do not see it in ourselves we shall never see it at all, although we read a thousand times the words which announce it. So with its gracious counterpart—" the gift of God is eternal life through Jesus Christ." These blessed words point us to the most consoling law in all the universe, but they point us away from themselves; and only by our souls coming into communion with a living God through a living Saviour can they behold the wonders of mercy and truth which are in that law.[1]

¶ Really, so far as spiritual vision is concerned, the angels must look upon this earth as a big blind asylum. We see close to us, but not afar off; we see the surface, and miss the depths; we see not as wide awake, but as those who rub their eyes hardly knowing whether they wake or sleep. Have I seen the "wondrous things" out of God's law—the things which accompany salvation. Many feel the intellectual interest of God's Word, enjoy its eloquence, extol its moral worth, or they appreciate its prudential wisdom, like Napoleon, who put it in the political section of his library; but they do not grasp its spiritual, saving message. They gather shining pebbles and painted shells, and overlook the pearl of great price. Oh! to see the wondrous depths of redeeming love! Whilst I study systems of theology and search the commentaries of exegetes do I sufficiently remember the promised Revealer and wait His illumination? "Ye have an unction from the Holy One, and know all things."[2]

III.

1. The most wonderful of all laws are God's moral and spiritual laws. They are the laws of God in a far higher sense than other laws. The laws of the physical world might have been quite

[1] Robert Flint.　　　　[2] W. L. Watkinson.

different from what they are. God made them to be what they are
by making the physical world itself what it is. If He had made quite
a different material world with quite other laws, He would have
been none the less God, the true object of our worship. But He
did not make the fundamental laws of moral life to be what they
are by any mere forthputting of His will. They are eternal and
unchangeable. That God should alter them would be for Him
to cease to be wise and righteous and holy and loving. It would
be for Him to cease to be God. The wonders of these laws are
thus the wonders of the Divine nature, and far greater, therefore,
than any wonders of created nature. At the same time, these
laws are the laws of our natures, of our spirits, of what is much
higher and much more wonderful than anything else to be beheld in
nature. "On earth," it has been said, "there is nothing great but
man, and in man there is nothing great but mind." And certainly
a soul is a far more wonderful thing than even a star, a spiritual
being than a material world, and its laws are far more wonderful. It
is spiritual law that determines men's relations to their God and to
one another, and it is on obedience or disobedience to it that the
weal or woe of individuals or societies chiefly depends, so that all
the marvels and mysteries of human nature and destiny gather
round it.

¶ I am not quite sure that the sole, or even chief, end of
punishment is the reformation of the offender. I think a great
deal of *law*. Law rules Deity; and its awful majesty is above
individual happiness. That is what Kant calls "the categorical
imperative," that is, a sense of duty which commands categorically
or absolutely—not saying "it is better," but "thou shalt." Why?
Because "thou shalt," that is all. It is not best to do right—
thou must do right; and the conscience that feels that, and in that
way, is the nearest to Divine humanity. Not that law was made,
like the Sabbath, for man, but man was made for it. He is beneath
it, a grain of dust before it; it moves on, and if he will not move
before it, it crushes him; that is all, and that is punishment. I
fancy that grand notion of law is what we have lost, what we
require to get, before we are in a position to discuss the question
of punishment at all, or to understand what it is.[1]

2. To behold fully how wonderful the law is—how sacred God
regards it to be—how terrible disobedience to it is—it is to the

---

[1] *Life and Letters of the Rev. F. W. Robertson*, 236.

cross we must look; to the cross, towering high above all other subjects, in the midst of the ages, in the presence of the nations, to show sin in all its hideousness and righteousness in all its perfections. If we can see no wonders in the law which Christ died to satisfy and glorify, if we do not see it to be unspeakably more wonderful than all the other laws, assuredly our blindness is great indeed, and we cannot too earnestly cry to a merciful God, " Open Thou mine eyes."

¶ In a letter to her father Miss Nightingale says :
"What I dislike in Renan is not that it is fine writing, but that it is all fine writing. His Christ is the hero of a novel; he himself, a successful novel-writer. I am revolted by such expressions as *charmant, delicieux, religion du pur sentiment*, in such a subject. . . . As for the 'religion of sentiment,' I really don't know what he means. It is an expression of Balzac's. If he means the 'religion of love,' I agree ,and do not agree. We must love something loveable. And a religion of love must certainly include the explaining of God's character to be something loveable —of God's 'providence,' which is the self-same thing as God's Laws, as something loving and loveable. On the other hand I go along with Christ, not with Renan's Christ, far more than most Christians do. I do not think that 'Christ on the Cross' is the highest expression hitherto of God—not in the vulgar meaning of the Atonement—but God does hang on the Cross every day in every one of us; the whole meaning of God's 'providence,' i.e. His laws, is the Cross. When Christ preaches the Cross, when all mystical theology preaches the Cross, I go along with them entirely. It is the self-same thing as what I mean when I say that God educates the world by His laws, i.e. by sin —that man must create mankind—that all this evil, i.e. the Cross, is the proof of God's goodness, is the only way by which God could work out man's salvation without a contradiction. You say, but there is too much evil. I say, there is just enough (not a millionth part of a grain more than is necessary) to teach man by his own mistakes,—by his sins, if you will—to show man the way to perfection in eternity—to perfection which is the only happiness." [1]

IV.

Man's eyes are veiled, so that he sees but a little way into God's law. Our intellectual perception of law is one thing and

[1] Sir Edward Cook, *The Life of Florence Nightingale*, i. 486.

our spiritual perception of God in law is a very different thing. To see law itself we need only a clear and disciplined understanding. To see God in law we need spiritual discernment. The eye sees only what it brings with it the power of seeing. And neither mere bodily vision nor mere intellectual vision will enable us to behold spiritual reality. The things of the spirit must be spiritually discerned.

¶ When on a serene night millions of stars sparkle in the depths of the sky, any man who has bodily eyes, although he may have no talent and culture, has only to raise them upwards to embrace at a glance all the splendours of the firmament, and thereby to receive into his soul, at least in some measure, the impressions which so sublime a spectacle is fitted to produce. But there may stand beside him one whose intellectual ability is far greater, and who has improved that ability to the utmost by diligent and carefully directed exercise, yet if Providence have denied to him the blessing of sight, in vain for him will there be all magnificence. There is another sky, and one far grander than the azure vault which is stretched over our heads, and this mystic sky is filled with the stars of Divine truth, the wonders of creative power, the mysteries of infinite wisdom, the bounties of Divine beneficence, the beauties of absolute holiness, the marvels of redeeming love, the riches of the Godhead, the glories of Father, Son, and Spirit, shining far more bright and pure than the sun at noonday. And yet to great men, to the wise of this world, to the most scholarly and the most scientific of men, they may be quite invisible, although they are lighting up with their Divine radiance the path of the simple peasant and causing his heart to leap and sing with joy as he beholds them.[1]

¶ I remember very well when Sir Redvers Buller came home from South Africa, in almost the first speech he made after landing at Southampton, he drew attention to the immense superiority of the Boer over the Briton in the matter of vision. Accustomed to the clear atmosphere and vast distances of South Africa, the Boer had brought his sight faculty to such a pitch of perfection that he could see a moving object a mile or two farther off than the average Englishman could, with the result that he was aware of the approach of the English soldier long before the Englishman became aware of his nearness. And Sir Redvers did not hesitate to set down some of our calamities and disasters and defeats to this cause.[2]

[1] Robert Flint.   [2] J. D. Jones, *Elims of Life*, 126.

1. One cause of this blindness is *a hereditary defect in the unbelieving heart*, a natural congenital blindness, which the lapse of years has not cured. We are all born blind, and remain blind to moral and spiritual truth long after birth. Discernment between right and wrong, a sense of duty, a sense of failure and secret shame in consequence, is a state or faculty into which we can grow only after we have lived as mere animals about four or five years. It takes some years longer before we grow into knowledge of the ideas of character, of trustworthiness in parents, of their unselfish love, and of the intense kindness of that discipline which at first we resisted and resented. Before that development we were blind, we could not discern spiritual things; we could not know what true love is, for love is the most spiritual of all human faculties. It crowns the climax of all strictly human qualities. But, though it seems incredible, it is true that some men and women have grown up without any moral sense being developed, and also without any knowledge or sense of true love.

¶ I came across a man well advanced in years who confided to me that he believed neither in God nor in a future life. I at once asked him: "Did you ever really love any one in the world?" After some days' reflection, he replied to me: "No, I don't think I ever did love anybody—at least, not as you define true love." Now, if you cannot get as far as love in human development, you must, of course, be blind to God. You cannot see Him, cannot take any pleasure in the thought of Him, but must be practically dead towards Him.[1]

2. Another cause of blindness is to be found *in the conditions of life which are either forced upon us or have been chosen by ourselves*. The worst and most widespread of these conditions is absorption in the concerns and pleasures of this life. Rich and poor alike suffer from this absorption, yet the rich suffer from it far more than the poor. Want and distress may open our eyes to God, fulness and luxury never. So long as our hearts are fixed wholly on worldly good and animal indulgence, our souls are utterly blind to God and to all spiritual things.

¶ Christian saw in Interpreter's House two boys, Passion and Patience. Passion had a bag of gold in his hand, but Patience was willing to take his Governor's advice and wait for his good

---

[1] Charles Voysey.

things till the next year. And these two boys, says John Bunyan, are typical of the worldly man and the true Christian. The worldly man, with his favourite proverb of " A bird in the hand is worth two in the bush," wants his good things at once; he wants his bag of gold in the hand, not seeming to realize that his money must perish with him; but the Christian is willing to do without this world's wealth, because he looks not at the things which are seen, but at the things which are not seen.[1]

¶ A scientist delivered a lecture a little time ago in which he maintained, on the basis of studies started by the observation of the eye of a wounded bird, that all diseases of the body register themselves in the eye, that it was even possible to judge the location of the disease by the part of the pupil affected. Whether this can be demonstrated or not, there is no doubt that the eye has its connexion with organs of the body that are less honourably placed, and is affected by their accidents and disquietudes. Diseases of the blood and of the digestive functions cloud and vex the sight. You shall not be careless of your eating and drinking and maintain clear vision. The mists and the filmy globes which float before the eye are the indices of things wrong in parts of the system that are remote from the eye itself, and to be remedied by neither eye-lotions nor glasses. So neglect of the spiritual life results in blurred spiritual vision.[2]

3. Above and beyond these things which naturally darken our souls, there lie *the conditions which we may create for ourselves.* Not knowing anything about the soul and the spiritual life, some steep themselves in studies and occupations which prevent all entrance of light into their minds concerning God and His ways. They keep the company of irreligious and unbelieving men like themselves. They pore over essays and volumes which not only throw not a gleam of light upon the spiritual world, but are purposely written to shut it out, to make it more and more difficult to see God, to deepen the darkness in which they started on their search for what they call " Truth." Thus, blind at the beginning, they take for their guides men and books still more blind than themselves, and flounder on with ever less and less power to recover their sight. And all the while they studiously neglect those means by which their eyes may be opened. They never lift up their

---

[1] J. D. Jones, *Elims of Life*, 134.
[2] W. C. Piggott, *The Imperishable Word*, 68.

hearts to God. They avoid all thoughts of religion unless only to sneer at it, or to look down upon it with supercilious curiosity. They never attend public worship or put themselves in the way of hearing what they never have heard. "What is the use," cry the more intelligent among them—"what is the use of praying to a God who is absolutely unknowable?" But they forget that God is unknowable only to those who think Him to be so, to those who never pray. If they did but confer with those who have lifted up their hearts to God and have found Him, they might be brought to go down upon their knees to pray, "Lord, open Thou mine eyes that I may see."

¶ A little steam vessel in which I was sailing round the coast of Arran, emitted such a thick pall of smoke as to blot out the vision of Goat Fell. And sometimes our souls create those obscuring clouds and hide the glory of God. It may be the vapour of pride. It may be the steam of unclean passion. It may be the smoke of timidity and fear.

> O may no earth-born cloud arise
> To hide Thee from Thy servant's eyes.[1]

Night comes; soon alone shall fancy follow sadly in her flight
Where the fiery dust of evening, shaken from the feet of light,
Thrusts its monstrous barriers between the pure, the good,
    the true,
That our weeping eyes may strain for, but shall never after view.
Only yester eve I watched with heart at rest the nebulæ
Looming far within the shadowy shining of the Milky Way;
Finding in the stillness joy and hope for all the sons of men;
Now what silent anguish fills a night more beautiful than then:
For earth's age of pain has come, and all her sister planets
    weep,
Thinking of her fires of morning passing into dreamless sleep.
In this cycle of great sorrow for the moments that we last
We too shall be linked by weeping to the greatness of her
    past:
But the coming race shall know not, and the fount of tears
    shall dry,
And the arid heart of man shall be arid as the desert sky.
So within my mind the darkness dawned, and round me
    everywhere
Hope departed with the twilight, leaving only dumb despair.[2]

[1] J. H. Jowett.   [2] A. E., *Collected Poems* (1913), 25.

V.

The Psalmist does not ask for a new faculty, but for clearer vision. The eyes are there already; they need only to be opened. It is not the bestowal of a new and supernatural power that enables a man to read the Bible to profit, but the quickening of a power he already possesses. A man will never grow into the knowledge of God's Word by idly waiting for some new gift of discernment, but by diligently using that which God has already bestowed upon him, and using at the same time all other helps that lie within his reach. There are men and books that seem, beyond others, to have the power of aiding insight. All of us have felt it in the contact of some affinity of nature which makes them our best helpers; the kindred clay upon the eyes by which the great Enlightener removes our blindness (John ix. 6). Let us seek for such, and if we find them let us employ them without leaning on them. Above all, let us give our whole mind in patient, loving study to the book itself, and where we fail, at any essential part, God will either send His evangelist Philip to our aid (Acts viii.) or instruct us Himself. But it is only to patient, loving study that help is given. God could have poured all knowledge into us by easy inspiration, but it is by earnest search alone that it can become the treasure of the soul.

1. If we are to get spiritual sight our prayer must be sincere. The old Hebrew poet, speaking with a true insight confirmed by experience, says: "If thou seek him, he will be found of thee; yea, if thou seek him diligently with thy whole heart." That is the secret. It will not do to be seeking God with a heart looking back to the idol which had taken His place. It will not do to be wanting to have God and the idol at one and the same time. God has made that to be impossible for the soul of man. One God or idol at a time, or not God at all. And while any lingering love for the idol remains, there is no room for God to enter in. It is not His fault, or His unwillingness, or His jealousy. But it is our own Divine incapacity to trifle or dissemble with Him; it is our own Divine necessity for wholeness, for uprightness and sincerity, that makes any attempt at double-mindedness futile.

¶ An old colleague and friend of Denholm Brash writes :—

"Chief among my impressions of his excellences is that of his utter sincerity. It was so invariable that it bewildered the average man. He never troubled about maintaining any position he might have taken up yesterday. He told you what he thought to-day ; every passing mood was faithfully reflected in his words ; the fleeting opinion or feeling was not concealed. You were allowed to trace processes in his thought which most men hide from view. . . . I have seen him confound an old fox of a man by sheer candour. He left the enemy breathless with surprise at a simplicity he had thought faded out of the world with Eden. The man's arts would have been a match for any arts they encountered, but artlessness dumbfounded him. The armour of light not only defended the wearer, but dismayed the assailant. Never was this servant of truth 'off duty,' and with the audacious simplicity of love he would attack an apparently impregnable fortress, and with one well-planted shot would bring a whole pile of hypocrisies toppling down. He had a short method with some of these Goliaths which worked wonders."[1]

2. We must bring our hearts into harmony with the law. At South Kensington there is a clock made above 500 years ago under the hammer of a Glastonbury monk. It has measured out the moments of fifteen generations of men. That piece of mechanism has done and is still doing its maker's will. It has served its maker's purpose. It fulfils his praiseworthy intention and so praises him. Every stroke of its pendulum is to the glory of the Glastonbury smith. The thing has done good and done right. It keeps (so to say) its maker's commandment. What he meant it to do it has done well and truly. Perhaps it may seem a little strained to apply such phraseology to a piece of inanimate mechanism, but it will surely aid us in seeing what the moralist means by telling men to live as they were meant to live. Think of this clockwork of the brain, this delicate mechanism of thought and feeling. Year in, year out, the restless wheels of desire and feeling, of thought and passion, play into one another and mark results on the solemn dial of life. Matters may be so mismanaged as to put the machinery into a whirl of wild confusion. It is, on the other hand, possible to secure

[1] *Love and Life : The Story of J. Denholm Brash*, 163.

such inward adjustment, such balance, such regulative control, such true impulse, as to make the soul a splendid harmony and the life a utility which men acknowledge with reverence and benediction. With God's works as with man's the essential thing is to be true to the Maker's purpose. There is a commandment, a Divine intention, to which every one must be true. "Thy hands have made me, and fashioned me; give me understanding that I may learn thy commandment."

¶ The Lord will draw us and securely lead us to Himself, in a way contrary to all our natural will, until He have divested us thereof, and consumed it and made it thoroughly subject unto the Divine will. For this is His will: that we should cease to regard our own wishes or dislikes; that it should become a light matter to us whether He give or take away, whether we have abundance or suffer want, and let all things go, if only we may receive and apprehend God Himself; that, whether things please or displease us, we may leave all things to take their course and cleave to Him alone. Then first do we attain to the fulness of God's love as His children, when it is no longer happiness or misery, prosperity or adversity, that draws us to Him, or keeps us back from Him. What we should then experience none can utter; but it would be something far better than when we were burning with the first flame of love, and had great emotion but less true submission; for here, though there may be less show of zeal, and less vehemence of feeling, there is more true faithfulness to God. That we may attain thereunto, may God help us with His grace. Amen![1]

3. In proportion as we love and obey the law, its wonders unfold themselves to our cleansed vision. Emerson says in his essay on Nature, "The health of the eye seems to demand a horizon. We are never tired so long as we can see far enough." It is quite true that wide vision is refreshing. We have all been more depressingly tired in our own houses than on the broad upland and under the open sky. The mountaineer in his loftiest adventure knows no such oppressive weariness as the woman who sits "in unwomanly rags plying her needle and thread." The man with the widest and furthest vision is the man with the most exuberant energy. Jesus, even with Gethsemane and Calvary before Him, is not so weary of life as Judas. St. Paul in

---

[1] *Tauler's Life and Sermons* (trans. by Susanna Winkworth), 297.

labours more abundant is never so jaded as Nero. The
early Christian martyrs, with their vision of the Name, amid
all the unspeakable horror of their torture, were not so weary
of their sufferings as their persecutors were weary of their
persecution. They might still sing, as Chesterton splendidly
puts it in the " Ballad of the White Horse,"

> That on you is fallen the shadow,
>   And not upon the Name;
> That though we scatter and though we fly
> And you hang over us like the sky,
> You are more tired of victory
>   Than we are tired of shame.
>
> That though you hunt the Christian man
>   Like a hare on the hill side,
> The hare has still more heart to run
>   Than you have heart to ride.
> That though all lances split on you,
>   All swords be heaved in vain,
> We have more lust again to lose
>   Than you to win again.

LIBERTY IN GOD'S LAW.

LITERATURE.

Bramston (J. T.), *Fratribus*, 125.
Campbell (L.), *The Christian Ideal*, 109.
Farrar (F. W.), *The Voice from Sinai*, 85.
Ferguson (F.), in *Sermons on the Psalms*, 115.
King (E.), *The Love and Wisdom of God*, 294.
Knight (W.), *Things New and Old*, 172.
Roberts (A.), *Miscellaneous Sermons*, 295.
Selby (T. G.), *The Strenuous Gospel*, 380.
Stanley (A. P.), *Sermons in the East*, 123.
Thomas (J.), *Myrtle Street Pulpit*, iii. 19.
Christian World Pulpit, xxxvii. 355 (M. Bryce); l. 121 (E. King).
Preacher's Magazine, ii. 220 (W. Hawkins).
Sunday Magazine, 1891, p. 171 (S. A. Tipple).
Treasury (New York), xxi. 675 (H. C. Swentzel).

LIBERTY IN GOD'S LAW.

I have seen an end of all perfection;
But thy commandment is exceeding broad.—Ps. cxix. 96.

THIS psalm throbs throughout with true religion, and is evidently the production of some venerable father in Israel who had endured greatly and had not fainted; who had been 'divinely taught and chastened by the toils, the troubles, and the temptations of life; who had striven to live in loyalty to the law revealed to him, and was left at once ardent about right doing, and devoted to meditation; at once sadly conscious of infirmity and weakness, and joyfully trustful in God's goodness and mercy. Nevertheless, though thus confident, the writer of the psalm confesses, "I have seen an end of all perfection." There is a sound of weariness and depression in the words; we can hear speaking in them a man who had suffered disenchantments and disappointments, who had tried things that looked inviting to find them less charming than they looked, void of what they had promised; a man who had aimed sanguinely in vain, and had sorrowfully learned that it must always be in vain; who had nursed bright expectations that had not been fulfilled, although again and again he had felt sure that they were going to be, and who knew now they never could be.

¶ This was the favourite text of Dean Stanley, a choice characteristic alike of the man and of his work: "I see that all things come to an end; but Thy commandment is exceeding broad." [Prayer-Book Version.] These words are inscribed on his own and his wife's tomb in Henry VII.'s chapel in Westminster Abbey.

I.

THE UNSATISFACTORINESS OF OUR EXPERIENCE.

1. It was no young man who spoke the words of the text; young people have not seen "an end of all perfection," have not

arrived at the conclusion that every radiance is stained by the shadow of defect, that the fullest is not full, the most complete incomplete. On the contrary, they are setting out to climb to the top of delectable mountains descried in the distance, where they shall build their tabernacle and stay. They have visions of the perfect, and count on realizing them—would infallibly realize them, they say to themselves, if only such or such circumstances were granted them; and what is there to which they may not attain with all the world-before them? No; he who uttered the exclamation of the text must have been a comparatively old man —a man, at all events, who had lived much, who had passed through many vicissitudes; who had found out with oft-repeated trial how much he could not do of what he once thought himself capable of doing, the delusiveness of many an apparent possibility.

¶ There was much in 1850 to sadden Watts; the want of response, except amongst his own personal friends, to all the enthusiasm with which he had returned to England, full of faith in a revival of great art, was making itself felt with chilling effect year by year. In a moment of depression he writes: "I do not expect at most to have the opportunity of doing more than prepare the way for better men—and not that always; more often I sit among the ruins of my aspirations, watching the tide of time." No wonder that in such a mood he once signed "Finis" in the corner of one of his pictures. But the challenge to despair was given by Mr. Ruskin, who, on reading the word, took up the charcoal and added beneath, "et initium." If the end, then a beginning; and so it proved to be.[1]

2. Perhaps the disillusion which depressed the Psalmist, and for which he had found an antidote in the permanence and magnitude of the Divine law, was not limited to the religious aspect of life only. By his own simple pathway he had reached the conclusion, familiar to modern thinkers, that the present world is not of unimpeachable perfection, but a chaos of knotted problems, amazing anomalies, clashing interests, contending principles. He set out with other views, but he reminds himself that moral processes go on working themselves out upon a scale of immeasurable greatness, when the secular movements which

[1] *George Frederic Watts*, i. 126.

once promised amelioration are threatened with arrest and defeat. God's inward law, larger than the designs appearing in the history of contemporary nations, forms the centre round which his baffled and faltering faith rallies. Spiritual ends are continued in that larger kingdom of the unseen. God's changeless and ever-enlarging law of right satisfies that sense of moral greatness which the course of secular events so often seems to mock.

¶ I am old enough to be done with work, only that I feel that my best words have not been said after all, that what has been said is not its full expression. All is incomplete, and I must wait for the fresh, strong life of immortality, in the hope that through the mercy of Him who "knoweth our frame" and our weaknesses, I may be enabled to do better with the talent He has given me than I have done.[1]

¶ The longer we live the less we are inclined to be hero-worshippers, seeing more failings in the men and things we revered in the enthusiasm of youth. "I have seen an end of all perfection"; but it is well if we can add, "thy commandment is exceeding broad." The more, however, we get to know the temptations and trials of men, and feel how our own accomplishment falls short of our ideal, the more charitable we become.[2]

> One day I grieved because our greatest gain
>   Grows pale beside the smallest loss we feel;
>   One hour of wrong can years of right repeal;
> One faulty link can spoil the strongest chain;
> One little thorn can cause a cruel pain
>   That twice ten thousand roses cannot heal;
>   One harsh discordant note can straightway steal
> All harmony from e'en the sweetest strain.
> To these my doubts there came an answer sure—
>   "God's laws are right if rightly understood!
>   Man's patent of perfection lies in this,
> That nought imperfect can his soul endure:
>   The highest natures seek the highest good
>   Till they are perfect as their Father is."[3]

[1] *Life and Letters of J. G. Whittier*, ii. 657.
[2] John Ker, *Thoughts for Heart and Life*, 13.
[3] Ellen Thorneycroft Fowler, *Verses, Wise or Otherwise*, 189.

II.

THE SATISFACTORINESS OF GOD'S LAW.

1. Everything earthly is only partial; it covers only a part of life. Whether it be wealth, fame, knowledge, power, it has a limit; its territory is not commensurate with the whole life of man. Though I have all knowledge, said the Apostle, and understand all mysteries, and have not love, it profiteth me nothing. Knowledge is measurable. There are heights and depths of spirit which it cannot fill. There is a limit to it. The only thing immeasurable is love, for love is the Infinite Himself. Nothing can endure for ever except that which touches the deeps of life, for that which is only fragmentary and partial must pass away. So there is an end to it also in the sense of termination because the limited must terminate; and, because there is an end to it, it will not satisfy us. We must have something without an end, because the spirit of man is larger than time, larger than any finite period; and, however man may have sometimes tried in the perverseness of his heart to deny it, he is still a child of immortality, and nothing less than immortality filled to the brim with possession will ever satisfy the yearning of man. "Broad is thy command exceedingly." That is, it is immeasurable, it has no limit. This must be the Psalmist's meaning, otherwise the contrast fails, and the command of God, being limited, must be declared inadequate like all other perfections. But the word of God has no limit whatsoever. Immeasurable! As soon as we touch the command of God with our heart and soul and spirit, at once we know that we are at the centre of immeasurableness. It reveals to us straight away the infinite God, the soul, and immortality.

¶ "There are two things," said Kant, "that fill me with amazement, the starry heaven above me, and the moral law within me." Both of them immeasurable, stretching away into infinity, with man at the centre of them; yet God's word is higher than the heavens, and when the moral law has touched the life of man he knows that he belongs to the infinite vast, and cannot be satisfied without it.[1]

[1] J. Thomas.

¶ Man feels capacities within him that ask an eternity for bloom and fruitage. There is in nature something that sends him in yearning search beyond and above nature.

> That type of perfect in his mind
> In nature can he nowhere find.
> He sows himself on every wind.

In the entire universe, as revealed to man by his senses, there is nothing perfect; and the central impulse in all man's noblest striving is derived from the aspiration of his spirit towards a perfect truth, a perfect beauty, a perfect happiness, which are exemplified nowhere in the world. Art, religion, and the impetuous career of the race towards a higher grade of civilization, depend alike upon universal imperfection of the material world and the impossibility that a God-related spirit, which man is, should be contented therewith.[1]

2. Our advance is towards this infinite. It is in an unbroken advance towards it that human excellence consists. The standard of perfection lifts itself on new heights with the march of each new day and month. The perfection of yesterday ceases to be the perfection of to-day, because the commandment is ever adding increments to the demands it makes upon us, and binding the conscience with fresh sanctions. As men are emancipated from the senses and ushered into more delicate spheres of perception and experience, they find themselves face to face with new laws that have to be kept, new decalogues that must be reverently obeyed, new obligations that must be strenuously fulfilled.

¶ The law which the God of righteousness, and the Father of all the families of the earth, may impose upon the children of men is obviously larger in its range of applications than the law congruous to the sovereignty of one known chiefly as the Lord of Hosts, and the Defender of an isolated group of clans. The precepts breathed into the conscience by One who has come into immediate converse with His worshippers exceed in scope and surpass in fine discriminations the precepts enjoined by a Divine King who dwells apart and is adored from afar by a people smitten with fear because of His majesty. To know the length and breadth, the depth and height of the love which surpasseth knowledge means that the soul is brought face to face with ranges of the commandment hitherto unexplored by human thought. The

[1] P. Bayne, *Lessons from My Masters,* 284.

law cannot possibly be the same for an Israelite who stands before the flame-girt Horeb and the believer who bows wondering before the Cross where the Man of Sorrows bears the burdens of mankind. The commandment is broad before the vision of the man, to whom all life is becoming a theophany.[1]

¶ Christ is the personification not of one part only, but of the whole of the law of God. His character has not the littleness of a mere teacher, nor the narrowness of a hermit or a saint, nor the eccentricity of genius. "His shoulder," as the Prophet says, is broad enough " to bear the government " and the sins of the whole world. His mind is wide enough to sympathize with all our infirmities, as well as with all our efforts after good in every direction. No griefs of life are more trying than those which arise from the half-goodness or the half-wisdom of those whom we wish to love and respect. It is when we think of these things that the Perfect Law and the Perfect Mind of Christ is so inexpressibly consoling.[2]

3. Unlike that story of the iron shroud or room, which enclosed its prisoner, day by day, within a narrower and narrower circle, the chamber of duty and of God's commandment widens, and opens, and expands with new interests, new enjoyments, new affections, new hopes, at every successive step we take, till we find ourselves at last in that Presence, where there is indeed "fulness of joy and pleasures for evermore."

Our earthly life, the earthly life of those whom we have known and loved, is cut short by that dark abyss into which we cannot penetrate, and over which our thoughts can hardly pass. But God's commandment—and the fulfilment of God's commandment—is "exceeding broad"; it is broad enough to span even that wide and deep river which parts this life and the next. For it is this that makes this life and the next life one. Knowledge, prophecies, gifts of all kinds pass away, but the love of God and the love of man never fail. They continue into the unseen world beyond the grave ; the remembrance of these things, as we have known them here, enables us still to think of them there ; the unselfish purpose, the generous sympathy, the deep affection, the transparent sincerity, the long self-control, the simple humility, of those to whom the commandment of God has been precious—

---

[1] T. G. Selby, *The Strenuous Gospel*, 394.
[2] A. P. Stanley, *Sermons in the East*, 129.

these are the arches of that bridge on which our thoughts and hopes cross and re-cross the widest and most mysterious of all the chasms which divide us; the gulf which divides the dead and the living, the gulf which divides God and man.

¶ In Stark's Life of Murker of Banff we have this portrait of a church member: The last day on which her pastor saw Elspeth alive he asked, "Have you no fears at all in crossing the Jordan?" "No," was the reply, "what should I be fear'd for, when I see Him who is the life an' the resurrection on the ither side. His word drives awa' a' the mists. I'm just like a bairn that's been awa' on the fields pu'in' flowers, an' I maun confess whyles chasin' butterflies, and noo when the sun's fa'en I'm gaun toddlin' hame. I've a wee bit burnie to cross; but, man, there's the stappin'-stanes o' His promises, an' wi' my feet firm on them, I've nae cause tae fear." After awhile she again opened her lips, and was heard to say, "He is wi' me in the swellings of Jordan."[1]

III.

The Value of Dissatisfaction.

1. The Psalmist had desired and purposed to keep God's law, to be and to do the best according to his light, and had never been able to accomplish his object, had been always falling short of it; the perfection he craved and sought had always evaded him; he had striven worthily, and had more or less done worthily too; but it did not satisfy him—there was an excellence to be reached that was not reached. Or he had had conceptions of duty that had seemed to him all-comprehending, embracing all that could be required of him. Here, he had thought, was the whole duty of man; but in acting out, or endeavouring to act out, these conceptions, others, larger and loftier, had risen upon him. In following his standard of right, the standard rose, leaving him far behind when he fancied himself nigh; in yielding to the demands of conscience, the demands increased; the more he did, the more his obligation grew; so that he would have said with a modern poet—

> I see the wider but I sigh the more,
> Most progress is most failure.

[1] J. Stark, *John Murker of Banff*, 188.

Nothing satisfied the Psalmist; the present discredited the past, only to be in its turn discredited; every seeming fulness proved shortly an illusion, and why? Because a Divine commandment had been revealed to him which continually transcended all, which was continually showing something more and greater to be done, and continually urging him on when any height was gained. The more he looked into it, the more it enlarged for him the field of duty. When he fancied he had fulfilled all, it would straightway be whispering in his ear some fresh claim; when he meditated repose, it would still be disturbing him. Had he not known this commandment, he might have known the peace of satisfaction; it was its presence with, and pressure on, him that made an end of perfection, and kept him always discontented with the best that had been wrought. Yet our Psalmist would not have been without the commandment. " Oh, how I love thy law !" he cries, in the very next verse. This, in fact, was his distinction, his dignity, and blessedness—that he had it to his perpetual restlessness and dissatisfaction, and could not be as careless and happy as the heathen, though he should propose to be; that he had a vision of the right and of the good which robbed him of ease, and before which every highest attainment paled to poorness.

Here is the beautiful Divine secret of our troubled dissatisfaction with things; that we bear within us a commandment greater than ourselves, and are more than we are or can be. Our everlasting sense of limitation means that our illimitableness, our unappeasable hunger is due to our self-transcending capacity; nothing contents us because we are more than everything, because we are not a mere part of the visible system, but include, so to speak, something supernatural; capabilities, susceptibilities, not adjusted like the powers of other creatures to the scope and conditions of this mortal life, but overshooting them. And here, in the grander than ourselves, or the world—for the world is always insufficient for it, and we are always inferior to it—here in the grander than ourselves or the world which, possessing us, keeps us ever insatiable, ever unable to find perfection, let the world yield us what it will, or let us grow to what we may—here is the God of whom we dream and never hear or see, and whom men seek in vain to prove.

We feel, do we not? that we are capable of developments in knowledge and virtue which are never reached, that we are always imperfect at our best and greatest, and yet that there is no goodness or greatness to which we may not aspire; that there are no limits to our possible progress. We are burdened with an ideal which, strive and attain as we may, is always reproaching, depreciating, condemning us, always looking down on us with eyes of disdain. There is that in us which declares continually that we might be and ought to be what we cannot be, what with all our wistfulness and effort we are perpetually hindered from being. And what does it signify but that we are invaded by the Infinite —that God is in us? Our weary unrest, our successive disenchantments and disappointments, our scorn of what we have gained or wrought, our sighs, as we "look before and after, and pine for what is not"—these are the hints and tokens of God.

¶ Inward distaste—emptiness—discontent. Is it trouble of conscience, or sorrow of heart? or the soul preying upon itself? or merely a sense of strength decaying and time running to waste? Is sadness—or regret—or fear—at the root of it? I do not know: but this dull sense of misery has danger in it; it leads to rash efforts and mad decisions. O for escape from self, for something to stifle the importunate voice of want and yearning! Discontent is the father of temptation. How can we gorge the invisible serpent hidden at the bottom of our well,—gorge it so that it may sleep? At the heart of all this rage and vain rebellion there lies —what? Aspiration, yearning! We are athirst for the infinite —for love—for I know not what. It is the instinct of happiness, which like some wild animal is restless for its prey. It is God calling—God avenging Himself.[1]

2. It would not answer even for the Christian who has meant to surrender his will, and really wants to be perfected in the will of God, to be made safe in his plans and kept in continual train of successes. He wants a reminder every hour—some defeat, surprise, adversity, peril; to be agitated, mortified, beaten out of his courses, so that all that remains of self-will in him may be sifted out of him, and the very scent of his old perversity cleared. If we could be excused from all these changes and somersets, and go on securely in our projects, it would ruin the best of us. Life

---

[1] *Amiel's Journal* (trans. by Mrs. Humphry Ward), 271.

needs to have an element of danger and agitation,—perilous, changeful, eventful; we need to have our evil will met by the stronger will of God, in order to be kept advised, by our experience, of the impossibility of that which our sin has undertaken. It would not do for us to be uniformly successful even in our best meant and holiest works, our prayers, our acts of sacrifice, our sacred enjoyments; for we should very soon fall back into the subtle power of our self-will, and begin to imagine, in our vanity, that we are doing something ourselves. Even here we need to be defeated and baffled now and then, that we may be shaken out of our self-reliance and sufficiency, else the taste of our evil habits remains in us, and our scent is not changed.

We trust and fear, we question and believe,
From life's dark threads a trembling faith to weave,
Frail as the web that misty night has spun,
Whose dew-gemmed awnings glitter in the sun.

While the calm centuries spell their lessons out,
Each truth we conquer spreads the realm of doubt;
When Sinai's summit was Jehovah's throne,
The chosen Prophet knew His voice alone;
When Pilate's hall that awful question heard,
The heavenly Captive answered not a word.

Eternal Truth! beyond our hopes and fears
Sweep the vast orbits of thy myriad spheres!
From age to age, while history carves sublime
On her waste rock the flaming curves of time,
How the wild swayings of our planet show
That worlds unseen surround the world we know.[1]

[1] Oliver Wendell Holmes.